Personality and Psychop

May 2013

To Shady

In appreciation for the good work you've done at Williams.

JM.

Shady:
It's been a pleasure to be part of your journey. Thanks and godspeed!
Margi

Shady,
I've enjoyed working with you and seeing your thoughtful and compassionate work — Thank you.
Hedy

Shady,
It's been wonderful to have you as part of the team. Wishing you all the best,
Judith

To Shady —
Wonderful getting to know you.
Best wishes —

Shady,
It's been a pleasure to share the work with you. Wishing you well in your work & growth!
Karen

Shady,
I so appreciate your contributions to our team this year & wish you all the best. I hope our paths continue to cross in your work & life.
Paul

Shady!
Wishing you the best as you continue your professional journey. Cheers!
Beverly

Craig Piers
Editor

Personality and Psychopathology

Critical Dialogues with David Shapiro

 Springer

Editor
Craig Piers
Williams College Health Center
105 Knoll Road
Williamstown, MA 01267
craig.piers@williams.edu

ISBN 978-1-4419-6213-3 (hardcover)   ISBN 978-1-4419-6214-0 (eBook)
ISBN 978-1-4614-6817-2 (softcover)
DOI 10.1007/978-1-4419-6214-0
Springer New York Heidelberg Dordrecht London

Printed on acid-free paper

Springer is part of Springer Science+Business Media (www.springer.com)

Contents

Preface

When I approached David Shapiro with the idea of putting together a book of essays on various aspects of his work, my reasons were obvious. Shapiro's writings have influenced countless clinicians from virtually every theoretical orientation, including psychoanalysts, cognitivists, existentialists, and humanists. Since its publication in 1965 and subsequent translation into six languages, *Neurotic Styles* alone has become one the most widely read books on personality and psychopathology. Dr. Shapiro's response, as I might have expected, was somewhat different. He mentioned that he had always found the *Library of Living Philosophers* book series very interesting because the format entailed a conversation between the featured theorist and distinguished contributors. I concluded that a similarly structured collection of exchanges between Shapiro and invited contributors was an ideal format because it would facilitate a revealing and penetrating discussion of key psychological concepts.

This book brings together leading figures in psychodynamic thought to critically evaluate essential aspects of Shapiro's work. Although the contributors were selected because their work overlaps with his in significant ways, it is important to note that, in several instances, the contributors have arrived at different conclusions. To highlight areas of convergence and divergence, Shapiro has written a formal response to each chapter and the contributors were invited to conclude the exchange with a rejoinder. Through dialogue, elaboration, and clarification, the principle aim of the book is to advance the understanding of personality, psychopathology, and treatment.

The book opens with Dr. Shapiro's intellectual autobiography. In this chapter, he recounts the teachers, colleagues, ideas and schools of thought that most influenced the development of his distinctive perspective. This provides a historical context in which to situate and understand his individual pieces of work, while also reveals central themes that weave their way through his writings.

The main body of the book is broken into five parts. Part I focuses on psychotherapy, relational theory, and development. Herbert Schlesinger opens the section with a discussion of psychotherapy, with special attention paid to Shapiro's psychotherapeutic emphasis on not only what the patient says, but how he or she says it. This leads to a discussion of transference and the place of causal, historical interpretations in psychotherapy. Paul Wachtel's chapter highlights the critical role of context in understanding an individual's psychology, and reviews relational, inter-subjective theory and its implications for Shapiro's conceptualization of character. Virginia Demos' discussion of development in terms of dynamical systems research and affect theory closes the first section. Her conceptualization points to the significance of volition and agency in development, while at the same time, raises questions about Shapiro's discussion of prevolitional modes.

Part II focuses on personality and psychosis. The section opens with Sidney Blatt's review of the theoretical and empirical basis of his two fundamental psychological dimensions – relatedness and self-definition – and addresses their relationship to Shapiro's two fundamental prevolitional modes – rigid, rule-based, and passive-reactive modes. In his chapter, Louis Sass joins Shapiro in seeing autonomy as important in understanding schizophrenia, but raises questions about whether the diminishment of autonomy is always present in schizophrenia.

Part III takes up the subject of defense or dynamics of self-estrangement. Morris Eagle addresses the notion of defense (including its adaptive and maladaptive consequences), levels of consciousness, varieties of self-knowledge, and the defensive response to trauma. In the second chapter of this section, Mardi Horowitz reviews his research on defensive control processes, discussing their adaptive and maladaptive expressions and how they organize the patient's conscious state and interpersonal communications.

Part IV focuses specifically on the subject of self-deception. Michael Schober and Peter Glick examine the psycholinguistic evidence for self-deceptive speech, and review the findings of their own empirical research that has identified several lexical markers of self-deceptive/defensive speech. The section closes with Lawrence Josephs' discussion of self-deception from an evolutionary perspective, suggesting that self-deception may serve an important role in mate selection and reproduction.

Part V has as its focus contemporary extensions and empirical applications of Shapiro's theorizing. In my chapter, I examine Shapiro's work from a systems perspective, suggesting that much of his clinical theory and observations are largely congruent with complex systems theory. Mindy Greenstein's chapter reviews the addiction literature, as well as her empirical research on the role of diminished intentionality in addiction. The section closes with Andreas Evdokas's and Ali Khadivi's review of their empirical investigation of the role of motivated activity and the suspension of self-criticism in hypomania.

The quality and wide-ranging nature of these conversations reflects the depth and breadth of David Shapiro's seminal contribution to our understanding of the mind.

Craig Piers

Autobiographical Notes

I had no thought of being a psychologist even as late as my B.A. degree. I assumed, at least since high school – Stuyvesant High, in New York – that I would go into some "hard" science, physics, or chemistry. In my last year of high school, my family moved to Los Angeles and after graduating I enrolled at UCLA, majoring in physics, but soon changing to mathematics. In my senior undergraduate year I changed my major again, this time to philosophy. I was influenced particularly in this by courses with the logician and philosopher of science, Hans Reichenbach, but the change was also on account of a broadening of my interests. I graduated, in 1945, by then much involved in student left politics. I was nineteen and had no idea what to do next. I had done some student journalism and I thought of writing, but that thought came to nothing. An application for a junior position as a mathematician with the U.S. Geodetic Survey, brought an appointment, months later, by telegram, but by that time I was no longer interested.

After answering an ad in the college paper, I did get an interesting temporary job. It turned out to be with the Institute for Social Research, the exiled German "critical theory" group of social philosophers led by Max Horkheimer and Theodor Adorno. They were located at the time in Los Angeles. Adorno was working on the project on anti-Semitism and authoritarian personality in collaboration with psychologists at UC Berkeley and the immediate task was to condense, in American English, what he had written for a report. That was not hard, and my boss, Friedrich Pollock, an economist, was pleased with my work. But Adorno was a different story; he was certain that any condensation of his work was simply beyond anyone's capability. (His words, I recall, were, "Mr. Shapiro has worked hard, but it would take God..."). Adorno's proposal therefore was to leave his work intact and eliminate the Berkeley contribution altogether. My job with the Institute was in any case interrupted when I was drafted into the postwar army, which, in 1946, was already being demobilized.

In a year I was out of the army and the GI bill opened new possibilities. I had by that time a passive interest in psychoanalysis, but I had an active interest in finding a career. That meant returning to the university. The difficulties of my situation, not only vocational, but, as it happened, now personal as well, prompted me to enter a psychotherapy group I had heard about. It was conducted by a left wing analyst, Dr. Alexander Wolf, who called his method group psychoanalysis. It involved each person in turn telling what he or she thought about each of the others. I have no idea now of the therapeutic effects of that experience, but I found it extremely interesting. In fact, I enjoyed it. Meanwhile, I was encouraged by some friends to apply for a new graduate program in clinical psychology that they had entered. The program had been developed in response to postwar needs of veterans and it combined university seminars and classes with paid clinical training at Veterans' Administration psychiatric facilities. I decided to apply and, after making up some psychology courses, I was accepted into the program at the University of Southern California, and began training at Brentwood V.A. Hospital in Los Angeles. Our supervisors hadn't much training themselves, but our morale was high. The hospital was visited frequently by local psychologists and psychoanalysts. Some were helpful, some not, but for me it was the beginning of serious interest in clinical work and psychoanalysis. I was especially interested in the psychoanalytic ideas of Wilhelm Reich, in his book *Character Analysis*. My initial interest in Reich, actually, was on account of his reputation as a Marxist, as I considered myself to be, and in some measure still do. But as it turned out, I found no special value in Reich's Marxism, while his ideas on psychoanalysis and character were much more compelling than I had anticipated.

Not long after I began the training program an unexpected and unusual opportunity presented itself. Dr. Ruth Tolman (wife of the physicist Richard Tolman and sister-in-law of the well known psychologist Edward Tolman), who was in charge of the V.A. program in Southern California, knowing of my by now strong interest in psychoanalysis, of my student's budget and perhaps, also, of my still somewhat unsettled outlook, offered to arrange a cost-free psychoanalysis for me. An analyst-in-training she respected, settling in Los Angeles after returning from the military and working for the time being at a different V.A. facility, had expressed interest in finding an "appropriate" patient for psychoanalysis whom he would see where he worked. I was happy to be recruited. I began the analysis, which was to continue for several years, though no longer cost free after we both left the V.A.

The V.A. training program was supposed to last four years, but in my case it was interrupted after two years. The McCarthy Red-scare was getting underway in 1949 and President Truman, probably trying to preempt McCarthy, instituted a loyalty investigation of his own covering all Federal employees. I had by that time joined the Communist Party and, although my membership was, strangely, not among the particular charges presented to me, I was found, by a board of volunteers recruited for their patriotism, to be disloyal to the United States, and fired. Luckily, I had already begun work on my dissertation and was able to complete it quickly and get my degree. I managed to get a part-time job at a nonprofit psychiatric clinic and actually began seeing private patients for psychotherapy, using mainly what I had learned in my own analysis.

I was making a living, but I was not satisfied either with my work or its prospects as a career. I wanted to learn psychoanalysis more deeply, not only its therapeutic method, but also its theoretical ideas; but in those days, psychoanalytic institutions were closed to nonmedical people. I happened, then, to go to a lecture at UCLA by David Rapaport, who was giving several talks on psychoanalytic theory in Los

Angeles. His lecture was far more interesting, reasoned and scholarly, altogether more impressive than anything I had heard from psychoanalytic or psychiatric teachers before. I learned that Rapaport worked at a small psychoanalytic hospital in a rural part of Western Massachusetts. The staff at what was then called the Austen Riggs Foundation (later changed to Austen Riggs Center to forestall requests for funds) also included Erik Erikson, whose reputation I knew (Erikson had recently left UC Berkeley after refusing to sign the new California loyalty oath) and, as Medical Director, Robert P. Knight, a very well-known analyst, who had been Medical Director at the Menninger Clinic. A few weeks after Rapaport's lecture I wrote to him at Riggs asking if post-doctoral training positions for psychologists were available there. A reply came from Roy Schafer, then the staff psychologist. There were no post-doctoral fellowships at Riggs (at that time), but he, Schafer, was going to leave in a year and they were looking for someone to replace him. If I wished to apply, let him know.

Austen Riggs Center

I went to work at Riggs in 1952. It was what I had hoped for. The staff was a small group of about a dozen people. Case conferences, in which everyone, junior as well as senior members, was expected to participate, were held two or three times a week. Seminars were conducted during the week by the senior staff – Erikson on his current work, Rapaport on various aspects of psychoanalytic theory, Margaret Brenman, whom Knight had brought from Menninger's, on her work. There were, also, regular Friday evening seminars for the staff alone by visiting luminaries in psychoanalysis and sometimes in related fields. And, for junior staff, there was weekly supervision of intensive psychoanalytic psychotherapy. New junior staff began with a year of weekly supervision with Dr. Knight. Following that, I was able to arrange a year with Erikson, and another year or so with Dr. Joseph Chassel, an analyst of the so-called Washington school. Everyone seemed to work hard, but, I think, we all felt some pride that we were at the forefront of psychoanalytic thinking. No staff member was permitted any outside practice. Even Riggs' location in the small New England town of Stockbridge seemed, perhaps on account of what it lacked otherwise, to concentrate interest in work.

Several years after I began work at Riggs, my situation there, also, was threatened by politics. I was called one day by an agent of the area FBI office asking for an appointment, and I thought I could not refuse. I decided to tell Dr. Knight of the situation, and I asked him if he was willing to be present during the interview. He agreed and, over the strenuous objections of the FBI agents, we met in Knight's large office instead of my small one. The agents asked for information about others in the Party, as I expected they would, and I refused it. At some point, to my surprise, Dr. Knight spoke up: he didn't blame me for refusing information, considering the political atmosphere in the country. The agents were taken aback and confused by this intervention and there was not much more to be said. As we left

Knight's office, one of them remarked to me that I was lucky to have a boss like that. Later, talking to Knight, I offered to leave Riggs if my presence created problems, but there was no further trouble.

Everyone on the staff, except for David Rapaport, was expected to see patients in psychotherapy, but the special responsibility of the staff psychologist was psychological testing. Psychological testing was greatly respected, in fact often relied on, and I did a great deal of it. I generally found it tedious, but I accepted it as a cost against other benefits. As it turned out, it introduced me in a special way to a great number of patients and many kinds of psychopathology, and, after a time, I found certain theoretical interests and value in it, particularly in the Rorschach test.

Interpretation of the Rorschach test generally relies on two kinds of data, the ideational content of the images and their formal qualities (use of color, quality of form, etc.) and manner of presentation. I had always, even as a student, been skeptical of the facile psychoanalytic interpretations particularly of certain images that were popular then. But the formal qualities of the subject's response, the ways things were seen and described, was clearly expressive of general ways of thinking, of attitudes and, together with the image content, of qualities of subjective experience. I became particularly interested in the perceptual qualities of different responses to color and I developed a theory, building on some theoretical work of Rapaport's, relating these to different qualities of subjective experience and kinds of psychopathology.

Another idea occurred to me in connection with test interpretation in general. We had been using the picture of an individual's attitudes and ways of thinking that emerged from the psychological tests to draw conclusions about the defense mechanisms characteristic of him or her. It seemed to me, though, that this translation was an unnecessary step, and one that tended to gloss over fine differences. The attitudes and styles of thinking were themselves clearly restrictive and limiting to conscious experience, in the way that an unvarying careful, fastidious style of thinking limits spontaneity. The ways of thinking and seeing things, in other words, seemed themselves to constitute presumably anxiety-forestalling defenses. This idea was the beginning of my work on *Neurotic Styles*.

I had for some time been in doubt about whether my personal psychoanalysis had accomplished all that I had thought, and I was considering further analysis. Several of the younger members of the staff were or had been in analysis with senior staff members and I thought I might do the same. I talked with Erikson; he was agreeable and we began, but the arrangement met with objection from Dr. Knight, who wanted Erikson's time to be available. It happened, though, that I had been deeply impressed by a talk given at Riggs by an older analyst I had never heard of, Hellmuth Kaiser. He had recently left the Menninger Clinic and was establishing a practice in Connecticut. (Kaiser was actually a Ph.D. in philosophy who, having published a literary article in a psychoanalytic journal, had been admitted to psychoanalytic training in Berlin on the strength of an appreciative letter from Freud. I learned later that in his student years he had been a roommate of my philosophy professor, Hans Reichenbach.) I had been struck, listening to Kaiser's lecture, by the acuteness of his understanding of his patient and the quiet directness and simplicity of his communication. I had been introduced to him before his talk by David Rapaport and afterward I asked Rapaport about him. Rapaport spoke of him very respectfully, but I could not help noticing some hint of reservation; evidently Kaiser was in some way, probably theoretically, unorthodox.

Nevertheless, a little guardedly, I began therapy with Kaiser. Almost from the beginning, I found this experience remarkable, even exciting, both as a patient and as a therapist myself. It was different from what I had experienced in my earlier analysis, and from what I had learned and practiced before, but I could not put my finger on what the difference was. At first it seemed to me simply that Kaiser had a method, that there was a consistency about the nature of his interest that distinguished what he said from the sometimes arbitrary-seeming, yet conventional, interpretations that were familiar to me. I gradually realized that it was not mere consistency, but the scope of his attention that was different. It was a more encompassing attention than I had been used to. It particularly included notice of how I said what I said. He took notice, before I did, for instance, that I was not much interested in what I was talking about, or that I was trying to persuade him, and myself, of something I didn't really believe. In short, his attention was not totally absorbed in what I was producing, but was also on me, as I was producing it. I learned only after I had known him for some time that Kaiser had been an early student of Wilhelm Reich. Reich's influence, his therapeutic precept, pay attention not only to what the patient says, but how he says it, was obvious.

I came to realize that the therapeutic significance of that kind of interest is very great. To pay attention consistently to how someone says what he says is to pay attention to the person, as he or she is with you, at that moment. It is to pay attention to what they are doing by saying what they are saying, and therefore to the immediate reason for doing that. Sometimes that reason is simply the wish to share what that person feels or believes. Sometimes, though the speaker himself may not be aware of it, his wish is to persuade himself that he feels or believes something else. Perhaps he tries insistently to show that he is no less important than his listener, or perhaps he believes he is, and tries to feel, hopeless, or angry when he only thinks he should be hopeless or angry. Altogether, when a therapist's interest expands to include, consistently, not only what the patient is saying, but what the patient is doing right there, a new picture emerges of psychological dynamics. It is a picture of defensive efforts that are driven, unwittingly, by the activity of a consciously purposeful person, according to his ways and attitudes, rather than by particular unconscious memories, fantasies, or internalized images. This was undoubtedly the direction that Wilhelm Reich's work was taking before he badly overshot the mark. Reich's early work and, after that, Kaiser's and then, I believe, my own constitute a logical extension of the psychoanalytic development known as ego psychology. That development broadened psychoanalytic interest almost, but not quite, to the activity of the person as a whole.

After several years of therapy with Kaiser and a year or so spent in supervision with him, we became friends.

Neurotic Styles

I left Riggs in 1960, after eight years, to return to California. I had learned what I came to learn, and at the same time, from another source, I had learned a more effective method of psychotherapy. I felt confident of my ability to help patients and I was eager to return to independent practice. I was eager, also, to write about neurotic conditions from the formal standpoint of their characteristic ways and attitudes. I had presented at Riggs much of what was to become the chapter on obsessive-compulsive character in my book *Neurotic Styles*. Dr. Knight, in particular, had liked it and urged me to do similar studies of other kinds of psychopathology in a book.

My aim in *Neurotic Styles* was simple, to describe the ways of thinking and acting, the styles, and the qualities of subjective life characteristic of various kinds of neurotic conditions, and to show that their typical symptoms were special expressions of these styles. I wanted to show that all symptoms were "in character" because they are products of character. The study of attitudes and formal characteristics of thinking also made it possible to understand more clearly the relationships between different kinds of psychopathology, for example, that between obsessive and paranoid conditions, that are not apparent from the content of their symptoms. And it was possible to show, as I have mentioned, that on account of the restrictiveness of these ways of thinking that whole aspects of subjective life, not just particular ideas or wishes, were excluded from consciousness.

Autonomy and Rigid Character

Another interest, in the subject of autonomy, had grown out of my therapeutic work. It had both theoretical and practical aspects. The theoretical issue had to do with the attenuation and weakening of autonomous self-direction, or agency, in neurotic conditions, most conspicuously in obsessive–compulsive symptoms. The practical interest arose as I realized that the great preponderance of the patients I saw had obsessive symptoms of one kind or another. I suspect that is true of most outpatient psychotherapy practices.

The fact that symptomatic behavior is invariably in character means that there is no clear distinction between symptomatic behavior and characteristic, consciously purposeful or volitional behavior in general. Yet it seems that neurotic people, and schizophrenics more so, regularly experience their own behavior, particularly the behavior we describe as symptomatic, as less than autonomous. That is, they experience their behavior as not fully their own free choice, as obligatory in some way, a compulsion or in some other way not really or completely intended or desired ("I drank more than I wanted last night"), or simply as strange and "not like me." This disjunction between the objectively characteristic nature of symptomatic behavior and its subjective alienation reflects an estrangement from the self that cannot be explained as an intrusion of particular unconscious wishes. The case is, rather, that the neurotic person does not know himself in a more general sense; he is estranged from, does not recognize, whole attitudes and aims of his conscious subjective life.

As I mentioned, it was not only the theoretical problem of autonomy but, also, a special interest in obsessive conditions that led me to take up the whole subject of autonomy and volitional action and their distortions in rigid character. That general subject, in turn, came to include sadomasochistic attitudes and sexuality, long associated clinically with rigid, moralistic character, and paranoid character.

I was particularly interested in the old problem of masochism, again partly for theoretical reasons, and also because I had seen masochistic attitudes and behavior, so-called "moral masochism," in my practice frequently, and much more frequently among women than men. Studying masochistic attitudes as expressions of rigid, essentially obsessive character showed them in a new light. What has often been described as an abject seeking, or embrace, of suffering victimhood for its own sake showed itself, on the contrary, to be a principled and determined defense of self-respect. The exaggerated suffering and humility, the "nursing" of grievances, that one sees in masochism actually constitutes a refusal, on the part of one who feels humiliated and powerless, to allow that humiliation to go unremembered, unnoted, and therefore unanswered. To keep defeat or humiliation alive, to remind oneself of it constantly, obsessively, is to summon moral authority against it. Masochism is a defensive effort of the less powerful; that is why it is a defensive effort primarily of women.

But the understanding of sexual masochism and sadism presented a problem. How could a character structure or a way of thinking explain the existence of a sexual drive? In the psychoanalytic tradition the explanation is in the other direction. But in fact, what is or is not sexually exciting to a particular person is determined not simply by a drive, but by a mind. It is determined, again, by attitudes, ways of thinking. To rigidly controlled, moralistic individuals sex and sensuality are dirty and degraded, even humiliating. It follows that sexual objects and situations that seem dirty and degraded, or at least the idea of such objects and situations, become especially erotic. Similarly, if erotic sensuality, to the rigidly controlled, moralistic person is an abandonment of morality, of self-control, and therefore of self-respect, then the wanton, abject figure, that is, the woman, who surrenders to the will and discipline of another, the man, will be especially erotic. A curious implication of these attitudes is that, from both a sadistic and a masochistic standpoint, the focus of sexuality is the submissive female.

I had wanted, since *Neurotic Styles* to take up Freud's discovery of the relation in the male of unconscious homosexuality to paranoia. Now, with the effects of rigid attitudes on the content of sexual fantasy in mind, that relation was clarified. Like many others, I took up the famous case of Schreber, the German jurist whose paranoid delusion that he was being transformed into a female led Freud to his discovery. Schreber, a rigid man by anyone's standards, upright, dutiful, by his own lights "morally unblemished," was horrified by the idea and the sensation that despite his great efforts of will he was being transformed into a wanton, voluptuous female, subjugated and tortured. Here, too, the subjugation and surrender of will which is abhorrent to the rigid character, is precisely what is especially sensual and erotic. Understanding paranoia as a variety of rigid character, in other words, makes clear both the erotic attraction of Schreber's fantasy and the horror it inspired in him.

I was satisfied by these solutions and considered them confirmation of my idea that attitudes or the general form of thinking determine, within limits, the specific nature of the ideational symptom.

Psychotherapy of Neurotic Character

During these years, from 1960 to 1989, I was almost entirely occupied profession-ally with my psychotherapy practice. I did teach as an adjunct at the UCLA School of Social Welfare, where some psychology graduate students, who remain friends to this day, joined my class. I also lectured here and there, and I spent part of a semester as visiting professor at Simon Fraser University in British Columbia. But it was doing psychotherapy that absorbed my professional interest for nearly thirty years, that and writing.

The therapeutic approach that I had learned from Kaiser and made my own had shown its effectiveness and I wanted to present it in a convincing way. That meant two things: making explicit the understanding of neurotic conditions which the therapy rests on, and showing how therapy can be done according to this approach.

The general characterological theory was already well developed. The neurotic condition consists essentially of the strains generated by the restrictive neurotic character. Anxieties arise as those strains are exacerbated by circumstances, requir-ing the individual to act, according to his character, in ways that forestall or dispel those anxieties. Usually that defensive action aims to reinforce the characteristic restrictive style. Thus, the obsessive person, confronted by a personal choice is thrown into confusion and anxiety; he says that he doesn't know what he wants. He searches for rules to determine what he "should" do, and if he can find or devise them, his anxiety is dispelled, but he remains cut off, estranged, from what he actu-ally wants. As far as psychotherapy is concerned, this picture of the neurotic condi-tion immediately indicates a revision of the idea of "therapeutic material." The therapeutic material is no longer to be sought in presumed derivatives in the patient's narrative of particular, largely ideational, unconscious conflicts. It actually consists of the more robust dynamics of the whole character, the whole person, manifest at that moment in his action, in what he is doing by producing that narrative.

I knew from my own experience as well as from supervising others that learning to pay attention to what the person is doing, as well as what he is saying, is not as easy as one might think. It is especially difficult for therapists already trained in psychoanalytic therapy. The psychoanalytic tradition does not encourage that kind of attention. The traditional arrangement in which the analyst sits behind the patient, whose expression cannot be seen and evidently is not thought necessary to be seen, reflects the more or less exclusive focus in psychoanalysis on the content of the patient's narrative and associations.

I found a useful concept in the idea of the speech act. I was introduced to it by a philosopher friend, Dr. David Gordon of Los Angeles, who sent me to the book, *How to Do Things with Words*, by the English philosopher, J.L. Austen. Austen's concept of speech acts is a specification of what the logicians call the instrumental use of language. Austen describes how certain kinds of speech constitute actions that have effects other than their simple communicative value. An example is the statement "I do" in the marriage ceremony. Another example is the statement "I'll be back at three o'clock"; it may be a threat, or it may be a promise. In these examples, as Austen says, saying something is doing something. Austen specifies certain kinds of speech that have certain kinds of effects, but in fact all speech is action; it has a purpose, a point. Sometimes that purpose is simply to communicate information, to share an idea or experience.

Our patients, who typically speak more or less throughout the therapy hour, are doing something as they are with us. They may simply be sharing an idea or a feeling, or they may be persuading themselves that they feel or believe what they think they should feel or believe. They may be, without realizing it, showing us, by their exaggerated deference, that they "know their place," or they may be showing us, and assuring themselves, that they are at least our equals. In ways such as these, the patients' dynamics are lived in front of us, in the "here and now."

As I mentioned, I wanted also to develop, and to offer, an understanding of the psychology of therapeutic change. This returned me to my interest in autonomy or agency and what seemed, actually, the rather obvious notion that introducing someone to himself, making it possible for him to experience clearly what he wants to do, in the current phrase raising his consciousness, increases his autonomy and actually raises the volitional level of his action.

A Professor

My professional life had been, I suppose, rather isolated since the years at Riggs, although I didn't feel particularly isolated. I had never collaborated in work and although I held some nominal memberships I had not participated in professional organizations. I lectured occasionally here and there and, as I mentioned, I did teach as an adjunct or a visitor. The idea of a regular academic position seemed attractive from time to time, but I never sought one and had never been offered one. I enjoyed my practice and pursued my writing in Los Angeles without much thought to other arrangements. My wife, Gerry Shapiro, who is an architect, had built a vacation home for us in rural Western Massachusetts, near old friends and not far from where we had lived before. We began to consider ways of spending more time there than the usual vacations. A response to an inquiry of mine from Dr. Herbert Schlesinger, who was then Director of the clinical program at the Graduate Faculty of the New School for Social Research in New York, inviting me to teach there, was attractive, and we decided to move East. I resumed a small practice, at first at our home in Massachusetts, and, commuting once a week to New York, I began to teach part time at the Graduate Faculty. Before long, my association with the school became full time and eventually, after Schlesinger's retirement as director of the program, and a few more years in which I was able to avoid it, I became director. Unexpectedly, I had begun a new career in my sixties.

It was a more diverse work life than I was used to. I continued to see patients, now mainly in New York City and continued to write, in addition to teaching and some administrative work. I enjoyed being around colleagues and students and, though one isn't supposed to, I generally enjoyed even faculty meetings. The intellectual atmosphere in the department and the Graduate Faculty was lively. At the invitation of Dr. Arien Mack, a professor in the department and editor of the Graduate Faculty journal *Social Research*, I contributed some articles that I would not have written otherwise. In particular, work on the article, *On the Psychology of Self-Deception*, allowed – actually, required – me to think through the conundrum that subject has posed to philosophers. I was able to show that the internal defensive process of self-deception is essentially the same as coerced self-deception, as in brain-washing.

Working in an academic setting also brought my attention and sometimes my interest to experimental and theoretical psychological work I would not have known. I supervised research projects for the first time and some of my students did studies of psychopathology that were interesting and valuable to me. Still, my overall exposure to experimental clinical research did not erase my reservations about much of it. There was, though, a further important benefit of being a professor. I now had student assistants for library work. They not only saved time in locating literature, but also located some that, on my own, I might easily have missed, or, more likely, simply skipped. This was particularly useful for the project I had in mind, which became my book *Dynamics of Character*.

Dynamics of Character: Self-Regulation in Psychopathology

I had thought for some time of deepening and, also, extending to hypomanic and schizophrenic conditions the work on pathological styles I had begun in *Neurotic Styles*. I had already shown formal or structural relations between symptomatically disparate neurotic conditions. I thought it would be possible to identify more fundamental formal dimensions of psychopathology that would apply to psychotic as well as neurotic conditions.

Although I was well aware that there is no simple continuity between the two, it became evident to me that the defensive styles of neurotic conditions did in fact share certain formal characteristics with schizophrenic thought and affect. A loss of objective reality in schizophrenia was commonly supposed to distinguish it from nonpsychotic conditions, but this is not true; a loss of objective reality, in more moderate, more subtle, but nevertheless actual, forms, as, for example, in exaggerated obsessive worrying, could be shown in neurotic conditions as well. A degradation, or "flattening," of affect, similarly, was considered distinctively schizophrenic, but the shallowness of hysterical affect or the emotional indifference of the psychopath were clearly moderate, but formally similar versions of a reduced quality of emotionality. And most central, a weakened or attenuated experience of agency and a corresponding actual abridgment of normal volitional processes, including volitional direction of attention, already well known in schizophrenia ("loss of will") was apparent also in neurotic conditions.

The finding that these formal dimensions of schizophrenic symptoms are intrinsic also to nonpsychotic conditions argues that similar dynamics are at work in both. It argues, in other words, that schizophrenic symptoms are the product not of a collapse of an existing defense structure, but of its radical extension. It remains a fact of course that when a transition occurs from a neurotic to a schizophrenic state, a qualitative reorganization takes place. I offered a conjecture based on some well-established clinical data to explain that reorganization. I, like others, assume that the particular vulnerability of some individuals to such a radical reorganization has to do with biological factors. The psychological manifestations of any such biological vulnerability would presumably be, again, of a formal or very general kind, such as unusual sensory thresholds, as was once suggested, I believe, by Dr. Sybille Escalona, rather than particular cognitive capacities.

Postscript

Since the completion of *Dynamics of Character* and retirement, except for one seminar, from my position at the New School, I have been entirely occupied again with doing and supervising psychotherapy, and writing. That professional life feels very familiar and comfortable to me, and somehow liberates me to take up topics that interest me without considering, or almost without considering, organizing them into a book. Those topics have included the two meanings, moral and psychological, of responsibility; the distinction between conscience dependent on rules and conscience of conviction; the muddled issue of self-control and loss of control; even the ancient problem of free will. These projects, diverse as they seem, will probably turn out to have some common aim, since they occur to the same person, if only to wrestle with obscurities that have bothered me.

New York, NY
July, 2010

David Shapiro

Contributors

Sidney J. Blatt, Ph.D. is Professor of Psychiatry and Psychology at Yale University and a faculty member at the Western New England Institute of Psychoanalysis. His most recent books include: *Polarities of Experience: Relatedness and Self-definition in Personality Development, Psychopathology and the Therapeutic Process* (APA, 2008) and *Experiences of Depression: Theoretical, Clinical and Research Perspectives* (APA, 2004). He is also coeditor, with Diana Diamond and Joseph Lichtenberg, of *Attachment and Sexuality* (Analytic Press 2007) and with Jozef Corveleyn and Patrick Luyten of *The Theory and Treatment of Depression: Towards a Dynamic Interactionism Model* (Lawrence Erlbaum, 2005).

E. Virginia Demos, Ed.D. is a senior staff psychologist and a past Erikson Scholar at the Austen Riggs Center. A clinical and developmental psychologist, infant researcher and teacher, she is Assistant Clinical Professor of Psychology in the Department of Psychiatry at Harvard Medical School. Dr. Demos has been a teacher of early development and a clinical supervisor for over 20 years in training hospitals and at the Harvard Graduate School of Education where she was the director of the Program in Counseling and Consulting Psychology. She was also the director of a private psychotherapy clinic in Boston. Dr. Demos edited *Exploring Affects: The Selected writings of Sylvan S. Tomkins* (Cambridge University Press, 1995) and has published numerous articles and book chapters on affective development in early childhood and the central role of affect in shaping psychic organization. She has received several research fellowships and is a founding member of the International Society for Research in Emotion (ISRE).

Morris N. Eagle, Ph.D. is Professor Emeritus and Clinical Professor, Derner Institute of Advanced Psychological Studies, Adelphi University and former President of the Division of Psychoanalysis, American Psychological Association. He is the author of approximately 150 scientific articles. Dr. Eagle is also the author of *Recent Developments in Psychoanalysis: A Critical Evaluation* (Harvard University Press, 1987); and co-editor of *Interface between Psychology and Psychoanalysis* (APA, 1992); *Psychoanalysis as Health Care* (Analytic Press, 1999); and *Attachment: Current Research, Theory, and Clinical Practice* (Other Press, 2002). Dr. Eagle maintains a private psychotherapy practice in Los Angeles, CA.

Andreas Evdokas, Ph.D. is Assistant Professor of Psychiatry and Behavioral Science at the Albert Einstein College of Medicine and Adjunct Professor of Psychology at the New School for Social Research. He is also the Administrative Director of the Department of Adult Psychiatry at Bronx-Lebanon Hospital Center and is in private practice in New York City.

Peter J. Glick, M.A. is a doctoral student in clinical psychology at the New School for Social Research.

Mindy Greenstein, Ph.D. received her doctorate in clinical psychology from the New School for Social Research, and her A.B. in English Literature from the University of Chicago. She was a forensic psychologist with the Federal Bureau of Prisons, where she conducted psychotherapy with inmates and court-ordered evaluations of pre-trial defendants' criminal responsibility and competency to stand trial. Dr. Greenstein later trained in psycho-oncology at Memorial Sloan-Kettering Cancer Center, where she was a National Institute for Mental Health AIDS Research Fellow and Chief Clinical Fellow in the Department of Psychiatry and Behavioral Science. While there, she designed the meaning-centered group psychotherapy intervention for the hospital's existential psychiatry program. Dr. Greenstein is currently consulting with the Psychiatry Department at Sloane-Kettering on interventions for geriatric oncology patients. She lives in New York City with her husband and two sons.

Mardi J. Horowitz, M.D. is Professor of Psychiatry at University of California-San Francisco, originator of the diagnosis of PTSD, and contributor to the diagnoses of Histrionic and Narcissistic Personality Disorders, as well as author of 17 books and approximately 300 papers.

Lawrence Josephs, Ph.D. is Professor of Psychology at the Derner Institute of Advanced Psychological Studies of Adelphi University. He is also a member of the North American Editorial Board of the *International Journal of Psychoanalysis*. In years past, Dr. Josephs published a book on character styles, *Character Structure and the Organization of the Self* (Columbia University Press, 1992) that was reprinted as *Character and Self-Experience* (Aronson, 1995) and a book on character analysis, *Balancing Empathy and Interpretation* (Aronson, 1995). More recently Dr. Josephs has been writing on the dynamics of seduction and betrayal in the context of love triangles. He has also been interested in examining Freudian views of human sexuality in the light of recent developments in evolutionary psychology.

Ali Khadivi, Ph.D. is Associate Clinical Professor of Psychiatry and Behavioral Science at the Albert Einstein College of Medicine and Adjunct Professor of Psychology at the New School for Social Research. He is also Chief of Psychology at the Bronx-Lebanon Hospital Center.

Craig Piers, Ph.D. is a senior psychologist and psychotherapy supervisory in the health center at Williams College, and formerly, Associate Director of Admissions and a senior supervising psychologist at the Austen Riggs Center. Dr. Piers frequently presents his work nationally and his published articles and book chapters have addressed personality disorders and assessment, psychotherapeutic impasse, suicide and complex systems theory. Dr. Piers is coeditor (with John Muller and Joseph Brent) of *Self-Organizing Complexity in Psychological Systems* (Aronson, 2007), an Associate Editor of *Psychoanalytic Dialogues*, and serves as a reviewer for several other professional journals.

Louis A. Sass, Ph.D. is Professor in the Department of Clinical Psychology, Graduate School of Applied and Professional Psychology, at Rutgers – the State University of New Jersey. He also serves as a Faculty Affiliate in Rutgers University's Program in Comparative Literature, as a Research Associate in the Rutgers Center for Cognitive Science, and as a fellow of the Rutgers Center for Cultural Analysis. Dr. Sass's primary areas of interest include psychopathology (especially borderline, schizoid, and schizophrenia-spectrum disorders), phenomenology and hermeneutics, psychodynamic theory, cultural psychology, and the nature of the self in modernism and postmodernism. Dr. Sass has been awarded fellowships from the National Endowment for the Humanities, the Institute for Advanced Study (Princeton, New Jersey), and the Fulbright Foundation. Dr. Sass has published over 80 articles. He is the author of *Madness and Modernism: Insanity in the Light of Modern Art, Literature, and Thought* (Harvard University Press, 1998); and *The Paradoxes of Delusion: Wittgenstein, Schreber, and the Schizophrenic Mind* (Cornell University Press, 1995). A fellow of American Psychological Association, he is on the editorial board of the journals *Philosophy, Psychiatry, Psychology*; *Phenomenology and the Cognitive Sciences*; *Theory and Psychology*; *Psychiatrie, Sciences Humaines, Neurosciences* (Paris), and *Psicothema* (Oviedo, Spain); he has served on the editorial board of *Cultural Anthropology*.

Herbert J. Schlesinger, Ph.D. is Professor of Clinical Psychology at Columbia University. He is also Director, Clinical Psychology, and Psychologist-in-Chief at NewYork–Presbyterian Hospital, and a Training and Supervising Psychoanalyst, Columbia Center for Psychoanalytic Training and Research. Formerly, Dr. Schlesinger was Director of Clinical Psychology Training Program of the Graduate Faculty of New School University as Alfred J. and Monette C. Marrow Professor of Psychology. Dr. Schlesinger's research and writing on clinical topics has been published widely in refereed journals and now includes four books, most recently, *Promises Oaths, and Vows: On the Psychology of Promising* (Analytic Press, 2008). He served on the editorial boards of several journals, and for 20 years was Editor of *Psychological Issues Monograph Series*. His research into the effects of mental health care on the use of medical care services was supported for many years by the National Institute of Mental Health (NIMH), the Congressional Budget Office, and the McArthur Foundation. He also served for several terms reviewing grant applications to the NIMH, and was appointed to the Advisory Council of the Alcohol, Drug Abuse, and Mental Health Administration and an adviser to the World Health Organization.

Michael F. Schober, Ph.D. is Dean and Professor of Psychology at the New School for Social Research. His published research examines dyadic conversation, perspective-taking, and the joint construction of meaning in various face-to-face and mediated settings, including interviews and chamber music performances. He is Editor of the multidisciplinary journal *Discourse Processes*.

David Shapiro, Ph.D. is Professor Emeritus at the New School for Social Research, where he was formerly Director of Clinical Psychology Training. He has practiced psychotherapy for many years in Los Angeles and New York City since leaving the Austen Riggs Center where he was Chief Psychologist. His writing on neurotic character is well known, particularly his book *Neurotic Styles* (Basic Books, 1965), which is considered a classic and has been translated into six languages. He is also the author of *Autonomy and Rigid Character* (Basic Books, 1981), *Psychotherapy of Neurotic Character* (Basic Books, 1989) and *Dynamics of Character* (Basic Books, 2000).

Paul L. Wachtel, Ph.D. is CUNY Distinguished Professor in the doctoral program in clinical psychology at City College and the Graduate Center of the City University of New York. His most recent book is *Relational Theory and the Practice of Psychotherapy* (Guilford, 2008). He is a cofounder of the Society for the Exploration of Psychotherapy Integration.

Part I
Comparative Analysis

Chapter 1
Another View of Psychotherapy?

Herbert J. Schlesinger

Over the years, David Shapiro's career and mine have intersected productively several times. I think we have a talent for bouncing ideas off one another. This piece is about one such encounter, or perhaps it was a mythical encounter for my recollection of it lacks detail. In any case, I prefer not to check on the veridicality of my memory; it serves me well enough, whether or not it tells me the truth in any absolute sense about this occasion of enlightenment. As you will see, I take a narrative view toward truth-telling, and I will leave it to Dr. Shapiro to vet my recollection of the founding incident. In his modest way, he may disown having been the source of my inspiration. I accept that risk. It will make no essential difference to my conclusions, and in view of our long acquaintance, I prefer to be grateful to him rather than to one of his antecedents; if he feels he has not met all of his obligations to his intellectual forbearers, they are for him to acquit. Anyway, enough throat clearing, or to unmix the metaphor, enough pen wiping or pencil sharpening; let me get on with it already.

Once upon a time, I don't remember the occasion; quite possibly it was when Dr. Shapiro and I both were discussing a student's case presentation at The New School, which was our most frequent meeting place, I heard Shapiro utter quietly a few simple words that were entirely apt for the occasion, but that rang out loudly to me as having wide application and enormous clinical and intellectual power. They have stayed with me and the more I have thought about them, and quoted them to generations of students; the more I see them as central to my own thinking, the keystone, if you will forgive me the extravagant comparison, to my own intellectual arch. I hope you are dying of curiosity rather than boredom at this self-indulgent delaying; the phrase Shapiro uttered on that fateful occasion was, "The clinical material is what the patient is doing, not just the words the patient is saying."

There! So why all the fuss? Some readers may react with "Huh?" Others with, "of course, what's new about that?" And still others may comment patiently, "But

H.J. Schlesinger (✉)
Professor of Clinical Psychology in Psychiatry, College of Physicians and Surgeons,
Columbia University, 630 West 168th Street, New York, NY 10032
e-mail: hjs1@columbia.edu

C. Piers (ed.), *Personality and Psychopathology: Critical Dialogues with David Shapiro*,
DOI 10.1007/978-1-4419-6214-0_1, © Springer Science+Business Media, LLC 2011

isn't saying words also a kind of doing?" I see that I shall have to deconstruct this simple phrase to make its clinical power obvious.

Of course, my third commentator is right, saying is doing, and he might have added that Shapiro probably was referring to the other doings of the patient, that is, other than tongue wagging, including his posture and other expressive movements.

However, there is another important sense of "saying is doing" embedded in Shapiro's phrase. Words have not only a dictionary sense but when spoken by the patient to the therapist[1] they also convey intention, mostly not fully conscious intention. That is, the patient may be aware that he harbors these intentions, or he could easily be made aware of owning them. But he is likely to be less aware that his speaking right now is imbued with intention. To put the matter succinctly, if dogmatically, all patient speech is tendentious; it is suffused with action. To borrow from Roy Schafer, another member of our small group (Schafer 1976), patients do not have to be taught, as analysts must be taught, to speak in "action language." In that additional and essential sense, the patient is "doing" something with his words (Austen 1967). The patient intends his words to do something to the therapist, or to get him to do something to, or for, or about, the patient. Of course, the patient equally could intend a negative sense, that is, to get the therapist to stop doing something to, or for, or about, the patient. The knowledgeable reader will understand that I am making a glancing reference to transference, but not only to transference. We rely on the skill of the therapist to discern the degree to which the intentionality of the patient's words derives from his unremembered past, that is, from sources other than the immediate and realistic aspects of their relationship.[2]

Let me pause to consider a more personal question, could I have arrived at these ideas without imagining them as stemming from Shapiro's remark? Perhaps I am only fitting them into the existing body of my own thinking because they are so congruent; after all Dr. Shapiro and I grew up in the same tradition and have had teachers and colleagues in common. It could be so, but I am grateful to him nonetheless, for this utterance struck me as containing a basic truth.

Let me spell out where I think our ideas converge and perhaps where they diverge. If we can agree that the clinical material is what the patient is doing, it seems to me a safe implication that the patient is doing what he must do, that is, his speaking is determined in large part by the neurotic tangle that brought him to psychotherapy. To the extent that it is so determined, he will be forced to repeat in action what he cannot remember in words, so that his speaking becomes a retelling it via reenacting it. In short, the patient is forced to repeat *with* the therapist the script of that neurosis. I underlined *with* to emphasize that the retelling is not *to* the therapist but with him; that is, with the therapist's willing or (usually) unwilling

---

[1] As I will discuss only the words spoken by the patient to the therapist in the psychotherapy setting, I will only note here that my remarks apply equally, if most often with less urgency, to words spoken by either party in any social setting.

[2] If space permits, I will spell out some of the implications of this statement; if not, I leave the issue with the advice that it is best to assume that all patient speech, however realistic, bears some stamp of the patient's past; but it is not safe to assume that this stamp necessarily is of immediate clinical significance.

participation in the act of retelling. It is just this conjunction, "with" that makes transference such a powerful form of clinical communication. This phrasing invites the question, "If the telling is not to the therapist, to whom is it directed?" Fair question; the retelling is directed at the transference object who seems for the moment to be embodied by the therapist, but not the therapist qua therapist. The reader will note that this formulation requires the therapist to recognize that he has dual identities, we might call them "therapeutic ally" and "transference object," and like Pooh Bah, in Gilbert and Sullivan's Mikado (Gilbert and Sullivan 1865), must figure out which of his multiple identities is being addressed at the moment. Therapists, like the rest of us, prefer to think of themselves as unitary. For many of us, the idea of having even two identities is foreign, and in the therapeutic situation, the transference object described by the patient is so often such an odious character that the thought of being taken for him/her is repellant. That is one more reason why the therapist must learn to tolerate the therapeutic split, actually to cultivate it, so as to allow him to parse the patient's communications usefully (Sterba 1934; Zetzel 1956). Maintaining one's therapeutic split is a delicate achievement, one easily lost in the hurly-burly of the therapeutic situation. When the patient accuses the therapist of being a revenant of the countless others who have taken advantage of the patient, a revenant who now has inflicted the most egregious and insulting disappointment of all, the therapist needs a sturdy split both to be able to bear the accusation rather than to defend himself, and to be able to join the patient in confronting the transference object so as to examine how the transference object has failed him once again. It is a natural tendency to defend one's reputation when one feels unjustly attacked. The disciplined therapist might restrain that impulse and maintain a high-minded silence under attack, or perhaps might attempt a seeming non-defensive "pointing out" of the error in the patient's thinking, which the patient is likely to understand as a counter-attack by the transference object. However, if the therapist had been able to maintain his therapeutic split, in his identity as therapeutic ally, he could have helped the patient discover why it felt necessary to attack the transference object just at that moment, that is, what just happened that resonated with the ancient hurts? There is more to say about the delicacy of the therapeutic split, but first I want to return to the take-off point of this digression in Shapiro's aphorism.

I think it remarkable that we can derive a good bit of the theory of transference from that laconic statement. It may take the reader a little thought to agree about the necessity of the implications I have drawn, not to say their correctness, but consider, I take license from the exclusiveness inherent in the phrase, "the clinical material"; THE clinical material is, of course, the stuff the therapist MUST attend to. It is the closest statement we have, I think, to a clinical absolute. It is one of the few matters I am comfortable in being dogmatic about.[3] As I develop this argument further, I will propose corollaries to that statement in the form of maxims such as, "The patient is doing the best he can," and "The patient is always right" (Schlesinger 2003).[4]

---

[3] That is, I can't think of any others at the moment but want to leave open the possibility that there may be others. I am afraid I am not cut out to be a dogmatist.

[4] That is, it is up to the therapist to discover the faulty premises from which the patient logically drew his realistically incorrect opinions.

If the reader has followed me this far, he probably will have seen that by implicating the phenomenon of transference in Shapiro's aphorism, we are well on the way to deriving from it a working theory of the psychotherapy of neurosis. Neurosis is no longer a fashionable term in the official diagnostic scheme, but it captures for me, as I think it does for Shapiro, the notion of a psychopathology based more or less on unconscious conflict, that is, conflict that the patient cannot express in pure symbolic form as a non-tendentious narrative. Like the Ancient Mariner (Coleridge 1798), the patient must reenact his guilt and shame-ridden story with all comers, including especially the therapist. This is not to say that I believe there are no other sources of psychopathology, but rather to affirm that no matter what other psychopathology patients suffer from, like all non-patients, they are burdened by such unresolved conflicts (Kubie 1954, 1967).[5]

Perhaps it should not be surprising that this seemingly simple idea in Shapiro's aphorism is so difficult to get across to students in any effective way. By effective way, I mean of course, in a way that would enable them to apply it regularly.[6] Instead, I have found it to be one of two mantras that I have to intone regularly in every case that I have supervised and every conference in which clinical material is presented, which is to say, all of them. The other mantra, which seems easier to apply, is "Why now?" This mantra actually is a reinforcer of Shapiro's aphorism; it stresses that the patient's telling, that is, his doing, is taking place now, while the matter the patient is telling about, if it happened at all, happened at another time; it reinforces the admonition to focus on the *telling* as well as on what is *being told*. I do not actually intone these words as often as the situation would call for and try to find other ways to make the same points lest I be thought to have nothing else to say. But as a teacher, I wonder, why is it so difficult to apply these simple truisms?

I think the answer to that question is to be found in the coercive nature of transference which, of course, most commonly does not involve direct accusations of, or invitations to the therapist, but consists of more subtle action tendencies. Let me clarify the distinction by comparing the situation of the therapist with his patient with that of a member of the audience of a play. The author of the play has provided a script, of course, but the words have no life until actors are taught, spurred, and coaxed by a director to enact the author's words and to strive for maximum effect. The intention of the playwright and the acting company is to move the audience emotionally. Indeed, the members of the audience have come to the theater to be moved. They attend voluntarily hoping to lose themselves in the world of the play; they are willing to suspend disbelief for an hour or two, and to identify themselves with a character they find sympathetic. If the play was well written and is well acted, the members of the audience will be able to lose themselves safely in the

---

[5] The knowledgeable reader will recognize that I have not offered a complete theory of transference to which one would have to add the contribution of role theory and cognitive theory.

[6] I do recognize that it may be an excessive expectation that students will grasp this principle and be able to apply it regularly in the course of one semester with their first patients.

lives of the characters, characters that are embodied on stage but that exist only in the author's imagination. If the play is badly written, if the characters are unconvincing, and the actors cannot make them come to life on the stage, only the most susceptible of the members of the audience will be stirred. If the rest of the playgoers are unable to do so, they will count the evening as lost. To believe the critics, that unfortunate outcome is all too prevalent.

How is it with the therapist and his patient? Consider, the patient we think suitable for psychotherapy will generally be a good and willing story teller. His one story is the script of his unconscious fantasy, and as he does not fully remember it, he tells it as he must, by reenacting it. A good story teller, whether or not he tries to dramatize his telling, provides a compelling experience for the listener.

Like a member of the audience of a play, or the reader of a novel for that matter, the listener tends to lose himself in the story being told. He tends to project himself imaginatively into the scene being described. Figuratively, as the lights dim, the therapist-listener loses awareness that the story he is hearing is about past events, and he experiences the events of the story as if they are occurring now; he feels surprise, anxiety, joy, and fear as might be appropriate for a contemporary participant or witness of the events described, and he even may want to intervene, to encourage or caution the patient, to prevent his story from coming out disastrously, as it now seems inevitable.

This degree of involuntary participation whenever one listens to a well told story is, I think, universal.[7] To this point, we do not need to invoke the phenomenon of transference. I think the phenomenon of losing oneself in another's story owes much less to conflict based psychopathology than to the millennia mankind spent in the oral tradition. Before the invention of writing, the transmission of culture depended on memorizing the sacred stories that bound people together. It is only in recent times that one would be allowed to take a critical attitude toward the traditional texts which were supposed to be passed on unchanged to the next generation.

By referring to unchanging traditional texts, I might give the wrong impression that the patient literally repeats a story of childhood trauma. Like the Ancient Mariner (Coleridge 1798), some patients do that repeatedly, and nearly all can tell that story on request, as when a new therapist "takes a history." But most patients when left to their own devices tell about what is going on in current life, but the stories, in a formal sense, relate the theme of the old script with current characters; for instance, the unappreciative and misunderstanding father of yore is represented metaphorically by the current unappreciative boss. The ancient script is not just a recipe for story telling but is a script for living. The patient lives out a metaphoric recycling of that script, a condition we call neurosis.[8] Another implication I must address is, if the therapist recognizes the presence of transference in the patient's

---

[7] One might invoke the concept of regression to explain it.

[8] This may be the point to remind the reader that transference is a Latinate translation of the German Übertragung, literally to carry across, and that metaphor is a Greek term with the same literal meaning.

metaphors, must he draw the patient' attention to it, or in more technical terms, interpret it? I think that answering this question would require too many qualifications of the "it depends" variety to permit a prescriptive generalization; it is a matter best left to art of psychotherapy rather than to science. To discuss the matter in somewhat more general terms, consider that any interpretation is also functionally an abortion; it interrupts the patient's story telling to inform him about what he is "really saying." Consider too that the patient, like all of us, resorts to metaphor when he is unable to speak, or is fearful about speaking more directly. At the very least, the therapist ought to weigh the advantage he sees in interrupting the patient's efforts to communicate in spite of his reservations by imposing on him the therapist's view of clarity against the advantage of allowing the patient to work his way through a possible transference bind with less directive assistance. For instance, the therapist, when feeling called upon to contribute something at such a juncture, instead of blurting out an interpretation, might offer what I have come to call an "umbrella statement," such as remarking that what the patient has said about "x" could also apply to others in the patient's life. Such a statement has a diagnostic as well as supportive intent. By observing the patient's response; does he continue on the same theme? Does he try to include only the more distant others the therapist had alluded to as being under the "umbrella?" In short, the therapist soon will see how ready the patient is to accept that the metaphor includes the therapist (i.e., transference object). Not infrequently, the therapist will notice that the patient suddenly has become more uncomfortable and may want to drop the subject. Here is a point when the therapist can suggest that the patient has just had an unwelcome thought, to which the patient might (and so often does) say: "Well I thought you might think I was referring to you." Guess which approach I prefer.

Unlike the professional story-teller, the patient in psychotherapy does not tell his story to provide an esthetic experience for the listener. He tells his story because he must, and in the vain hope of escaping from it; but as for the Ancient Mariner, it always comes out the same way. As the telling progresses, the story takes on life and the patient experiences afresh in the telling the old hopes, fears, disappointments, and resentments. As the narration slips into reenactment, the dramatization requires more than a script, it requires actors. The patient as playwright and director must make do with the persons he has at hand; he recruits the therapist to play the parts opposite the role the patient takes himself. The therapist, of course, did not volunteer to join in the re-enactment of the patient's script, or even to participate emotionally in the patient's retelling; he only signed on to help if he can. But most patients are good story tellers, deeply invested in the story they want to tell, and in the oral tradition, the therapist as audience is likely to relax and participate by visualizing the events being narrated. He will tend to lose his focus on the telling of the story as he surrenders his therapeutic split until suddenly he realizes that he is on the stage, so to speak, having joined willy-nilly in the reenactment. He has been jerked out of his safe role as auditor and has been forced to play the parts as the patient needs him to; in short, he is experiencing transference.

The seasoned psychotherapist is well aware that transference is coercive, but the well-meaning beginner will be disconcerted to find himself in the situation of mythic Laocoön who tried desperately to rescue his children from the serpents only to find himself trapped in their coils (Virgil, ca. 29–19 BC). When the young therapist for the first time feels helpless, impotent, without any way to help the patient or to extricate himself, it may signal the beginning of clinical wisdom; he may be ready to hear the advice, in effect to, "Put on your own oxygen mask first, then you can help your patient." In more proper terms, "anxiety has led you to give up your therapeutic split, look after it. By regaining it you will regain your therapeutic leverage."

As an aside, occasionally a patient tells his story in a way that is unconvincing; it does not inspire belief in the therapist who even begins to doubt that the patient believes what he is saying. This situation calls on the skill of the therapist; how to decide if the patient is a poor story teller doing the best he can, or if the patient's intention is expressed in the very distance he takes from the telling? Does the patient intend to imply, "I don't expect you to believe me, no one in my family does?" Again, if the therapist keeps his main focus on the telling of the story, he might find that such a meaning comes alive for him rather than becoming bored by a dull story.

As I have described transference as deriving from the unremembered past, I must deal with the question if the therapist must attempt to restore the patient's missing memory. Older theory would have it so, and the accompanying theory of change held that therapeutic change follows only after the arrival of "insight." My own experience in conducting psychoanalysis and psychotherapy is that some patients do recover memories that help to make sense of their neurotic behavior and make change possible. Others find that some memories they help to reconstruct fit plausibly into their histories whether true or not; their progress in therapy does not seem to depend on the convincing recovery of memory. Many patients, in psychotherapy particularly, seem able to accomplish their aims in therapy by working only with the metaphoric expressions of unconscious fantasy. The question, "What really happened?" or "What must have happened?" arises in any therapy that entertains the possibility that something in one's development has contributed to, if not caused, one's current misery. I see no need in most therapies, however, to try to recover missing memories as a primary activity. For some patients, the pursuit of elusive memories serves as an enjoyable distraction from facing difficult decisions that are all to plain to see. My own experience does not accord with the expectations of older theory; in particular I have noticed that most often insight, including recovery of significant memories, follows therapeutic change. That sequence makes sense to me in the same way that patient's memories of their parents change when it is no longer necessary to blame one's misery on their evil ways.

Let us return again to our takeoff point in Shapiro's aphorism. Becoming shanghaied into the enactment of transference is not the only way in which the "doing" inherent in patient's speech affects the therapist. The therapist's loss of distance under the almost hypnotic sway of the patient as story teller is duplicated when the therapist repeats the story to a supervisor and again to a case conference. If the presenter does not keep his nose in his notes as he reads them, and sometimes even then, one can see the glint in the presenter's eye, he is eager to give his listeners the same exciting experience he had when he heard the story for the first time. It is an example of what has been called "parallel process," a phenomenon familiar to supervisors; the student therapist tells the supervisor about the baffling experience he had with the patient by reproducing it so that the supervisor will feel as helpless as the student did, an example of transference in the supervisory situation.

You might think that I am about to suggest that the young therapist should deal with the potential hazards of transference by immunizing himself against the emotional contagion of persuasive stories by taking a critical and objective attitude toward them. You would be only partially correct. For, if the therapist were able to immunize himself against being moved by the patient's efforts, he would in effect tune out much of the patient's message and would become therapeutically useless. Becoming immune to the patient's blandishments, temptations or accusations is not the point. The therapist has an even harder lesson to learn; he has to both allow the patient to influence him, to allow the transference to settle on him, as it were, and at the same time observe the patient doing it and his own reactions from some distance away. The image that comes to mind is that the patient and transference object are at the end points of a line of action while the therapist (i.e., the therapeutic ally) is on a line at right angles to the line of action so as to able to observe and empathize with the regressed aspect of the patient and with the patient's projection of the transference object, as well as with the therapist himself (Schlesinger 1981). The task is somewhat the same as that of the anthropologist who must learn to be a participant-observer, able to join in the lives of the people under study so as to be accepted by them, and to study them at the same time, while avoiding "going native."

As I noted earlier, this knack of participating in the transference and observing the actions of transfer-er and transfer-ee at the same time is one of the most difficult skills for the therapist to learn. The therapist has to realize that the patient has dual and overlapping images of him as transference object and as therapeutic ally and tends to shift, seemingly without warning, between engaging with one or the other. As the therapist gains skill, he may become familiar enough with the metaphoric repetitions of the patient's script to be able to sense when the transference is about to shift. The skill the therapist needs calls on the capacity all of us have to split ourselves, that is, to split our sense of ourselves into object and observer. At the beginning of one's career, as our students are, they already feel inadequate to the task of helper. They feel highly vulnerable to be manipulated, teased, or shamed. If one already feels vulnerable and suddenly feels suffused by any strong emotion, one becomes even more vulnerable. One naturally attempts to reduce the sense of vulnerability by sealing up the split between participant and observer, between therapeutic ally and transference object. The image that comes to mind is the scene in a Western movie when the Indians swoop over the hill and threaten attack; the settlers draw their wagons into a tight circle and prepare to defend themselves. The anxious therapist, fearful of saying the wrong thing, not sure he understands enough to say anything is in no position, he thinks, to cultivate openness to experience and to trust his innate ability to observe what is going on between the patient and the transference object. Preoccupied by the need to defend his shaky sense of worth from what he experiences as the patient's demands upon him (actually, the patient's demands on the transference object), he hardly is able to listen to the patient, let alone understand him. He feels impotent, over a barrel; nothing useful comes to mind.

Dear reader, I had to stop writing at this point and did not get back to it for many days. By chance, I stumbled upon an old e-mail from Craig Piers to which he had attached an autobiographical note by Dr. Shapiro. I read it avidly hoping to answer the question of where my organizing quotation came from, and there it was. He credited the idea to Hellmuth Kaiser, Shapiro's analyst at Riggs, who had credited Wilhelm Reich for it. Here is another point at which Shapiro's and my career paths crossed. During the short time they remained in Topeka, the Kaisers, Hellmuth and Ruth became my good friends, and Hellmuth was a fellow instructor at the Topeka Psychoanalytic Institute. I also claim him as a significant teacher. I was so taken with his ideas about systematic analysis of resistance (Fierman 1965), which seemed to clarify the murky teaching about technique at the Institute that I sat in on one of his courses. I also enjoyed his account of Fenichel's attack (Fenichel 1935) on his position about the analysis of resistance (Kaiser 1934), an attack that must have served to put Kaiser beyond the pale of some quarters of the psychoanalytic establishment.

At any rate, I can see now why the aphorism I credited to Shapiro resonated so. The words I credited to Shapiro had never occurred to me as such, but when I heard them, they captured a central conception that had long since been become part of my way of listening to patients (Schlesinger 1994). Of course, couching these ideas in the context of how to deal with resistance begs the question I began with. Recall that we began with the notion that the clinical material is what the patient is doing. If we take the position that what the patient is doing is best described as resisting, we must necessarily assume that as the patient is in conflict, he prefers to present only one side of it.[9] How much freedom the patient feels he has in acting on that preference is a major issue for the therapy. I will assume, however, that the patient is doing, at least at the times of high clinical interest, what he feels he *must* do, whether or not he is fully aware of having chosen.[10] And it is only a further small step to assert that the patient is doing the best he can, considering that he is of at least two minds about the major issues of his life. And it is only another small step to assert, counterintuitively, that the patient is always right, with the proviso that by "right" we mean that his behavior is consistent with the patient's premises. From the point of view of common sense, this statement might seem absurd, but considered as a heuristic, it points to the responsibility of the therapist to help the patient discover the premises that would make the patient's odd behavior or peculiar ideas

---

[9] I weaseled by stating the patient's choice of what to present and what to withhold as a preference, thus avoiding taking a stand on whether the patient is aware of being in conflict and by implication the whole issue of "the unconscious." I did so because I want to engage Dr. Shapiro on the larger matter of the derivation of much of what I (and I believe he too) do clinically from his aphorism without descending (or rising) to discussing whether we need to invoke any variety of metapsychology.

[10] Clearly, having taken the coward's path in regard to metapsychology, after asserting that the patient does as he must, you will expect me to follow suit by dodging the issue of "free will."

"right," that is, consistent with his script, and to understand what they were for and why they are here now. I think these notions are a reasonable, if overly simple, way of describing one of the intentions of psychoanalysis or psychoanalytic psychotherapy. I believe I have demonstrated that we can understand patient behavior without resorting to the concept of resistance.

I would like to offer an alternative approach to the relevance of the patient's "transferring" as an aspect of his "doing" to which the therapist should attend. Transference is a ubiquitous phenomenon, present continuously in the clinical situation as elsewhere. Nevertheless, discussions of transference invariably refer to clinical applications, probably because mainly it is clinicians who find the term useful. The clinical situation, in which distractions are minimal and which discussion is perforce focused on personal issues rather than on general topics, seems well designed to permit transference to flower. The situation of everyday life, in contrast, minimizes the opportunity for transference to appear; the task orientation of "external reality" tends to constrain, but not prevent, the idiosyncratic attributions of qualities of relationship that characterize transference, let alone permit their expression.

I would like to suggest that transference is a particular expression of the more general process by which we are prepared by memory and expectation to find that the social situation we are about to enter is familiar or strange.[11] Therapists take for granted that the field of operation for psychotherapy is the patient's psychological world; to help the patient, one must be able, as it were, to view the world as he or she experiences it. Still, therapists, like the rest of us tend to take for granted that the world that the patient lives in is similar in many respects to that of the therapist, and to the version that might be called consensual reality, but also is deviant in important respects such that the patient's expectations of important others are regularly thwarted. The patient is frustrated and indignant with the (mis)behavior of others who do not do as the patient believes they should. When therapist and patient look into the matter, they generally discover that the patient has long held expectations of others that are anachronistic, expectations that might have been reasonable at a much earlier time in the patient's life, perhaps during infancy, but are no longer valid, and the others of today will not honor them.

Following this formulation, the patient will have become increasingly frustrated and likely increasingly non-functional, because he or she continues to press an idiosyncratic view of reality on a resistant and rejecting social environment. The patient "knows" that "it" (whatever he has been doing) doesn't work, but seems unable to learn from the disappointing experiences, continuing to "hit his head against the wall" as if expecting that in time and with sufficient effort the wall would give way. When the patient comes (or is brought more or less unwillingly) for treatment, it is this capacity, (perhaps better this necessity) of the patient to

---

[11] I allude here to the necessity of turning to cognitive theory and social psychology to understand the full complexity of the general phenomenon of expectation, of which transference is a component.

assume that the patient's view of the world is held by all, that generates the peculiar behavior we call transference.

By linking the patient's transference experiences of the clinical situation to the patient's behavior in everyday life, I mean to develop the more general view that the "reality" we all believe we hold in common is a private construction, that "reality is relative," (Laforgue 1940). However, if we take seriously the point of view that experience is idiosyncratic, that reality is relative, we invite the obvious question how can we account for that we seem able to take for granted that we share the same world; that in our daily exchanges with others our expectations generally are mostly met unexceptionably.

Here are some thoughts that may help to reconcile these observations. Consider, much of childhood education, at home as well as in school, consists of the teaching of "manners," that is in how to conduct oneself with others so that one's needs can be met, more or less, while meeting the needs and expectations of others, more or less. In short, the major lesson of childhood is how to survive and thrive in a reality, that is, a social environment that one has inherited and how to reconstruct it sufficiently to make it one's own; it is not one that one invents de novo. The child eventually becomes reconciled to the necessity of joining the "adult" world, a world he did not make, and learns how to appreciate it, adapt to it and to make it his own while at the same time, gain awareness that the way he experiences "the world" is likely to be different in important ways from the way others experience it. He learns that in order to thrive, he must remain in a workable relationship with others must negotiate the sense of reality that will govern their mutual experiencing, or in other words, so that the expectations each has of the other will be met. The child learns that negotiating the nature of the ongoing relationship is a continuous process. In conversation, we assure ourselves that we are "in tune," "on the same page," nonverbally through facial expression, eye contact and posture. Then too, our verbal exchanges are interrupted periodically with phrases intended to hold the interest of the other and to assure the speaker that the other is paying attention and following along; "Y'know what I mean?" and such. The child learns these lessons without awareness that he has absorbed them; they become installed in procedural memory. In short, to assume that we may take for granted that we all live in the same social reality is safe in only the most general sense and only as long as the conversation has little emotional weight.

For the therapist, the clinical function of much of the "manners" of the "beginning," the tentative, mutual feeling-out that characterizes the initial encounter with a patient, consists of discovering the nature of the patient's psychological world, his sense of reality, while the patient tries to figure out what the therapist really wants from him and whether he can be useful. The therapist wants to learn the patient's characteristic "rules of behavior," how he organizes his world including the expectations the patient brings to the clinic, as well as those he holds of life in general, and at the same time, to help the patient learn the "rules" of the clinic and clinician, what he may expect and how to go about it. This matter is sometimes discussed in terms of informing the patient about the policies of the clinic or "establishing the frame." The therapist of any degree of experience "knows" that despite his best intentions and "normal" behavior (that is, for a clinician) the patient will attempt to impose his or her sense of reality on the therapist and will develop expectations that the therapist cannot possibly meet and should not attempt to meet.

Sadly, many clinicians tend to think of this inevitable clash of values and differing views of reality as that the patient "distorts" REALITY, has "delusions," or shows a "failure of reality testing." The therapist who insists that his or her sense of reality is the correct (i.e., universally accepted) one, and that the patient must learn to adapt to it, commits the major error of defining the patient's behavior in terms of what it is not rather than in terms of what it is. That therapist also misses the opportunity to learn about the ways in which the patient's way of doing things works for him and how he has constructed his world so as to confirm his "rightness." That therapist is not likely to find out the circumstances when the patient is "right," not wrong, and how to help the patient appreciate that when he pursues conflicting agendas he inevitably trips up. Before the therapist can help the patient to recognize and perhaps accommodate to the differences in the way he or she sees things and the idiosyncratic view held by a significant other, or with the consensual view, the therapist must appreciate "where the patient is coming from."

I anticipate that the reader might easily extrapolate this point of view to an impossible extension, to the polar, "libertarian" stance that if everyone is entitled to his own view of things, that one view must be as good and right as any other, that there is no such thing as psychopathology and that psychotherapy and the whole psychiatric enterprise is a form of psychic tyranny and colonialism. A point of view approximating this caricature was offered by R. D. Laing (1965) and is worth reading as a useful corrective to any temptation to push these ideas beyond their useful limits.

To summarize, when we unpack the aphorism, "the clinical material is what the patient is doing, not just what the patient is saying," we find that much of what we understand as essential in doing psychotherapy is either stated in it or is implied by it. I am grateful that I was a receptive listener when I overheard Shapiro say it, and I am grateful too for this opportunity to refresh my memory and to state my appreciation for this token of what Dr. Shapiro has contributed to all of us.

References

Austen, J. L. (1967). *How to do things with words*. Cambridge: Harvard University Press.

Coleridge, S. T. (1798). The rime of the ancient mariner. In E. H. Coleridge (Ed.), *The complete poetical works of Samuel Taylor Coleridge*. London: Oxford University Press (1912).

Fenichel, O. (1935). Concerning the theory of psychoanalytic technique. In H. Fenichel (Ed.), *The collected Papers of Otto Fenichel* (First Series, pp. 331–348), New York: David Lewis (1953).

Fierman, L. B. (1965). In L. B. Fierman (Ed.), *Effective psychotherapy; the contribution of Hellmuth Kaiser*. New York, Free Press.

Gilbert, W. S., & Sullivan, A. S. (1865). The Mikado, or the Town of Titipu. In *The complete plays of Gilbert and Sullivan*. New York, Norton (1976).

Kaiser, H. (1934). Problems of technique. In M. S. Bergmann & F. R. Hartman (Ed.), *The evolution of psychoanalytic technique* (pp. 383–413). New York: Basic Books (1976).

Kubie, L. S. (1954). The fundamental nature of the distinction between normality and neurosis. *The Psychoanalytic Quarterly, 23,* 167–204.

Kubie, L. S. (1967). The relation of psychotic disorganization to the neurotic process. *Journal of the American Psychoanalytic Association, 15,* 626–640.

Laforgue, R. (1940). The relativity of reality; reflections on the limitations of thought and the genesis of the need of causality (trans: Jouard, A.). New York: Nervous and Mental Disease Monographs.

Laing, R. D. (1965). *Divided self: an existential study in sanity and madness.* New York: Penguin.

Schafer, R. (1976). *A new language for psychoanalysis.* New Haven: Yale University Press.

Schlesinger, H. J. (1981). *The process of empathic response, psychoanalytic inquiry* (Vol. 1, No. 3, pp. 393–415). New York: International Universities Press.

Schlesinger, H. J. (1994). How the analyst listens: The pre-stages of interpretation. *International Journal of Psycho-analysis, 75,* 31–37.

Schlesinger, H. J. (2003). *The texture of treatment. On the matter of psychoanalytic technique.* Hillsdale, NJ: The Analytic Press.

Sterba, R. (1934). The fate of the ego in analytic therapy. *International Journal of Psycho-analysis, 15,* 117–126.

Virgil (ca. 29–19 BC). *The aeneid* (Book 6, trans: Fagles, R.). New York: Viking (2006).

Zetzel, E. (1956). Current concepts of transference. *International Journal of Psycho-analysis37,* 369–375.

Reply to Herbert Schlesinger

David Shapiro

The precept, pay attention to what the patient is doing, that is Herbert Schlesinger's focus is indeed central to psychotherapy. That kind of attention automatically enlarges the scope of the therapeutic material from what the patient produces to the *person* who is producing. At the same stroke, it brings the therapist's attention to the immediate present. The precept, as Schlesinger says, has particularly direct and easy application to understanding the patient's relationship with the therapist, or the transference. That relationship, because it exists in the immediate present (the "here and now") opens itself more or less continuously to the question, what is the patient doing? Thus, the therapist does not have to rely, for his understanding of the patient's attitude toward him, on a presumed associative or metaphorical significance of occasional references to other figures, or even the much rarer direct references to the therapist himself. He will see the patient's attitude far more reliably expressed in action; as Schlesinger says, in what the patient is doing with, or to, or, I would add, before, the therapist. There is, though, a question here for which Schlesinger and I have different answers. I notice that, although he makes the point emphatically that the patient's transference is expressed in what he is doing, Schlesinger seems in his further comments to give greater emphasis to the metaphorical interpretation of verbal content. I will return to that question later.

In his further discussion of transference, Dr. Schlesinger identifies two ways in which patients talk to therapists: as the therapist really is, or, unrealistically, as a "transference object." He raises the interesting and rarely mentioned problem for the therapist of distinguishing between these ways. How does the therapist know when he has become a transference object for the patient? I want to suggest an answer to that problem. We can say that in talking to the therapist as the therapist really is, on the one hand, or as a transference object, i.e. unrealistically, the patient must be doing two different things. How to define that difference? I would say that in the first case, when the patient is talking to the therapist as he really is, he is simply sharing the anxieties that are on his mind, often, though not necessarily always, mindful that he is talking to someone who might be able to help him. In the second case, the patient does not know what these anxieties are and is unable to share them with therapist. Instead, these anxieties cause him to regard the therapist with biases and to act in ways that mitigate or avoid those anxieties. Those biases and that kind of action is manifest in talking to the therapist unrealistically or as a transference object. This kind of talking is not what could be called communicative talking. It is different from communicative talking not only in the distorted and unrealistic perception of its object; it involves different internal processes from those of communicative talking.

When the patient is talking to his therapist as a transference object he is not only doing something to his therapist but, also, talking for his own ear. That is, he is not only transforming his therapist in some way that suits his defensive needs, but is transforming himself. It is a kind of talking that will sound different from genuinely communicative or expressive talking.

Here is an example:

A new patient, a tense, serious looking man in his early thirties, announces almost immediately upon meeting the therapist that he doesn't think much of psychotherapy. In fact, he has written a paper proving this. He himself comes only on account of a vocational question concerning whether to remain in his present technical field, nothing more; he has had some trouble with his boss, as well as some bosses in the past. He proceeds to describe this trouble angrily; he has been passed over for a promotion by a man he considers his inferior. He goes into some detail, loudly and angrily, in describing that person's, as well as his boss's, inadequacies. In this and the following several sessions he seems to avoid the use of the therapist's formal title, in fact addressing him from the beginning by his presumed nickname. Several sessions later, after his insistence, in connection with arrangements, that his time was as valuable as the therapist's, the therapist suggests that he seems concerned to make it clear that the therapist is no more important a person than he is. He responds angrily, "You're not!"

It is easy to infer from the verbal content of this patient's speech alone that the therapist is for him a "transference object." It is not hard to grasp, not only from what he says, but from his disdainful manner, a quality of what this patient is doing. He is demeaning those he sees, and unwillingly (and unknowingly) respects, as of higher rank than himself. He does this presumably to restore his own wounded dignity. These figures include his boss and, at present, the therapist. Still, how can we be sure that this is in fact an instance of talking to the therapist as a transference object? How can we be sure, for instance, that we, ourselves, have not been condescending, talking to him as to an inferior, and that his reaction to the therapist may not be to the therapist as he really is? We can never be sure that we see ourselves objectively, but there is something strange about the patient's way of talking that is independent of us. We can see in the quality of the patient's speech that he is not speaking only to the therapist, but in some sense is also addressing himself. He is not simply telling a story, however angrily and disdainfully. He does not simply express disdain; he *announces* his disdain, from the very beginning, in the manner of a declaration that has been rehearsed. It is not merely that he speaks, loudly and repetitiously, of his superiors' offenses and their unentitled satisfaction with themselves. He says these things in the way of a politician trying to arouse a crowd to anger with a fiery speech. He is doing this to himself, while ostensibly talking to the therapist, and it gives his speech an artificial, ungenuine, quality. It is this quality of ungenuineness that Hellmuth Kaiser, whom Schlesinger referred to as both his friend and teacher and mine, identified when he said neurotic patients do not "talk straight." It is what I have called self-deceptive speech. This patient is creating, or trying to create, primarily for himself, an image of himself as like the lion harassed by hyenas. It is a defensive image, that is, an image that in some measure, insufficiently in this case, forestalls clear consciousness of his genuine feelings about himself. And it is an image that requires the creation of complementary images of certain figures around him. All this, in my opinion, describes the creation of "transference objects."

As Dr. Schlesinger says, he and I grew up in the same tradition, even with some of the same teachers and colleagues. We share many, probably most, ideas and attitudes about psychotherapy – that is undoubtedly why the precept, pay attention to what the patient is doing, was so immediately congenial to him. I know exactly what he means, and I agree absolutely, when he says that "the patient is always right," or "the patient is doing the best he can," or that the therapist must understand and respect "where the patient is coming from." If we were both to see a patient we would probably take notice of more or less the same things and arrive at more or less the same impressions. We would certainly agree that the neurotic patient, as Schlesinger says, suffers from the burden of unresolved internal conflicts. Still, our respective ideas of the exact nature of those conflicts are different. That difference shows itself in connection with the concept of transference and transference objects.

Transference objects are conceived to be present figures, mainly the therapist, who stand for figures of the (unremembered) past. In the example of the accusing patient that he cites, Schlesinger speaks of the therapist as a surrogate for all those who have taken advantage of her. In the case I cited above, Schlesinger's interest, I assume, would take him to the same question he asks himself about her: "to whom is this defensive anger (unconsciously) directed?" He understands such anger as anachronistic. My interest goes to different questions. It goes to the questions, what is the present frame of mind, the present attitudes that generate this anger? What requires this man to launch these angry speeches? Is his anger like the prideful-but-poor man's bitter resentment of the rich? Is it inflamed by the poor man's unwilling and unrecognized shame at his own shabby clothes? Is this patient's arrogance and condescension, as well as his anger toward his boss and me, an effort to mitigate, that is, a less than successful defensive action, some unarticulated, humiliating and hateful idea that we are his betters?

In my view, in other words, the patient's reaction is not anachronistic, even though it is certainly not a reaction to things as they really are. It is the understandable, even inevitable, reaction to certain figures around him as he, according to his character and point of view ("where he is coming from"), is bound to see those figures. There is no reason to assume, and in my experience such an assumption would very often be incorrect, that there was a figure in the patient's early history who is now represented by his boss or therapist. In other words, from this standpoint, the engagement of the image of the therapist by the dynamics of the patient's personality makes that image an immediate focal point of those dynamics, but is not in itself or in its history necessarily central to the neurotic conflict.

But here is the thing that puzzles me about Dr. Schlesinger's view. I have just contrasted my thinking about the patient I described with Schlesinger's. Yet, I believe that all the questions I have asked and the interests they reflect would be shared by Schlesinger as well. This is confirmed by his attention to what the patient is doing and in the importance and meaning to him of where the patient is coming from. Furthermore, Schlesinger makes it clear that he does not regard the patient's recovery of memories of early family dynamics, or of the figure for whom the therapist is now presumed to be surrogate, to be necessary or even important for therapeutic change. Why, then, assign those presumed sources of the neurosis such a central role in the present neurotic condition and in the therapist's thinking about the patient's relationship with him? Given a therapeutic interest in what the patient is doing and where he is coming from, isn't Schlesinger's special interest in whom the transference object stands for at best superfluous?

Psychoanalysts in general, Schlesinger obviously far less than most, are, in my opinion, distracted from the dynamics of the present personality, the unconscious conflicts of attitudes, by these assumptions of the continued presence of early family dynamics in neurotic conflict and specifically in the relationship with the therapist. There is of course no question that the internal dynamics of personality manifest themselves in the patient's engagement with others and, often, in his relationship with the therapist. And I assume, as Schlesinger does, early family dynamics are a principal source of the present dynamics of the personality. But between those early family dynamics and the present engagement with the therapist a character has developed. That character has its own self-protective restrictive ways and attitudes which are responsible for new conflicts and anxieties. These attitudes and the conflicts they engender have an autonomous present standing. On this account, I don't agree with Dr. Schlesinger that the patient's anxieties are anachronistic. This is the issue I hope he will address in his reply.

Psychoanalysis began to recognize a dynamics of the personality with the advent of its structural theory, and further with the development of its ego psychology. That is the tradition in which Schlesinger and I grew up. It is possible to push this development further (as I mentioned in Chapter 2 of this volume in connection with the work of Erikson) to a dynamic psychology of the *volitional person*. That psychology must recognize the unconscious attitudes that shape consciousness and share responsibility for purposeful, often defensive, self-deceptive action. This includes of course speech action. That is the dynamic psychology that leads to the therapeutic interest in what the patient is doing. And, again, I am quite sure that Schlesinger would share this view with me.

There is another element in this theoretical development whose importance for me Schlesinger recognized in his remarks. I described in the Autobiographical Notes in this volume the important influence of Hellmuth Kaiser on my work and thinking. I didn't know until now that Dr. Schlesinger knew and admired Kaiser too. As he mentions, Kaiser was an early student of Wilhelm Reich who then made important therapeutic discoveries and innovations himself. In particular, Kaiser was a very close observer of the ways patients talked. He concluded that the neurotic schism in the personality – manifest, I would say, in neurotic self-deception – has the general effect of an ungenuineness in patients' speech. It is an extremely valuable observation for therapists.

It is worth making a few remarks about Reich's place in this development. It is well recognized that Reich made a critical contribution to psychoanalytic psychotherapy in his book *Character Analysis*. It is less well recognized (for which Reich himself is in no small part to blame), that his was the major therapeutic contribution consistent with, and advancing, the ego psychology of his day. When Reich says the therapist must pay attention not only to what the patient says, but to how he says it, he is in effect expanding our attention from the patient's words to the person producing those words. He is calling our attention to that person's attitudes and, actually, to what that person is doing with his words.

Response to David Shapiro

Herbert J. Schlesinger

I am impressed by the care with which Dr. Shapiro addressed my chapter. The issues are central to the teaching and belief systems that we tend to broadcast to the (unheeding) world but rarely discuss in the way that the format of this book allows. In this response, I will direct myself to specific parts of Shapiro's reply. I suspect that Shapiro will agree with most, if not all, of my clarifications of my position and show that once again, clinicians with somewhat different personal histories, starting from somewhat different positions, may be drawn by experience with patients into converging paths. One more demonstration that patients are our best teachers – if only we would listen!

Dr. Shapiro focuses much of his reply on how the therapist can distinguish the patient's experience of therapist as he really is from the patient's experience of the therapist as a transference object. To this end, he suggests that the nature of patient's speech, as either communicative or ungenuine, assists greatly in making this distinction.

Before moving to the substance of his distinction, I want to clarify one point; Shapiro suggests that the distinction I make between the therapist as he really is and as a transference object is rarely mentioned in the psychoanalytic literature. Actually, this is an accepted distinction for most, or at least many, analysts. The rest, who subscribe to the "totalistic view," call everything the patient says to or about the therapist as transference. They do not seem bothered by retaining two terms for what they regard as one phenomenon. Actually, I go further along this line when teaching by distinguishing between the "transference object" and the "therapeutically." This distinction helps students make sense of the confusing behavior of patients who seem to be living in two places at the same time, and so make demands they "sort of know" are unrealistic, but persist truculently nevertheless. Elsewhere, I have spelled out for the therapist a way of distinguishing between the transference object and therapeutic ally (Schlesinger 1981). I don't like this categorizing of what in reality is a rather fuzzy and vacillating distinction, but it seems to help students and so I swallow my distaste.

For the most part, I agree with the distinction Shapiro makes between communicative talking and ungenuine talking, if we may assume that the person in the "first case" who is talking "communicatively" is relatively unanxious. In my experience, people are not fully aware of what they are anxious about, although they may have given a name to a putative cause. Transference is expressed more obviously in the "second case." I put it this way because I believe that transference is always present, at least in potential form, and because, as I believe Shapiro suggests in his reply, transference is an expression of character; one might say a particularization of character for the current interpersonal situation.

In describing the way the patient's ungenuine speech not only transforms the therapist but also the patient's experience of himself, Shapiro makes a most important point; one usually overlooked when discussing transference. Transference involves regression both in the identification of the object and of the self doing the transferring. As I use the term here, regression does not necessarily refer to an ontogenetically earlier state, such as Freud proposed in the idea of regression to fixation points in personal development, but to an earlier and now generalized outlook we refer to as character. For instance, "that's the way they all treat me" expresses an expectation that the therapist, like all others in authority, will put him down. The regression is to a character position which seems safer, i.e., more familiar and less anxiety arousing than the uncertainties of the new encounter. To be fair to the usual psychoanalytic position about transference, the putative person of early history was presumably a figure in infantile history as he was perceived by the infantile self, and most likely was a composite of many experiences rather than a single retrievable actual person at a definable time, although in clinical short-hand (and sadly, in the view of some who have not thought through these issues) as "THE mother" or "THE father."

Dr. Shapiro goes on to suggest that "transference objects" represent an aspect of the patient's defensive effort to forestall clear consciousness of his genuine feelings about himself. That is to say, success in deceiving himself about his genuine feelings requires "the creation of complementary images of certain figures around him." I would agree, with some reservations. The sense of ungenuineness the therapist hears in the patient's speech comes from hearing a different emotional meaning in the way the patient spoke the words. The patient cannot be "genuine" in the limited sense of being all here and in the same emotional place because he has at least two messages to convey and is "genuinely" of mixed minds about them. Also, the patient is ungenuine only with respect to the therapist whom he is encountering newly as a stranger, but he has rehearsed this anxiety-arousing encounter with the characters built into his character structure, into what analysts call his unconscious fantasy, and cognitive psychologists call, his script or schema. In other words, the patient is "right" but in a different context than the one in which he ostensibly is engaged. One could say, and I make the point frequently in class, that while the therapist begins with the patient when he walks into his office the first time, the patient has begun the therapy at the point he first considered obtaining it. In other words, the therapist begins in the middle of the patient's therapy. From this point of view, instead of responding as the therapist did in Dr. Shapiro's clinical example, in which the therapist tends to hold himself off from the patient, the therapist might have said, "Yes, I am no more important a person than you, and my time is no more valuable than yours." The patient would likely feel a bit non-plussed by the therapist's unexpected agreement and likely would respond in some way that expresses feeling disarmed. The therapist might then remark that the patient was expecting a different reception. I should add that I see no need to wait several sessions to take up this issue.

Another distinction the therapist must be prepared to make about genuineness occurs on the occasion when he believes he is hearing a "genuine" expression of transference about which the patient feels uncomfortable because he also has opposing feelings and views, and on the occasion when the patient seems to be "putting on" the therapist, deliberately trying to fool or control him. In the latter instances, it might be a total "put on," but might also reflect that the patient is experiencing transference that is so uncomfortable that he tries to control it by "riding the tiger," as it were, pretending to be in control. Not an easy distinction to make, but not uncommon in the clinics in which our students train.

In closing, Dr. Shapiro asked me to clarify my interest in sorting out who the transference object represents in the patient's past, particularly given my emphasis on what the patient is doing in the clinical situation. He adds that he thinks that I give greater emphasis to determining who this figure is than to what is expressed in what the patient is doing, and wonders if my interest is superfluous. First, I hadn't intended to give more weight to one than the other. But as to my retained interest in determining who the therapist is standing in for, it may be enough to say that it derives from the philosophical position that the past in some sense determines the present, and from the clinical position that holds the extent to which the philosophical position is true for any patient at any time is a matter to be determined in the therapy. The over-riding principle is expressed in the clinical mantra, which I believe Shapiro also expresses in his carefully crafted argument is, "Why now?" That is, everything has a history, but why is the patient acting this way now? What makes it hurt now? I would add that blaming the past for the miseries of the present is as pointless as ignoring the past.

Reference

Schlesinger, H. J. (1981). The process of empathic response. *Psychoanalytic Inquiry, 1*, 393–415.

Chapter 2
Personality in Context: Reflections on the Contributions of David Shapiro

Paul L. Wachtel

The enormous contribution of David Shapiro to our understanding of personality and of clinical phenomena arose in the context of a psychoanalytic world that was largely dominated by what has now come to be called the one-person point of view. In this chapter, I will reexamine Shapiro's contribution from the vantage point of the two-person, intersubjective viewpoint that has emerged as a central contribution of psychoanalytic thought in recent decades.

More broadly, Shapiro's thinking evolved in the context of the ego psychological tradition. In certain respects it continued to reflect the assumptions and proclivities of psychoanalytic ego psychology. In other respects, it departed quite considerably from the ego psychological approach and, at least implicitly, presented important challenges to that point of view. I aim here to consider both the aspects of Shapiro's thinking that reflect his having been trained in the ego psychological tradition and the ways in which he reworked those assumptions and modes of thought and introduced important new ideas and perspectives. In doing so, I will offer some additional thoughts on his work from the vantage point of the theoretical tradition that has most potently challenged ego psychology – the relational point of view.

Phenomenological Virtuoso

As what I have said thus far implies, I will offer, later in this chapter, some elements of critique of Shapiro's viewpoint and some suggestions for alternative ways to frame the important observations he offers us. But I wish to begin with (and indeed to concentrate on) an *appreciation* of his work, because that pole of my response to his contribution is so much stronger. In a review of *Autonomy and Rigid Character* (Shapiro 1981), I referred to Shapiro as a "phenomenological virtuoso" (Wachtel 1982). Few writers in our field have even come close to him in capturing the subtleties

P.L. Wachtel (✉)
Distinguished Professor, City College and the Graduate Center of the City University of New York, 365 Fifth Avenue, New York, NY 10016
e-mail: paul.wachtel@gmail.com

C. Piers (ed.), *Personality and Psychopathology: Critical Dialogues with David Shapiro*,
DOI 10.1007/978-1-4419-6214-0_2, © Springer Science+Business Media, LLC 2011

of subjective experience – and, especially, in illuminating how *consequential* subjective experience is. Rather than treating subjectivity as an epiphenomenon, the byproduct of "deeper" forces or of physiological or neurological processes, Shapiro's writing illuminates how powerful an understanding we gain by examining the way the person experiences and structures his world. As I further stated in my review, he "pierces to the heart of subjectivity, revealing a structure to conscious experience so elaborate and so fateful that one is forced to rethink entirely the relation between conscious and unconscious or the easy equation of the former with the superficial and the latter with the deep." Traditional psychoanalytic formulations are usually rooted in the archaeological vision that so captivated Freud and in Freud's ambitions as a discoverer (Wachtel 2008). These twin sources led to a construction in which conscious (or conscious/preconscious) was sharply and dichotomously distinguished from unconscious, rendering the unconscious as a radically separate hidden realm – a formulation that, not incidentally, magnified the import of Freud's having "discovered" the theretofore buried roots of mental life. Through the lens of this model, consciousness appeared to be a superficial covering, of interest more as a barrier to the true gold that lay beneath than in its own right. As Ricoeur (1970) has noted in a different context, consciousness in the psychoanalytic model was largely *false* consciousness – *fool's* gold, we might say, in relation to the metaphor I introduced in the previous sentence. What was *really* of interest for most analysts was what was seen as lying "below" consciousness. Consciousness itself largely *obscured* the true nature of personality.[1]

Shapiro, in contrast, *delved into* consciousness. Consciousness was, for him, not a superficial "cover" for what is "really" important, but itself the key indicator of who we are. The consciousness he *saw*, however, was rather different from the consciousness seen by most analysts. The perceptions of consciousness by analysts who regarded consciousness largely as the "superficial" layer of personality (cf. Wachtel 2003) were, well, superficial. Shapiro, however, saw consciousness in depth. So much of interest lay in consciousness as it was revealed by Shapiro that it became in his hands not just the royal road to the unconscious, as Freud called dreams, but the royal road to the personality as a whole. Shapiro rooted his psychoanalytic vision in a phenomenological rather than a structural or quasi-physical mode of thought. In place of an emphasis on theoretical terms such as forces and energies, or on geographic locations containing different systems (e.g., System Cs-Pcs and System Ucs, or Ego, Id, and Superego), depicted from a point of view external to the experience of the person herself, Shapiro presented an account of personality that was rooted in the person's own vantage point. He showed that if we understand how the world looks to the person, we can understand most of the phenomena addressed in the psychoanalytic literature in a fresh way. Defensive

---

[1] A parallel devaluing was directed toward the events and experiences of daily life, rendering them too, through the lens of traditional psychoanalytic thought, as relatively "superficial" and leading to a tendency, prevalent to this day, for many analysts – even relational analysts (see Wachte 2008) – to pay insufficient attention to the impact and the dynamics of daily life.

processes that protect our conscious experience from noticing what would disturb us remained at the center of his account, but he differed from standard psychoanalytic ways of understanding those defensive processes in a number of important ways. These differences, it is interesting to note, derived not from a departure from the core insights of psychoanalytic ego psychology but from Shapiro's taking those insights *more* seriously than most of the writers who saw themselves, or were seen as, writing within the ego psychological mainstream. Very much at the heart of the clinical and observational impetus[2] for Freud's formulations in *The Ego and the Id* (Freud 1923) was the increasing recognition that consciousness was not in fact as crucial a criterion as had been thought for whether or not a defended against psychic content had been assimilated in a way that led to cure and psychological health. What Freud recognized, and what later ego psychological writers elaborated, was that the defenses were far more variegated and complicated than had previously been appreciated. Although Freud recognized from the very beginning of his psychoanalytic work that intellectual insight alone could not lead to cure, it was only after practicing for some decades that he really appreciated how varied and labyrinthine were the ways that threatening material could be excluded from self-experience.

More often than not, the means of such exclusion was *not* really the neat mechanism of repression that left the person totally unaware of the threatening material. Much more often what happened was more complex and more subtle. In various ways, we were rendered *both aware and not aware*. This more complicated reality was alluded to in the conference theme of the 2008 meetings of the Division of Psychoanalysis of the American Psychological Association: "Knowing, Not-Knowing, & Sort-of-Knowing." It was acknowledged as well, in a different way, by Freud himself, when he noted, well before he wrote *The Ego and the Id*, that,

> Forgetting impressions, scenes or experiences nearly always reduces itself to shutting them off. When the patient talks about these 'forgotten' things he seldom fails to add: 'As a matter of fact I've always known it; only I've never thought of it.' He often expresses disappointment at the fact that not enough things come into his head that he can call 'forgotten' – that he has never thought of since they happened (Freud 1914, p. 148).

Shapiro goes further than this, building on the later observations that became the foundation of ego psychology. It is not only that the patient has always known it but just not thought of it; it is also often the case that he *has* thought of it. But he has thought of it in a particular way, a way that renders it not fully *experienced* as self or that is assimilated to a larger style of thought, affect, and interaction with the world that constitutes a "defense" but also the person's very way of being in the world, his way of being a person. In light of Shapiro's insights, we may see that the person's very way of seeing certain things is what enables him not to see them,

---

[2] I refer to the "clinical and observational" impetus, because there were also *abstractly theoretical* sources, stemming from the contradiction between defenses being seen as belonging to the System Cs/Pcs since they defended that system against the Unconscious, yet also, by the logic of the same topographic theory, belonging to the System Ucs, since they were dynamically unconscious.

his very way of feeling certain things is what enables him not to feel them, and his very way of knowing certain things is what enables him not really to know them – at least, not to know them in a way that leads to what knowing usually leads to, but instead serves to protect him from the dangers (and responsibilities) that knowing in the more familiar ways might introduce.

Staying close to the clinical data, Shapiro avoided conceptions of defense *mechanisms* or of contents neatly placed in some subterranean vault – valuable "originals" stored for safekeeping while distorted copies ("derivatives") might be permitted to pass through customs and give a hint of the riches hidden down below (cf. Schimek 1975). He eschewed sharply dichotomous formulations in which some things remained "in the unconscious" while others were permitted to pass through to consciousness. He regarded *gradations* of consciousness and *qualities* of consciousness, not *absence* of consciousness, as crucial to the understanding of defense – and of personality.

In carrying forth this essentially phenomenological version of psychoanalytic thought (cf. Atwood and Stolorow 1984; Stolorow and Atwood 1984), Shapiro restores both personhood and agency to the psychoanalytic vision. As he put it in his book on *Psychotherapy of Neurotic Character* (Shapiro 1989), "The conception of an unconscious agent of behavior, an anomalous and irrational intruder into adult attitudes,... clouded the individual's responsibility for his own behavior, seeming to make him a mere passive – or even unwilling – witness of it [and] reduced the role of the individual's consciousness to that of a compliant and innocuous bystander" (p. 19).

Addressing the same theme from a somewhat different vantage point, he argues in *Autonomy and Rigid Character* (Shapiro 1981) that "even symptomatic behavior is directed not by internal *forces and needs* according to their 'aims,' – as traditional 'dynamics' sees it – but rather by the neurotic *person* according to his aims, his thinking, and his point of view" (p. 4, italics added). Where traditional psychoanalytic accounts leap to formulations of unconscious motives "virtually without regard to (the person's) conscious disposition" (p. 21), Shapiro concerns himself with the conscious – though not necessarily fully articulated (cf. Stern 1997) – frame of mind that makes symptomatic acts seem like simply "the thing to do."

Vicious Circles, Critiques of "Received" Understandings, and Consonances with the Point of View of Karen Horney

Looking more closely at the dynamics implied by this point of view, we may see that in Shapiro's account, it is not merely that the person's frame of mind makes the next step in the neurotic process feel like "the thing to do"; it is also that the frame of mind that led to this disposition is *maintained* by the very consequences it produces. Having *done* "the thing to do" makes it more likely to seem *again* like the thing to do. As Shapiro puts it in *Neurotic Styles* (Shapiro 1965), "[the neurotic's] makeup and the way he sees things... move him to feel, think, and do things that continue the neurotic experience and are indispensable to it…. He seems to think in such a way and his attitudes and interests are such *as to continue and sustain* the neurotic process" (p. 18, italics added). Relatedly, in *Psychotherapy of Neurotic Character* (Shapiro 1989), he states, "Thus a circularity is established in the workings of neurotic personality: the restrictive dynamics of the personality prevents the articulation of certain aspects of subjective experience; the unarticulated discomfort or threat of that subjective sensation, in turn, propels this dynamics. It is this circularity that is responsible for the irreversibility of the neurotic process without external intervention" (p. 131).

This emphasis on vicious circles, in which the effect of one round of the repetitive process is the cause of the next, is one of the things that initially drew me to Shapiro's work. At the time that *Neurotic Styles*, came out, I had not yet explicitly formulated my own cyclical psychodynamic account (e.g., Wachtel 1977, 1987, 1993, 1997, 1999, 2008), which also placed central emphasis on the role of vicious (or virtuous) circles in perpetuating the dynamics of personality; but it is clear to me in retrospect that this emphasis in Shapiro's thinking was one of the primary reasons it "spoke to me" so eloquently, much as I was similarly drawn, at around the same time, to the writings of Horney (e.g., 1939, 1945), which also highlighted the circular nature of the casual sequences in human experience.[3]

I don't know how much attention Shapiro had paid to Horney's work in formulating his own ideas (her name does not appear in the indexes of any of his books), but I see many important parallels in their theoretical constructions (as, of course, important differences as well). Horney shares with Shapiro not only a strong emphasis on the vicious circle dynamics in neurotic difficulties but also a strong emphasis on character and on holism – that is, on the consistency of character and inclination across a wide range of circumstances. Moreover, in developing their centrally characterological conceptions, both raise probing questions about the ways that psychoanalytic theorizing has relied on explanations centered in the concepts of drive or libido and about the ways that analysts have centered their explanations of present symptoms and character traits in the events and experiences of the past.

A number of these shared theoretical predilections have informed and stimulated my own thinking in important ways. Especially salutary, in my view, is the strong emphasis on character that is shared by both writers. Shapiro contends, for example, that, "Every reader with clinical experience and, for that matter, every sensitive person will know that symptoms or outstanding pathological traits regularly appear in contexts of attitudes, interests, intellectual inclinations and endowments, and even vocational aptitudes and social affinities with which the given symptom or trait seems to have a certain consistency." Similarly, Horney (1939) argues that "The so-called symptoms of neurosis, which are usually regarded as the criteria for their classification, are not essential constituents. Neurotic symptoms such as

---

[3]It is important to note that circular patterns are responsible for the perpetuation of *positive* character traits as well, and play a central role in the creation and maintenance of attachment patterns (Wachtel 2008, 2010a).

phobias, depressions, fatigue, and the like may not develop at all. But if they develop they are an outgrowth of the neurotic character structure and can be understood only on that basis" (p. 239). Especially in an era when both tendentious ideological arguments by proponents of some therapeutic schools (see Wachtel 2006, 2010b; Westen et al. 2004) and the economic self-interest of the large corporations that fund health care converge on a preference for a narrow focus on isolated symptoms, it is important to be reminded that we are treating *people*, not symptoms, and that the suffering that brings people to see us is almost always rooted in the way of life they have created for themselves under the exigencies of the desperate, and therefore often short-sighted, effort to cope with guilt, shame, and anxiety.

The shared emphasis on understanding character enabled both Shapiro and Horney to see clearly the limits of certain perspectives that appeared "obvious" to most other psychoanalytic writers. Regarding the role of the past and of childhood experiences in the difficulties about which the patient complains today, both clearly acknowledge the importance of childhood experiences in shaping the direction of personality development. But both as well highlight the ways in which this influence has frequently been misunderstood, to the detriment both of therapy and of our understanding of personality and its development. Much of Horney's work is a critique of the over-emphasis on the past in psychoanalytic thought, a critique undertaken not from a vantage point that dismisses the importance of early experiences, but rather from one that understands their influence in a way that puts the evolution of the person's *character* at the center. Horney's approach to the role of early experiences begins with a *question*: she asks *why* do childhood attitudes persist into adulthood and *when* does this happen? This leads her to the question of "what factors *in the present character structure* demand the persistence – even though it may be in a different form – of attitudes developed in the past?" (Horney 1939, p. 141). In exploring this theme, she notes that "the sum total of childhood experiences brings about a certain character structure," then revises this statement noting that it is more accurate to say that it *starts* the development of character, which continues to evolve in different ways and to different degrees in different people. Thus, she notes that "we cannot draw one isolated line from a later peculiarity – such as hatred of a husband which is not provoked essentially by his behavior – to a similar hatred of the mother, but that we must understand the later inimical reaction *from the structure of the whole character*"(p. 153).

In a similar vein, Shapiro (1965), building on an observation of Erikson's (1950),[4] criticizes the "marionette" view of personality in which "pieces of history intrude themselves into the contemporary behavior of the individual, bypassing his

---

[4] I will have more to say shortly about the relation between Erikson's ideas and Shapiro's. The affinities between Shapiro's ideas and Erikson's are even more obvious than those between Shapiro and Horney. Shapiro had direct contact with Erikson at Austen Riggs, and Erikson, of course, was a leading figure in the ego psychology movement out of which Shapiro's ideas evolved. I had originally intended to include a section in this chapter on the relation between their ideas, but in fact the section got too long to include, and I will have to discuss this topic elsewhere.

contemporary modes of functioning and leaving him, again, as a passive witness of his own manifest behavior and the victim of his history" (p. 21). He goes on to say that,

> the question here is not about psychological determinism, historical causation, or unconscious motives; the question concerns the bypassing of consciousness and contemporary modes of functioning, which these views imply. From our point of view, the neurotic person is no longer merely a victim of historical events in the sense described; his way of thinking and his attitudes – his style, in other words – having also been formed by that history, are now integral parts of that neurotic functioning and move him to think, feel, and act in ways that are indispensable to it" (p. 21).

The "marionette" metaphor was originally introduced by Erikson in relation to the concept of libido, in relation to which Erikson said that "while we must continue to study the life cycles of individuals by delineating the possible vicissitudes of their libido, we must become sensitive to the danger of forcing living persons into the role of marionettes of a mythical Eros – to the gain of neither therapy nor theory" (p. 64). This implicit critique of the way the libido theory had been employed in psychoanalytic discourse was also a central element in the writing of both Horney and Shapiro. Horney's critique of the libido theory was more direct and provocative. Regarding the idea of derivatives and disguised expressions of libidinal aims, for example, she notes wryly that, "the substitution of one pleasure striving for another does not prove that the second is in any way akin to the first.... If a monkey cannot obtain a banana and finds a substitute pleasure in swinging, this is not conclusive evidence that the swinging is a component drive of eating, or of the pleasure found in eating" (Horney 1939, p. 52). She goes on to say that, "If the libido concept led only to a peculiar interpretation of sexual deviations or of infantile pleasure strivings the question of its validity would not be so important. But its real significance lies in its doctrine of the transformation of instincts, which makes it possible to attribute to a libidinous source the majority of character traits, strivings and attitudes toward the self and others" (p. 53). In pursuing this line of thought further, she comes to a conclusion that has much in common with the position that is central to Shapiro's thinking about the issue.

> In other words, should not the greediness shown in eating or drinking be one of many expressions of a general greediness, rather than its cause? Should not a functional constipation be one of many expressions of a general trend toward possessiveness, control? The same anxiety which may compel a person to masturbate may compel him to play solitaire. It is not at all self-evident that the shame in playing solitaire results from the fact that in the last analysis he is pursuing a forbidden sexual pleasure. If he is, for instance, a type for whom the appearance of perfection is more important than anything else, the implication of self-indulgence and lack of self-control may be sufficient to determine his self-condemnation (p. 61).

In another statement that bears many similarities to Shapiro's point of view, Horney notes that, "a person does not have tight lips because of the tenseness of his sphincter, but both are tight because his character trends tend toward one goal – to hold on to what he has and never give away anything, be it money, love or any kind of spontaneous feeling" (p. 62). She goes on to root this tendency not in a particular libidinal impulse that is being defended against or surreptitiously and indirectly expressed through "derivatives," but to the person's "general attitude to others and to himself."

Like Horney, Shapiro does not reject the concept of instinctual drive altogether, but he too places it in a context in which the role of character takes center stage. He notes that "the unfolding of new drives with new urges and motivations, new potentialities of subjective experience, objects of interest, kinds of activity, and modes of activity, certainly have an impact on the existing fabric or configuration of mental organizing forms." But he asks, "what is the outcome of this impact?" (Shapiro 1965, p. 181). He considers the proposal that "each phase of instinctual drive development freshly stamps and reshapes all forms of mental functioning according to its own mode," but he rejects this idea as inconsistent with the facts of observation. In the first place, he says, "there simply is no evidence that the cognitive modes, general forms of subjective experience, and the like, are in fact subject to such radical upheavals. On the contrary, all that we can see points in the opposite direction, to their relative stability and slowness to change." Moreover, he emphasizes, the implications of any upsurge of drive tension are not direct but are mediated by the individual's already existing psychological organization.

In further elaborating this latter point, he notes that,

> A drive tension cannot spring into being fully developed and sharply articulated. On the contrary, it must initially be exceedingly diffuse subjectively, an impetus, let us say, toward certain external objects and actions. This diffuse impetus is enough, however, to move its subject into the external world, to move it toward actions and toward objects... In the course of this actual experience and depending on the nature of the external object and circumstances, the initially diffuse tension becomes organized into new qualities of subjective experience, new qualities of affect and satisfaction, and new kinds of behavior (Shapiro 1965, p. 183).

This formulation bears much in common with Donnel Stern's (1997) conception of unformulated experience, an idea that has become increasingly influential in the literature of the relational point of view. Here, and in the broader theme of critiquing the way personality has been viewed as organized primarily by the actions of drives, Shapiro's point of view has interesting and important affinities with the relational point of view. In other respects, however, Shapiro's conceptualization differs significantly from the relational conceptualization, and it is to these differences that I now turn.

Holism and the "One-Person" Point of View

Horney and Shapiro, with their emphasis on vicious circles, and their related emphasis on the critical role of character in perpetuating psychological proclivities in the present that may have had their origins in the distant past, are among the thinkers in our field who have most valuably contributed to my own understanding of personality and its dynamics. But their accounts of the vicious circles that are generated by certain features of neurotic character were rooted in a radically holistic outlook about which I wish to raise some questions. Put differently, in certain respects their theories were formulated in a fashion that, from a contemporary vantage point, could be described as "one-person" in nature.

This characterization of their theorizing as reflecting a one-person point of view may seem to some readers like a rather idiosyncratic way to view these two thinkers. Horney, after all, is usually grouped with the interpersonalists, a group of theorists whose work was part of the inspiration for the "two-person" critique of the "one-person" point of view. And Shapiro includes fairly prominently among the consequences of the neurotic frames of mind he articulates the way the person relates to others. I will take up shortly what I mean by the "one-person" features of their theorizing, but in laying the groundwork for this discussion I will begin with the aspect of my characterization of them as theorists that is more likely to seem accurate to most readers – their holism.

Shapiro's holistic viewpoint, like Horney's, is one of the great strengths of his theoretical perspective, as it is simultaneously one of the potential limitations. Shapiro notes that his point of view is rooted in "the simple fact of human consistency over broad areas of functioning (Shapiro 1965, p. 3)." This theoretical focus enables Shapiro, like Horney, to call our attention to common meanings and modes of experience that can be found behind diverse specific actions and perceptions. It enables us to notice how these diverse specifics cohere and are organized into a structured character that persists over time. In doing so, it sheds light in useful and insightful ways on a wide range of psychological experiences and phenomena. But what seems to me missing in both Shapiro's and Horney's holism is sufficient attention to the other pole of human reality, the enormous *variability* in our behavior and, indeed, in our very experience of ourselves, from one context to another. Holism enables us to see connections that might otherwise not be noticed, but it may also simultaneously obscure *differences* or *variations* in behavior and experience from context to context that are more readily seen from a less thoroughly holistic vantage point.

I first became acutely aware of the need to include in our theoretical models the remarkable diversity in our behavior and experience from one context to another in addressing the empirical and theoretical challenges presented by behavior therapists and social learning theorists (see especially, Mischel 1968; cf. Wachtel 1973, 1977). As I attempted to come to grips with the findings they presented – and with the experiences of everyday life that they reminded me to pay closer attention to – I increasingly came to realize two things. First, just as the coherence in individual functioning is, as Shapiro notes, evident from everyday experience, so too is the diversity. We are each *enormously* different with our parents, our children, our friends, our acquaintances, our sexual partners, our boss, our subordinates, etc., and we are similarly different at work, in school, on the playing field, or in bed. This variability is as obvious and subjectively striking as is the coherence. Neither can be ignored except through the filter of a prescribed theory or ideology that filters one perspective out.

Second, in thinking about whether the challenge to psychoanalytic thought introduced by Mischel and other social learning theorists really had any weight, it became clear to me that Mischel's critique applied more to some versions of psychoanalytic thought than others. In particular, it became apparent that the interpersonal version of psychoanalytic thought was not at all threatened or challenged by the observations that Mischel and others were highlighting. Rather, the variability in behavior and experience from context to context could be seen as an essential feature of its theoretical vision, at the heart of how it differed from other psychoanalytic viewpoints while retaining an equally strong interest in unconscious motivation and thought processes and the fearful or guilty shrinking from our own experience that was at the heart of the psychoanalytic point of view. Much more than other strands of psychoanalytic thought, interpersonal theory was a *contextual* version of psychoanalysis, a way of incorporating the observations that were the intrinsic contribution of psychoanalysis, but in a fashion in which the interpersonal context and the impact of ongoing and reciprocal transactions between people played a central role in shaping which of the various psychological configurations that were a part of the overall structure of the individual personality (in Sullivan's terminology, which of the dynamisms) were called into play. There was no essential contradiction between being committed to psychoanalytic ideas of conflict, defense, unconscious motivation, and so forth and being attentive to the remarkable variability in experience and behavior from one context to another (see, for example, Wachtel 1977, 1981).

Over time, the psychoanalytic foundation for my overall integrative approach evolved from a primarily interpersonal focus to a theoretical perspective grounded in the broader *relational* point of view in psychoanalytic thought (Wachtel 2008). In immersing myself in the relational literature, I was struck by the prominence in that literature of the concept of multiple self-states (e.g., Bromberg 1998; Mitchell 1993; Harris 1996; Davies 1996; Slavin 1996). As I studied this literature, it became clear to me that the concept of multiple self-states represented another way of addressing the differentiation I have just been emphasizing. But in contrast to the accounts of variability and differentiation in the social learning literature, this relational account is attentive to the phenomena that have always been the singular strength of the psychoanalytic point of view – conflict, character, affect, representations of self and other, and so forth. The inner world, from this vantage point, is not ably characterized as reflecting fixation or arrest at a particular developmental level, since multiple "developmental levels" may be evident in the different states of mind illuminated from this perspective, and, viewed through the lens of the concept of multiple self-states, neither is character well described as having a singular essence or set of attributes. From this vantage point, character is a plural noun; there are *multiple* configurations of affect, motivation, and thought that are characteristic of the individual, each evident at different moments in the course of the person's life or in the psychotherapy session.

Viewed from this angle, Shapiro's writings appear not so much to provide a description of the entire character but rather to offer extraordinarily acute portrayals of people's *self-states*. Those self-states each have qualities of quite elaborate organization; they are not a random set of inclinations, but rather, just as Shapiro describes, remarkably coherent ways of being and experiencing. Moreover, it remains very useful to consider that, much as Shapiro describes, people may be characterized by the particular configurations that are their "signature" way of being in the world and experiencing the world. But, it is important to note, that signature configuration is not the person's *exclusive* configuration. Of equal importance in certain respects is the ways (and the times) that the person *departs* from this modal way of being, the ways and times she is *different* from the way she usually behaves and usually experiences herself and others.

What Shapiro has offered us remains one of the most remarkably perceptive accounts available to us of the complexity, organization, and quality of subjectivity. But I am suggesting that this account would be of even greater clinical value – and even more sharply accurate – if we *contextualized* it, attending to the question of *when* a particular neurotic style is manifested by the individual and when, in contrast, another mode of experiencing may come to the fore, either more neurotic or more adaptive in nature. It does not diminish the value of Shapiro's contribution to treat the styles and modes of functioning he has so exquisitely described as varying with varying social, emotional, and relational contexts. Their complexly coherent configurational and organizational qualities do not become mere artifacts or epiphenomena when we do so, nor is the difference diminished between Shapiro's depictions of complex human beings *actively making sense of* their varying contexts and the image that emerges from a simple stimulus-response psychology. The problems with the latter do not lie in their attention to how our behavior varies with changing stimulus conditions; that is their *strength*. The problem lies in failing to do precisely what it is that Shapiro does – see the meaning and organization in the way we interact with and respond to our contexts, making clear that, indeed, the *context*, in any meaningful psychological sense, cannot be usefully reduced to a set of "stimuli."

Reframing Shapiro's descriptions in this way, attending to the variability as much as to the holistic consistency, enhances considerably the clinical applicability of the understanding we achieve. If the modes of experiencing Shapiro describes are taken to be too pervasive, too airtight as it were, then it becomes difficult to see how to intervene effectively. If, instead, we take them to be descriptions of how the person *can* function, even of how the person *frequently* functions, then we can also ask the crucial question, "when is he or she *different*?" Attending to these variations, and, as part of that, attending to the patient's hidden *strengths*, to the kernels of a different way of experiencing and behaving that constitutes the path toward therapeutic change, is a key foundation of effective psychotherapy (Wachtel 1993).

The two-person perspective, unfortunately, has often been limited in the relational literature to accounts of the reciprocal influence between patient and analyst and to the epistemological status of our formulations about patients (Wachtel 2008). But if we move beyond the distinction between one-person and two-person thinking to an understanding of the differences between *contextual* and *acontextual* accounts of personality, then we may see that the more fundamental problem in much of the literature that has been criticized as reflecting a "one-person" point of view is that it describes people acontextually, largely divorced from the reciprocal transactions with other people that give a complexly bidirectional structure to our lives and from the ways that the classroom, the boardroom and the bedroom call forth different aspects of our multifaceted selves. Accounts of people as "monadic" (Mitchell 1988, 1995), as driven by "internal" states and representations that are sealed off from influence by the events of the person's contemporary life, are limited and misleading. Indeed, even the concept of multiple self-states is at times unsatisfactory, because depictions in the literature often present the varying self-states as configurations that appear and disappear as a mysterious product of internal fluctuations rather than in a way that clearly delineates how they are responses to the varying relational experiences in which the person is immersed from moment to moment.

I have suggested that the one-person versus two-person distinction, although a useful initial pointer to important differences in theoretical strategies, is too course-grained to take us as far as we need to go in refining our understanding (Wachtel 2008). In offering a reexamination of Shapiro's conceptualization from the vantage point of the two-person point of view, one also comes up upon the limits of that point of view. It is not really satisfactory to describe Shapiro's formulations as "one-person" accounts. In so many ways, his approach to personality is so much subtler, so much more human, so much more addressing a *person* rather than a "specimen" (the ultimate source, in large measure, of what is wrong with the one-person approach) that to refer to it as a one-person approach does not seem quite right. Consider, for example, this discussion of the claim that therapeutic work is depleting for the therapist:

> In personal relations in general, a gain for one is also a gain for the other, not a loss; a satisfactory experience for one is satisfactory experience for the other. It is so in psychotherapy as well. The achievement of contact with a patient who was previously cut off from himself, and therefore from the therapist, is a satisfying experience for both.... What is taxing and depleting is the effort to give sympathy when it is not there – to be concerned, to be interested, or to look interested, when one is bored....And this is especially so when, though not experiencing contact or communication with the patient and, consequently, not genuinely interested, the therapist feels obliged to behave as if he were." (Shapiro 1989, pp. 156–157)

I have, only half in jest, referred to the one-person – two-person distinction as more accurately depicted as one between one-and-a-quarter-person theorists and one-and-three-quarter-person theorists (Wachtel 2008). Putatively one-person thinkers are rarely as inattentive to the relational context or to the role of the observer as their two-person critics imply; and putatively two-person thinkers are rarely as free from "monadic" elements in their accounts of personality as the one-person, two-person language implies. In this, admittedly whimsical, framework, Shapiro might be characterized as a one-and-a-*half* person theorist, offering a point of view that lies between those of the contending camps. His attentiveness to the relationship and to the patient's mode of living *in the world*, as well as his framing of character very largely in terms of how the person perceives and makes sense of *what is presently going on*, reflect important differences from the views of those more appropriately labeled as one-person thinkers, as does his emphasis on the patient's actions in the world. But his strong emphasis on consistency, his relative neglect of the variability of experience and sense of self from one context to another, distinguish his view from a strong two-person emphasis. So too does his primary reliance on an interpretive, essentially insight-centered approach, in contrast to an emphasis on the central role of new relational experiences (e.g., Frank 1999; Aron 1996; Mitchell 1997; Stern et al. 1998; Wachtel 2008). Shapiro certainly lies on the more sophisticated and experiential end of the insight pole, and almost *no* therapist today is inattentive to or rejecting of the impact of new relational experiences on therapeutic change. But it nonetheless seems to me, as I read him, that his primary focus is on helping the patient to *see* what he is doing, rather than on offering the kind of alternative experience that, from Alexander, to Weiss and Sampson, to Kohut, to contemporary relationalists, has been the other polarity in therapeutic strategy.

Shapiro, Ego Psychology, and Relational Psychoanalysis

Since the time when Shapiro began his writings on neurosis, character, and psychotherapy, psychoanalysis has changed very substantially. The hegemony of ego psychology has come to an end. Psychoanalysis has become more pluralistic, and the relational point of view in particular has become an at least equally influential paradigm, especially in the United States. The label relational, however, is more an umbrella term than a name for a very specific theoretical position (Wachtel 2008). There are *multiple* meanings to the term, as used by different writers. Relational thinkers share in common the fact of having some significant divergences from the prior ego psychological consensus, but they do not necessarily completely agree with each other or, for that matter, diverge from the prior consensus in the same way. Several themes, however, are common enough among relational writers, if not necessarily totally consensual, that they are usefully described as "relational" views. These include the two-person critique of the one-person position; an emphasis on relationships rather than drives as the central shaping influence on personality development; a constructivist view of the patient's experience and the events of the session; a greater readiness to challenge traditional clinical guidelines such as neutrality, anonymity, and abstinence; a consequent greater readiness to self-disclose, or at least to see self-disclosure or *non*-disclosure as equally needing to be examined and considered (Wachtel 2008); and an inclination to see new relational experience of one kind or another as at least as important as insight in the promotion of deep and meaningful therapeutic change. In many ways, Shapiro's extension of ego psychology moves in similar directions as the relational turn; in other ways it remains closer to the traditional psychoanalytic viewpoint out of which it emerged.

Shapiro's work overlaps in interesting ways with the relational position on a number of these themes. Regarding the role of drives, for example, I have already noted both the ways that Shapiro, like Erikson, raises questions about the role of drives as invisible controllers of the strings of "marionettes" manipulating the direction of personality development and the individual's choices, as well as the convergences between Shapiro's approach to the drives and some of the relational contributions of Stern (1997) regarding unformulated experience. The ways in which Shapiro reconceptualizes the role of the unconscious, stressing degrees of articulation and qualities of experiencing rather than a separate realm of fully formed but buried thoughts, wishes, and fantasies similarly overlaps very substantially with Stern's account. (Consider the following passage, for example: "It is precisely its strange, unarticulated, and therefore comparatively undifferentiated, nature that accounts for the neurotic dynamics of such experience.... It is the essentially unarticulated and undifferentiated nature of certain feelings and aims – the fact that awareness of them is only vague and incipient, global and without proportion – that makes their sensation as threatening as it is." [Shapiro 1989, p. 131])

It should also be clear that the relational emphasis on constructivism (see especially Aron 1996; Hoffman 1998) has strong resonances with Shapiro's approach to the way that the individual creates meaning and makes sense out of the experiences and situations he encounters. For Shapiro, as for many writers in the relational movement, these acts of meaning-making are at the very heart of what a psychoanalytic point of view can contribute. Shapiro is not frequently listed among the ranks of the constructivist pantheon, and his constructivism is more evident by example than by prescription. He does not trot out the heavy philosophical artillery that many writers on constructivism elaborate, but his approach to understanding people seems to me clearly constructivist through and through.

On the other hand, Shapiro's account of the therapeutic process and the therapeutic relationship does not seem to me to resonate as closely with the dominant relational viewpoints with regard to such issues as neutrality, anonymity, or self-disclosure. While clearly not an advocate of the "hard-line" or ideological traditionalist views, he does not seem as clearly to be an "implicit critic of neutrality and anonymity" as he is an "implicit constructivist." The vantage point of his depictions of patients and of the therapist's stance in *Psychotherapy of Neurotic Character* (Shapiro 1989) seems closer to the traditional one-person mode of thought in certain respects, more directed toward a kind of neutral observer perspective on the therapist's role, a "pointing out" role more than a "participant" role. In this regard, he also seems to me, as I have noted above, more toward the insight end of the spectrum than the new relational experience end (bearing in mind that virtually no one – certainly neither Shapiro nor the most important relational writers) operates from an either-or way of thinking regarding these two poles).

Perhaps what is most evident in thinking about Shapiro's contribution and that of the relational movement is that Shapiro seems to have given little thought to or paid little attention to the latter point of view. This is certainly understandable. His work originated in – though very significantly transformed – the ego psychological perspective that is one of the chief targets of the relational critique, and the thinkers with whom he was in contact, and in relation to whom he shaped his ideas (if even with regard to opposition and critique), were those in the ego psychology movement. By the time the relational movement was a powerful influence in the psychoanalytic world, Shapiro's views had already been largely shaped. *Psychotherapy of Neurotic Character*, for example – Shapiro's mature statement of the implications of his viewpoint for therapeutic practice, and a work that is perhaps better viewed as the culminating statement of his theoretical viewpoint than his one later, and very brief additional book, *Dynamics of Character* (Shapiro 2000) – appeared just a year after Mitchell's (1988) *Relational Concepts in Psychoanalysis*, the book that could be said to have been the very first explicit statement of the relational viewpoint.[5] It clearly was mostly being written before Mitchell's book was published. Thus, Shapiro had completed the lion's share of his contribution *before there was* a relational movement.

I had concluded my review of *Autonomy and Rigid Character* with the complaint that after his two brilliant contributions to the understanding of personality, Shapiro owed his readers a "moral debt" – his insights were just too sharp and important for him not to provide us with a book on how to apply them therapeutically. Some years later, Shapiro did in fact make good on that "debt." *Psychotherapy of Neurotic Character* described in valuable detail just how he approached the therapeutic process. Now I wish to end the present chapter with another request. I cannot here claim that Dr. Shapiro has incurred another moral debt. He has provided us with more than enough enrichment of our understanding already. But, in light of what I have just been discussing, I would love to see a detailed accounting from Shapiro of how he sees his ideas in relation to the relational point of view. Where does he find the relational perspective complementing his own point of view or adding something useful to it? Where does he find it incompatible with his own views? Where does he find it misleading or wrong, or, for that matter, simply containing old wine in new bottles? When Dr. Shapiro began his seminal work, ego psychology was, in the eyes of many, virtually synonymous with psychoanalysis, especially in the United States. Today that is no longer the case. A strong case could be made, in fact, that it is the relational viewpoint that is today the most influential psychoanalytic paradigm. It would be a wonderful addition to the many insightful illuminations that Dr. Shapiro has already offered us if he could give us his take on this movement, which has so significantly reshaped psychoanalysis in the years since he began and largely carried out his work.

---

[5]Mitchell's earlier book, in collaboration with Jay Greenberg, *Object Relations in Psychoanalytic Theory* (Greenberg and Mitchell 1983) could at most be said to be a *proto*-relational work or a *precursor* of the relational point of view.

References

Aron, L. (1996). *A meeting of minds: Mutuality in psychoanalysis*. Hillsdale: Analytic Press.

Atwood, G. E., & Stolorow, R. D. (1984). *Structures of subjectivity: Explorations in psychoanalytic phenomenology*. Hillsdale: The Analytic Press.

Bromberg, P. M. (1998). *Standing in the spaces: Essays on clinical process, trauma, and dissociation*. Hillsdale: Analytic Press.

Davies, J. M. (1996). Linking the "pre-analytic" with the postclassical: Integration, dissociation, and the multiplicity of unconscious process.Contemporary Psychoanalysis, 32, 553–576.

Erikson, E. H. (1950). *Childhood and society*. New York: Norton.

Frank, K. A. (1999). *Psychoanalytic participation*. Hillsdale: Analytic Press.

Freud, S. (1914). *Remembering, repeating, and working through* (Standard Edition, 14). London: Hogarth Press.

Freud, S. (1923). *The ego and the id* (Standard Edition, 19). London: Hogarth Press.

Harris, A. (1996). The conceptual power of multiplicity. *Contemporary Psychoanalysis, 32*, 537–552.

Hoffman, I. Z. (1998). *Ritual and spontaneity in psychoanalysis: A dialectical-constructivist view*. Hillsdale: Analytic Press.

Horney, K. (1939). *New ways in psychoanalysis*. New York: Norton.

Horney, K. (1945). *Our inner conflicts*. New York: Norton.

Mischel, W. (1968). *Personality and assessment*. New York: Wiley.

Mitchell, S. A. (1988). *Relational concepts in psychoanalysis*. Cambridge: Harvard University Press.

Mitchell, S. A. (1993). *Hope and dread in psychoanalysis*. New York: Basic Books.

Mitchell, S.A. (1995). Interaction in the Kleinian and interpersonal traditions. *Contemporary Psychoanalysis, 31*, 65.

Mitchell, S. A. (1997). *Influence and autonomy in psychoanalysis*. Hillsdale: The Analytic Press.

Ricoeur, P. (1970). *Freud and philosophy*. New Haven: Yale University Press.

Schimek, J. G. (1975). A critical re-examination of Freud's concept of unconscious mental representation. *International Review of Psychoanalysis, 2*, 171–187.

Shapiro, D. (1965). *Neurotic styles*. New York: Basic Books.

Shapiro, D. (1981). *Autonomy and rigid character*. New York: Basic Books.

Shapiro, D. (1989). *Psychotherapy of neurotic character*. New York: Basic Books.

Shapiro, D. (2000). *Dynamics of character*. New York: Basic Books.

Slavin, M. O. (1996). Is one self enough? Multiplicity in self-organization and the capacity to negotiate relational conflict. *Contemporary Psychoanalysis, 32*, 615–625.

Stern, D. B. (1997). *Unformulated experience: From dissociation to imagination in psychoanalysis*. Hillsdale: Analytic Press.

Stern, D. N., Sander, L. W., Nahum, J. P., Harrison, A. M., Lyons-Ruth, K., Morgan, A. C., Bruschweilerstern, N., & Tronick, E. Z. (1998). Non-interpretive mechanisms in psychoanalytic therapy: The 'something more' than interpretation. *International Journal of Psychoanalysis, 79*, 903–921.

Stolorow, R. D., & Atwood, G. E. (1984). Psychoanalytic phenomenology: Toward a science of human experience. *Psychoanalytic Inquiry, 4*, 87–105.

Wachtel, P. L. (1973). Psychodynamics, behavior therapy, and the implacable experimenter: An inquiry into the consistency of personality. *Journal of Abnormal Psychology, 82*, 324–334.

Wachtel, P. L. (1977). Interaction cycles, unconscious processes, and the person situation issue. In D. Magnusson & N. Endler (Eds.), *Personality at the crossroads: Issues in interactional psychology* (pp. 317–331). Hillsdale: Lawrence Erlbaum Associates.

Wachtel, P. L. (1981). Transference, schema, and assimilation: The relevance of Piaget to the psychoanalytic theory of transference. *Annual of Psychoanalysis, 8*, 59–76. New York: International Universities Press.

Wachtel, P. L. (1982). Phenomenological virtuoso: A review of David Shapiro's "autonomy and rigid character." *Contemporary Psychology, 27*, 681–682.

Wachtel, P. L. (1987). *Action and insight.* New York: Guilford.

Wachtel, P. L. (1993). *Therapeutic communication.* New York: Guilford.

Wachtel, P. L. (1997). *Psychoanalysis, behavior therapy, and the relational world.* Washington, DC: American Psychological Association.

Wachtel, P. L. (1999). *Race in the mind of American: Breaking the vicious circle between blacks and whites.* New York: Routledge.

Wachtel, P. L. (2003). The surface and the depths: The metaphor of depth in psychoanalysis and the ways in which it can mislead. *Contemporary Psychoanalysis, 39*, 5–26.

Wachtel, P. L. (2006). Psychoanalysis, science, and hermeneutics: The vicious circles of adversarial discourse. *Journal of European Psychoanalysis, 22*, 25–46.

Wachtel, P. L. (2008). *Relational theory and the practice of psychotherapy.* New York: Guilford.

Wachtel, P. L. (2010a). One-person and two-person conceptions of attachment and their implications for psychoanalytic thought. *International Journal of Psychoanalysis, 91*, 561–581.

Wachtel, P. L. (2010b). Beyond "ESTs": Problematic assumptions in the pursuit of evidence-based practice. *Psychoanalytic Psychology, 27*, 251–272.

Westen, D., Novotny, C. M., & Thompson-Brenner, H. (2004). The empirical status of empirically supported psychotherapies: Assumptions, findings, and reporting in controlled clinical trials. *Psychological Bulletin, 130*, 631–663.

Reply to Paul Wachtel

David Shapiro

Dr. Wachtel makes several interesting points. I will try to take them up consecutively.

I think he is quite right in his assertion that I have neglected the work of Karen Horney and failed to give her the credit she deserves. I knew some of her work as a young student, but it was essentially overlooked in my later training. The reason for this, I believe, was that Horney herself lacked a systematic theory and was somewhat alienated from the prevailing psychoanalytic theoretical work of the time. In any case, it is clear that particularly in one respect she was ahead of her time, and ahead of some of the theoretical systematizers: her psychology is a psychology of *persons*, as Erik Erikson's is, and as mine is. There is no doubt that the systematic ego psychologists laid a theoretical basis in psychoanalysis for that kind of psychology, but they did not quite get there. Horney did get there, but without much of a system. Erikson's work was perhaps an unselfconscious bridge in this development. He jokingly said that, on being told by David Rapaport that his work was ego psychology, he felt like the bourgeois gentleman in Moliere's play who was happily surprised upon learning that he had been speaking prose all his life. The fact is that Erikson went a step further than ego psychology.

Wachtel raises the question of whether my work in developing a picture of relatively stable, self-regulating pathological character fails to do justice to the considerable variability or fluctuations in any individual's behavior and experience in different contexts, especially different interpersonal contexts. The existence of such fluctuations and their regulation by a superordinate organization in response to varying contexts I have always taken for granted. It is important to keep in mind that the character styles I have analyzed and described are restrictive or limiting, anxiety forestalling styles. That is to say, these styles limit conscious experience, particularly self awareness, in certain ways; they do not actually describe *all* subjective experience. For instance, the characteristic symptoms and traits of a rigid, compulsive character who has arranged his life in a fairly predictable, routine way may not be much in evidence within those boundaries. Furthermore the exact nature and definition of those boundaries, the special circumstances and the rationalizations which allow transgressions not to be experienced as transgressions – the number of martinis or the friends whose company he needs to diminish his self consciousness, the person with whom he feels sexually most comfortable – all such countless and individual particulars of context will be determinants of his experience and behavior. The superordinate organization of this individual's personality which accounts for such variations could in principle be defined, and to a certain extent he, himself, or, better, those who know him well, could probably define it ("Oh, Joe is lively and funny with a few friends, but he's shy at a big party"). No doubt generalizations of that kind could be made not only about individuals, but about character styles more subtly differentiated than those I have described, though I have not attempted to do it to any extent.

All this, however, is quite different than the idea that the variations of experience and reaction in various contexts can be regarded as multiple selves. That idea seems to me no more than a rhetorical evasion of the problem, and a misleading and therapeutically disadvantageous evasion at that.

Dr. Wachtel expressed interest in my view of relational psychoanalysis. I can summarize that as follows: I think the relational school has presented some valuable research and useful theoretical and therapeutic ideas, but its proponents tend to stretch those ideas beyond their usefulness and exaggerate their innovation.

The emphasis of the relational school on interpersonal transactions in infancy and the research they have sponsored or embraced is important. Their rejection of certain features of Freudian metapsychology is justified, as far as I am concerned, but at this point amounts to demolishing a straw man (I have not heard any psychoanalytic worker speak of drive energy discharge for many years). No one can reasonably doubt the importance of early relationships in the development of personality, and therefore to the nature of psychopathology, where that exists. But the assertion that personality and psychopathology are constructed virtually entirely of early interpersonal transactions and internal representations of them is more than doubtful.

Interpersonal patterns or templates or schemas created by early relationships, important as they may be for development, do not constitute a personality. On the contrary, the idea that such structures constitute the dominant forms of adult experience and behavior makes understandable, perhaps inevitable, the conclusion that there is no such thing as a relatively stable, relatively integrated personality or self. Hence the inevitability of the vacuous concept of multiple selves. I do not see, either, how an understanding of psychopathology that is limited to such interpersonal schemas or conflict between them can account for the specific facts of the individual's internal conflict with himself or the specific symptoms of the various kinds of psychopathology. I have referred elsewhere in this volume (see my reply to Sidney Blatt) to the conception of the rigidity of obsessive-compulsive and paranoid character as an internalized (or introjected) product of early interpersonal relations, presumably with figures of severe authority. It is true that there are instances in which that hypothesis seems to be born out, but in my experience there are far more cases where it is not. In general, it seems to me that the relatively direct derivation of adult character or psychopathology from early experience and behavior, inasmuch as it gives short shrift to development, is bound to be oversimplification. The effort brings to mind Piaget's complaint about psychoanalysis, that it was "too much a science of the permanent."

Some of the therapeutic principles of the relational school that are basically valuable and important are, also, in my opinion spoiled to some extent by overreaching. It is certainly past to abandon the tradition of the austere analyst, meeting questions with silence. But self-disclosure (the term hints at a spy story) can also be deliberately used in the hope of encouraging the perception of therapeutic empathy and an equalitarian relationship. That seems to me too close to salesmanship. Empathy and the achievement of a genuinely communicative contact and relationship are certainly therapeutically central. But a therapist's need to show that he or she is empathic is something quite different and in my opinion is inimical to an authentically communicative relationship.

Similarly, the emphasis by the relational school on therapeutic communication focused on the immediate situation, the "here and now," is very important. As is the recognition in that connection that communications between the patient and the therapist are relational acts. Certainly every communication must be regarded not only as a transmission of content, but as a purposeful, speech act. But are the patient's communications, or utterances, always and only relational, in the sense of being generated by and having their primary meaning in the interpersonal relationship in the office? Many times patients speak largely to themselves. They may, for example try, with exaggeratedly assured speech, to convince themselves of something they want to believe, but don't quite. In that case, the therapist is in effect a prop, an instrument, who serves as a listener to allow the patient to articulate, out loud and with more force, his effort to persuade himself. That, too, is a kind of relationship with the therapist, but it is not a genuinely communicative relationship, and it is a relationship that is decidedly secondary to the patient's relationship with himself.

Incidentally, apropos of the distinction between one person and two person psychology of which so much is made, shall I call my understanding of the kind of transaction I have just described the first or the second?

Convergences: Response to David Shapiro's Reply

Paul L. Wachtel

In elaborating on the ways that the character styles he articulates also lend themselves to accounts of variability ("Joe is lively and funny with a few friends, but he's shy at a big party") Dr. Shapiro's account converges still further with my own preferred way of seeing things. We may still differ in the degree to which we want to *highlight* those differences or variations in the course of the work – I find that explicitly examining with people the times when they are "different" from themselves is clinically very useful[6] – but the basic understanding is not really at odds so long as the character styles are understood as contextually responsive personality structures.

Although it seems he doesn't think so, I am actually in strong agreement with Shapiro about the problems with the concept of multiple selves. The concept I cited more approvingly was multiple self-*states*, which is quite different. The person is one person, the "same" person all the time, and yet can also be quite *different* at different times, in different moods, different roles, different relationships, different points or moments *in* the relationship, etc. Those differences are crucial to acknowledge in enabling the person to have a richer and fuller sense of "who he is." Indeed, it is the very ability to assimilate these varying experiences into the sense of sameness – "this is all the same me; it is all me even when I am different" that marks therapeutic growth. Here the view that I think Dr. Shapiro and I essentially share is very much like the understanding of Erikson's concept of identity – not a stultifying sameness, but a *sense* of sameness bridging and uniting the differences across time and varying contexts.

Dr. Shapiro and I converge in some of his critiques of the relational point of view as well. Clearly I am more identified with the relational movement than is Shapiro and (hence?) value it more highly. But my book on relational theory (Wachtel 2008) was both an embrace *and* a critique of relational thinking, or, put differently, an effort to sort out for myself the features of relational thought that were new and valuable and those that were old wine in new bottles, and not such good wine at that. In this, for example, I agree strongly with Shapiro's assessment that, "the assertion that personality and psychopathology are constructed virtually entirely of

---

[6] At times I have said to patients some variant of "you have to be a little more 'not like yourself' in order to be yourself." This has usually been in response to the patient noticing some variation on his or her own but saying either that other people don't think of it as the way he/she is or commenting on some such feeling as "I like it when I can be like this, but it doesn't feel quite like me." I am likely at such points to encourage the patient's experimentation with these "not like me" parts of himself, with comments that include that it still feels new and strange but will feel more and more "me-like" as he feels his way into it, especially if he senses that it is a way of expressing a part of himself that has previously been a source of anxiety or discomfort and hence has been submerged.

early interpersonal transactions and internal representations of them is more than doubtful," and also with his view that "the relatively direct derivation of adult character or psychopathology from early experience and behavior, inasmuch as it gives short shrift to development, is bound to be an oversimplification" Shapiro's evocation of Piaget in critiquing the latter point dovetails with my own interest in employing some of Piaget's concepts to point to an understanding of the dialectics of stability and change – the ways we experience new events in light of old schemas, but also the ways in which those schemas inevitably operate through accommodation as well (Wachtel 1981).One can, via such a conceptualization, account for the rigidities and persistences that bring people to therapy in a somewhat more complex and dynamic way that is both more theoretically satisfactory and more able to point toward possible ways of contributing to *modifying* that rigidity and persistence.

Finally, Dr. Shapiro ends by alluding to the overuse of the distinction between a one-person and a two-person psychology, and, in the question he raises, he implies, I believe, that the distinction is a rather blunt instrument. I myself view the one-person two-person distinction as an initially useful way of calling our attention to certain conceptual habits, but regard it as but a way station to a more adequate way of thinking about the issues. In discussing this previously, I have suggested that a more adequate formulation points us not toward "two-person" theory (there are many phenomena, after all, in groups, families, and such, where the dynamics between *more* than two people are crucial) but toward a *contextual* point of view (with the less satisfactory form of theorizing being *a*contextual). From this vantage point, I would suggest that patients often do "talk to themselves" in the manner Shapiro is suggesting, and that, as usual, Shapiro has captured beautifully an important phenomenological quality. But I would also suggest (and think that Dr. Shapiro would probably agree) that the quality of "talking to oneself" is different when one is doing it in the presence of a therapist, and thus that here too there is a contextual element that must be taken into account. Indeed, I have argued (Wachtel 2008, pp. 61–67) that even being *alone* must be understood in relation to context.

References

Wachtel, P. L. (1981). Transference, schema, and assimilation: The relevance of Piaget to the psychoanalytic theory of transference. *Annual of Psychoanalysis, 8,* 59–76. New York: International Universities Press.

Wachtel, P. L. (2008). *Relational theory and the practice of psychotherapy.* New York: Guilford.

Chapter 3
A New Developmental Foundation for David Shapiro's Work on Autonomy and Character

E. Virginia Demos

My task in this volume is to discuss David Shapiro's use of developmental theory in his ground breaking work on neurotic styles, as well as his more recent work on the treatment and the dynamics of rigid character. He writes explicitly about development in his two more recent books, *Autonomy and Rigid Character* (1981) and *Dynamics of Character* (2000), in which he argues that an abridgement of autonomy is an essential dynamic in all mental illness, and articulates how it manifests itself and functions in a range of diagnostic categories, which helps to clarify underlying dynamic similarities in the diverse symptomatology seen. I find Shapiro's phenomenological descriptions of the ways in which abridgements of autonomy are manifested in different kinds of mental illness and his discussions of these dynamics highly illuminating. I also believe that autonomy or agency is an essential factor in organizing the psyche, but that it is only part of what is essential, so I will introduce another basic human bias or priority that when impaired is also operating to constrict personality. I will further argue that both of these essential priorities are present at birth, thus I cannot accept Shapiro's assumption of the existence of prevolitional modes of functioning, and his further assumption that these modes are reverted to in adulthood when mental illness is manifested. He cites older stage theories of development, namely those of Werner and Piaget, as support for these assumptions, and possibly for notions of regression contained in such theories, although he does not use the term regression. I will also address his primary emphasis on cognition, which seems to leave little room for affects, except for the role of anxiety in evoking defensive organizations, and the presence of interest in expanding or constricting autonomy.

Let me begin with stage theories, which share several common assumptions, namely that development is governed by a master plan laid down in our genes or nervous system, and proceeds in a linear, step-by-step, invariant progression, consisting of homogeneous stages, roughly correlated with the child's age, and in the direction of getting better and better, or closer to some optimal functional end point of organization, control and effectiveness. Thus functioning at all ages is compared

E.V. Demos (✉)
Senior Supervising Psychologist, The Austen Riggs Center, 25 Main Street, Stockbridge, MA 01262
e-mail: virginia.demos@austenriggs.net

C. Piers (ed.), *Personality and Psychopathology: Critical Dialogues with David Shapiro*, 45
DOI 10.1007/978-1-4419-6214-0_3, © Springer Science+Business Media, LLC 2011

against a yardstick of optimal adult functioning, thereby defining all earlier stages as deficient. Piaget (1967), for example, labeled the period from age two to six, as the presymbolic stage of cognitive development, focusing only on young children's seeming inability to reason symbolically when given standard tasks, rather than on exploring children's actual engagement with the relevant people and objects in the context of their lived experience. In step with stage theory thinking, Shapiro, too, describes the infant and young child as being prevolitional, because in some situations they can be passive, seem to rely on reflexes or habitual routines, and seem unable to differentiate the means from the goal. He reserves the achievement of a truly volitional act for the child who possesses a self-reflective capacity, which he believes is necessary, in order to separate the means from the goal, and to actively plan or seek a goal not directly present.

There has been a marked shift, over the last four or five decades, in our understanding of developmental processes, based on advances in technology (e.g. the videotaping of infants, allowing slow-motion exploration of infant behaviors, which has revealed early organization and competence); neuroscience's exploration of brain functioning, which has revealed the dynamics of primary consciousness and procedural or implicit learning, stored separately in the brain from later linear, self-reflective, declarative learning; in theories of dynamic systems, with converging dynamic concepts from mathematics, physics, biology and psychology; and the motivational role of affects, represented in Silvan Tomkins' formulations, all producing vast amounts of new data. Many of the assumptions of stage theories have not been validated. The claim of homogeneous functioning across cognitive tasks has not held up (see Fisher and Pipp 1984). Logical reasoning deficits in infants and young children have also been disproved (see Baillargeon 1990 who demonstrated object constancy in 3 month-old infants; and Donaldson, 1979, who reported many studies which demonstrated that young children could perform Piaget's reasoning tasks if materials relevant to their lives were used).

A dynamic systems approach to development has largely replaced Piaget's and Werner's linear stage theories of development. Models of self-organizing systems in mathematics, physics, artificial intelligence, biology and human development all share the same dynamic principles, namely, that a few simple rules operating in the context of defined initial conditions and constraints can *intrinsically* generate complex dynamics and results. Small changes can lead to abrupt changes and shifts in organization, which are emergent and not predictable. In a dynamic systems model, there is no need to hypothesize the existence of a predetermined goal or outcome. The focus is on the conditions that promote the emergence of new organizations or behaviors, which is conceptualized as the result of a match that can occur in a dynamic exchange between the specific organizational characteristics of the system or organism (including the organism's intention to do something) and the specific characteristics of the context or task. For biological systems, including humans, which share an evolutionary history containing certain constraints and initial biases or values, individual variation and idiosyncratic, creative adaptations are the rule, thus longitudinal case studies are the method of choice.

Given this shift in thinking and the vast increase in data on very young infants, we can now more accurately locate the infant in a bio-psycho-social context as a being possessing considerable self-organizing capacities. I will argue that the capacity for volitional acts is present from birth, and that its optimal development is dependent on many factors. But first I will need to briefly summarize the current consensus about the basic capacities of neonates, as well as their limitations, (see Demos, 1992 for a more detailed presentation of these data, including supporting evidence for these results).

Neonates have the capacity to experience the full range of the basic affects, as described by Tomkins, namely enjoyment, interest, distress, anger, fear, startle, disgust and shame; they can recognize recurrent patterns of stimuli, can make fine discriminations between sounds and smells, can detect invariance in stimuli, and can detect contingencies between self-generated actions and effects on the environment; they can distinguish between internal and external events; and possess perceptual biases inherent in possessing a human nervous system, brain and body, e.g. can hear sounds only within certain frequencies, see colors only in certain wavelengths, perceive motion only at certain rates, and visually prefer light-dark contrasts and contours. Finally, neonates are capable of coordinating stimuli emanating from affective, perceptual, cognitive, memory and motor functions in order to try to bring about desired events or to try to limit or escape from undesired events. This latter capacity was demonstrated in a remarkable experiment reported by DeCasper and Carstens (1981), in which one-day-old infants quickly learned to lengthen the pauses between their bursts of sucking in order to turn on a recording of a female voice singing. Twenty-four hours later, these same infants became upset when placed in the non-contingent phase of the experiment, and recognized that lengthening their pauses could no longer produce the singing voice. This experiment reveals the amazing amount of mental organization and purposeful activity within the neonate, for success required the newborn to coordinate perception (detecting the contingency), emotion (interest in the stimulus), cognition (generating a plan to repeat this interesting event), motor patterns (*voluntarily* lengthening the pause between sucking bursts) and memory (remembering the plan and comparing the outcome to the goal).

These experimenters capitalized on their considerable knowledge of neonates. First of all, they tapped into one of the few well-developed motor patterns present at birth, namely the sucking reflex, and their knowledge that neonates are capable of sucking voluntarily. I believe that Piaget made a crucial error in assuming that only action on the external environment could lead to cognitive growth, which he saw as a slow step-by-step construction of schemas, and that if the infant could not perform such actions, (and of course the neonate's muscular abilities are very undeveloped), then nothing could be going on in the infant's mind. Thus Piaget was not aware of, nor did he perceive, that neonatal sensory capacities were already integrated at birth, along with many of the other capabilities listed above, and did not have to be slowly assembled. These experimenters also knew of the neonate's preference for the female voice, a bias already being learned in the uterus, as DeCasper would demonstrate in later experiments, and that such a recording would interest and hopefully motivate the neonates to actively alter their sucking pattern. They knew as well the time limits of the infant's capacity to remember a previous event. If the second phase of this experiment had occurred a week later, the neonates probably would not have recognized it as familiar. This experiment is a prime example of an optimal match between the organism's capabilities and the task presented. It was designed to demonstrate the neonate's exquisite sensitivity to contingency. It also illustrated the neonate's limits, for, in phase two of the experiment, when the stimulus was no longer contingent on the infant's sucking pattern, these infants became upset, as they were unable to repeat the earlier result, and they were unable to understand what had changed. I will return to the importance of being able to make sense of one's experiences with others and in the world later.

These infants' upset at no longer being able to control the stimulus in the second phase of the experiment, highlights an important characteristic of newborns, namely their capacity and preference for being an active agent in influencing events. The capacity to replace reflex sucking with voluntary sucking was reported by Brunner (1968), and Field et al. (1982) demonstrated the neonate's ability to imitate facial expressions. These examples in the literature underscore the infant's preference and intention to do voluntarily what has been experienced involuntarily. Such specific intentions are not innate, but seem to be generated in specific contexts, as if the infant thinks, "this is nice, but I'd rather do it myself." Tomkins (1978), in discussing these early phenomena, describes how such an idea might emerge, from a dynamic systems perspective:

> It represents an extraordinary creative invention conjointly powered by primitive perceptual and cognitive capacities amplified by excitement in the possibility of improving a good actual scene by doing something oneself. These are real phenomena and they appear to be highly probable emergents from the *interaction* of several basic human capacities. This is why I have argued that we have evolved to be born as a human being who will, with a very high probability, attempt very early and succeed in becoming a person. (p. 215)

Thus we have a neonate with pre-adapted capacities for feeling, thinking, perceiving, remembering, acting and coordinating these capacities in primary consciousness to produce voluntary acts and to learn from recent past experience. And although these capacities may be biased or organized in general ways, e.g. to facilitate transactions with other humans, they do not contain preformed contents or goals. This represents a departure from earlier formulations of an incompetent infant, embedded both in psychoanalysis and developmental psychology, but, as Bower (1974) has reminded us, such formulations ignored a basic evolutionary rule, namely that the more capable a species is in adulthood, the more capable is the newborn of the species.

Thus far the data have supported Shapiro's claim for the importance of agency in promoting mental health, and demonstrating that it is present at birth only underlines its primary importance. At this point, I want to elaborate on a further implication of locating the infant in a bio-psycho-social context and introduce another equally important factor, gleaned from the work of embryologists such as Bertalanffy (1952) and Weiss (1949) on the epigenesis of adaptive behaviors in biological organisms. Such organisms are characterized by two features – primary activity and organization, and adaptation is conceptualized in dynamic system terms. I have argued elsewhere (Demos 2007, 2008) that the two most basic human preferences or biases, which function by differentially weighting experience in such a way that they are felt to be of the highest priority, are that psychic coherence and organization is better than non-coherence, a bias in which the vicissitudes of affects play a central role, and that being an active agent in effecting the course of events is better than having no effect on events. Some psychoanalysts such as Ghent (2002) and Greenberg (1991) have also speculated that there may be early and basic tendencies or preferences for coherence and agency, which then dynamically generate "motivational systems" such as attachment. They suggest that Edelman's work (1987, 1992) on the tendency of neural networks to categorize and re-categorize successive experiences relates to the value of coherence. Neuroscience has taught us that the brain does not perceive the world directly, rather it has evolved to function as a reality simulator, constantly processing electrical and chemical signals through multiple synapses that can create within milliseconds a complex configuration or pattern of neural activity that represents a simulation of any "event." We are meaning making organisms. As these coherences of neural activity repeat over time, they can be recognized or matched, and the more they recur, the stronger the neural connections become, which allow the organism to learn from experience and to adapt to and/or create new responses.

Infant researchers, such as Sander (1969) and Wolff (1973) have argued for the centrality of state and state organization as a concept that can connect the biological and psychological levels, and studied the cyclical states along the sleep-wake continuum. Sander (1982) went on to argue that the infant's experiences of her own recurrent states represent the focal points around which the infant's inner awareness or consciousness consolidates, and argued further that the ego begins as "a state ego, rather than a body ego" (Sander 1985, p. 20). He stated that "the organization of state governs the quality of inner experience" (Sander 1985, p. 26), and described these waking states as alert inactivity, waking activity, alert activity and crying. In my own work, based on Tomkins' theory of affect (1962, 1963), and on the available evidence on infant affect facial expressions and correlated behaviors, I have argued that these waking states are distinctive affective states, such as interest, or distress or anger depending on the pattern and intensity of crying (Demos 1986, 1988, 1989b). Achieving internal state regularity and stability that can provide the background against which changes in coherent unities (states) can be perceived and recognized, both by the infant and the caregiver, is essential for adaptive functioning and requires coordination between the caregiver and neonate. Normal, full-term neonates with responsive caregivers can achieve this in the first week of life (Sander 1975). Infant characteristics (e.g. prematurity, or neonatal drug addictions) and/or caregiver limitations (e.g. excessive anxiety, neglect or abuse) can delay or impede the infant's ability to achieve some regulation of state coherence, which may create a vulnerability for developing psychotic states.

We saw in the DeCasper and Carstens experiment described earlier that the neonate was capable of organizing a coherent state of interest enabling an understanding of the situation and an effective adaptive response. But when the situation changed, the neonate could no longer "make sense" of the situation, could not adapt, and became upset. This highlights how the capacity to maintain coherence can be challenged when the organism cannot make sense of one's experience and/ or of events. In this example, the meaning of the change was beyond the infant's capacity to grasp, which can happen also in a young child's life when family dynamics or behaviors, including abuse, are not comprehendible. In many other cases, the threat to coherence comes directly from the inability of the infant to regulate affect states and the exposure to all kinds of stimuli. Whatever the source, threats to coherence can interfere with the emergence of self-generated goals and initiatives.

This brings us to the role of affect both in sustaining adaptive behavior and in compromising such behavior. I have relied heavily on the work of Silvan Tomkins in understanding affect dynamics and their adaptive functioning (see Tomkins 1962, 1963). He argues that the human organism evolved as a "multi-mechanism system" in which the affect mechanism is distinct from the sensory, motor, memory, cognitive, pain, and drive mechanisms, and is capable of acting independently, dependently, and interdependently with any or all of them. He theorized that affect functions as an analogue amplifier, and is composed of a correlated set of bodily responses that include facial muscles, vocal, respiratory, blood-flow changes, heightened skin receptor sensitivity, and other autonomic responses that together create an analog of the rate or intensity of stimulation impinging on the organism, thereby making "bad things worse and good things better" (Tomkins 1978 p. 203). He further states that this correlated set of responses has evolved to combine urgency, abstractness, and generality (e.g. a sense of "too much" or "too fast" or "just right") that is experienced as a qualitative affect state (e.g. anger, fear, or enjoyment) which is able to both capture consciousness, thereby causing the organism to care about what is happening, and with its qualitative valence, to shape and facilitate a response; affects, therefore, are the primary motivational system. It should be noted that Tomkins' formulations are in direct opposition to Freud's idea that affect operates as a discharge of tension, or that drives are the primary motivators. (See Panksepp (1999a, b) for a more recent neurological confirmation of many of Tomkins' concepts.)

If we now imagine a newborn infant, with the capacity to experience qualitative affect states, but with no prior experience to draw on, and who is hungry and begins to cry, we have to assume that she neither knows why she is crying, nor that anything can be done about it. This hypothetical initial cry represents a preprogrammed affective response to a continuous level of non-optimal stimulation, namely hunger, which in Tomkins' formulation triggers the rhythmical cry of distress, consisting of a correlated set of facial-muscles, blood-flow, visceral, respiratory and skeletal responses, which acts to amplify this level of non-optimal stimulation to produce an inherently negative experience for the infant, thereby making things feel worse, and so causing her to care about what is happening and about wanting relief from this distressing state. She is now motivated to pay attention to what happens next, to remember what these distressing sensations feel like, and to begin to connect them to antecedents (hunger) and consequences (comfort and food). Newborns are fed roughly every 2½ h around the clock, so this sequence is repeated eight or nine times a day, time for considerable learning to take place. If the caregiver has been responsive to the infant's cries, within 3 or 4 weeks the hungry infant will stop crying at the sight or the sound of the caregiver's approach, because the infant has already connected the experience of distress with the approach and comfort of the caregiver and thus is able to *anticipate* that the caregiver's approach means that relief will soon follow. This represents the achievement of an internal capacity for delay in this specific context. In *Autonomy and Rigid Character* (1981), David Shapiro in a footnote writes that "the precise nature of these internal tension-controlling or delaying processes and the manner in which they come into being, has never been entirely clear" (p. 45). The above description of the hungry crying neonate represents one way in which such processes can occur.

Tomkins' (1978) describes this phenomenon as the construction of an ideo-affect complex, which allows the hungry infant to stop crying and to wait. Ideo-affect is an abbreviation for ideo-perceptual-memorial-action-drive-affect complexes, which refers to the involvement of all of the critical subsystems that together constitute a human being. *The construction of ideo-affect complexes is the primary dynamic, creative process by which the infant gradually organizes her psychic life*. One of the assumptions operating here, implicit in much of our thinking about motivation, is that positive affect states feel better than negative affect states, and thus the infant is motivated to enhance, prolong, and repeat positive states (interest and enjoyment), and to limit, modulate, escape from or avoid negative affect states (distress, shame, disgust, anger, and fear).

On one's own, infants have a limited capacity to sustain positive affect states or to modulate negative affect states, and are therefore dependent on caregivers to titrate stimulation of all kinds, maintaining their stimulus worlds within an optimal range for processing information. This caregiver function involves regulating variables such as pacing, intensity, clarity and the optimal mix of redundancy and novelty. This can happen in many ways, for the caregiver not only responds to the infant's affect states, but is also engaged in expressing affect to the infant or within the infant's environment, and in evoking affects in the infant. In my longitudinal studies (Demos 1989a), the more the infants and young children received support in expanding, elaborating, sustaining, and communicating their states of interest and enjoyment and their related ideo-affect organizations, the more they were able to experience themselves as the source of interesting ideas and events, to sustain their interests when alone, to invest their interests readily and easily and to find a wide range of objects and activities interesting and enjoyable, all characteristics of autonomous functioning. By contrast, the more the infants and young children failed to receive support in expanding, elaborating, sustaining, and communicating positive affect and their related ideo-affect organizations, the more they constricted their interests, experienced boredom, engaged in repetitive behaviors, and were unable to sustain interests when alone, or derive enjoyment or excitement from their activities. In the realm of positive affects, it seems as if the rich get richer and the poor get poorer as early, preverbal patterns spontaneously build on themselves, and the developing child remains in the same non-responsive, or inhibiting environment. Such a child has considerably less capacity to act autonomously and becomes increasingly dependent on others for direction.

   The modulation of negative affect in infancy and early childhood is equally important and involves two aspects of the caregiver function: (1) protecting the infant and young child from traumatic experiences of negative affect that can threaten psychic coherence and the experience of psychic continuity, and set in motion massive defenses or an early splitting of the psyche; and (2) enhancing the infant's capacity to endure, tolerate and persist in the face of moderate intensities of negative affect in order to develop instrumental coping skills and effective volitional actions. If things go well, a sense of trust will develop within the infant and young child, namely a trust in the reliability and manageability of one's own inner states. Here we are in the realm of meaning for infants, for they will have learned that the onset of distress or anger or fear, does not evoke the need for a retreat, or obsessive rituals, or the dread of an escalation, but rather that such experiences can be tolerated or shared, that their causes can be resolved or known, and that they have a beginning, a middle and an end. Others and the world will also begin to feel trustworthy to the infant and young child, and will allow the young child to tolerate and explore the distress, anger, and fear in oneself and in others without excessive worry about being surprised, overwhelmed or disorganized by these states. But the salient task of organizing ones experiences in order to enhance psychic coherence is an ongoing process and must continue to be supported by the child's human environment.

   At this point in the discussion I need to make explicit two important formulations of infants and development that are implicit in all that has been stated so far. The first is that the objects that infants have the most dense, complex and frequent experience with are their caregivers, that therefore their early ideo-affect complexes are being constructed primarily in the context of these relationships, and that their earliest voluntary efforts involve the regulation of inner states and communications with caregivers long before they involve the manipulation of inanimate objects. Thus infants will look most competent in these contexts. Said another way, it is important to appreciate that all early learning, up through early and middle childhood, is deeply embedded in specific contexts, and that in order to understand infants and young children one must evaluate their capacities in contexts that are meaningful and familiar to them. For example, returning to our hungry infant, by 3 months of age, the infant can use the distress cry as a signal to the mother, namely by emitting a short cry combined with a look toward the mother and then a brief wait to see if mother responds, and then a repeat of this signal until the mother responds. Infants will also demonstrate the capacity to seek a goal that is not immediately present, if that goal involves a reunion with the caregiver. For instance, if their mother is out of sight, and they are being held by a stranger, infants will cry until the mother appears. Gaensbauer (1982) reported on a young infant girl who had been abused by her father in the first 3 months of life, but had a good relationship with her mother, and when removed from the home, this infant manifested a full grief response, and a month or so later she produced a differential fear response to a male stranger versus a female stranger, demonstrating the strength of learning based on fear. In terms of inanimate objects, immobile infants depend on being supplied with interesting objects. They cannot go after an object, but they demonstrate their agency by crying when it is removed, or becoming bored and looking away after it has lost its novelty.

The second set of formulations involves the issue of what is developing over time, given the infant's competence at birth. I have suggested at least four major kinds of changes going on (Demos 1992). One, the infant is going from being a generalist to becoming a specialist, e.g. a member of a specific culture, historical period, and family that can entail the loss of some general capacities (e.g. recognizing the phonemes of any language). Two, the infant's motor strength is increasing and thus his or her instrumental competence is increasing as the ability to move around in space increases and the child's world expands. Three, the infant is gradually learning to de-contextualize his or her knowledge of the world and her relation to and place in the world, e.g. through increasing mobility, the onset of language, and later through the ability to read and an ever widening social experience in school. And four, the fate of the infant's initial capacity for being an active agent and making sense of experiences is being determined through lived experiences in transactions with caregivers, and the inanimate world.

It is this latter issue that I would like to explore further by describing how the timing and content of the caregiver's responses can affect the infant's ability to develop and expand on his or her volitional capacities. Sander (1982) suggested that when a family can facilitate the infant's own efforts at goal realization and provide opportunities for the infant to initiate goal-organized behaviors, it will provide "the conditions which establish not only the capacity for self-awareness, but conditions which insure the use of such inner awareness by the infant as a frame of reference in organizing his own adaptive behavior" (p. 17). He went on to say that "the valence of this inner experience under these conditions of self-initiated goal realization will be felt as the infant's own" (p. 17). It follows then that this issue of the infant's agency and initiatives must be negotiated from the beginning within the family, for it will involve inevitable clashes of agendas between the infant's goals and the goals of other family members. If the family cannot make room for a new agent in its midst, then "abridgements of volition" will occur very early as the infant learns to turn away from or ignore internal cues as a frame of reference for action and becomes skilled at reading the cues of others. This is the beginning of what Winnicott (1971) called a false-self organization. I am emphasizing that this is not due to the infant's inability to differentiate self from the other, but represents a failure of parental fostering of the infant's initiatives.

Timing of the caregiver's response is an important element in determining the infant's continued use of inner cues as a frame of reference for action. Imagine an infant experiencing low-level distress, manifested by whimpering and motor restlessness, which gradually builds up into a rhythmical cry and more vigorous motor restlessness. At some point in this sequence, the infant will become aware of a distressed state (A), of an intention or wish to end or decrease it (I), and will begin to mobilize behaviors to achieve that goal e.g. sucking or searching behaviors (M). I refer to this entire process as AIM, and understand it as representing a dynamic coming together within the infant of an optimal level of affective arousal, combined with whatever past experience has accrued from connecting the antecedents and consequences of previous similar states, which results in the emergence of a goal and of an initiative to achieve that goal. If the caregiver times her intervention at that moment, and is able to match the specificity of the infant's goal (e.g. offering comfort or another appropriate remedy), the infant will experience this response as a recognition and validation of his or her own initiative, as well as a realization of the infant's goal. The effect of this entire transactional event will reinforce the infant's use of internal cues as a frame of reference for future action. If, however, the caregiver intervenes too early, before AIM has emerged within the infant, the infant will receive a remedy before any awareness of a problem has been experienced, and thus the caregiver's intervention will have no connection to the infant's own agenda, constituting a passive experience for the infant. If the caregiver intervenes too late, AIM will be disrupted by an increasing density of negative affect, so that the infant's sense of having some control will be overwhelmed and coherency may be lost, increasing the infant's dependency on the caregiver. The caregiver's acceptance of and valuing her infant as an active agent, her skill in assessing the optimal intensity of affective experience for her infant and accurately reading her infant's intentions are essential for supporting the infant's goals.

The content of the caregiver's response also plays a role in fostering the infant's goals. Imagine that an infant's interest is aroused by an object, that an intention to explore the object emerges, and that the infant mobilizes a reaching action, another manifestation of AIM.. Also imagine that given the infant's motor limitations, the effort fails and results in a low level of distress and/or frustration in the infant. If the caregiver facilitates the infant's efforts, the infant is likely to remain interested and persist. But if the caregiver is annoyed by the infant's fussing and puts the infant to bed, or becomes punitive, or simply ignores the infant, then the infant is likely to become more distressed. These different responses are experienced by the infant as affective sequences, e.g. in the first case a positive affect followed by a negative affect followed by a positive affect, versus in the second case a positive affect followed by a negative affect, followed by an intensification of negative affect. In this way the content of the caregiver's response helps to determine the motivational meaning of the whole sequence for the infant, namely what to expect when one experiences a particular affect state (interest) and tries to carry out one's intentions and actions mobilized by such a state (reaching). A positive-negative-positive sequence enhances the infant's agency and capacity to tolerate moderate levels of negative affect, so as to persist in the face of difficulties. In a positive-negative-negative sequence, which may also involve the caregiver berating the infant and/or leaving the infant alone to deal with the consequences, several aspects of the infant's engagement are at play simultaneously, and are challenged by the lack of caregiver support. Is it the interest or the frustration that is wrong? Is it the reaching behaviors that are wrong? Is it the wrong object? The infant tends to place a negative meaning on all three aspects, which can leave the infant in a defeated state. A steady diet of this latter sequence increases the infant's sense of helplessness, thereby undermining the infant's agency. The infant's positive affects have been minimized, the negative affects have been compounded and intensified, and then one is often left alone to cope with the consequences. I would argue that the infant has learned that his/her interests and goals do not seem to matter to the caregiver, thus the inclination to use one's inner awareness of AIM as a frame of reference for future actions is not supported, and that alone, he or she is unable to develop skills or solve problems, or to endure moderate negative affects and to reestablish positive affect states. This can lead to experiences of feeling devalued, ineffective, and helpless, states which heighten the need for parents, and leads the infant and young child to shift away from using inner states of interest and self-generated goals as guides for action, and to focus on how to obtain and sustain the caregiver's involvement. This strategy, while it retains a semblance of agency, substantially constricts the degrees of freedom open to the infant and young child by closing off access to inner sources of vitality and information.

The affect sequences described above, comprised of early, nonverbal, emotionally patterned communications between infants and caregivers, are occurring and being stored in implicit, procedural memory, which involve subcortical, limbic, right hemisphere circuits that tend to have less plasticity, when compared with the later developing neocortical circuits in the left hemisphere, the hippocampus, and the corpus callosum, involved in explicit, declarative, narrative learning, which is stored in a separate part of the brain, and continues to develop new dendrites and synapses throughout life. Early learning therefore can have long-lasting effects on psychological functioning, but these effects can be modulated and regulated by continued developments in the neocortex.

Sander (1975) has articulated an epigenetic series of issues that were negotiated, perturbed and then renegotiated between infants and their families from birth to 3 years of age, based on data from a longitudinal study done in the 1950s on 30 families and their first-born children. These issues describe the development of increasingly complex new organizations in the infant, as new, more focused states and intentionally initiated behaviors emerge and make new demands on the family, representing a progressive expansion of the scope of infants vis-à-vis the control of situations in their environments. From birth to roughly 3 months of age the initial regulation of coherent states of sleeping, waking, eating, elimination, and affect are being negotiated. From 4 to roughly 6 months, as the infant's awake states of interest become longer, reciprocal exchanges of smiling, vocal, motor responses are being negotiated and if engaged in, are being mutually enjoyed. Throughout this phase, the infant gradually becomes more active in initiating exchanges, which ushers in the next phase from roughly 7–9 months, called simply "initiative," in which the infant is more intentional and goal directed. From roughly 10 to 13 months, as the infant becomes able to move away from the caregiver, and now has to keep track of two moving objects, the infant's "focalization" on the mother becomes intensified. The infant has to determine how available the caregiver will be when the infant makes a bid for attention. This is the period of separation anxiety and stranger anxiety. Caregivers have very little privacy during this period, and have to renegotiate their availability. From 14 months to roughly 20 months as infant's become more mobile, they become more self-assertive about their goals, asserting them intentionally against the caregivers' wishes, requiring a new adjustment between caregiver and infant. This period is often called "the terrible twos," During the period of 18 months and 36 months, with the advent of language and secondary processing, the infant is more aware of his inner intentions, state, and fantasies and can now experience that another is aware of what he is aware of within himself, and becomes exquisitely aware of how small and less competent he is in relation to the big adults and more vulnerable to shame. Two issues are being negotiated. These new emergents make possible the self-reflective experience of "recognition" by another and of self-recognition. Many self-aware experiences of the toddler may or may not be recognized by the caregiver, or may be mislabeled, such as affect states, or intentions, increasing the likelihood of the toddler turning away from internal cues as a guide for goal directed behaviors and using only what the adult recognizes and values as a guide for goals. The other issue being negotiated at this time, which requires patience and flexibility in the caregiver, is the need for the toddler to disrupt and then restore mutual coordination with the other, through intentional aggressive and repair behaviors, so as to experience "continuity" in the self. An overly punitive response by caregivers will lead to compliance, if the bond between child and parent is strong, or to rebellion if it is weak.

The capacity to maintain coherent states and to generate and follow one's own goals and initiatives will continue to be developed and tested as young children enter into larger and more challenging contexts. In psychological terms, they will experience many ups and downs in their sense of competence and well-being. Their self-esteem can remain vulnerable for many years. When under stress they can become quite rigid and insist on only one way to proceed. At such times they seem to be at their limit to comprehend things, and require familiar routines to maintain some solace and comfort. But at other times, when they feel surer of their competence, they can be quite flexible and playful, e.g. when dealing with well mastered activities. Once again, context is everything. For example, early in her writing, my young granddaughter would insist that she had written the small case "e" in her name correctly. But later, she proudly showed me her name and said: "See, I did the 'e' right." At the earlier time, she needed to protect her self-esteem, even knowing the "e" was not right. It seems the louder the insistence, the greater is the threat to inner coherence or a sense of being able to make sense of the world. This last statement might be true at any age.

Our educational systems have developed optimally graded steps in presenting new materials which provide just the right mix of novelty and redundancy so that students of all ages can learn without feeling overwhelmed and defeated. Families may not be as skillful in matching the coping skills of their children to the challenges they present. Parental rigidities, excessive anger, or anxiety, or emotional lability, neglect, or abuse can overwhelm a child's capacity to make sense of, or to counteract parental actions, and put such a child in a defensive or passive position, resulting in a constriction of the child's inner freedom to use their own ideas, feelings, and wishes as guides for living. These constrictions represent fault lines in the child's psyche; namely the best solutions possible based on their capacities at the time to make sense of what was happening and to protect some areas of initiative. These fault lines may not show up for many years, until the child encounters the greater challenges of leaving home, going to college, or committing to a relationship or a career. While overwhelming challenges can come at any time in a person's life, those that have experienced such challenges earlier, which are often embedded in chronic maladaptive patterns of interactions in their families, are at greater risk for developing symptomatic behaviors in adulthood, which represent both an intensification of and the limitations of their earlier solutions. At all ages, as human beings, we are attempting to create meaning and to be in charge of our lives.

References

Baillargeon, R. (1990). *Young infants' physical knowledge*. Paper presented at the annual convention of the American Psychological Association, Boston.

Bower, T. G. R. (1974). *Development in infancy*. San Francisco: Freeman Press.

Brunner, J. 1968. *Processes of cognitive growth*. Worcester: Clark University Press.

DeCasper, A. J., & Carstens, A. A. (1981). Contingencies of stimulation: Effects on learning and emotion in neonates. *Infant Behavior and Development, 4*, 19–35.

Demos, E. V. (1986). Crying in early infancy: An illustration of the motivational function of affect. In T. B. Brazelton & M. Yogman (Eds.), *Affective development in early infancy* (pp. 39–73). Norwood: Ablex.

Demos, E. V. (1988). Affect and the development of the self: A new frontier. In A. Goldberg (Ed.), *Frontiers in self psychology: Progress in self psychology* (Vol. 3, pp. 27–53). Hillsdale: Analytic Press.

Demos, E. V. (1989a). Resiliency in infancy. In T. F. Dugan & R. Coles (Eds.), *The child in our time: Studies in the development of resiliency* (pp. 3–22). New York: Brunner/Mazel.

Demos, E. V. (1989b). A prospective constructionist view of development. *Annual of Psychoanalysis, 17*, 287–308.

Demos, E. V. (1992). The early organization of the psyche. In J. W. Barron, M. N. Eagle, & E. L Wolitsky (Eds.), *Interface of psychoanalysis and psychology* (pp. 200–233). Washington, DC: American Psychological Association.

Demos, E. V. (2007). The dynamics of development. In C. Piers, J. P. Muller, & J. Brent (Eds.), *Self-organizing complexity in psychological systems* (pp. 135–163). New York: Jason Aronson.

Demos, E. V. (2008). Basic human priorities reconsidered. *Annual of Psychoanalysis 36*: 246–265.

Donaldson, M. (1979). *Children's minds*. New York: Basic Books.

Edelman, G. M. (1987). *Neural Darwinism*. New York: Basic Books.

Edelman, G. M. (1992). *Bright air, brilliant fire: On the matter of the mind*. New York: Basic Books.

Field, T. M., Woodson, R., Greenberg, R., & Cohen, D. (1982). Discrimination and imitation of facial expressions by neonates. *Science, 218*, 179–181.

Fisher, K. W., & Pipp, S. L. (1984). Processes of cognitive development: Optimal level and skill acquisition. In R. J. Sternberg (Ed.), *Mechanisms of cognitive development* (pp. 45–80). New York: Freeman Press.

Gaensbauer, T. (1982). The differentiation of discrete affects. *Psychoanalytic Study of the Child, 37*, 29–65.

Ghent, E. (2002). Wish, need, drive: Motive in the light of dynamic systems theory and Edelman's selectionist theory. *Psychoanalytic Dialogues, 12*, 763–808.

Greenberg, J. (1991). *Oedipus and beyond: A clinical theory*. Cambridge: Harvard University Press.

Panksepp, J. (1999a). Emotions as viewed by psychoanalysis and neuroscience: An exercise in consilience. *Neuro-Psychoanalysis, 1*(1), 15–39.

Panksepp, J. (1999b). Drives, affects, Id energies and the neuroscience of emotions: Response to commentaries. *Neuro-Psychoanalysis, 1*(1), 69–89.

Piaget, J. (1967). *Six psychological studies*. New York: Vintage Books.

Sander, L. (1969). Regulation and organization in the early infant-caregiver system. In R. J. Robinson, (Ed.), *Brain and early development* (Vol. 1, pp. 311–332). New York: Academic Press.

Sander, L. (1975). Infant and caretaking environment: Investigation and conceptualization of adaptive behavior in a system of increasing complexity. In E. J. Anthony, (Ed.), *Explorations in child psychiatry* (pp. 126–166). New York: Plenum Press.

Sander, L. (1982). *The inner experience of the infant: A framework for inference relevant to development of the sense of self*. Paper presented at the 13th Margaret S. Mahler Symposium, Philadelphia.

Sander, L. (1985). Toward a logic of organization in psychobiologic development. In H. Klar & L. Siever (Eds.), *Biologic response cycles: Clinical implications* (pp. 19–37). Washington, DC: American Psychiatric Press.

Shapiro, D. (1981). *Autonomy and rigid character.* New York: Basic Books.

Shapiro, D. (2000). *Dynamics of character.* New York: Basic Books.

Tomkins, S. S. (1962). *Affect, imagery, consciousness: Vol. 1. The positive affects.* New York: Springer Publishing Company.

Tomkins, S. S. (1963). *Affect, imagery, consciousness: Vol. 2. The negative affects.* New York: Springer Publishing Company.

Tomkins, S. S. (1978). Script theory: Differential magnification of affects. In H. E. Howe Jr. & R. A. Dunstbier (Eds.), *Nebraska symposium on motivation* (pp. 201–236). Lincoln: University of Nebraska Press.

Von Bertalanffy, L (1952). Problems of life: an evaluation of modern biological thought. Oxford, England.

Weiss, P. (1949). The biological basis of adaption. In. Romano, John (Ed.). *Adaptation*, Ithaca, NY: Cornell University Press, pp. 1–22.

Winnicott, D. (1971). *Playing and reality.* London: Tavistock.

Wolff, P. (1973). Organization of behavior in the first tress months of life. *Association for Research on Nervous and Mental Disorders, 51,* 132–153.

Reply to E. Virginia Demos

David Shapiro

Virginia Demos' presentation of aspects of early volitional development, particularly affective ones, that are absent or slighted in my own work is a valuable supplement to that work, although I think Dr. Demos offers it both as a supplement and a correction. In any case, I much appreciate it. Still, there are some questions I would like to raise with her on several theoretical points, and I should also like to clarify my views on some matters Dr. Demos has touched on. I should also say at this point, for the sake of clarity, that Dr. Demos uses the terms "autonomy" and "agency" with a somewhat different meaning from mine. I use these terms to mean the developing capability of volitional self-direction and its associated subjective experience of intention or personal responsibility for action. I believe Dr. Demos uses these terms primarily to refer to the accomplishment of particular effective actions, a capability present virtually at birth, and the sense of competence and self-confidence that presumably accompanies that accomplishment. Thus she speaks of agency as a need or preference and as promoting mental health. In my sense, however, volitional self-direction, ultimately the capacity for self-reflective choice, is a general property of the mind, one which develops throughout childhood in all humans and may be compromised in various ways in psychopathology. The awareness of personal agency in connection with particular actions certainly may include a sense of competence, but it may also include an experience of anxiety or, in retrospect, dismay. If my understanding of Dr. Demos' meaning is wrong, I expect she will correct me.

As Dr. Demos observes, my discussion of the development of autonomy is largely concerned with cognitive developments and, except for consideration of anxiety, much less with motivation and affect. The general reason for this incompleteness is that I am concerned mainly with the development of psychological structure, primarily ways of thinking that determine ways of acting, rather than affects that motivate action. And, specifically, I believe the development of autonomy to be propelled primarily, though obviously not exclusively, by the opportunities opened progressively by cognitive development.

The picture of early cognitive and volitional development is clearly much richer today than it was when Piaget and Werner considered cognitive development. I do not underestimate the value of this recent work and, as I said, I am grateful to Dr. Demos for reminding me of it. However, I think certain objections Dr. Demos makes to their conceptions and implicitly to mine, and to its theoretical view of development in general, are not well-founded. In defending the competency of children against what she considers, perhaps correctly, the prejudices of earlier developmental work – a kind of adult chauvinism – she exaggerates the earlier pictures of the infant's mind, drawn by Piaget and Werner, and my own conception, as ones of complete passivity and virtual emptiness. Did Piaget really say that there is "nothing going on in the infant's mind"? I doubt it. I know I didn't. In the last chapter of my book *Neurotic Styles* I spoke of "innate organizing and form-giving configurations of psychological apparatus." In that place, also, I make the point that the infant is "not purely a passive agent" and that his function is not a product of drives and stimuli alone, but also of the organizing processes of an individual. At the same time that Dr. Demos exaggerates the emptiness and passivity of the earlier picture of infancy, I believe she makes the nascent volition of the infant seem more adult ("…as if the infant thinks, 'this is nice, but I'd rather do it myself'") than the evidence she presents indicates. I make this point not so much to defend the particulars of Piaget's and Werner's work – it is shown to be incomplete and perhaps incorrect in certain of its tendencies – as to assert that in spite of its failings, its general picture of the direction of cognitive development, of objectification of the external world and increasingly abstract thinking, shows us a cognitive basis for the development of reflective volitional action and the normal adult experience of personal responsibility. That development should not be blurred; it is critical for the understanding of psychopathology.

There is another, much discussed, issue, concerning the nature of developmental theory, raised by Dr. Demos that is of special interest to me. Dr. Demos characterizes Werner's, Piaget's and consequently my developmental conceptions as linear stage theories, as opposed to a view that recognizes development as a series of newly emergent qualities. I take "linear" to mean continuous development along a straight line; that is, a simple quantitative increase at a fixed rate of the same dimensions. I do not think that either Piaget's or Werner's ideas of developmental stages can be described that way. Indeed, what are stages, not just Werner's and Piaget's but also Erikson's and Freud's, if not representations of newly emergent qualities? Nor do I think my own picture of the development of volitional action in the child or the development of psychopathology in the adult can be described as linear. In connection with psychopathology I have repeatedly made the point that relatively small changes in formal features may result in major changes in symptomatic content, as in the development of paranoid from obsessive conditions. In connection with the development of autonomy I propose something comparable: a small increase in objectification of the external world results in the abrupt appearance of a significantly different and more active relationship with it. The discovery of marbles creates at the same stroke a marble player. The gradual awareness of a wider world by an adolescent creates at some point a person who noticeably starts to plan his adult life.

There is a special reason for my interest in Dr. Demos' discussion of the linear conception of development. She assumes that I rely, in my conception of psychopathology, on the (similarly linear) concept of regression, although, as she notes, I have never used that term. I have never used the term because I have never liked the concept; in fact, have explicitly rejected it. I have proposed an alternative conception, one whose subjective process is more understandable. It rests, to be sure, on a kind of stage conception, but it relies precisely on the existence of heterogeneity within stages. (Dr. Demos' characterization of stage conceptions as implying a homogeneity of function within stages is not justified; Werner, for example, pointed out that advances in cognitive mode do not leave earlier modes completely behind.) Adults are capable of deliberate, considered judgments but, equipped with an acute sensitivity to circumstances, they are also able to allow themselves various kinds of essentially more passive, spontaneous or rule-determined reactions, of a sort that are more predominant in childhood. Those earlier modes of thinking and action carry a diminished experience of personal agency or responsibility, as when the rigid person turns to a rule for what he "should" do or impetuous people disclaim deliberateness with the assertion that they simply follow their emotions. I have proposed that reliance on such modes or limitation to them, exactly on account of their diminished experience of agency, offers relief or protection from anxiety. In other words, such modes can serve defensive aims. This defensive diminishment or compromise of the experience of active agency, associated with a reliance on various forms of passively reactive or rigid modes, is what we see in all forms of psychopathology.

This conception in no way implies that different forms of psychopathology can sensibly be lined up on a linear scale of severity according to their characteristic experience of agency. They and their experiences of agency are much too different in quality for that. But it does make clear that effective psychotherapy, whatever may be the patient's initial pathology, will have the result of an increased experience of personal agency. To put it more simply, as I said in my reply to Louis Sass in this volume, if psychotherapy is successful, the patient will achieve a clearer sense of what he or she actually wants to do.

Continuing the Discussion

E. Virginia Demos

Dr. Shapiro's cogent reply to my presentation helps me see, as always, where I have not been as precise as I would have liked. Since Dr. Piers has allowed the commentators to have the last word, I have the opportunity to clarify my meaning and expand on some of the issues he has raised.

I do think that we are using the terms "autonomy" and "agency" in the same way, but that I have added a motivational component. Thus I accept his statement in *Dynamics of Character* (2000) that ordinary purposefulness involves "the wish to do something or effect some change in the external world" (p. 78). Earlier I cited evidence that purposefulness is present at birth and I could have cited other evidence demonstrating how motivating it is for infants, young children and other animals to try to do something and to succeed, how upsetting it is when they do not succeed, and how when they are the passive recipients of even desirable effects, it does not have the same motivational impact on them. The animal literature shows that more brain areas are activated in the act of self-initiated effort, than when the animal is passively stimulated, and that the self-initiated acts are intrinsically rewarding. All of these data suggest that given our long evolutionary history, agency is indeed "a general property of the mind." We start out life with a bias or preference for being an active agent, and only our lived experience will determine whether this capacity will thrive or be thwarted. I described both positive and negative affective sequences, and argued that when positive outcomes are more prevalent in a young child's life, it can lead to the expectation of success and to a feeling of competence. But if the child's initiatives are chronically met with failure or defeat, the wish to do something will evoke anxiety, an expectation of failure, a feeling of "why bother, nothing ever works out anyway," and can result in a curtailment or an avoidance of making an effort. Thus the capacity to use one's agency, or feel one has the right to or can own one's agency will, to some extent, depend on the consequences of having tried to do so early on and throughout ones childhood. So, yes I am saying that to be open to one's desires and to be free to be an active agent are signs of mental health, just as infringements of one's volition are symptoms of psychopathology.

By including the motivational component in the process of fostering and developing agency and autonomy, I am also challenging Dr. Shapiro's statement that such development "is propelled primarily, though not exclusively, by the opportunities opened progressively by cognitive development." I am arguing that motivation and cognition are equally important, for without the amplification of interest and curiosity, children cannot fully engage their minds, (the phenomenon of giving up or inhibiting exploration is observable early on) and thus cognitive opportunities will not be optimally exploited. There are many ways that parents fail to foster their children's interests and initiatives, e.g. neglect, criticism, humiliation, shaming, physical punishment, intrusive domination, etc. When children feel parental disapproval for their autonomous wishes or actions, they tend to hide their wishes and intentions from parental eyes and ears, and pursue them secretly, or outside of the home. Such strategies are conscious, responsive to context and do not evoke rigid defenses. Indeed, children may take pleasure in "getting away with it," and not be burdened with guilt. In more extreme situations, which evoke intense fear of parental intrusiveness, or punishments, children will not only inhibit their actions, but may also begin to control the contents of their minds more rigidly and defensively, lest they slip and make a mistake. Once that process takes hold, they can slowly become alienated from their own wishes.

I agree with Dr. Shapiro that children do have to rely on, and accept parental rules to a great extent, because they do not yet possess extensive knowledge or experience of the world. But he states that they do so passively, because it serves the child's spontaneous wishes, and I find this part of his argument problematic in two ways. First, it seems to allow for little variation, implying homogeneity, and thus has the sound of a categorical statement, based on the cognitive deficits of the child, typical of stage theory thinking. Second, it assumes that given the child's cognitive limitations, the child is necessarily passive in accepting parental expertise, and perhaps therefore, in Dr. Shapiro's thinking, is prevolitional, and lacking in self-direction. I am arguing that if agency is central to the psychodynamics of either health or pathology, then the task of having to adapt one's wishes to those of another always, at every age, involves a complex, active intra-psychological and inter-psychological negotiation. This task may require even more psychic effort in early childhood, when a child's wishes can seem so urgent. Earlier, I described Sander's work on the need for parents and children to continually renegotiate clashing agendas as the infant's and young child's initiatives become more focused, compelling, and intruding into more and more areas of family life. Young children are actively engaged in an ongoing process of developing new skills and possibilities, and in learning what they can and cannot master, what is and is not acceptable, when, how, in what contexts and with whom is it safe to pursue their aims. Such a process requires negotiation, which can become fraught with conflict, both internal and external, depending on how clear and consistent the rules are and how they are conveyed. Arbitrary rules, punitively enforced can lead to a compliance based on fear, or involve a grudging resentment and deep hurt that may have to remain hidden, and thus may evoke high anxiety and the need for more rigid defenses. But in more benign family environments, the child may comply in a spirit of mutual cooperation, and be freer to display a full range of mood related stances, including resistance, or rebellion, without fear of retaliation. There is quite a lot individual variation in how these issues get resolved over time, but it is never passive. I think this issue is central to either my misunderstanding of or to my disagreement with Dr. Shapiro, for if this process of complying with adult rules is active and quite variable, then there is no mode of "prevolition" that can be reverted to, and I do not understand what it adds to his already quite useful articulation of the ways that agency has been compromised in various psychopathologies.

I think the different ways we view the dynamics of development is relevant here. Dr. Shapiro believes that I have exaggerated the degree of underestimation of the infant's mind by Piaget, Werner, and himself, and have overestimated the infant's capacities by making them seem more adult, and thereby run the risk of blurring the real changes that do occur in development. Let me say at the outset that I do believe that real changes do occur in development, and that they do involve an increasing objectification and, what I could call an increasing de-contextualization of experience and thinking. But I am arguing that the basic capacities needed for learning are present at birth as exemplified in the DeCasper and Carstens experiment I reported, namely the ability to focus attention, and to co-ordinate perception, cognition, affect, and past experience, in order to try to act on the world. The duration of focused attention increases rapidly in infancy, as does their ability to remember events over longer time periods. They lack experience and knowledge, and the capacity for self-reflection, which does not develop until the middle of the second year of life. This later capacity represents a major transformation, and the beginning of a long process of de-centering ones experience, during which concepts will be repeatedly organized and reorganized into ever more encompassing new configurations, as the child moves into larger and larger contexts. But these early, preverbal experiences of self-initiated behavior are highly motivating and intrinsically rewarding, and may represent the beginnings of "owning" such behaviors that will later, when the world becomes more objectified, develop into a more elaborate sense of responsibility. Perhaps Dr. Shapiro wants to reserve the terms 'autonomous and agency for the self-reflective, fully aware, responsible form and call all earlier manifestations "prevolitional." Such a stance follows Piaget's use of such terms.

Before this transformation occurs, however, the task of trying to understand and describe the infant's mind presents a real challenge. The infant cannot use language to think; yet the infant does think, and produces actions that convey meaning and purpose. There is an extensive sensory-motor level of knowledge of the world and people that allows the infant to be active and to anticipate events. When interacting with an infant, one has the experience of being in conversation with a sentient being through facial, vocal and affective exchanges. I did exaggerate when I stated that Piaget did not believe that anything was going on in the infant's mind, but he did grossly underestimate the degree of organization and competence the infant possesses, by applying general rules of cognition, and ignoring the infant's most relevant contexts. He continued to underestimate the capacities of young children, because in a stage theory framework, the importance of context is overshadowed by the assumption that if a cognitive "structure" is present, it will be manifested across contexts, hence the implication of homogeneity. For example, he tested their understanding of the inclusion relation, namely that one class can be embedded in another, by using red and blue beads and asking, "Are there more red beads or more beads?" The children all answered there are more red beads, thereby failing the test. Piaget concluded that children in the "pre-symbolic stage" were not able to hold the two levels of classes in their mind at the same time, rather than that the children may have been more attracted by the difference between the red and blue beads. Subsequent research, (reported by Donaldson) using materials more meaningful to young children, namely sleeping cows and standing cows, found that when children were asked "Are there more sleeping cows or more cows?" they all said there are more cows, demonstrating that they could indeed hold two levels of classes in their minds, if the content of the class mattered to them. This newer research also demonstrates the importance of knowing what contexts are important to children, if one wants to learn how their minds work, for example many children's stories are told through the voices and adventures of animals.

In contrast to stage theories, a dynamic systems theory emphasizes the match between the child's focus and what the environment provides; with a good enough match, a genuine engagement in the task by the child can occur and result in a meaningful transaction with the world. The two approaches also differ in their understanding of the emergence of new behaviors or the emergence of cognitive shifts in organizing concepts. Stage theories postulate the existence of a genetically controlled timetable that gradually unfolds as the organism matures, and spend little time exploring the processes involved in such stage shifts. Here, I want to clarify my use of the term linear, in relation to stage theories, which I am using in a far narrower sense than Dr. Shapiro assumed. I mean it in a value-laden sense of the pejorative descriptions of the earliest stages as global, undifferentiated, passive, and basically incompetent, and the corollary assumption that we get better and better in every way as we develop. But progress is not always simple or in a straight line; we lose capacities as well, as we become more and more specialized. In a dynamic systems approach it is assumed that as biological organisms, we are self-organizing entities and thus there is competence at all levels, when the organism is seen in its proper context. There is no assumption of a preordained outcome, but rather an articulation of the initial conditions within which dynamic processes can occur. The focus is on the shifting balance between maintaining continuity and adapting to new situations by changing, and attempting to articulate the variables responsible for shifting or "tipping" the organism into a new organization in those relevant contexts. A dynamic systems approach also does not speak so much of structures, but of dynamic organizations that become increasingly strengthened as the number and speed of neural connections increase through frequent evocation of such organizations in active transactions with the world.

In conclusion, at times Dr. Shapiro seems to allow for variation and the existence of different capacities present in the same developmental time frame depending on context, and at such time uses conditional statements, but at other times he uses the term "prevolitional," which sounds categorical to my ears. I do not know if he imagines that there exists a "prevolitional mode" encapsulated somewhere in the psyche that remains invariant in some way, so that it can be "reverted to" in a process that does not constitute regression. For example, when discussing schizophrenia he states that this condition "presents a picture of an impairment or inhibition, or abandonment – or at any rate, a profound loss – of active, volitional self-direction" (*Dynamics of Character*, 2000, p. 128). But at another point he states that "the impairment of volitional direction in schizophrenia may also constitute an anxiety-forestalling reversion – in this case a radical one – to prevolitional modes," (ibid.) by which he seems to mean a lack of self-direction and "extreme passivity." No such modes are present in normal development, thus it would be more accurate to call them non-volitional modes. I would argue that extreme anxiety, namely terror, renders one helpless, and induces a paralysis of volition at any time of life. Why does it need to be seen as a "reversion?" What does he mean by that word? Dr. Shapiro does not address the effects of trauma, namely terror, on the psyche, particularly in childhood or the diagnosis of PTSD. This latter condition does contain elements of character variations, but the effects of chronic terror on the psyche seem to be a much more dominant force in determining the defenses.

Part II
Personality, Personality Disorders and Psychosis

Chapter 4
Two Configurations of Personality Development and Psychopathology: Etiologic and Therapeutic Implications

Sidney J. Blatt

David Shapiro, in an unpublished paper titled: *On two fundamental categories of psychopathology*,[1] notes that he and I via "different routes," have "arrived at the same conclusion that there are two fundamental categories of psychopathology." Shapiro notes "a general congruence" of his concepts of a "rigid mode" and a "passive-reactive mode" (e.g., Shapiro, 1981, 2000) and my formulations of anaclitic and introjective configurations of personality development, personality organization and psychopathology (e.g., Blatt, 1974, 1990, 1991, 2006, 2008; Blatt and Shichman, 1983).[2] But Shapiro also notes that "on a certain important point concerning both etiology and dynamics… [we] clearly diverge" and he discusses our divergence about "the dynamics of psychopathology and perhaps also its etiology." This paper articulates more fully this divergence and why I, in contrast to Shapiro, think it important to include aspects of the etiology and dynamics in formulations of the two configurations of psychopathology. I briefly cite studies that demonstrate the validity of some the assumptions about the etiology and dynamics of the anaclitic and introjective

---

S.J. Blatt (✉)
Professor of Psychiatry and Psychology, Yale School of Medicine,
300 George Street (Suite 901), New Haven, CT 06511
e-mail: sidney.blatt@yale.edu

[1] See Appendix A.

[2] Shapiro notes one "minor" (p. 3) exception between our formulations of two configurations or two modes of psychopathology – the issue of borderline personality disorder. Shapiro notes that he omitted borderline pathology from his formulations because it is "too vague symptomatically to permit any clear definition of form" (p. 3). He incorrectly notes, however, that I place borderline pathology in the anaclitic category. In fact, John Auerbach and I noted a number of years ago (Blatt and Auerbach 1987, 1988) the complexity of borderline pathology and distinguished two forms of borderline personality disorder – an anaclitic and an introjective form of borderline phenomena. Subsequent empirical research (e.g., Levy et al. 2007; Morse et al. 2002; Ouimette et al. 1994; Westen et al. 1992; Wixom et al. 1993) supports this distinction between one type of borderline personality disorder that is highly dependent and vulnerable to intense feelings of loneliness and interpersonal loss – an anaclitic borderline that conforms to the BPD diagnosis as described in DSM IV, and a more over-ideational introjective form of borderline pathology with obsessive-compulsive and paranoid features that has predominant concerns about issues of self-definition and self-worth.

C. Piers (ed.), *Personality and Psychopathology: Critical Dialogues with David Shapiro*,
DOI 10.1007/978-1-4419-6214-0_4, © Springer Science+Business Media, LLC 2011

configurations of personality organization and psychopathology and how these assumptions facilitate the articulation of a theoretically coherent and comprehensive model of psychological development, personality organization and psychopathology that has etiologic as well as therapeutic implications.

Shapiro correctly notes that my formulation of anaclitic and introjective configurations of personality organization and psychopathology is both a developmental and a dynamic theory – what I call a "dynamic structural developmental approach" (Blatt 2008). This approach stresses continuities between personality development, personality organization and psychopathology because they involve common developmental processes and have common developmental precursors. Shapiro, in contrast, discusses two types of character formation – a rigid and a passive-reactive character but has "less confidence in the psychoanalytic developmental model, especially as it is applied to adult psychopathology." Shapiro notes that he "cannot offer alternative suggestions for the etiology of each of these character forms" because he thinks "it is doubtful that they are heirs of childhood dynamics...." Thus, he states that he has "little to say about etiology" but is describing "two general forms of activity and thought characteristic of adult psychopathology."

Shapiro describes the phenomenology of two modes of functioning – how individuals in his rigid mode (or in my introjective configuration) "are to one extent or another, rule-directed... and] live with a continual awareness... of authoritative rules" and are dominated by the thought, "I should." Shapiro contrasts this rigid "rule-based, conscientiousness" with a more adaptive "autonomous conscientiousness of conviction." He notes that "the rules by which the rigid character lives, or tries to live, are often embodied in authoritative figures whom the rigid person attempts to emulate and identify... and... is constantly evaluating himself against these standards." But Shapiro notes that there is "little evidence that... [this] rigid conscientiousness necessarily reflects an internalization of rigid or strict parental control" and "may not be the *direct or simple* (emphasis added) product of introjection" ... and is unlikely to "rest on the slender foundation of developmental dynamics."

Shapiro raises similar questions about his passive-reactive mode or my anaclitic configuration. Consistent with my formulations about the anaclitic configuration (e.g., Blatt 1974, 1998, 2006, 2008; Blatt and Shichman 1983), Shapiro notes that concerns and problems in the passive-reactive mode are largely around interpersonal relations, in contrast to the concerns and problems in the rigid mode or introjective configuration which are primarily around issues of the self. But Shapiro doubts that the defense mechanisms and cognitive style associated with the passive-reactive mode are the "*direct* (emphasis added) products or expressions of earlier relational problems and particular developmental dynamics." Shapiro proposes "that the nature of the interpersonal issues and problems of these individuals can be derived from the general character form" – of being "unreflective and emotional reactive" and turning "away from introspection and toward external figures and events." Thus, Shapiro believes it "unnecessary" to see this type of functioning as "the effects of early relational problems" but prefers to view it as "particular expressions of the general character form [that] still allows [us] to recognize that early relationships will contribute to, perhaps determine, their specific content.... [and] that personal history and family dynamics will be a determinant of the general mode." Though Shapiro notes that the rigid person may attempt to emulate and identify with authoritative figures and that early relationships and personal history and family dynamics may be a determinant of the passive-reactive mode, he believes that the "assumption that the general quality of the adult psychopathology is the heir of the child's *early* (emphasis added) problems of relationships circumvents the intervening development of character." Shapiro stresses that adult symptoms are "expressions of adult character" that "differ in fundamental ways from the developmental problems that may have been their source.... Once that character has developed, the dynamics of the pathology has changed." The sources of anxiety are "not limited to revivals or representations of the original sources... [but] now by whatever threatens the attitudes and stability of that character...." But extensive recent research (see summaries in Blatt 2004; Blatt and Zuroff 1992) demonstrates impressive congruence between the nature of personality organization (anaclitic or introjective) and the type of life stressors (interpersonal loss or personal failure) that threaten "the attitudes and stability of that character."

Shapiro appears to repudiate any interest in the etiology and dynamics of adult psychopathology because he believes they distract from the articulation of character formation – of "the forms of activity and thought characteristic of adult psychopathology." Shapiro's disinterest in matters of etiology and dynamics seems to be the consequence of his belief that adult character and psychopathology are not the "direct or simple" expressions of earlier relational problems and are "not limited to revivals or representations of the original sources." I agree with Shapiro that adult psychopathology is not the *direct or simple* expression in adulthood of earlier childhood relational problems or limited to the revival or representations of the original sources. But research evidence (e.g., Blatt and Homann 1992) indicates important linkages between childhood experiences and impaired adult functioning and between the nature of personality organization and the life stressors that disrupt adult functioning (Blatt 2004; Blatt and Zuroff 1992). These linkages between childhood experiences and adult personality organization and psychopathology involve complex transformations, but the understanding of these complex transformations can elaborate more fully the nature of psychopathology in adults and contribute to its treatment.[3] But Shapiro, in fact, seems to acknowledge developmental antecedents of his two character modes in his comments that the character modes draw "on activity and thought ... characteristic of early childhood that continue to be available in normal adult life" – that the rigid character often "attempts to emulate and identify" with the rules "embodied in authoritative figures" and that "early relationships" and "personal history and family dynamics will contribute to, and perhaps... will be

---

[3] These linkages and complex transformations between childhood experiences and adult personality organization may be more apparent in psychopathology than in well-functioning adults because well-functioning adults are more open to changing environmental circumstances and opportunities. This openness to environmental opportunities is more restricted in disrupted functioning.

a determinant of the general [passive-reactive] mode." In contrast to Shapiro, I believe that understanding matters of etiology and dynamics does not circumvent but rather enrich and elaborate our understanding of the development of personality organization and its relationship to psychopathology and provide the basis for the specification of a coherent and theoretically comprehensive model of psychopathology that has both etiologic and therapeutic implications.

Shapiro notes that the rigid and passive-reactive character are not polar opposites but "actually they are very closely related [in that they are] opposites of full personal autonomy or ...self-direction. Both draw on modes of activity and thought that are *characteristics of early childhood* (emphasis added)" that in "psychopathology are defensively employed, restrictive and hypertrophied." As Shapiro further notes, "both modes attenuate volitional processes, (and) diminish the experiences of personal agency.... [F]rom this point of view... one should not be surprised to see evidence of both modes or symptoms of both categories in every kind of psychopathology." Research evidence (e.g., Blatt 1992; Blatt et al. 2007; Blatt and Ford 1994; Blatt and Shahar 2004; Fertuck et al. 2004; Shahar et al. 2003), however, clearly indicates the reliability and validity of classifying most patients as either predominantly anaclitic or introjective. Thus, I disagree with Shapiro that symptomatic expressions of both modes appear in every form of psychopathology, but I do agree that both configurations or modes of psychopathology are characterized by general restrictions of "personal autonomy" and "self-direction," as well as the quality of interpersonal relatedness.

Shapiro has made outstanding contributions to the understanding of the phenomenology of adult psychopathology, but he seems concerned that an interest in etiology and dynamics might diminish attention to the complexities and vicissitudes of psychopathology in adults. To the contrary, I found that the understanding of the complexities and vicissitudes of psychopathology is enriched by the recognition of the continuities between personality development, personality organization, and the two fundamental configurations of psychopathology because these processes are organized around the same fundamental psychological developmental issues: around (1) the development of the capacity for reciprocal interpersonal relatedness and (2) the development of a differentiated, integrated, realistic, essentially positive self-definition. In the remainder of this paper I briefly elaborate how the identification of these two fundamental processes in psychological development (interpersonal relatedness and self-definition) enabled us to establish conceptual continuity among *personality development* (from infancy to senescence), central aspects of *personality organization*, many forms of *psychopathology*, as well as aspects of the *therapeutic process* (see Blatt 2006, 2008 for a fuller explication of these issues).

Though my research and theoretical formulations of two configurations of personality development and psychopathology began with the articulation of two forms of depression (Blatt 1974, 1998, 2004; Blatt et al. 1976, 1982), these initial formulations were later extended to a broad range of psychopathology (e.g., Blatt 1990, 2006, 2008; Blatt and Shichman 1983). As colleagues and I have noted, many disorders are organized around two primary preoccupations and concerns – with problematic issues in one or the other of two most basic of developmental psychological processes – around issues of the development of the capacity for interpersonal relatedness or of the development of self-definition or identity. We also noted that a wide range of personality theories, from classic psychoanalytic theory (e.g., Freud 1930) to empirical investigations of personality organization (e.g., Wiggins 1991), are structured around these same two fundamental psychological developmental processes (Blatt 2006, 2008) and that psychological development involves a hierarchical synergetic interaction of these two fundamental developmental processes (Blatt and Blass 1990, 1996; Blatt and Shichman 1983).

It was the identification of the fundamental constructs of interpersonal relatedness and self-definition (or communion and agency; Bakan 1996) that facilitated our recognition of the two primary configurations of psychopathology and the conceptual links between aspects of *personality development, personality organization, psychopathology*, and the *therapeutic process* (Blatt 2006, 2008). Shapiro has also noted some of these linkages in his observations of the continuity between character formation and psychopathology, but he, in my judgment, underestimates the etiological and dynamic significance of noting that character and psychopathology are both organized around these two fundamental dimensions of personality development. In contrast, I believe that the observation of continuities among personality development (beginning in infancy), personality organization and psychopathology facilitates the articulation of a theoretically coherent and comprehensive model of personality development in which various forms of psychopathology are viewed not as separate and independent diseases, with assumed, but as yet often undocumented, biological origins as considered in DSM-IV, but as maladaptive modes of functioning that develop over the life span (e.g., Blatt and Luyten in press, b).

Personality Development

Colleagues and I (Blatt 1974, 1998, 2006, 2008; Blatt and Blass 1990, 1996; Blatt and Shichman 1983) proposed a "two polarities" or "two configurational" model in which processes of interpersonal relatedness and self-definition (or attachment and separation) are fundamental psychological dimensions in personality development, variations in normal personality organization and concepts of psychopathology, as well as in processes of therapeutic change. We elaborated the theoretical implications of these two fundamental dimensions (relatedness and self-definition) in personality development and organization by proposing that personality development evolves, from infancy to senescence, through a *complex dialectic transaction* between these two fundamental psychological dimensions – between the development of increasingly mature, intimate, mutually satisfying, reciprocal, interpersonal relationships and the development of an increasingly differentiated, integrated, realistic, essentially positive sense of self or identity. These two fundamental developmental processes evolve through a life-long, *complex, synergistic, hierarchical, dialectic transaction* such that progress in one developmental line usually facilitates progress in the other. An increasingly differentiated, integrated, and mature sense of self emerges out of constructive interpersonal relationships and, conversely, the continued development of increasingly mature interpersonal relationships is contingent on the development of a more differentiated and integrated self-definition and identity. Meaningful and satisfying relationships contribute to the evolving concept of self, and a revised sense of self leads, in turn, to a capacity for more mature levels of interpersonal relatedness. The specification of this normal synergistic developmental process provides a basis for identifying adaptive and maladaptive variations of this fundamental developmental process.

Personality development throughout life, from infancy to senescence, proceeds through a hierarchical series of synergistic dialectical interactions between two fundamental developmental processes – between the development of the self and the development of a capacity for interpersonal relatedness. Progress in each of these two dimensions facilitates the development of the other. Throughout life, meaningful interpersonal experiences contribute to a fuller articulation, differentiation and integration of the sense of self that, in turn, facilitates the establishment of more mature forms of interpersonal relatedness. Though the relative balance between these two developmental dimensions and the specific life experiences that contribute to the development of a sense of self and the capacity for interpersonal relatedness varies across individuals and across cultures, these two fundamental dimensions essentially evolve through a basic synergistic developmental process.

Based on these formulations about the processes of personality development, we (Blatt and Blass 1990, 1996; Blatt and Shichman 1983) expanded Erikson's developmental model by including an additional psychosocial stage, cooperation versus alienation, around the age of 4–6 years with the emergent awareness of the triadic structure of the family (the Oedipal phase), the development of operational thinking (e.g., Piaget 1954) and the beginning of cooperative peer play (e.g., Whiteside et al. 1976) and placed this phase at the appropriate point in Erikson's developmental sequence between the "phallic" stage of "initiative versus guilt" and the psychosocial issues of latency – "industry versus inferiority." This extension of Erikson's formulations enabled us to identify one developmental dimension (self-definition or individuality) as evolving from early experiences of separation and autonomy from the primary caregiver, to a capacity to initiate activity first in opposition to the other and later proactively, to industry with sustained goal-directed activity that has direction and purpose, to the emergence of individuality and a "self-identity." The addition of an intermediate stage of cooperation to the Erikson model facilitated the identification of phases in the development of interpersonal relatedness that evolve from the sharing of affective experiences between mother and infant (e.g., Beebe and Lachmann 1988; Stern 1985) with a concomitant sense of basic trust (e.g., Erikson 1950), to a capacity for cooperation and collaboration with parents and peers, to the evolution of a close friendship with a same-sex chum (Sullivan 1953), to the development of mutual, reciprocal, enduring intimacy. Thus, the articulation of the processes of interpersonal relatedness and self-definition enabled us to identify two fundamental developmental pathways (e.g., Fischer et al. 1997; Sroufe 1997) in both normal and disrupted psychological development and to recognize their synergistic developmental interaction.[4]

Although this broadened Eriksonian model is still too sketchy to capture fully the details of the infinitely complex processes of human psychological development (Blatt and Luyten, in press, a), it docs articulate the reciprocal synergistic development of two dimensions throughout life, from infancy through the early developmental years until adolescence at which time the developmental task is to integrate these two developmental dimensions of relatedness and self-definition (or attachment-separation or communion-agency) into the comprehensive structure Erikson called "self-identity" (Blatt and Blass 1990, 1996) or a self-in-relation (Blatt 2006, 2008). Hence, adolescence is a crucial time for a synthesis that can result in the formation of a consolidated identity or the emergence of many forms of psychopathology, particularly personality disorders that are characterized by failures to integrate these two fundamental developmental processes (Blatt and Luyten, 2010b).

Personality Organization

Well-functioning personality organization involves an integration or balance in the development of interpersonal relatedness and of self-definition. Each individual, however, even within the normal range, places a somewhat greater emphasis on one or the other of these dimensions. Some individuals, more often women, tend to place somewhat greater emphasis on relatedness (an anaclitic personality organization), while other individuals, more often men, place somewhat greater emphasis on self-definition (an introjective personality organization). We (Blatt 1974; Blatt and Shichman 1983) used the term *anaclitic* for the personality organization focused predominantly on interpersonal relatedness, a term taken by Freud (1963) from the Greek *anklitas* – to rest or lean on, to characterize all interpersonal relationships that derive from dependency experienced in the context of the mother–child relationship (Laplanche and Pontalis 1974; Webster et al. 1960).

---

[4]The evolving capacities for autonomy, initiative, and industry in the self-definitional developmental dimension progress in an alternating sequence with the development of relational capacities. For example, one needs a sense of basic trust to venture in opposition to the need-gratifying other in asserting one's autonomy and independence, and later one needs a sense of autonomy and initiative to establish cooperative and collaborative relationships with parents and peers. Development begins with a focus on interpersonal relatedness – specifically with the stage of trust versus mistrust – before proceeding to two early self-definitional stages: autonomy versus shame and initiative versus guilt. These early expressions of self-definition are then followed by the newly identified stage of interpersonal relatedness, cooperation versus alienation, and then by two later stages of self-definition, industry versus inferiority and identity versus role diffusion. These more mature expressions of self-definition are followed by the more advanced stage of interpersonal relatedness, intimacy versus isolation, before development proceeds to two mature stages of self-definition, generativity versus stagnation and integrity versus despair (Blatt and Shichman 1983).

The term *introjective* refers to a personality organization primarily focused on self-definition, a term used by Freud (1917) to describe the processes whereby values, patterns of culture, motives, and restraints are assimilated into the self (e.g., made subjective), consciously or unconsciously, as guiding personal principles through learning and socialization (Webster, 1966; Webster et al. 1960).

This relative emphasis on interpersonal relatedness and self-definition delineates two basic personality or character styles, each with a particular experiential mode; preferred forms of cognition, defense, and adaptation; unique qualities of interpersonal relatedness; and specific forms of object and self-representation (Blatt 2006, 2008; Luyten et al. 2005a, 2005b). Thought processes in the *anaclitic personality style* are more figurative and focused primarily on affects and visual images, characterized by simultaneous rather than sequential processing and an emphasis on the reconciliation and synthesis of elements into an integrated cohesion rather than a critical analysis of separate elements and details (Szumotalska 1992). The anaclitic personality style is characterized by a predominant tendency to seek fusion, harmony, integration, and synthesis. The focus is upon personal experiences – on meanings, feelings, affects, and emotional reactions. These individuals are primarily field dependent (Witkin 1965), very aware of and influenced by environmental factors. Thought processes in the *introjective personality style*, in contrast, are much more literal, sequential, linguistic, and critical. Concerns are focused on action, overt behavior, manifest form, logic, consistency, and causality. These individuals tend to place emphasis on analysis rather than on synthesis, on the critical dissection of details and part properties rather than on achieving a total integration and an overall gestalt (Szumotalska 1992). These individuals are predominantly field independent (Witkin 1965), their experiences and judgments are primarily influenced by internal rather than environmental factors. Thus, the two personality dimensions of relatedness and self-definition develop through the life cycle, each influencing the shape and meaning given to psychological experiences (Blatt 2006, 2008). Extensive research demonstrates the validity of the distinction of anaclitic and introjective personality styles in nonclinical samples (see summaries in Blatt 2004, 2008; Blatt and Zuroff 1992; Luyten et al. 2005a; Zuroff et al. 2004).

Extensive research (see summary in Blatt and Homann 1992) documents the unique developmental antecedents of these two types of personality organization. This research is based primarily on retrospective reports of childhood experiences and though some questions have been raised about the accuracy of these retrospective reports (e.g., Lewinsohn and Rosenbaum 1987), Brewin and colleagues (Bewin et al. 1990, 1993) demonstrated the validity of retrospective reports. Though only a handful of prospective longitudinal studies are available (e.g., Gjerde et al. 1991; Koestner et al. 1991; Lekowitz and Tesiny 1984), their results support the conclusions of Brewin and colleagues (1990) about the validity of retrospective reports and the relation between adverse early experience and later psychopathology, often involving severe parental maltreatment. Consistent with the extensive research on attachment styles that demonstrates the continuity of secure and insecure attachment styles from early childhood (12–18 months) into adulthood, longitudinal research by Koestner and colleagues (1991) found that mothers' reports of parenting practices collected when their children were 5 years old was significantly related to the children's report of self-critical tendencies at age 12 and disrupted functioning at age 31. Children of mothers who had been rated by observers as rejecting and restrictive when their children were age 5, were more likely to be self-critical at age 12. In females, this self-criticism was still evident when these children were adults (31 years). Self-critical 12-year-old boys, however, tended not to be self-critical at 31 years, but instead reported greater aggressive impulses, although not necessarily aggressive actions. Thus, the findings of Koestner et al. (1991) indicate that rejecting, restrictive parenting in earlier childhood predicted self-criticism at age 12 in both boys and girls, especially when received from the same-sex parent, and that this self-criticism at age 12 had continuity with problematic functioning in adulthood.

Noteworthy is a recent report by Beebe and colleagues (2007) that demonstrated how mother's personality organization influences infant's development of self- and interactive regulation as early as 4 months of age. Using the Depressive Experiences Questionnaire (DEQ; Blatt et al. 1976, 1979), Beebe and colleagues assessed, 6-weeks post delivery, the extent to which primiparious mothers of a healthy first-born child in an ethnically diverse, low-risk sample of well-educated women experienced feelings of dependency or disturbances in self-worth and self-criticism (anaclitic and introjective issues) – the two dimensions I consider central in personality development, personality organization, and psychopathology. Beebe and colleagues examined the impact of these feelings of dependency and self-criticism in the mothers on interactive play patterns these mothers had with their infants 4 months after the infants' birth. Using well-established split screen analyses of mother–infant interaction, Beebe and colleagues (2007) found that elevated maternal scores on dependency and self-criticism both significantly predicted lower infant self-regulation at 4-months of age. But these two dimensions predicted very different patterns of mother-infant interactive regulation at 4-months. Dependent mothers had heightened facial and vocal coordination with their infants – an "attentional vigilance" that was accompanied by heightened emotional activation of the infants. Infants of these dependent mothers showed a similar emotional vigilance and an intense reactivity to shifts in mother's affective shifts. This heightened vigilance and dyadic symmetry of mother and infant indicates excessive maternal concern about the infant's availability that limits the infant's individuation and affect regulation.

In contrast, mothers with elevated scores on self-criticism had difficulty sharing their infant's attentional focus and emotional variations. These mothers appeared to try to compensate for their disengagement with their infants by touching their infants more frequently, a more neutral type of engagement than sharing facial expressions, voice quality or visual gaze. In response to the disengagement of self-critical mothers, their 4-month old infants seemed to disengage from their mother by withdrawing vocal quality coordination. This distancing and disengagement in self-critical mothers and in their infants appear to be the precursors of dismissive insecure attachment. The intense involvement of dependent mothers and their infants, in contrast, appear to be the precursors of preoccupied or anxious-ambivalent insecure attachment. It remains for subsequent research to examine the relationship among these early interpersonal interactive patterns observed at 4 months of age, attachment patterns observed in the second year of life, and the development of anaclitic and introjective forms of personality organization and psychopathology. Of course, mothers with relatively low levels of dependency and self-criticism, mothers who effectively and appropriately engage with their infants, would be expected to contribute to the development of a secure attachment pattern in their infants.

Psychopathology

Biological predispositions and severely disruptive environmental events can interact in complex ways to distort the integrated synergistic developmental process of relatedness and self-definition (see also Cicchetti and Gunnar 2008) and lead to a defensive and exaggerated emphasis on one developmental dimension at the expense of the other. These deviations can be relatively mild in normal personality or character variations, as discussed above, but these deviations can also be quite extreme. The more extensive the deviation, the greater the exaggerated emphasis on one developmental line at the expense of the other, the greater the possibility of psychopathology. Severe disruptions of the synergistic dialectic developmental process at different points in development can lead to various forms of psychopathology described in Axis I and Axis II of the DSM, from schizophrenia and depression to the personality disorders. The nature of this distorted one-sided emphasis identifies two primary configurations of psychopathology. *Anaclitic* forms of psychopathology (e.g., undifferentiated schizophrenia, abandonment depression, and the borderline, dependent and histrionic personality disorders) all involve, at different developmental levels, a distorted one-sided emphasis on interpersonal relatedness. *Introjective* forms of psychopathology (e.g., paranoid schizophrenia and the paranoid, obsessive-compulsive, self-critical depressive, and narcissistic personality disorders), in contrast, are characterized, at different developmental levels, by a distorted and one-sided emphasis on self-definition (Blatt 2006, 2008; Blatt and Shichman 1983).[5]

Again, considerable research evidence (e.g., Blatt 2004, 2006, 2008; Blatt and Zuroff 1992) supports the validity of this distinction of two primary configurations of psychopathology. Anaclitic and introjective patients have very different early and later life experiences and different concerns and preoccupations (e.g., Blatt and Homann 1992; Blatt and Zuroff 1992) and respond differentially to different types

---

[5] Although psychopathology in most patients is organized primarily around one configuration or the other, some patients may have predominant features from both the anaclitic and introjective dimensions and their psychopathology could derive from both configurations (see Blatt et al. (1982) and Shahar, Blatt and Ford (2003) for investigations of patients with mixed anaclitic and introjective characteristics, and Blatt (2008), for a corresponding clinical example).

of therapeutic interventions (e.g., Blatt 1992; Blatt et al. 2008; Blatt and Ford 1994; Blatt and Shahar 2004; Blatt and Zuroff 1992; Fertuck et al. 2004). Clinical investigators from different theoretical orientations (e.g., Arieti and Bemporad 1978; 1980; Beck 1983; Blatt 1974, 1998, 2004; Bowlby 1988a, b), for example, have identified two fundamental dimensions in depression (Blatt and Maroudas 1992) – an anaclitic dimension centered on feelings of loneliness, abandonment, and neglect and an introjective dimension focused on issues of self-worth and feelings of failure and guilt. Extensive empirical investigations (see summaries in Blatt 2004; Blatt and Zuroff 1992; Luyten et al. 2005) have consistently indicated differences in the current and early life experiences of these two types of depressed individuals (Blatt and Homann 1992) as well as major differences in basic character style, relational and attachment style (Luyten et al. 2005b), and clinical expression of depression (Blatt 1974, 1998, 2004; Blatt and Zuroff 2005) as well as therapeutic response (Blatt 2004, 2008; Blatt and Zuroff 2005). These differences are also found in postpartum depression (Besser et al. 2008), suggesting that it is more productive to focus on underlying personality dynamics as the basis for the classification of depression than on manifest symptoms.

The differentiation between individuals preoccupied with issues of relatedness and with issues of self-definition has also enabled investigators to identify an empirically derived, theoretically coherent, replicated taxonomy for the diversity of personality disorders described in Axis II of the DSM. Systematic empirical investigation with both inpatients and outpatients found that various Axis II personality disorders are meaningfully and in theoretically expected ways, organized into two primary configurations – one organized around issues of relatedness and the other around issues of self-definition (for reviews, see Blatt 2004, 2008). Congruent with theoretical assumptions (e.g., Blatt and Shichman 1983), these studies have generally found that individuals with a dependent, histrionic or borderline personality disorder have significantly greater concern with issues of interpersonal relatedness than with issues of self-definition, while individuals with a paranoid, schizoid, schizotypic, antisocial, narcissistic, avoidant, obsessive-compulsive or self-defeating personality disorder usually have significantly greater preoccupation with issues of self-definition than with issues of interpersonal relatedness. These findings are supported further by attachment research showing that personality disorders can be similarly organized in two-dimensional space defined by attachment anxiety reflecting anaclitic concerns, and by attachment avoidance reflecting introjective issues (Blatt and Luyten 2010b; Meyer and Pilkonis 2005). As noted earlier (footnote # 1), several studies have provided evidence for a distinction between an anaclitic versus an introjective type of borderline personality disorder (Blatt and Auerbach 1988; Levy et al. 2007; Morse et al. 2002; Ouimette et al. 1994;Westen et al. 1992; Wixom et al. 1993).

Thus, the two configurations model establishes conceptual continuity between processes in normal psychological development, variations in normal personality or character organization and concepts of psychopathology. In this view, psychological development is a life-long personal negotiation between two fundament dimensions in human affairs, interpersonal relatedness and self-definition.

Psychological development, from infancy to old age, occurs as a synergistic inter-action between these two fundamental polarities, with most individuals favoring to varying degrees either the relatedness (anaclitic) or the self-definition (introjective) dimension, and with the two polarities existing in dynamic tension in normal func-tioning (Blatt and Blass 1990, 1996; Blatt and Shichman 1983). Extensive empiri-cal research (see summaries in Blatt and Zuroff 1992; Blatt 2004) supports the validity of two broad types of personality organization and documents how these two types of individuals engage and experience life in very different ways.

These same two dimensions, anaclitic concerns about interpersonal relations and introjective concerns about self-definition and self-worth, are central in psychopa-thology. Exaggerated emphasis on one of the two developmental dimensions at the expense of the other is expressed at different developmental levels in a wide variety of psychological disorders. A broad array of empirical research supports this view of psychopathology, not as clusters of present or absent symptoms, but rather as compensatory exaggerations of the normal polarities of relatedness and self-defini-tion. This conceptualization not only establishes conceptual continuity between personality development and psychopathology but it also has important therapeutic implications. Anaclitic and introjective persons respond differently to specific dimensions of the therapeutic process and express therapeutic progress in different ways in a wide variety of therapeutic approaches.

The Therapeutic Process

Research evidence with both inpatients and outpatients in both long-term intensive and brief treatment (Blatt 1992; Blatt et al. 2007; Blatt and Ford 1994; Blatt and Shahar 2004; Blatt and Zuroff 2005; Fertuck et al. 2004; Vermote 2005) indicates that anaclitic and introjective patients are differentially responsive to different aspects of the treatment process and express therapeutic progress in different, but equally constructive ways – they express therapeutic progress along dimensions most relevant to their personality organization. Therapeutic change in the long-term intensive inpatient treatment of seriously disturbed treatment resistant anaclitic patients occurred primarily in the quality of their interpersonal relations with other patients and staff and in the quality of their representation of the human form in responses to the Rorschach. Therapeutic change in introjective patients occurred primarily in the frequency and intensity of their manifest symptoms and in the level of their cognitive functioning on psychological tests – a significant increase in IQ (Blatt and Ford 1994). Both anaclitic and introjective patients had substantial reduction in thought disorder on the Rorschach, but on different types of thought disorder. Significant reduction in thought disorder in anaclitic patients occurred mainly in thought disorder indicating disturbances in establishing and maintaining boundaries between independent objects or thoughts (Contamination responses) and between realistic experiences and intense personal reactions to these experi-ences (Confabulation responses), responses that indicate difficulty maintaining the boundary between inside and outside the self. Significant reduction in thought disorder in introjective patients, in contrast, occurred primarily on responses that expressed referential thinking in the attribution of an arbitrary and inappropriate relationship between separate and independent objects because of their spatial or temporal contiguity (Fabulized Combination responses). It seemed consistent that therapeutic progress in seriously disturbed anaclitic patients who have intense and sometimes primitive longings for merger and interpersonal closeness, would be expressed primarily in a reduction of thought disorder expressing disturbances in establishing and maintaining boundaries. It also seemed consistent that therapeutic progress in seriously disturbed over-ideational introjective patients would be expressed primarily in a reduction of the attribution of arbitrary and illogical relationships between independent percepts (Blatt et al. 2007).

Anaclitic patients appear to have a more constructive therapeutic response to the supportive dimensions of the treatment process that inhibit associational and referential activity, whereas introjective patients have a better therapeutic response to the more interpretative dimensions of the treatment process (Blatt and Shahar 2004; Fertuck et al. 2004) that encourage associational activity. Anaclitic patients appear to do better in a supportive therapeutic context that contains these affective labile, emotionally overwhelmed and vulnerable patients whereas a more intensive, exploratory and interpretative therapeutic context appears to facilitate the therapeutic response of the more distant, interpersonally isolated introjective patients (Blatt 1992; Blatt and Shahar 2004). These differences in therapeutic response suggest fundamental differences in the dynamic organization of these two groups of patients.

The formulations of the two configuration model of personality development and psychopathology suggests that the fundamental synergistic developmental interaction of processes of interpersonal relatedness and self-definition in normal psychological development, as discussed earlier, also appears to occur in processes of therapeutic change (Blatt 2002) indicating a common developmental pathway in effective treatments. Effective interventions act through experiences of engagement and disengagement, of attachment and separation, of gratifying involvement with others and experiences of incompatibility with aspects of that involvement in the treatment process, as it does throughout life (Behrends and Blatt 1985; Blatt and Behrends 1987). Sustained and consolidated progress in psychotherapy seems to involve the reactivation of the normal synergistic developmental process in which interpersonal experiences in the therapeutic relationship contribute to revisions in the sense of self that lead to more mature expressions of interpersonal relatedness that in turn contribute to further refinements in the sense of self (Blatt 2002). Findings by Safran and Muran (2000) in the study of the repair of ruptures in the therapeutic alliance provide empirical support for this view of the reactivation of the normal synergistic developmental process in the later phases of the treatment process (Blatt et al. in press).

Safran and Muran (2000), discussing the resolution or repair of ruptures in the therapeutic alliance, distinguish two types of ruptures: withdrawal and confrontation (or complaints). Withdrawal ruptures include denial, minimal response, shifting the topic, intellectualization, storytelling, and extensive talking about others. Confrontation ruptures include attacks on the therapist as a person or on his or her competence, irritation about the activities or parameters of the therapy, the lack of therapeutic progress or dissatisfaction about being in therapy. Withdrawal from involvement with the therapist would be more typical for interpersonally oriented anaclitic patients while confrontation would be more characteristic of self-oriented introjective patients.

Safran and Muran (2000) found that empathic statements by the therapist to withdrawal ruptures evoke experiences of disavowed unmet needs for nurturance that underlie the extensive interpersonal demands of the patient. The direct expression of these intense needs for nurturance is, according to Safran and Muran, "an important act of self-assertion" because it enables the patient "to begin to take responsibility for ... (these) demands, rather than expressing them indirectly" (p. 154). Thus, the resolution of withdrawal ruptures, typical of the more passive dependent anaclitic patients, involves an assertive, agentic expression of disavowed needs for nurturance. The resolution of confrontational ruptures in the more interpersonally isolated introjective patients, in contrast, involve the exploration of the "construal of the futility of the situation... and the underlying feelings of desperation." Safran and Muran (2000) noted how these explorations lead to the emergence of underlying "fears of abandonment... and access to feelings of vulnerability and the need for nurturance" (p. 174). Thus, the resolution of confrontational ruptures, typical of self-oriented introjective patients, leads to the emergence of underlying interests in interpersonal relatedness (anaclitic issues), feelings that are defended against in introjective individuals. In contrast, the resolution of withdrawal ruptures, typical of interpersonally oriented anaclitic patients, lead to the emergence of self-assertive (introjective) activity. Thus, therapeutic progress appears to involve the emergence of the other voice.

The reactivation of the normal synergistic developmental process in treatment results in modifications and revisions in the representation of self and significant others (Blatt and Behrends 1987; Blatt et al. 1996; Harpaz-Rotem and Blatt 2005, 2009). Sequential experiences of engagement and disengagement in the treatment process result in the reduction and revision of distorted, impaired, possibly pathological, representations of self and significant others and to the development of new, revised, more articulated, differentiated, and integrated representations of self, of others, and of their actual and potential relationships (e.g., Blatt et al. 1996, 2008; Diamond et al. 1990; Gruen and Blatt 1990; Harpaz-Rotem and Blatt 2005, 2009). Activation of distorted representations of self and of significant others in the treatment process provides the patient and the therapist the opportunity to observe, understand and revise distorted interpersonal representations and to establish more adaptive schemas. These revised internalizations are expressed behaviorally and psychologically in more mature levels of self-definition and of interpersonal relatedness and in symptom reduction and the development of enhanced adaptive capacities (Blatt et al. 2010).

From this perspective, change in representational structures in the therapeutic process is similar in fundamental ways to the processes of normal psychological development. These changes include differentiated and integrated representations of self and others that are necessary for understanding interpersonal relationships and to effectively navigate the social world. The systematic study of these revisions in representations or cognitive-affective schemas of self and of others provides a method for assessing the extent and nature of therapeutic change – the reparative interpersonal therapeutic process in which individuals are able to move toward more mature levels of self-definition and more mature levels of interpersonal relatedness with a capacity to find personal satisfaction in mutually enhancing and facilitating interpersonal relationships (e.g., Blatt et al. 1998, 1996; Calabrese et al. 2005; Eklund and Nilsson 1999; Phillips et al. 2006; Piper et al. 2002). Thus, the aim of treatment is not just to reduce symptoms or improve interpersonal functioning, but to enable individuals to resume normal psychological development.

Summary

Research findings support the anaclitic-introjective diagnostic differentiation in both non-clinical and clinical samples as well as assumptions about the developmental antecedents and some of the dynamic issues inherent in these two personality styles and two configurations of psychopathology. Focus on etiology and dynamics facilitated the identification of continuities between personality development, personality organization, and psychopathology because they are all organized around the fundamental issues of interpersonal relatedness and self-definition. This focus also provides an alternative to the DSM model of psychopathology – an alternative comprehensive theoretical model that stresses that psychopathology results primarily from disruptions of normal developmental processes and are not separate diseases that have presumed, but as yet frequently undocumented, biological antecedents. So, while Shapiro and I agree about two fundamental categories of psychopathology, we differ about the etiologic and dynamic implications of our observations of two modes of character (passive-reactive and rigid) or the two primary configurations of personality development, personality organization and psychopathology (anaclitic and introjective). While research findings support the differentiation of the two character modes and the two configurations of personality organization and psychopathology, research findings also provide support for the formulation of a dynamic structural developmental model of personality development and psychopathology – a model that identifies conceptual continuities between personality development, personality organization, and different types of psychopathology, which has etiological as well as therapeutic implications.

References

Arieti, S., & Bemporad, J. R. (1978). *Severe and mild depression: The therapeutic approach*. New York: Basic Books.

Arieti, S., & Bemporad, J. R. (1980). The psychological organization of depression. *American Journal of Psychiatry, 137*, 1360–1365.

Bakan, D. (1966). *The duality of human existence: An essay on psychology and religion*. Chicago: Rand McNally.

Beck, A. T. (1983). Cognitive therapy of depression: New perspectives. In P. J. Clayton & J. E. Barrett (Eds.), *Treatment of depression: Old controversies and new approaches* (pp. 265–290). New York: Raven.

Beebe, B., Jaffe, J., Buck, K., Chen, H., Cohen, P., Blatt, S. J., Kaminer, T., Feldstein, S., & Andrews, H. (2007). Six-week postpartum maternal self-criticism and dependency predict 4-month mother-infant self- and interactive regulation. *Developmental Psychology, 43*, 1360–1376.

Beebe, B., & Lachman, F. M. (1988). The contribution of the mother-infant mutual influence to the origins of self- and object representations. *Psychoanalytic Psychology, 5*, 305–338.

Behrends, R. S., & Blatt, S. J. (1985). Internalization and psychological development throughout the life cycle. *Psychoanalytic Study of the Child, 40*, 11–39.

Besser, A., Vliegen, N., Luyten, P., & Blatt, S. J. (2008). Systematic empirical investigation of vulnerability to postpartum depression from a psychodynamic perspective: Commentary on issues raised by Blum (2007). *Psychoanalytic Psychology, 25*, 392–410.

Blatt, S. J. (1974). Levels of object representation in anaclitic and introjective depression. *Psychoanalytic Study of the Child, 29*, 107–157.

Blatt, S. J. (1990). Interpersonal relatedness and self-definition: Two personality configurations and their implications for psychopathology and psychotherapy. In J. L. Singer (Ed.), *Repression and dissociation: Implications for personality theory, psychopathology & health* (pp. 299–335). Chicago: University of Chicago Press.

Blatt, S. J. (1991). A cognitive morphology of psychopathology. *Journal of Nervous and Mental Disease, 179*, 449–458.

Blatt, S. J. (1992). The differential effect of psychotherapy and psychoanalysis on anaclitic and introjective patients: The Menninger Psychotherapy Research Project revisited. *Journal of the American Psychoanalytic Association, 40*, 691–724.

Blatt, S. J. (1998). Contributions of psychoanalysis to the understanding and treatment of depression. *Journal of the American Psychoanalytic Association, 46*, 723–752.

Blatt, S. J. (2002). Patient variables: Anaclitic and introjective dimensions. In W. Sledge & M. Hershen (Eds.), *Encyclopedia of psychotherapy* (pp. 349–357). New York: Academic Press.

Blatt, S. J. (2004). *Experiences of depression: Theoretical, clinical and research perspectives*. Washington, DC: American Psychological Association.

Blatt, S. J. (2006). A fundamental polarity in psychoanalysis: Implications for personality development, psychopathology, and the therapeutic process. *Psychoanalytic Inquiry, 26*, 492–518.

Blatt, S. J. (2008). *Polarities of experience: Relatedness and self-definition in personality development, psychopathology, and the therapeutic process*. Washington, DC: American Psychological Association Press.

Blatt, S. J., & Auerbach, J. S. (1987). Three types of "Borderline" patients and their differential responses to psychological tests. In L. Yazigi & I. Z. Succar (Eds.), *Rorschachina XVI* (pp. 199–205). Bern: Huber.

Blatt, S. J., & Auerbach, J. S. (1988). Differential cognitive disturbances in three types of borderline patients. *Journal of Personality Disorders, 2*, 198–211.

Blatt, S. J., Auerbach, J. S., & Aryan, M. (1998). Representational structures and the therapeutic process. In R. F. Bornstein & J. M Masling (Eds.), *Empirical studies of psychoanalytic theories: Vol. 8. Empirical investigations of the therapeutic hour* (pp. 63–107). Washington, DC: American Psychological Association.

Blatt, S. J., Auerbach, J. S., & Behrends, R. S. (2008). Changes in representation of self and significant others in the therapeutic process: Links among representation, internalization and mentalization. In A. Slade, E. Jurist, & S. Bergner (Eds.), *Mind to mind: Infant research, neuroscience and psychoanalysis* (pp. 225–253). New York: Other Press.

Blatt, S. J., & Behrends, R. S. (1987). Internalization, separation-individuation, and the nature of therapeutic action. *International Journal of Psychoanalysis, 68,* 279–297.

Blatt, S. J., Besser, A., & Ford, R. Q. (2007). Two primary configurations of psychopathology and change in thought disorder in long-term, intensive, inpatient treatment of seriously disturbed young adults. *American Journal of Psychiatry, 164,* 1561–1567.

Blatt, S. J., & Blass, R. B. (1990). Attachment and separateness: A dialectic model of the products and processes of psychological development. *Psychoanalytic Study of the Child, 45,* 107–127.

Blatt, S. J., & Blass, R. (1996). Relatedness and self definition: A dialectic model of personality development. In G. G. Noam & K. W. Fischer (Eds.), *Development and vulnerabilities in close relationships* (pp. 309–338). Hillsdale: Lawrence Erlbaum Associates.

Blatt, S. J., D'Afflitti, J. P., & Quinlan, D. M. (1976). Experiences of depression in normal young adults. *Journal of Abnormal Psychology, 85,* 383–389.

Blatt, S. J., & Ford, R. (1994). *Therapeutic change: An object relations perspective*. New York: Plenum.

Blatt, S. J., & Homann, E. (1992). Parent-child interaction in the etiology of dependent and self-critical depression. *Clinical Psychology Review, 12,* 47–91.

Blatt, S. J., & Luyten, P. (2009) A structural-developmental psychodynamic approach to psychopathology: Two polarities of experience across the life span. *Development and Psychopathology, 21,* 793–814.

Blatt, S. J., & Luyten, P. (2010a). Reactivating the psychodynamic approach to classify psychopathology. In T. Millon, R. Krueger, & E. Simonsen (Eds.), *Contemporary directions in psychopathology: Toward DSM-V, ICD-11, and beyond* (pp. 483–514). New York: Guilford.

Blatt, S. J., & Luyten, P. (2010b). Relatedness and self-definition in normal and disrupted personality development. In L. Horowitz & S. Strack (Eds.). *Handbook of interpersonal psychology* (pp. 37–56). New York: Wiley.

Blatt, S. J., & Maroudas, C. (1992). Convergence of psychoanalytic and cognitive behavioral theories of depression. *Psychoanalytic Psychology, 9,* 157–190.

Blatt, S. J., Quinlan, D. M., Chevron, E. S., McDonald, C., & Zuroff, D. (1982). Dependency and self-criticism: Psychological dimensions of depression. *Journal of Consulting and Clinical Psychology, 50,* 113–124.

Blatt, S. J., Sanislow, C. A., Zuroff, D. C., & Pilkonis, P. A. (1996). Characteristics of effective therapists: Further analyses of data from the NIMH TDCRP. *Journal of Consulting and Clinical Psychology, 64,* 1276–1284. (Published as a special feature.)

Blatt, S. J., & Shahar, G. (2004). Psychoanalysis: For what, with whom, and how: A comparison with psychotherapy. *Journal of the American Psychoanalytic Association, 52,* 393–447.

Blatt, S. J., & Shichman, S. (1983). Two primary configurations of psychopathology. *Psychoanalysis and Contemporary Thought, 6,* 187–254.

Blatt, S. J., Wein, S. J., Chevron, E. S., & Quinlan, D. M. (1979). Parental representations and depression in normal young adults. *Journal of Abnormal Psychology, 88,* 388–397.

Blatt, S. J., & Zuroff, D. C. (1992). Interpersonal relatedness and self-definition: Two prototypes for depression. *Clinical Psychology Review, 12,* 527–562.

Blatt, S. J., & Zuroff, D. C. (2005). Empirical evaluation of the assumptions in identifying evidence based treatments in mental health. *Clinical Psychology Review, 25,* 459–486.

Blatt, S. J., Zuroff, D. C., Hawley, L., & Auerbach, J. S. (in press). Processes that contribute to sustained therapeutic change. *Psychotherapy Research, 20,* 37–54.

Bowlby, J. (1988a). Developmental psychology comes of age. *American Journal of Psychiatry, 145,* 1–10.

Bowlby, J. (1988b). *A secure base: Clinical applications of attachment theory*. London: Routledge & Kegan Paul.

Brewin, C. R., Andrews, B., & Gotlib, I. H. (1993). Psychopathology and early experience: A reappraisal of retrospective reports. *Psychological Bulletin, 113*, 82–98.

Brewin, C. R., Firth-Cozens, J., Furnham, A., & Andrews, B. (1990). Self-criticism in adulthood and perceived childhood experience. *Journal of Abnormal Psychology, 101*, 561–562.

Calabrese, M. L., Farber, B. A., & Westen, D. (2005). The relationship of adult attachment constructs to object relational patterns of representing self and others. *Journal of the American Academy of Psychoanalysis and Dynamic Psychiatry, 33*, 513–530.

Cicchetti, D., & Gunnar, M. R. (2008). Integrating biological measures into the design and evaluation of preventive interventions. *Development and Psychopathology, 20*, 737–743.

Diamond, D., Kaslow, N., Coonerty, S., & Blatt, S. J. (1990). Change in separation-individuation and intersubjectivity in long-term treatment. *Psychoanalytic Psychology, 7*, 363–397.

Eklund, M., & Nilsson, A. (1999). Changes in object relations in long-term mentally ill patients treated in a psychiatric day-care unit. *Psychotherapy Bulletin, 9*, 167–183.

Erikson, E. H. (1950). *Childhood and society* (2nd ed.). New York: Norton.

Fertuck, E., Bucci, W., Blatt, S. J., & Ford, R. Q. (2004). Verbal representation and therapeutic change in anaclitic and introjective patients. *Psychotherapy: Theory, Research, Practice Training, 41*, 13–25.

Fischer, K. W., Ayoub, C., Singh, I., Noam, G., Maraganore, A., & Raya, P. (1997). Psychopathology as adaptive development along distinctive pathways. *Development and Psychopathology, 9*, 749–779.

Freud, S. (1963). Three essays on sexuality. In J. Strachey (Ed. & Trans.), *Standard edition of the complete works of Sigmund Freud*, (Vol. 7, pp. 135–243). London: Hogarth Press (Original work published in 1905.).

Freud, S. (1957). Mourning and melancholia. In J. Strachey (Ed. & Trans.), *The standard edition of the complete psychological works of Sigmund Freud* (Vol. 14, pp. 243–258). London: Hogarth Press. (Original work published 1917.)

Freud, S. (1961). Civilization and its discontents. In J. Strachey (Ed. & Trans.), *The standard edition of the complete psychological works of Sigmund Freud*, (Vol. 21, pp. 64–145). London: Hogarth Press. (Original work published in 1930.)

Gjerde, P. F., Block, J., & Block, J. H. (1991). The preschool family context of 18 year olds with depressive symptoms: A prospective study. *Journal of Research on Adolescence, 1*, 63–91.

Gruen, R. J., & Blatt, S. J. (1990). Change in self- and object representation during long-term dynamically oriented treatment. *Psychoanalytic Psychology, 7*, 399–422.

Harpaz-Rotem, I., & Blatt, S. J.(2005). Changes in representations of a self-designated significant other in long-term, intensive, inpatient treatment of seriously disturbed adolescents and young adults. *Psychiatry Interpersonal and Biological Processes, 68*, 266–282.

Harpaz-Rotem, I., & Blatt, S. J. (2009). A pathway to therapeutic change: Changes in self-representation in the treatment of adolescent and young adults. *Psychiatry Interpersonal and Biological Processes, 72*, 32–49.

Koestner, R., Zuroff, D. C., & Powers, T. A. (1991). The family origins of adolescent self-criticism and its continuity into adulthood. *Journal of Abnormal Psychology, 100*, 191–197.

Laplanche, J., & Pontalis, J. B. (1974). *The language of psycho-analysis* (trans: Micholson-Smith, D.). New York: Norton.

Lekowitz, M. M., & Tesiny, E. P. (1984). Rejection and depression: Prospective and contemporaneous analyses. *Developmental Psychology, 20*, 776–785.

Levy, K. N., Edell, W. S., & McGlashan, T. H. (2007). Depressive experiences in inpatients with borderline personality disorder. *Psychiatric Quarterly, 78*, 129–143.

Lewinsohn, P. M., & Rosenbaum, M. (1987). Recall of parental behavior by acute depressives, remitted depressives and non-depressives. *Journal of Personality and Social Psychology, 52*, 611–619.

Luyten, P., Blatt, S. J., & Corveleyn, J. (2005a) Introduction. In J. Corveleyn, P. Luyten, & S. J. Blatt (Eds.), *The theory and treatment of depression: Towards a dynamic interactionism model* (pp. 5–15). Leuven, Belgium: University of Leuven Press.

Luyten, P., Blatt, S. J., & Corveleyn, J. (2005b). Towards integration in the theory and treatment of depression. In J. Corveleyn, P. Luyten, & S. J. Blatt (Eds.), *The theory and treatment of depression: Towards a dynamic interactionism model* (pp. 253–284). Leuven, Belgium: Leuven University Press.

Meyer, B., & Pilkonis, P. A. (2005). An attachment model of personality disorders. In M. F. Lenzenweger & J. F. Clarkin (Eds.), *Major theories of personality disorder* (2nd ed., pp. 231–281). New York: Guilford Press.

Morse, J. Q., Robins, C. J., & Gittes-Fox, M. (2002). Sociotropy, autonomy, and personality disorder criteria in psychiatric patients. *Journal of Personality Disorders, 16*, 549–560.

Ouimette, P. C., Klein, D. N., Anderson, R., Riso, L. P., & Lizardi, H. (1994). Relationship of sociotropy/autonomy and dependency/self-criticism to DSM-III-R personality disorders. *Journal of Abnormal Psychology, 103*, 743–749.

Philips, B., Wennberg, P., Werbert, A., & Schubert, J. (2006). Young adults in psychoanalytic psychotherapy: Patient characteristics and therapy outcome. *Psychology and Psychotherapy: Theory, Research and Practice, 79*, 89–106.

Piaget, J. (1954). *The construction of reality in the child* (trans: Cook, M.). New York: Basic Books. (Original work published 1937.)

Piper, W. E., Joyce, A. S., McCullum, M., Azim, H. F., & Ogrodniczuk, J. S. (2002). *Interpretive and supportive psychotherapies: Matching therapy and patient personality*. Washington, DC: American Psychological Association.

Safran, J. D., & Muran, J. C. (2000). *Negotiating the therapeutic alliance: A relational treatment guide*. New York: Guilford Press.

Shahar, G., Blatt, S. J., & Ford, R. Q. (2003). The identification of mixed anaclitic-introjective psychopathology in young adult inpatients. *Psychoanalytic Psychology, 20*, 84–102.

Shapiro, D. (1981). *Autonomy and rigid character*. New York: Basic Books.

Shapiro, D. (2000). *Dynamics of character*. New York: Basic Books

Sroufe, L. A. (1997). Psychopathology as an outcome of development. *Development and Psychopathology, 9*, 251–268.

Stern, D. N. (1985). *The interpersonal world of the infant: A view from psychoanalysis and developmental psychology*. New York: Basic Books.

Sullivan, H. S. (1953). *The interpersonal theory of psychiatry*. New York: Norton.

Szumotalska, E. (1992). *Severity and type of depressive affect as related to perceptual styles: Relationship of anaclitic versus introjective depressive configuration to holistic versus analytic similarity judgment*. Unpublished doctoral dissertation, New School for Social Research, New York.

Vermote, R. (2005). *Touching inner change: Psychoanalytically informed hospitalization*. Doctoral dissertation. University of Leuven.

Webster, N. (1966). *Third new international dictionary*. Springfield: G. & C. Merriam.

Webster, N., Gore, P. B. et al. (Eds.) (1960). *The third new international dictionary*. Springfield: Merriam.

Westen, D., Moses, M. J., Silk, K. R., Lohr, N. E. et al. (1992). Quality of depressive experience in borderline personality disorder and major depression: When depression is not just depression. *Journal of Personality Disorders, 6*, 382–393.

Whiteside, M. F., Busch, F., & Horner, T. (1976). From egocentric to cooperative play in young children: A normative job study. *Journal of the American Academy of Child Psychiatry, 15*, 294–313.

Wiggins, J. S. (1991). Agency and communion as conceptual coordinates for the understanding and measurement of interpersonal behavior. In W. W. Grove & D. Cicchetti (Eds.), *Thinking clearly about psychology*, Vol. 2: *Personality and psychotherapy* (pp. 89–113). Minneapolis: University of Minnesota Press.

Witkin, H. A. (1965). Psychological differentiation and forms of pathology. *Journal of Abnormal Psychology, 70*, 317–336.

Wixom, J., Ludolph, P., & Westen, D. (1993). The quality of depression in adolescents with borderline personality disorder. *Journal of the American Academy of Child & Adolescent Psychiatry, 32*, 1172–1177.

Zuroff, D. C., Mongrain, M., & Santor, D. A. (2004). Conceptualizing and measuring personality vulnerability to depression: Commentary on Coyne and Whiffen (1995). *Psychological Bulletin, 130*, 489–511.

Reply to Sidney Blatt

David Shapiro

Since Dr. Blatt refers in some detail to an earlier, unpublished, paper of mine in which I discussed his work, I shall limit myself here to a further clarification of those issues which separate us, and also some corrections of his characterization of my views and interests. The issues, as Blatt indicates, have to do with his understanding and mine of what seem to both of us to be two general categories of psychopathology, which he describes as anaclitic and introjective configurations and I understand as passively reactive and rigid styles. More is involved here than choice of words.

First, the corrections. Blatt attributes to me an indifference to matters of etiology and dynamics. As far as etiology is concerned, perhaps he had in mind that I have in the past, perhaps too modestly, but also for a specific reason, disclaimed any extensive proposals regarding the causes of psychopathology. However, I have offered, in my book *Autonomy and Rigid Character*, a view of the development of personal autonomy, to which cognitive development as well as personal relationships was central. In my last book, *Dynamics of Character*, I returned to that subject and proposed a general conception of the defensive reliance on early modes in psychopathology as an alternative to the psychoanalytic idea of regression; the regression concept has always seemed too vague psychologically to me. But I have never proposed a theory of first causes and, in fact, have none to speak of. Many years of clinical work have left me far less confident of such theories than I was at the beginning of my career. It has also left me with the conviction that a deep and reliable understanding of the causes of psychopathology can be achieved only *after a clear and specific* understanding of its nature. To attempt otherwise – and there has been no scarcity of such attempts – with plausible surmises about causes made on the basis of insufficiently specific understanding of the object of explanation leads, with enough simplification of complicated phenomena, to the inevitable, but illusory confirmation of those surmises.

As to Blatt's notion that I "repudiate" interest in the subject of the dynamics of psychopathology; I am puzzled. I have discussed that subject in each of my books, and it is the title and main subject of my last book *Dynamics of Character: Self-regulation in Psychopathology*. I can think of two reasons for Blatt's mischaracterization. As I have said in my Introduction to a recent edition of *Neurotic Styles*, I originally did not make the defensive function of those styles sufficiently emphatic, although it is the explicit subject of the last two sections of the book. At any rate, my analysis of those defensive styles has been taken as merely descriptive by some readers. The reason for that failing of mine, if it was that, is that what clinicians actually see of neurotic conditions is not so much anxiety, but the means by which anxiety is avoided, and these are what I described and analyzed in *Neurotic Styles*.

However, there may be another, more interesting, reason for Blatt's impression, namely that my conception of the dynamics of psychopathology is different from his. Blatt's is a dynamics of particular early needs and their developmental derivatives, and defensive compensations for them. Mine is a conception of an agency-restricting, therefore anxiety-forestalling, character structure, under strain on account of its defensively restrictive nature, though generally elastic enough to be stable. I will return to this subject later.

Blatt's assertion of two general categories of psychopathology, his general description of those two categories, his rejection of the psychiatric picture of symptomatically diverse conditions in favor of an understanding of psychopathology emerging from personality – all this, supported by extensive research, is valuable and persuasive. Certainly it is consistent with my own conclusions. It is the claim of a universal dynamic significance of two fundamental needs, the need for interpersonal relatedness and the need for self-definition, underlying the two categories that I question. Interpersonal relatedness and self-definition are broad concepts and a lot can be squeezed into them and their sometimes remote derivatives. But they cannot include everything, at least not without vagueness, a blurring of distinctions and a loss of understanding of the specific processes involved. Maybe one can find the need for self-definition within obsessive regret or paranoid projection, but it is hard to see how it can characterize those processes. Maybe one can see the hysteric's faintness of personal authority and responsibility as caused by problems of interpersonal relatedness, but it is much easier to see it the other way round: the exaggerated perception of the authority of the other, and dependence, as the consequences of that faintness of personal authority.

But there is another, perhaps more important, issue here to which I have already alluded: the issue of character structure and its relation to dynamics. By psychological structure I mean something analogous to its architectural meaning: the structure is what holds the building up and gives it its essential form. Blatt says his conception is structural as well as a dynamic, but it is not. It has structural elements – he refers, for instance, to cognitive styles – but it presents no picture of a relatively stable, self-regulated personality. In adult neurotic conditions such a personality, or character, has been formed and gives symptoms their shape. This character, its organization of attitudes or ways of thinking, serves defensive aims; that is, it serves to forestall or dispel anxiety by restricting self-awareness, particularly the experience of personal agency. Insofar as it is restrictive of the experience of personal agency – the experience of oneself wanting and choosing to do something and doing it – it curtails spontaneity in one person, deliberateness in another. Neurotic character, because it is restrictive of subjective life, is never altogether free of tension, and neurotic people are never altogether free of some incongruence between what they think or feel and what they believe they think or feel; that is, never free of some self-deception. Under special circumstances this defensive self-deception is strained, and an experience of anxiety or discomfort will impel some self-protective reinforcement of the restrictive character style; in other words, the rigid person will become more rigid. Neurotic character, therefore, is self-regulating, even if not comfortable. It is this total process that may be described as its dynamics.

At the same time, this character, its attitudes and its "ways of being," even in their exaggerated forms, can also serve adaptive aims: the industriousness of the obsessive, the charm of the hysteric, even the psychopath's decisiveness. Altogether, neurotic character is, despite its tension and self-deception, still in ordinary circumstances a working and relatively stable, to some degree elastic, organization of attitudes and ways of being. Its stability can in fact be measured by its considerable resistance even to therapeutic change. It is an autonomous, self-regulating organization, an emergent phenomenon, in the sense that Craig Piers describes. That is why it is easy to detect childhood antecedents of adult personality or psychopathology, but impossible, so far, to predict them. Its dynamics are no longer energized by or dependent upon those sources originally responsible for its existence, or their derivatives, no longer limited to its original defensive functions and no longer threatened only by its original anxieties. What excites anxiety and impels defensive or self-protective measures in the neurotic character is what threatens its present stability, what is incompatible with its present attitudes: thus, spontaneity in the rigid character, assertiveness in the timid ("Gee, I hope I'm not becoming a tough New Yorker!"). What is threatening therefore will include whole classes of circumstances, actions, aims; perhaps above all, attitudes contained in aims or actions that enlarge the experience of personal agency. Particular, historically important anxieties may still be active, but they will be to the extent that the perspective of the present character has revived them and given them their significance.

Blatt describes the introjective conditions as ones in which the person is defensively engaged with himself, whereas the anaclitic individual's neurotic preoccupation is with interpersonal relations. But in fact the individual is engaged in conflict with the self in all neurotic conditions, in hysterical character no less than in obsessive-compulsive character. Self-consciousness, which is the signature of obsessive conditions, should not be confused with the existence of internal conflict. It is only that such conflict is less conspicuous, less consciously in evidence, in the hysterical case, as in passively reactive conditions in general, precisely because the defensive inhibition or avoidance of reflectiveness makes it so. Blatt sees the focus on interpersonal relations in hysterical character as the central one from which all other traits and symptoms flow. But how, for example, does the ephemeral quality of these individuals' emotionality, their impetuousness and, for that matter, the inconstancy of their attachments follow from an exaggerated dependence on others?

There are also problems with Blatt's second, "introjective," category, comprising mainly obsessive compulsive and paranoid conditions. We know these conditions – speaking for the moment mainly of obsessive and compulsive conditions – to be characterized by a special, rigid form of conscientiousness. However, the supposition that this kind of conscientiousness is the result of early internalization, or introjection, of, presumably severe, authority has little or no justification. In some cases that supposition does seem justified, as I myself have said elsewhere, but by no means all. It is not unusual – judging from my own practice it is more the rule than the exception – that even severely obsessive or compulsive, even paranoid individuals have in fact not been subject to such parental authority. One can only conclude from this that other etiological factors are, not only involved, but may be decisive.

I have pointed out one such likely factor, in cognitive development. It has to do with the fact that the strict conscientiousness of rigid characters is of a special kind, as Blatt notes. It is a conscientiousness of rules, that is, a continual awareness of obligatory rules, experienced usually as a subjective experience of "I should…." A normal conscientiousness, on the other hand, is a conscientiousness of personal conviction; it is largely unselfconscious and consists, one might say, of educated values. All young children are full of rules and are often quite rigid in following their requirements. These are certainly in large part adopted on the strength of parental authority. However, they are not infrequently rules of their own making, based only on precedent – it has been that way, therefore it must be that way again – and often exasperating to the adults around them. Some years ago the famous psychologist Kurt Lewin noted that this phenomenon was particularly exaggerated in intellectually retarded children (called "feebleminded" at the time). In fact, he noted that this "strict adherence to the rules" had "an appealing appearance of moral rectilinearity (sic)." In other words, it strongly resembled the moralizing rigidity of obsessive compulsives. However, this "moral rectilinearity" was not based on internalized authority, or introjection, but on cognitive limitations. I am not suggesting, of course, that the rigidity of the neurotic adult is a matter of cognitive limitations. But it may be that the source of the particular kind of rule based conscientiousness characteristic of individuals within Blatt's introjective category is not entirely introjective at all. It may, in fact, be an attitude common to the early cognitive development of all of us, only employed, with both historical and contemporary materials, and exaggerated to satisfy defensive requirements, in some of us.

There is one other matter I would like to discuss further with Dr. Blatt. As he mentions, in my view, that is, from a formal standpoint, the two categories of psychopathology, rigid and passively reactive, are not actually polar opposites, though they may seem to be. They are in fact very closely related, each being an anxiety forestalling or defensive restriction of personal autonomy and experience of agency. Both draw on modes of activity and thought characteristic of early childhood and, though superseded by more mature modes, both continue to be available in normal adult life. In psychopathology they are, as I indicated, hypertrophied and defensively employed; in one case, agency is ceded to the authority of rules, in the other to immediate and unreflective reaction to external figures and circumstances. From this standpoint the distinction between the two modes is not as sharp as Blatt's, basically content-defined, categories implies. Blatt does agree that both modes are characterized by restrictions of personal autonomy, but he disagrees that symptomatic expressions of both are to be found in all psychopathology. But in fact a flighty, hysterical character is never altogether without "shoulds," and an obsessive person faced with a personal choice will, if he cannot find a decisive rule, make the choice with an impulsive leap. In other words, neither the rigid nor the passively reactive person is able to make a deliberate decision on the normal basis of what he or she wants. This shifting from one mode to another is especially clear in young children where one sees rigidity, of the established-precedent sort that I described, and an immediate reactiveness and distractibility side by side. I would be interested in Dr. Blatt's comments on that phenomenon and, also, any observations from his work with chronic schizophrenics he may have in respect to this matter.

Interpersonal Relatedness and Self-definition: Fundamental Developmental Psychological Dimensions

Sidney J. Blatt

I want to express my appreciation to Craig Piers for inviting me to engage in this dialogue with David Shapiro about our shared formulations of two primary configurations or modes of psychopathology and to David Shapiro for clarifying his position on matters of etiology and dynamics and for raising important questions that allow me to clarify further my formulations of two primary configurations of personality development, personality organization and psychopathology.

Shapiro and I not only concur that many forms of psychopathology are organized in two primary configurations, or two primary modes of adaptation in Shapiro's terms, but both of our efforts are based on the premise that understanding of the causes (as well as the treatment) of psychopathology can only be achieved with a full understanding of the nature of psychopathology. Understanding the nature of psychopathology is essential not only for investigating the etiology of psychological disturbances, but it is also essential for developing effective modes of intervention and prevention. Shapiro's articulation of two primary experiential modes – the rigid and the passive-reactive modes – and my formulations of the anaclitic and introjective configurations of personality development and psychopathology provide important clarification of the nature of psychopathology that have facilitated clinical practice and clinical research.

Shapiro's original comments on my formulations of two primary configurations of personality development and psychopathology, and his response to my reactions to his initial comments, makes it clear that despite the considerable congruence in our views about the nature of psychopathology, Shapiro has primary concerns about my assertion of the universal dynamic significance of two fundamental developmental processes of interpersonal relatedness and self-definition or identity in personality development, personality organization, psychopathology and in the therapeutic process. Shapiro seems concerned that I use these developmental constructs too broadly, in ways that are vague and lead to blurring of distinctions and a loss of understanding. Before responding to these concerns, let me note that I think of these two psychological dimensions of interpersonal relatedness and self-definition, not as" needs" as Shapiro seems to view my formulations, but as two fundamental developmental psychological processes that usually progress through life, from infancy to senescence, in a hierarchically organized, dialectic, synergistic transaction, such that progress in one developmental line reciprocally facilitates development in the alternate developmental line. And I view psychopathology as the consequence of severe disruptions, at various points in development, of this fundamental dialectic developmental process. These developmental disruptions not only contribute to individuals defensively developing exaggerated preoccupation with one of these developmental dimensions to the neglect of the other, but these exaggerated preoccupations are associated with particular modes of adaptation: (a) with particular types of defenses (counteractive or avoidant), (b) with particular types of cognitive functioning in which, in one mode of adaptation, differences are exaggerated to keep things separate and independent; or in the other mode of adaptation, differences are minimized in an effort to reduce conflict and contradiction in an effort to bring things together, and (c) with an emphasis on things and objects or on feelings and interpersonal relationships. These two modes of adaptation can range from relatively subtle and flexible modes of adaptation expressed in normal variations of personality or character organization or in relatively exaggerated, inflexible modes of (mal)adaptation in psychopathology. A grossly exaggerated imbalanced emphasis on one mode of adaptation, at various developmental levels, characterizes two primary configurations of psychopathology. Thus, while I agree with Shapiro that one should always be cautious about the elasticity of concepts and the tendency to use constructs too broadly, I think Shapiro seriously underestimates the power of these two developmental dimensions or processes that are fundamental in psychological development and in adaptive and maladaptive functioning including the rigid and passive-reactive modes of functioning that Shapiro has so meaningfully articulated.

I initially became aware of the importance of these two fundamental developmental dimensions early in psychoanalytic training in my analytic treatment of two depressed patients (e.g., Blatt 1974) when I noted major differences in preoccupations and modes of functioning between a patient whose depression focused on issues of loneliness and feelings of neglect and abandonment and a patient whose depression focused on issues of self-worth, responsibility and guilt. Subsequently, I realized that these two fundamental developmental processes of relatedness and self-definition were central in personality development (e.g., Blatt and Shichman 1983; Blatt and Blass 1990, 1996) and that these two developmental processes, at different developmental levels, are central in a wide range of psychopathology ranging from schizophrenia to the personality disorders and the neuroses (e.g., Blatt and Shichman 1983). And even later, I discovered that these two fundamental processes had been extensively considered in a wide range of theoretical formulations of personality development and personality organization – from classic psychoanalytic formulations (e.g., Freud 1930) to empirically based research investigations (e.g., Wiggins 1991).

The two dimensions of interpersonal relatedness and self-definition (or identity), have actually been viewed as fundamental in personality theory for many years. Angyal (1941, 1951) discussed surrender and autonomy and Bakan (1996) discussed communion and agency as two fundamental modalities of human experience. And much of Freud's theoretical model of personality development, from the beginning to the very end of his vast contribution, is constructed around this fundamental polarity of interpersonal relatedness and self-definition. Freud (1930, p. 142), for example, noted that "the development of the individual seems to be a product of the interaction between two urges: the urge toward happiness, which we call 'egotistic' and the urge toward union with others in the community, which we call 'altruistic'."

The fundamental polarity of relatedness and self-definition is expressed in Freud's oft-quoted statement that the two major tasks in life are "to love and to work" as well as his (Freud 1914, 1926) distinctions between object and ego (or narcissistic) libido (investment in others or in the self), as well as between libidinal instincts in the service of attachment and aggressive instincts necessary for autonomy, mastery, and self-definition. Freud (1914, 1926) also differentiated two types of object choice: an *anaclitic* choice based on the mother who feeds and/or the father who protects and a narcissistic choice based on what one is, was, or wants to be. An anaclitic choice involves developing affectionate, need-satisfying relationships, whereas a narcissistic choice involves the use of others to enhance the self.

Freud (1930) extended this polarity of relatedness and self-definition (attachment and individuation) to concepts of psychopathology by distinguishing between two fundamental forms of anxiety. One source of anxiety derives from the internalization of superego (moral) authority and involves feelings of guilt and fears of punishment that are related to ego instincts (issues of self-assertion and mastery) that Freud viewed as opposing the progress of civilization. The second source of anxiety, "social anxiety," involves the fear of loss of love and contact with others. Freud (1914, 1926) also linked these two primary dimensions of relatedness and self-definition (or attachment and individuation) to concepts of psychopathology in his differentiation of four primary dangers or traumas: (a) relational dangers involving feelings of helplessness associated with the loss of the mother or the loss of her love, and (b) self-definitional dangers involving a loss of superego approval and the fear of punishment because of assumed transgressions of omission or commission. Freud viewed the sense of helplessness that derives from separation from a loved object (Freud 1905, 1926) as particularly related to aspects of feminine development and he (Freud 1914, 1923, 1926) viewed the loss of superego approval and the threat of punishment, expressed in self-reproach and feelings of guilt, as more characteristic of masculine development. Hartmann et al. (1949) suggested that the fear of loss of the primary love object and her love (i.e., mother) is related to conflicts involving affectionate (libidinal) strivings; whereas the loss of superego approval and the threat of punishment (often from the father) are related to conflicts involving aggressive strivings and the struggle for individuation and identity. Impressed with the extent to which this fundamental polarity pervaded Freud's wide-ranging contributions, Loewald (1962, p. 490) commented that "these various modes of separation and union.... [identify a] polarity inherent in individual existence of individuation and primary narcissistic union – a polarity that Freud attempted to conceptualize by various approaches and that he recognized and insisted upon from beginning to end [in]... his dualistic conception of instincts, of human nature, and of life itself."

As reviewed in my recent (2008) book, *Polarities of Experience*, this fundamental duality or polarity was also central in a wide range of other psychoanalytic (e.g., Adler 1933; Rank 1929, 1945; Horney 1945, 1950; Sullivan 1953; Bowlby 1988a, b; Balint 1959; Shor and Sanville 1978; Kohut 1966) and non-psychoanalytic formulations (e.g., Angyal 1951; Bakan 1966; Benjamin 1974; Deci and Ryan 1985, 1991; Helgeson 1994; Helgeson and Fritz 1999; Markus and Oyserman 1989;

McAdams 1985; McClelland 1986; White 1959; Wiggins 1982, 1991, 1997) of personality development and organization.

These two fundamental personality developmental dimensions of interpersonal relatedness and self-definition are central in a number of contemporary personality theories including (a) *Beck's cognitive theory* (1983, 1999) in which Sociotropy (social relations) and Autonomy (individuality) are considered fundamental in depression and personality disorders, (b) *contemporary interpersonal theory* (e.g., Horowitz et al. 2006) which is organized around two primary orthogonal dimensions – communion (or nurturance and affiliation) and agency (or social dominance), (c) in *contemporary attachment theory and research* (e.g., Mikulincer and Shaver 2007; Meyer and Pilkonis 2005; Sibley 2007) that has identified two fundamental attachment patterns, attachment anxiety (e.g., fear of abandonment) and attachment avoidance (e.g., defensive self-sufficiency and social isolation), and (d) and in *Self Determination Theory* (e.g., Deci and Ryan 1985, 1991) in which the constructs of relatedness and autonomy and competence are central. Thus, the formulation of the two configuration model is congruent with a number of contemporary formulations of personality organization.

The fundamental polarity of relatedness and self-definition has also been central in empirical personality research beginning with Henry Murray and David McClelland and colleagues (e.g., McAdams 1985; McClelland 1961, 1986; Winter 1973) who investigated extensively "affiliation and achievement or power" in personality organization. Jerry Wiggins (1991), a major proponent of the Five Factor Model (FFM), noted that the "meta-concepts of agency and communion" provide a higher order structure for the Five Factor Model of personality organization (e.g., McCrae and Costa 1990) as well as for the Interpersonal Circumplex personality model, two empirically derived personality theories prominent in contemporary conceptualization and measurement of personality dimensions (Luyten and Blatt, in press).

Thus, clinically-derived, theory-dominated, as well as empirically-based approaches to personality development, personality organization, and psychopathology all converge in indicating that interpersonal relatedness and self-definition (or attachment and autonomy) are two fundamental psychological developmental dimensions that provide a theoretical matrix for understanding personality development and for developing a classificatory system of psychopathology that links concepts of psychopathology to processes of personality development, variations in normal personality organization, as well as to processes of psychological development that can occur the in therapeutic process (Blatt 2008; Blatt and Behrends 1987; Mikulincer and Shaver 2007; Pincus 2005; Skodol and Bender 2009; Wiggins 1991). The identification of the centrality of interpersonal relatedness and self-definition as fundamental psychological processes has facilitated the establishment of a theoretical model of personality development and psychopathology that is theoretically coherent, one that has important implications for clinical practice and research (Luyten and Blatt, in press).

References

Adler, A. (1933). On the origin of the striving for superiority and of social interest. In H. L. Ansbacher & R. R. Ansbacher (Eds.), *Alfred Adler: Superiority and social interest* (pp. 29–40). New York: Viking Press. (Original work published 1933.)

Angyal, A. (1941). *Foundations for a science of personality*. New York: Viking Press.

Angyal, A. (1951). In E. Hanfmann & R. M. Jones (Eds.), *Neurosis and treatment: A holistic theory*. New York: Wiley.

Bakan, D. (1966). *The duality of human existence: An essay on psychology and religion*. Chicago: Rand McNally.

Bakan, D. (1996). Origination, self-determination, and psychology. *Journal of Humanistic Psychology, 36*, 9–20.

Balint, M. (1959). *Thrills and repression*. London: Hogarth Press.

Beck, A. T. (1983). Cognitive therapy of depression: New perspectives. In P. J. Clayton & J. E. Barrett (Eds.), *Treatment of depression: Old controversies and new approaches* (pp. 265–290), New York: Raven.

Beck, A. T. (1999). Cognitive aspects of personality disorders and their relation to syndromal disorders: A psychoevolutionary approach. In C. R. Cloninger (Ed.), *Personality and psychopathology* (pp. 411–429). Washington, DC: American Psychiatric Press.

Benjamin, L. S. (1974). Structural analysis of social behavior. *Journal of Psychological Review, 81*, 392–345.

Blatt, S. J. (1974). Levels of object representation in anaclitic and introjective depression. *Psychoanalytic Study of the Child, 29*, 107–157.

Blatt, S. J. (2008). *Polarities of experience: Relatedness and self-definition in personality development, psychopathology, and the therapeutic process*. Washington, DC: American Psychological Association Press.

Blatt, S. J., & Behrends, R. S. (1987). Internalization, separation-individuation, and the nature of therapeutic action. *International Journal of Psychoanalysis, 68*, 279–297.

Blatt S. J., & Blass, R. B (1990). Attachment and separateness: A dialectic model of the products and processes of psychological development. *Psychoanalytic Study of the Child, 45*, 107–127.

Blatt, S. J., & Blass, R. B. (1996). Relatedness and self-definition: A dialectic model of personality development. In G. G. Noam & K. W. Fischer (Eds.), *Development and vulnerabilities in close relationships* (pp. 309–338). Hillsdale,: Erlbaum

Blatt, S. J., & Shichman, S. (1983). Two primary configurations of psychopathology. *Psychoanalysis and Contemporary Thought, 6*, 187–254.

Deci, E. L., & Ryan, R. M. (1985). *Intrinsic motivation and self-determination in human behavior*. New York: Plenum.

Deci, E. L., & Ryan, R. M. (1991). A motivational approach to self: Integration in personality. In R. Dienstbier (Ed.), *Nebraska Symposium on Motivation, 1990: Vol. 38. Perspectives on motivation. Current theory and research in motivation* (pp. 237–288, xiv, 369 pp). Lincoln: University of Nebraska Press.

Freud, S. (1905). Three essays on sexuality. In J. Strachey (Ed. & Trans.), *Standard edition of the complete works of Sigmund Freud* (Vol. 7, pp. 135–243). London: Hogarth Press.

Freud, S. (1914). On narcissism: An introduction. In J. Stachey (Ed. & Trans.), *The standard edition of the complete psychological work of Sigmund Freud* (Vol. 14, pp. 73–102). London: Hogarth Press.

Freud, S. (1923). The ego and the id. In J. Strachey (Ed. & Trans), *The standard edition of the complete psychological works of Sigmund Freud* (Vol. 19, pp. 12–66). London: Hogarth Press.

Freud, S. (1926). Inhibitions, symptoms and anxiety. In J. Strachey (Ed. & Trans.), *The standard edition of the complete psychological works of Sigmund Freud* (Vol. 20, pp. 87–172). London: Hogarth Press.

Freud, S. (1930). Civilization and its discontents. In J. Strachey (Ed. & Trans.), *The standard edition of the complete psychological works of Sigmund Freud* (Vol. 21, pp. 64–145). London: Hogarth Press.

Hartmann, H., Kris, E., & Lowenstein, R.M. (1949). Notes on the theory of aggression. *Psychoanalytical Study of the Child, 3/4*, 9–36. New York: International Universities Press.

Helgeson, V. S. (1994). Relation of agency and communion to well-being: Evidence and potential exploration. *Psychological Bulletin, 116*, 412–428.

Helgeson, V. S., & Fritz, H. L. (1999). Unmitigated agency and unmitigated communion: Distinctions from agency and communion. *Journal of Research in Personality, 33*, 131–158.

Horney, K. (1945). *Our inner conflicts: A constructive theory of neurosis*. New York: Norton.

Horney, K. (1950). *Neurosis and human growth*. New York: Norton.

Horowitz, L. M., Wilson, K. R., Turan, B., Zolotsev, P., Constantino, M. J., & Henderson, L. (2006). How interpersonal motives clarify the meaning of interpersonal behavior: A revised circumplex model. *Personality and Social Psychology Review, 10*, 67–86.

Kohut, H. (1966) Forms and transformations of narcissism. *Journal of the American Psychoanalytic Association, 14*, 243–272.

Loewald, H. W. (1962). Internalization, separation, mourning, and the superego. *Psychoanalytic Quarterly, 31*, 483–504.

Luyten, P., & Blatt, S. J. (in press). Integrating theory-driven and empirically-derived models of personality development and psychopathology: A proposal. Clinical Psychology Review.

Markus, H. R., & Oyserman, D. (1989). Gender and thought: The role of the self-concept. In M. Crawford & M. Gentry (Eds.), *Gender and thought: Psychological perspectives* (pp. dams, D. P.100–127). New York: Springer-Verlag.

McAdams, D. P. (1985). *Power, intimacy, and the life story: Personological inquiries into identity*. Homewood: Dorsey.

McClelland, D. C.(1961). *The achieving society*. New York: Free Press.

McClelland, D. C. (1986). Some reflections on the two psychologies of love. *Journal of Personality, 54*, 334–353.

McCrae, R. R., & Costa, P. T. Jr. (1990). *Personality in adulthood*. New York: Guilford Press.

Mikulincer, M., & Shaver, P. (2007). *Attachment in adulthood: Structure, dynamics, and change*. New York: Guilford Press.

Meyer, B., & Pilkonis, P. A. (2005). An attachment model of personality disorders. In M. F. Lenzenweger & J. F. Clarkin (Eds.), *Major theories of personality disorder*(2nd ed., pp. 231–281). New York: Guilford Press.

Pincus, A. (2005). A contemporary integrative interpersonal theory of personality disorders. In M. F. Lenzenweger & J. F. Clarkin (Eds.), *Major theories of personality disorder* (2nd ed., pp. 282–331, xiii, 464 pp). New York: Guilford Press.

Rank, O. (1929). *Truth and reality* (J. Taft, Trans.). New York: Knopf.

Rank, O. (1945). *Will therapy and truth and reality*. New York: Knopf.

Shor, J., & Sanville, J. (1978). *Illusions in loving: A psychoanalytic approach to intimacy and autonomy*. Los Angeles: Double Helix.

Sibley, C. G. (2007). The association between working models of attachment and personality: Toward an integrative framework operationalizing global relational models. *Journal of Research in Personality, 41*, 90–109.

Skodol, A. E., & Bender, D. S. (2009). The future of personality disorders in DSM V? *American Journal of Psychiatry, 166*, 388–391

Sullivan, H. S. (1953). *The interpersonal theory of psychiatry*. New York: Norton.

White, R. W. (1959). Motivation reconsidered: The concept of competence. *Psychological Review, 66*, 297–333.

Wiggins, J. S. (1982). Circumplex models of interpersonal behavior in clinical psychology. In P. C. Kendall & J. N. Butcher (Eds.), *Handbook of research methods in clinical psychology* (pp. 183–221). New York: Wiley.

Wiggins, J. S. (1991). Agency and communion as conceptual coordinates for the understanding and measurement of interpersonal behavior. In W. W. Grove & D. Cicchetti (Eds.), *Thinking clearly about psychology*, Vol. 2: *Personality and psychotherapy*, (pp. 89–113). Minneapolis: University of Minnesota Press.

Wiggins, J.S. (1997). In defense of traits. In R. Hogan, J. Johnson et al. (Eds.), *Handbook of personality psychology* (pp. 95–141). San Diego: Academic Press.

Winter, D. (1973). *The power motive*. New York: Free Press.

Chapter 5
Autonomy and Schizophrenia: Reflections on an Ideal

Louis A. Sass

> The choice which we make of our life is always based on a certain givenness. My freedom can draw life away from its spontaneous course, but only by a series of unobtrusive deflections which necessitate first of all following its course—not by any absolute creation.

Maurice Merleau-Ponty (1962, p. 455).

[Note: DC = Shapiro, Dynamics of Character; AR = Autonomy and Rigid Character]

Introduction

Here I shall consider an assumption that is widespread in psychoanalysis, psychiatry, and clinical psychology, and that is presented with characteristic subtlety in the writings of David Shapiro. This is the notion that the essential touchstone or yardstick of mental health is a person's capacity for what Shapiro alternatively terms "autonomy," "agency," "intentionality," or "self-directed action." Corollary ideas are (1) that degrees of psychopathology correlate with a person's or patient's distance from this ideal, and (2) that the essential purpose of psychotherapy will be to increase one's sphere of self-awareness and personal agency.[1] Shapiro's presentation of this extremely influential notion or assumption is the richest and clearest of which I am aware in clinical psychology or psychiatry. I will criticize the adequacy of this notion in relation to what is perhaps the most severe form of psychopathology: the schizophrenic disorders, a topic Shapiro mentions in

L.A. Sass (✉)
Professor, GSAPP— Rutgers University, 152 Frelinghuysen Road, Piscataway, NJ 08854
e-mail: lsass@rci.rutgers.edu

[1] Shapiro writes that all psychopathology "will involve some loss of autonomy … probably the more severe the pathology, the greater the loss" (AR p. 31). He describes the "essential aim of psychotherapy" as to introduce the patient to his own "authorship of his own actions… and to enlarge his experience of it" (p. 10). See also *Dynamics of Character*, pp. 19 and 127, where Shapiro cites Roy Schafer and Helmuth Kaiser.

C. Piers (ed.), *Personality and Psychopathology: Critical Dialogues with David Shapiro*,   99
DOI 10.1007/978-1-4419-6214-0_5, © Springer Science+Business Media, LLC 2011

Autonomy and Rigid Character (AR, published in 1981) and treats at length in *Dynamics of Character* (DC 2000). Part of my discussion focuses on the nature of schizophrenic symptoms in particular. The other part concerns the ambiguity of the psychological *concepts* in question – namely, personal "autonomy" as well as closely related notions including agency, volition, self-direction, and free will.

In the books just mentioned, Shapiro gives particular emphasis to this autonomy ideal, and describes it in both subjective and objective terms. "All psychopathology," he writes in *Dynamics of Character*, involves "diminished volitional experience…a diminished experience of self-direction (as in decision) or personal responsibility, or agency" (p. xii; also AR p. 31). Presumably, this diminished *experience* of self-direction corresponds to a diminishment of the degree to which action and thought are *in fact* under volitional control: It is "not only the subjective experience of agency that is diminished," writes Shapiro. "The subjective loss of agency is associated with some actual limitation or impairment of volitional action" (DC p. 14).[2] Instead of action that is "volitional or self-directed," (p. 48) "planful and considered" (p. 57), "directed according to conscious aims" (p. 48) or "reflective conscious direction," (p. 57) persons with significant psychopathology will, according to Shapiro, always manifest one of what he describes as the two "varieties of general modes of diminished agency" (p. xi): what he calls "passive reactive" or "rigid … prevolitional modes" (DC p. 133). The first mode is "a comparatively unreflective, spur-of-the-moment planlessness', the second a form of "rigidity, direction by fixed, internal rules" (DC p. xii). Whereas the first supposedly hearkens back to the "passive reactiveness [of] the child's immediate and quasi-reflexive response to an external provocation," the second recalls the young child's "passive enactment of a fixed, internal program, in this case a memory" (DC p. 50).

According to Shapiro, the loss of volition and agency is particularly extreme in schizophrenia. He speaks of a "reversion to prevolitional modes" that is "radical" and "severe"; and cites classic authors (Goldstein, Angyal, Bleuler, Kraepelin, Jung) who spoke of "impairment of volition, will or intentionality, or … a condition of extreme passivity" involving "inability, or unwillingness … to initiate a course of action, to make a considered choice, or even to concentrate, to focus or shift attention at will" (DC p. 128). Shapiro also argues that this loss of agency has some very global consequences – hypothesizing that it is, in fact, the main cause of the loss of the sense of reality, weakening of ego boundaries, and degradation of affect that are such prominent features of this illness.

A complicating factor is that Shapiro sees the loss of agency as itself resulting, in some deeper sense, from defensive processes – namely, from what he calls the "anxiety-forestalling surrender of volition and agency." In Shapiro's view, diminished autonomy in schizophrenia (the purported cause of most other symptoms of the illness) is not itself (or is not primarily) the sign of some innate or acquired

---

[2] Shapiro speaks of "a loss or weakening of the experience of self-direction (synonymous in my use with agency) and a corresponding attenuation of the actual processes of volitional action" (DC p. 126).

defect or deficiency; it is, rather, a motivated attempt or "defensive retreat" (DC p. 147) to avoid anxiety by denying the sense of agency on which anxiety depends. He wants, in this sense, to show the kinship that psychotic pathology bears to defensive processes in pre-psychotic and neurotic conditions (DC p. 110). His hypothesis is that "schizophrenic symptoms are the product not of a collapse of an existing defense structure but of its radical extension" (DC p. 130).[3]

No one would deny, of course, that persons with schizophrenia do indeed demonstrate a diminished degree of *normal* autonomy or agency – if by this one refers to the exercise of *standard* forms of action and thought that are directed toward the achievement of *conventional* purposes within the *accepted* social order. (What else could we mean by calling them "psychotic" or "insane"?) One point that Shapiro neglects, however, is that while persons with schizophrenia certainly do manifest very pronounced diminishments of agency or autonomy, in terms both of experience and action, they may also, at times, experience *heightened* forms of personal agency, or may think and act in ways that suggest *exaggerated* autonomy – at least according to a number of the standard meanings of "autonomy." As Henry Maudsley once noted, those who "have practical experience of the insane know well what a power of self-control they sometimes evince when they have sufficient motive to exercise it" (in Barham 1984, p. 17). This duality may be difficult to conceptualize or to explain. It is, however, very much in keeping with the generally paradoxical nature of this illness, which so often seems to defy normal or common-sense forms of psychological understanding or explanation.

Shapiro's clinical descriptions and accounts of many particular psychological disorders show a deep appreciation of the paradoxical complexities than can occur in psychopathology; I will describe these in the following section. It seems to me, however, that, in his account of schizophrenia, Shapiro's signature subtlety and appreciation of complexity is sometimes lacking. Also, his *overall* characterization of diminished agency or autonomy is, I believe, somewhat unclear and even, in some ways, potentially misleading. One source of confusion derives from Shapiro's tendency, on occasion, to equivocate between speaking of *distorted* and of *diminished* autonomy. This is a minor problem, since the notion of diminishment is clearly more dominant in his texts. Unfortunately, however, the *meaning* of this diminishment is not entirely clear, since Shapiro offers no precise definition or philosophical analysis of how he understands the psychological quality or characteristic in question. Instead, he offers a series of near-synonyms

---

[3] Shapiro asks whether "the loss of volitional direction of thought and attention" is "the primary deficiency in schizophrenia from which its other symptoms derive; and, if the latter, whether it can be understood as a defensive reaction or, on the contrary, is a directly biological deficiency" (DC p. 134). "Thus we are led to the possibility that the impairment of volitional direction in schizophrenia may also constitute an anxiety-forestalling reversion – in this case a radical one – to pre-volitional modes" (DC p. 127f). He describes his hypothesis as follows: "that the symptoms of schizophrenia, though not themselves defensively purposeful, are products of a radical surrender of volitional direction of thought that is defensive in origin" (DC p. 135).

from everyday language – such as "agency," "autonomy," "volitional action," "self-direction," "intentionality," "directedness of behavior" (DC p. 126, Shapiro 1965, pp. 35) – and relies on his readers' common-sense linguistic intuitions and grasp of clinical examples. This is often a wise approach. Indeed, a reading of recent, technical-philosophical discussions of agency and autonomy is unlikely to inspire optimism about imminent consensus on how to conceptualize these phenomena. Still, a perusal of this literature can perhaps sharpen our intuitions concerning the essentially ambiguous nature of our everyday concept of autonomy/agency: in one recent article, for example, eight distinct meanings of the word "autonomy" are described (Arpaly 2004). It may also alert us to some of the alternative ways in which autonomy might more precisely be defined.

An adequate understanding of schizophrenic psychopathology requires one to appreciate not only the surprisingly antithetical nature of many schizophrenia symptoms, but also the way in which, in normal experience, such opposite characteristics as autonomy and dependence, or agency and passivity, may, in fact, typically coexist in various forms of complex complementarity. Among the most subtle descriptions of this sort of multiplicity and complementarity can be found in the writings of David Shapiro himself. I would argue, in fact, that some of Shapiro's *generalizations* about diminished autonomy and agency are in tension with his own, most distinctive (and in my view *indispensable*) descriptive and interpretative contributions to the study of psychopathology. Although I will criticize some of his prominent claims, my own critique is actually very Shapiro-esque in nature and will sometimes rely on insights inspired by or taken directly from his writings.[4] There is, in fact, little in what I have to say that does not find its echo or precursor in Shapiro's writings, in one fashion or another.

Indeed I do not wish to deny either the reality or the importance of any of the structural relationships or dynamic possibilities that Shapiro describes in his rich and illuminating account of the loss or surrender of volition in schizophrenia. I believe, however, that there are some very important *additional* aspects that he neglects. I will argue that Shapiro tends – very uncharacteristically for him – to oversimplify the schizophrenic condition by neglecting a variety of important ways in which such patients often show forms of *exaggerated* autonomy. Once recognized, these are likely to make one prefer a somewhat different overall account. The difference in our views concerns, then, both some overall generalizations about autonomy and psychopathology and also the degree to which certain complexities of autonomy are associated with schizophrenia in particular.[5]

---

[4] I consider myself something of a disciple of Shapiro's. I was fortunate to have been assigned *Neurotic Styles* in one of the first psychology courses I took as an undergraduate, and Shapiro's perspective has profoundly influenced my thinking ever since. Together with Laing's *Divided Self* and Merleau-Ponty's *Phenomenology of Perception*, Shapiro's book inspired me to study clinical psychology.

[5] Some related issues are discussed in Sass (2007).

Before proceeding, however, I would like to acknowledge the essential reasonableness of Shapiro's way of understanding the term "autonomy." I acknowledge as well that my own approach to the concept is indeed somewhat non-standard – at least from the standpoint of how these issues are typically understood in the mental health professions. It is certainly true, for instance, that the heightened autonomy to be found in schizophrenia seldom corresponds to what would typically be viewed as autonomy, or to what is required for successful functioning in society. (For this reason, my own approach may even strike some readers as somewhat perverse.) Still, I believe there is considerable value in adopting this non-standard perspective. Only by pursuing the insights it reveals can one appreciate certain aspects of schizophrenia that are all too easily neglected, and thereby grasp the true nature and complexity of the psychological processes at issue. The latter goal is, of course, fully congruent with – indeed identical to – the central thrust and achievement of Shapiro's life work.

Shapiro on Autonomy

One of the most striking features of Shapiro's writings – and one of the reasons they stand as *classic* contributions to psychopathology – is, in fact, precisely their acknowledgement of the heterogeneous, complex, often paradoxical quality of many aspects of psychological functioning, both normal and abnormal. Of all the prominent theorists in the broad psychodynamic tradition, Shapiro is the one who sticks most closely to the actual experiential phenomena at issue. For the most part, it seems to me, he eschews the grand, meta-psychological generalizations of both the developmental and ego-psychological models, with their respective emphases either on fixation/regression or on purported "deficits" of ego functioning. Shapiro appears to be far more interested in capturing the specific *qualitative* features of differing modes and styles of psychological being. His natural inclination, it seems, is to reject oversimplifying Procrustean tendencies in favor of a close, descriptive concern with "the things themselves" of actual psychological life[6]; and this brings him, in some ways, closer to the spirit of the phenomenological tradition than to that of some of his psychoanalytic colleagues. A typical expression in Shapiro's writing is this cautionary note: "But the facts are more complicated" (DC p. 108).

---

[6] *Neurotic Styles* begins as follows: "This book had its beginnings in the noticing of certain facts about various pathological conditions and certain specific clinical conclusions—long before I would have considered these to represent a 'point of view.' … if I take some pains in this introduction to explain its orientation, it is not with an interest in theoretical argument, but to guide the reader in his understanding of the clinical chapters that follow" (p. 1) Some pages later in his Introduction: "I will have little to say about the possible origins of the neurotic styles to be discussed here … Careful study of the styles themselves and a clearer, more detailed picture of the forms of cognition, activity, emotional experience, and so on, that characterize various pathological conditions is, I am convinced, an indispensable prerequisite to an understanding of origins" (p. 15).

In light of this general trend (to my mind, the very heart of his approach), Shapiro's attempt to capture the essence of pathology in terms of any single dimension – such as "diminished autonomy" – seems somewhat out-of-character for a theorist of his ilk. It is noteworthy that these generalizing attempts are sometimes accompanied by developmentalist speculations (often offered in what seems a passing, somewhat half-hearted fashion) – as when Shapiro suggests that defensive styles involve "hypertrophy" of developmentally early modes of "diminished self-awareness and sense of agency" (DC pp. 32, 76); or when he writes, "It is well known that the condition of schizophrenia harks back to the early lack of polarity between subject and object" (AR p. 172).[7]

Shapiro's appreciation for the complexity of autonomy is clear from his account of its vicissitudes, which he describes as being imbued with "ambiguities and circularities" and surrounded by "paradoxes" (DC pp. 65, 73). In *Neurotic Styles* (p. 59), for instance, Shapiro describes paranoid suspicion as "rigidly intentional," and paranoid people as being "not merely capable of remarkably active, intense, and searching attention" but "essentially incapable of anything else." They and other rigid personalities show what he calls forms of "tense purposefulness." Here the engagement of forms of *heightened* activity (active, searching attention; purposefulness) is itself described as lying beyond the subject's active control.

Shapiro is well aware of the at least *seemingly* autonomous aspects of rigid personalities. Indeed, he ascribes to such persons many of the defining features of agency or free will, including "an extraordinary degree of articulation and self-consciousness of aim and purpose, an often excruciating consciousness of choice and decision, and great deliberateness of action" (AR p. 19). For such people, he writes, "Areas of life that are normally considered spontaneous ... become matters of serious deliberation, often full of complex purposes" (AR p. 69). Shapiro recognizes that such persons do not merely manifest such tendencies, but take these tendencies as objects of explicit attention and concern: "Among people of rigid character," he writes, "autonomy itself is a matter of preoccupation and concern. These people are concerned with the issue of 'giving in,'" and may harbor "an exaggerated notion of the power of will and self-discipline, and ... an illusion of a kind of self-transcendence through them" (AR p. 85). Shapiro notes that such a person's "purposiveness" may be "very intense: careful, determined, tense, with his attention fixed on aims." Such purposiveness and demand for control "does not brook deviation or distraction" (AR p. 70) and hence is "rigid" – not itself under the patient's volitional control.

---

[7] In my view, this would better be described as a widely held *claim* (in psychoanalysis), rather than an item of "*knowledge*." Shapiro writes that in one respect (absence of "clear, objective picture" of the world), "the rigidity of adult psychopathology is not different from the child's" (DC p. 76), even though one is due to incapacity and the other to defensive dynamics. But if one is concerned with assessing forms or degree of autonomy, the latter would seem to be a *crucial* difference—as I will show.

A similar appreciation of contradictory features emerges in Shapiro's description of hypomanic conditions – not only of the *"driven spontaneity"* of such persons (DC p. 12) but of their failure to "second guess" themselves. The hypomanic person, writes Shapiro, *"consciously rejects* any need for second thoughts and *asserts the right* to do so" (p. 98, emphasis added). What Shapiro describes here seems a kind of *third*-order, quasi-reflective awareness that rejects (*"consciously* rejects") the need for any *second*-order reflective awareness. Such a person seems, at one level, to be *devoid* of reflective awareness; yet this very lack of reflection derives from a form of overarching meta-awareness and choice. Shapiro is, then, well aware of the subtle intertwining of deficiencies and defensive processes that is so typical of psychological functioning. As he notes, for instance, a deficiency of reflectiveness may truly exist in psychopathic individuals, yet this very deficiency can also be exaggerated and exploited by such individuals for the defensive purpose of forestalling anxiety (DC p. 62, 65). Shapiro recognizes the difficulty of characterizing such common psychological conditions in any unilateral way: "... there is something to be said for either view, that the supposed failure of self-control is what it is presented as being, and at the same time that it is not" (DC p. 53). In a passage on rigid personalities (DC p. 71), Shapiro poses a similar set of options: "Is rigidity an excess of will or a disability of will? Is it helplessness or refusal?" he asks. The correct response, one might expect, would be to recognize the truth in *both* these views. It is somewhat surprising, then, that, when it comes to generalizing about autonomy both in "rigid" personalities and in schizophrenia, Shapiro seems to opt for a rather uni-dimensional position.

Shapiro does acknowledge that one's *first* impression of rigid personalities is likely to be of an overdeveloped will, namely, of what he aptly describes as "an active and deliberate self-directedness that stands at the opposite pole from impulsiveness or other kinds of passive-reactiveness." Such purposiveness and deliberateness "may easily appear to be the result of an overdevelopment of volitional direction and control and the overdevelopment of a detached and objective attitude – the opposite extreme of the subjectivity, the immediacy, and the passivity of reaction of early childhood" (AR 74). But Shapiro goes on to argue that this apparent exaggeration of volition and control is essentially an illusion: "the condition of rigidity reflects not so much an overdevelopment of volitional direction and control as a miscarriage of that development. Flexibility – not rigidity – of behavior stands at the opposite pole from the immediacy and the passivity of reaction of early childhood" (p. 74).

The term "miscarriage" is vague in this context; it could cover a number of different kinds of deviations from the norm. "Rigidity" can also mean various things. A careful reading of Shapiro shows, however, that he views the disturbed autonomy of rigid and especially of schizophrenic persons as essentially a *diminished* autonomy involving a rather straightforward lack of free will (the "rule-following" he describes is of a quasi-automatic kind) which he compares to the forms of "rigidity" to be found in early childhood ("... in its absence of a clear, objective picture of the external figure or situation of interest, the rigidity of adult psychopathology is not different from the child's"; DC p. 76). "To put the point more generally," writes Shapiro in a passage on schizophrenia, "a greater rigidity implies a further diminishing of the sense of agency" (DC p. 153).

Let us now turn to the central question: To what extent is it accurate to characterize schizophrenia as being, in essence, a condition of diminished agency or autonomy?

Loss of Autonomy in Schizophrenia

One must begin by acknowledging that many characteristic symptoms and signs of schizophrenia do indicate a striking diminishment of agency or autonomy that is, indeed, quite "distinctively schizophrenic" (DC p. 130). Perhaps the most obvious examples are the well-known Schneiderian "first-rank symptoms" ("positive symptoms"). One patient, for example, said that, when eating, he had the feeling that someone else's tongue was operating in his mouth (DC p. 118); clearly he had lost the normal sense of being the owner and agent of his own bodily action. Another patient periodically had the idea that an evil "Mind" would possess him, making him feel terror and the sense that he had lost all of his will power (Hackett 1952, in Landis 1964, p. 361). Such thoughts and actions seem to lack the key feature of "self-determined or willed actions" – namely, that they be experienced "precisely *not* as an occurrence caused by a different agent but as an initial act of the ego-center itself," as actions which the "ego-center" initiates or to which it at least "assents" (Pfander 1911, p. 20; Ricoeur 1966; both quoted in Ryan et al. 1997, p. 707).

The so-called "negative" and "disorganization" symptoms provide other examples. One patient with *abulia* complained of being "without energy or will" and stated, "It is impossible for me to reflect about something at will. My head feels like a washcloth." He described his own loss of volition very explicitly: "I don't perceive my will and do everything mechanically. ... I, myself, can't bring the sensation of will, that is the sensation of the expression of the will to the level of consciousness" (Heveroch 1913, p. 427, quoted in Landis 1964, p. 347). A catatonic patient of Arieti's experienced himself as "solidifying," becoming "like a statue of stone" (in DC p. 153). The speech of patients with prominent formal thought disorder may seem to follow random sound-associations or irrelevant alternative meanings of words or phrases rather than pursuing a conscious or purposeful aim; the patients themselves may have the sense that the words come out all by themselves rather than expressing any will to meaning. One might also mention individuals who feel obliged to follow command hallucinations, or who engage in repetitive behavior in accord with rigid self-imposed rules.

Symptoms such as the above are certainly among the most prominent schizophrenic symptoms. It is understandable that one would be tempted to see in them the expression of an underlying essence, fundamental feature, or core disturbance of the illness (what Minkowski [1927] called the *trouble genérateur*). But before one accepts this as a *sine qua non* or essential defining and explanatory feature of schizophrenic psychopathology, it is important to recognize that there are, in fact, other symptoms or features, also very typical of schizophrenia, that would seem to indicate just the *opposite* tendency. Such persons may, in fact, experience themselves either as passive and machine-like or as divine or all-powerful, either as bodies devoid of mental or spiritual substance or as disembodied minds; these experiences are perhaps complementary and – paradoxical though it may sound – may even occur simultaneously (Stanghellini 2004; Sass 1992, Chapter 11).

Many schizophrenia patients (slightly more than half in one sample; Stanghellini and Monti 1993) will report a combination of passivity experiences (thoughts, body, or will being controlled from without) *together with* experiences of abnormal degrees of activity or control – such as the sense of being able to transmit one's thoughts directly to others at will, to tune in intentionally to others' thoughts, or to exert intentional mental control over objects and events in the outside world. Instead of feeling only passively manipulated, patients with schizophrenia may also have the sense of having unusual, supernatural powers: "I felt very strong and I thought I was a wizard," said one such patient regarding his ability to transmit thoughts to other people. This suggests that at least an *experience* of exaggerated autonomy or agency is, in fact, quite common in schizophrenia. More objectively observable forms of autonomy are suggested by what seems the willfully obstinate or anti-conventional behavior of many such individuals. Even some of the most prominent so-called "negative symptoms" – such as muteness and withdrawal – often have an active, goal-directed quality, reflecting "a self-protective mechanism that the person uses to avoid" failure and discouragement (Strauss 1989, p. 184).

In this paper I will discuss three distinct levels on which persons with schizophrenia can be said to demonstrate exaggerated forms of autonomy, whether experientially or in terms of more objective assessments of their modes of action or experience. The three levels can be ranged in a sort of hierarchy, defined by degrees of abstractness or explicit self-awareness: namely, the levels of *values*, of *action*, and of the *infrastructure* of action and experience. In discussing the first level I will introduce some recent concepts from analytic philosophy that are relevant to the question of autonomy or free will. My discussion of this level (values) is likely to arouse various objections to my position, and to elicit some rejoinders to my criticism of Shapiro's generalizations about autonomy and psychopathology. In the course of discussing all three levels, I will focus on these possible objections and rejoinders to my claims.

Before proceeding, I want to acknowledge the heterogeneous nature of schizophrenia, which comprises various subtypes and phases that can differ on many dimensions. I do not claim that the forms of autonomy I will emphasize are characteristic of *all* such patients, or present in *all* phases of the illness. These forms are, however, found in many patients at least some of the time, and must, therefore, be considered in our overall comprehension of this condition.

Values

The first level operates at a more abstract or "meta" level than that of mere wishes or desires, since it involves an evaluative attitude that is taken *toward* these wishes or desires themselves. This is the level of what the philosopher Harry Frankfurt (1971), in an extremely influential article called "Freedom of the will and the concept of a person," describes as "second-order desires" and "second-order volitions," or what Charles Taylor (1976), in another important formulation, describes as "strong evaluation." To engage in strong evaluation is not just to evaluate, to judge particular objectives or ends as good or bad; it is to have an attitude *about* one's own evaluations and thus *toward* the overall sort of person one wishes to be. Both Frankfurt and Taylor view this level as indispensable for what it is to have "free will" or to be a "person." Whereas animals demonstrate the capacity for *agency* – that of acting on the basis of a belief and a desire[8] – only human beings seem able to adopt an attitude *toward* their own attitudes and motivations; only they are fully persons for only they are able to take an active, potentially controlling stance toward the values by which they live. Frankfurt speaks of a "capacity for reflective self-evaluation [that is] manifest in the formation of second-order desires" (Frankfurt 1971, p. 7). In Frankfurt's analysis, this meta-level is identified as the locus of a kind of "true self."[9]

On Frankfurt's view, the presence of second-order desires (Taylor's strong evaluations) is a necessary condition for autonomy. It is not, however, a sufficient condition. To demonstrate autonomy or free will, in his view, one's first-order desires must also be in conformity with one's second-order desires and, in addition, one's actions must conform to, and serve to satisfy, these (meta-desired) first-order desires.

The case of schizophrenia is particularly interesting in light of these analyses, for a couple of reasons. First, such people will, very frequently, be especially preoccupied with the question of just what sort of person one ought to be. Persons with schizophrenia or schizotypal disorders often have great difficulty in deciding on or committing themselves to any particular set of values or way of being. Instead of getting on with the normal demands of life, they will often be preoccupied with larger or meta-questions, and may seem especially inclined to judge both their actions and those of others in light of these overarching systems.[10] This is particularly apparent in the "existential reorientation" and focus on ontological or metaphysical questions that are common in the early stages of the illness (Møller and Husby 2000). A second reason is that, in schizophrenia, the desire to be autonomous and idiosyncratic may be, in itself, the most prominent second-order desire. This latter fact, obvious to many

---

[8] This is Donald Davidson's definition: a movement is an action if it is caused, in a specific way, by the combination of a desire and a belief.

[9] The phrase comes from Susan Wolf (1993), who identifies Frankfurt and others inspired by his approach as offering "theories of the true self."

[10] For discussion of this aspect, see Laing (1965); also Sass (1992,Chapter 3). Hannah Arendt makes a useful distinction between what she calls "labor," "work," and "action." In the first, animal desire for bare existence is served. In the second, there is elaborate control of the environment; but each individual is interchangeable, merely serving a role in the production process. Only in the third – "action" – are the intentions and personal character of the agent made manifest. Persons in the schizophrenia spectrum sometimes seem particularly uninterested in both labor and work (witness their lack of interest in ADLs – activities of daily living – and in cooperative labor) and concerned only with "action" – the most individualized and expressive of the three modes. (I thank Jeffery Geller for alerting me to the relevance of Arendt's distinction.)

clinicians, is nicely described by the German psychiatrists Berze and Gruhle (1929, p. 118, quoted in Stanghellini and Ballerini 2007, p. 133): "The schizophrenic wants to be against. The schizophrenic is always ... if not anti-social – at least anti-traditionalist, anti-conventionalist." In the view of Berze and Gruhle, this oppositional behavior is no mere "defect" but the consequence of a "diverse will."

In a recent study of values expressed in transcripts of therapy sessions, Stanghellini and Ballerini (2007) found that patients with schizophrenia or schizotypal disorder were extremely likely to endorse the related values of independence and idiosyncrasy, and to disdain dependence and conformity. Stanghellini and Ballerini speak of "idionomia" and "antagonomia." The first refers to the patient's sense of "radical uniqueness and exceptionality" in his or her being, often felt as a gift involving a mission or superior, metaphysical understanding of the world. The second refers to the will to adopt an eccentric stance against shared assumptions and other people (see also Sass 1992, Chapter 3). Clearly, these involve "strong evaluations" or "second order desires or volitions" for they imply not so much any particular judgment or evaluation as a kind of overall, meta-attitude toward the *kinds* of attitudes, evaluations, or actions one ought to adopt.

The insistence on autonomy is very apparent in quotations from Stanghellini and Ballerini's patients. Here are some statements that imply "*Refusal of interpersonal bonds*":

"Interpersonal bonds have no reason to exist."

"I reject my tendency towards identifying myself with what the others say."

"What I detest more than anything else is being persuaded by others."

"I would like to be clear-headed to have intuitions. And for this I would like not to be too domesticated."

"I've always liked being different very much."

"I'm getting to be more humane. Will it ruin my brain? All this humanity is upsetting my special framework. It's polluting me."

Such persons may also show "Refusal of common sense knowledge and semantics":

"Mathematics, geometry, art, and justice are the improper certainties of human beings."

"By being by myself I am able to understand that nothing has a sense."

"My aversion to common sense is stronger than my instinct to survive."

Such refusal may lead them to prefer alternative modes of knowledge:

"Revelation is a subjective vision of the human condition disconnected from the 'common' idea to be or to belong to the human condition."

"Madness is necessary to human intelligence to get to the higher levels."

The refusal may also inspire them to *act* in non-conventional or contrarian ways:

"People buy a ticket to get on a train – that is the rule," said one patient. "But this rule is for them, not for me."

"It's time to change this objective handwriting into a subjective one," wrote another patient in a diary, after which the patient's handwriting shifted to an idiosyncratic alphabet.

As noted, the notion of "autonomy" can have a variety of different meanings – eight according to an article mentioned above. Of the meanings listed by Arpaly (2004), at least four are virtually synonymous with the values explicitly espoused by the patients described in Stanghellini and Ballerini's study and other reports, namely "independence of other people" (not depending on other people to survive), "independence of mind" (the opposite of being servile or submissive), "heroic autonomy" (being master of one's own fate), and "authenticity" (being true to one's values, which in this case are those of non-conformity etc.).[11]

Some Objections

We see, then, that, at least in terms of *espoused* values or *second-order* judgments, many schizophrenic individuals appear to be, if anything, even *more* individualistic or autonomous than the average person.[12] But what, really, a skeptic may ask, are the implications of this for the view that psychopathology implies *diminished* autonomy? I can think of three objections that such a critic might wish to address to the claim that such espousal of independence or nonconformity at the level of *expressed values* indicates a heightening of *actual* or *true* autonomy in schizophrenia.

The first objection concerns the internal *coherence* of this espousal:

1. *Might the patient's adherence to the ideal of independence/nonconformity be so extreme or unmodulated as to constitute, in itself, a form of (self-contradictory) rigidity?*

A second objection concerns the concrete, action-implications of this espousal:

2. *Is this consciously espoused value mere lip service - in the sense of not being truly associated with behavior or thoughts that are* in fact *especially autonomous?*

A third objection concerns the sources or causes of this espousal:

3. *Does the patient really* choose *non-conformity, or is she perhaps merely rationalizing an eccentricity over which she has no real control?*[13]

---

[11] Three of the four other types listed by Arpaly (2004) are not necessarily more absent in schizophrenia than in normal individuals or other forms of pathology; I would not however claim that they are especially prominent in schizophrenia. These are the following: (1) normative, moral autonomy, the ability to make one's own decisions free from intervention or false information. (2) Having a harmonious and coherent self-image, as in the case of a person who does not experience her desires as an external threat. (3) The ability to respond to reasons. The final type, "agent autonomy," refers to the issue of self-control or self-government: the ability to decide which motivational state to follow. This has affinities with Frankfurt's conception of autonomy, and is discussed in the course of this article.

[12] There is no control group in Stanghellini and Ballerini's (2007) study. It seems obvious however that the positions espoused by their schizophrenia-spectrum patients are more extreme than one would typically find in a normal population or in other diagnostic groups.

[13] Objections 1 and 3 are reminiscent of some recent philosophical criticisms of Frankfurt's view. See notes following.

The first objection argues that the schizophrenic person's very commitment to autonomy is so inherently absolute as to constitute, in itself, a form of rigidity, and that this commitment therefore conforms to the second of Shapiro's two patterns of *non*-autonomous conduct.[14] There is a kernel of truth in this point: the schizophrenic person's rejection of convention and dependency can indeed be very extreme, as if devoid of any sense of balance or nuance (thus reminiscent of the "exaggerated willfulness" that Shapiro describes in adolescence; AR 66f). Still, it seems unreasonable to deny the important difference between the nature of two forms of "rigidity" – between following an extreme meta-rule like "be autonomous!" and the kind of rigid, rule-boundedness that Shapiro describes. Whereas the first demands some critical distance from convention and the taken-for-granted, the latter tends toward mere automaticity and non-reflectiveness.

There is, admittedly, something unusual about taking autonomy/independence *itself* as one's explicit meta-goal – as opposed to letting it exist as a presupposition for, or emerge as the byproduct of, a shaping of one's life through actions oriented toward *other* purposes. This is not, however, a reason to ignore the reality of the autonomy itself. Indeed, such an orientation has affinities with certain rather abstract, ethical/esthetic ideals – often taken as paradigms of freedom – such as "making one's life a work of art" (often ascribed to Nietzsche and Foucault) or the more general injunction to be original or "make it new" (Ezra Pound), common in avant-garde and modernist movements in twentieth century art and culture (Sass 1992). An extreme and explicit aspiration to *be autonomous* may be, in some ultimate sense, ultimately unlivable and absurd; this does not change the fact that it does contain an autonomy-aspiration that is both powerful and real.

The second objection asks whether the autonomy-value has real implications for action, as opposed to being merely an empty assertion or claim. Posing this question is perfectly consistent with Harry Frankfurt's own position, for on Frankfurt's view free will requires (among other things) not only that one *have* particular second-order desires (whatever they may be), but also that one's actions and first-order desires be *congruent* with these higher-order commitments. This means having, not only second-order *desires*, but what Frankfurt calls second-order *volitions* – a second-order volition being the desire that a certain desire *constitute one's will*, namely, that it be the *actual cause* of one's action, the desire that moves one to action. To determine whether an individual manifests autonomy/free-will, one must ask, then, whether his actions and his effective or animating motivations are congruent with his second-order desires/volitions.

In the case of schizophrenic *idionomia* and *antagonomia*, the second-order desire is precisely to *be* autonomous or free. (As noted, there is a curious reflexivity here: with free will being demonstrated in actions whose point is precisely to

---

[14] This objection recalls criticisms of Frankfurt's position that question his privileging of second-order desires and volitions by arguing that there is, in fact, no reason to view these as necessarily capturing the person's authentic or autonomous will. Is it not possible, for instance, that a person could be incapable of being reflective about his second-order desires? See Watson (1975); also Thalberg (1978).

express this freedom.) The test of autonomy, then, will be whether the actions do *in fact* demonstrate a commitment to autonomy as such; if so, they would thereby demonstrate "agent autonomy" (Arpaly 2004), which involves exerting a kind of second-order control in deciding (or assent in allowing) which motivational state to follow. In schizophrenia, this often does seem to be the case – as I shall argue below in the section called "Action."

The third possible objection questions the freedom with which the second-order evaluation was adopted: One may ask whether, for the schizophrenic individual, the process of committing to the ideals of independence and nonconformity was *itself* under the person's control – or whether it might, rather, be rooted in a set of cognitive/affective deficits that render the person simply *incapable* of conventional behavior and social ties.[15] Rather than a mark of freedom, the commitment to independence/nonconformity would, on this view, simply be a sign of acquiescence to something that is determined and inevitable. Instead of being capable of self-transformation or self-correction in accord with autonomous and authentically held, second-order desires, the individual in question would rather be ruled by lower-order propensities that his second-order values would merely rationalize. The real controlling factor, then, would be a lower-level factor – in this case not even a *desire* but simply a cognitive-affective *deficiency* that *precludes* giving oneself over to the conformity of standard modes of action and perception.[16]

If such were the case, the situation of such an individual might be viewed as involving a kind of *forced* autonomy – in the sense that such an individual would be simply *unable* to depend on the taken-for-granted forms of life that are passively accepted and guide so much of the lives of normal persons, and *forced* instead to create patterns of existence on his own. Perhaps this helps to explain the apparent extravagance and manneristic behavior often found in schizophrenia (Binswanger 1987). Such a situation would undermine the capacity for *normal* autonomy, of course. Still, there might be an important sense in which the forced autonomy at issue actually represents a *heightened* autonomy of a non-normal kind. Indeed, as

---

[15] This objection recalls criticisms of Frankfurt that recommend focusing on the *process* through which second-order desires develop. See, e.g., Christman (1991). Christman emphasizes the *agent's* acceptance or rejection of the process of formation of his desire; an alternative approach might seek other, less subjective bases of evaluation of this process.

[16] One might wonder, in fact, whether the schizophrenic persons apparent autonomy is somehow akin to the way in which a neurological patient with involuntary motor tics may nevertheless find ways to incorporate these tics into action sequences that only *appear* to be purposeful. Still another objection might involve saying that the patient's statements of autonomy are, in some sense, "empty speech acts" devoid of meaningful or representational content (see Berrios 1991) – no more than a recycling of cultural clichés that are not really understood by the patient. Is it, perhaps, an over-extension of the famous "principle of charity" to interpret such statements as being meaningful in any straightforward sense?

Both these objections seem implausible. First, the actions in question often involve highly complex behavior-sequences that require executive functioning and have little in common with tics (see section on "Action" in this paper). Also, both the coherence of the patients' statements and the consistency of these statements with complex forms of non-automatic action, suggest that the speech acts could not be devoid of meaningful content or commitment.

we shall see somewhat later, there might even be a sense in which the underlying inability in question should itself be characterized as involving forms of exaggerated willfulness or volition.

The issues surrounding this third objection are especially complex and even paradoxical. They require us to consider in some detail the possible underlying abnormalities or infrastructure of action and cognition in schizophrenia; this is the topic of the penultimate section called "Infrastructure." But first we return to the second objection, which concerns the level of overt action.

Action

I have already acknowledged that the actions of persons with schizophrenia will frequently demonstrate diminished autonomy in various ways. The sense of volition may be lost (first-rank symptoms), for example, or the person may sense a diminishment of basic vital energy or ego-feeling that makes action or purposeful thinking almost impossible. These are key features of schizophrenia whose importance cannot be denied. But it is also true that such individuals will often engage in forms of action that are clearly volitional and that do seem to manifest – at times even to flaunt – the autonomy inherent in non-conformity and independence.

One young man whom I interviewed, for instance, was engaged in developing his own philosophical system, but refused to read any existing philosophical books since he did not want it to contaminate the purity of his own vision.[17] Another young man whom I knew ("Philip") would dance for hours while balancing on one foot, in order to develop his own, unique art form. In a letter, he declared his strong evaluation of independence/autonomy, writing that he refused to be limited by "ideas of a normal metabolism" and that "the importance of Reality is merely a social sanction (society inevitably ruled by those involved in reality)" (Sass 1992). The writer and man of the theatre, Antonin Artaud, who was floridly schizophrenic during much of the last ten years of his life, sought a form of autonomy that was utterly uncompromising: he claimed that he had neither father or mother but had, in fact, created himself; also, he rejected any form of normal linguistic syntax as a form of imprisonment, and sought to create an alternative mode of speech. "I used some words in order to express a concept entirely different from the usual one," said another patient. "Thus, I blithely employed the word *mangy* to mean *gallant*.... I would seek release in self-invented [words], as for example, *wuttas* for *doves*." "I'm enjoying so much wonderful freedom in my mental illness," said still another patient. "The life of a mental patient means being a prince, with all its freedoms and thoughts" (Lecours and Vanier-Clement 1976, p. 556; Bleuler 1978, p. 490).

---

[17] Minkowski (1927) describes a very similar case.

There is, of course, something bizarre, perhaps insane, about each of the above-mentioned attitudes or projects; maybe we should speak here of *"pathological* freedom" (Woods 1938). Such persons can obviously be described as lacking in *normal* autonomy. But the sheer bizarreness should not be allowed to obscure the fact that what accounts for the diminishment of *normal* autonomy is primarily the heightening of *other* forms of autonomy – namely, hyperbolic exaggeration of independence and rejection of convention. This heightening is not only perfectly real, in the sense of being expressed in real activity (actual bodily movements, ways of speaking, peculiar inventions, etc.). Also it conforms to the second-order commitments of the individual (for example, to "Philip's" rejection of the constraints of "Reality"; to Artaud's insistence on independence) – thus fulfilling Frankfurt's criteria for free will and personhood. Some of these individuals seem, in fact, to be clear examples of the type described in an autobiographical short story by the writer Robert Walser, who himself suffered from schizophrenia: each is a "connoisseur and gourmet of freedom," "always bowing inwardly to the pure image of freedom" (in Sass 1992 p. 140).

This kind of insistent living-out of an exaggerated ideal of freedom can be especially obvious, in non-psychotic form, in the schizoid or schizotypal personalities that are common in persons who later turn schizophrenic. It is surprising, therefore, to find that, in two pages on "Schizoid Personality" in *Dynamics of Character*, Shapiro (2000, pp. 154–155) describes only the "passive-reactive" qualities and "drifter" lives of such persons, noting "a lack or impoverishment of emotion" and "callous and unfeeling" tendencies, and comparing schizoid persons to (impulsive) psychopaths. All these traits can indeed be present; but it is crucial to recognize that, in schizoid personalities, they often co-exist with some antithetical qualities, such as (in many cases) a kind of affective hypersensitivity or thin-skinnedness as well as propensities for contrarianism, independence, and a kind of flaunted eccentricity (Sass 1992,Chapter 3).[18]

It is always possible to claim, of course, that these manifestations of extreme autonomy (whether in the schizoid or schizophrenic condition) are essentially *defensive* in nature, betraying some deeper level of experience at which the person

---

[18]Shapiro quotes from Harry Guntrip's writing on schizoid personality. However, he ignores the dialectical element in the accounts by Guntrip and Fairbairn, both of whom recognize the presence of an underlying and intermittently emergent sensitivity/vulnerability and a capacity for acute introspective awareness, as well as an insistence on autonomy (both at the level of values and of action) that are also common in many schizoid individuals (see also Laing 1965). Shapiro's comparison of schizoids with psychopathy seems odd, since schizoid individuals are typically dominated by forms of self-consciousness, hesitation, and psychological distancing mechanisms that have little in common with impulsive traits. See *Madness and Modernism* (Sass 1992, Chapter 3) for critical discussion of conceptions of schizoid personality, including both the uni-dimensional model implicit in DSM III and IV and the British object-relations approach.

fears and feels some kind of diminished autonomy – and thus to dismiss them as acts of reaction-formation or denial that are relatively superficial features of the person's overall psychic economy or organization.[19] This, however, has the ring of special pleading for the diminished-autonomy point of view. For one thing, it requires accepting complex hypotheses about unobservable psychic positions. But even if it were accepted that the exaggerated autonomy of such acts and thoughts is profoundly imbued with defensive motives (not an unreasonable proposition, admittedly), it seems questionable to dismiss its significance on these grounds. After all, the defense in question would seem to *require* certain commitments and certain underlying capacities and propensities – in this case, none other than capacities and propensities for *autonomous functioning*. Also, as Shapiro more than anyone else teaches us, defenses themselves are not peripheral automatisms or routines that are merely "*used* by the person" but, rather, forms of intentionality and conscious life that constitute the very substance of selfhood or personality itself; they are "processes, constituents, of the person" (DC p. 30).[20] If the defense demonstrates exaggerated autonomy, then (in some sense) so does the person.

The defensive element is perhaps especially obvious in the case of certain patients with chronic schizophrenia who withdraw into a quasi-delusional imaginative world of pure fantasy, over which they can exert a kind of godlike control. A good example is the patient and *art brut* artist Adolf Wölfli, whose decades in the Waldau Asylum in Switzerland were spent creating paintings and collages and writing stories about imaginary worlds (Sass 1997, 2004). It seems likely that such withdrawal does indeed serve (among other things) as a way of avoiding the more anxiety-laden demands inherent in exercising autonomy in the real world. But this does not change the fact that such patients *are* opting to live in a world – albeit virtual or imaginary – in which they do exercise a kind of extreme autonomy. In these cases, in fact, the autonomy in question has something in common with one of our primary cultural icons of independence: the artist's creating of virtual or imaginary worlds.[21]

---

[19]Shapiro offers this sort of analysis in his treatment of adolescence. He recognizes that adolescents are "concerned with the right, in principle, to hold their own views, to follow their own lights, to be in charge of themselves. They are explicitly and consciously aware of and concerned with the matter of autonomy or self-determination itself ..." He speaks of forms of "exaggerated willfulness, defensiveness, and other symptoms of an unsteady, self-conscious, and sometimes simply artificial assertion of autonomy and personal authority" (AR 66–67), thus characterizing these acts and assertions as mere *pseudo*-autonomy.

[20]In this sense the term "mechanism" in the phrase "defense mechanisms" is somewhat misleading.

[21]One might wish to impose, as a *criterion* of autonomy, that the person remain in basic touch with consensual reality, and to argue that this is not the case with such patients. However, some such withdrawn, schizophrenic persons do show significant recognition of the merely virtual nature of their delusional or quasi-delusional worlds. Good examples are the famous patients Paul Schreber and Adolf Wölfli; discussed by Sass (1994, 1997, 2004).

Infrastructure

I turn now to the third and most foundational of the levels at issue: that of what might be called the psychological infrastructure of action and experience. We will be speaking now, not about value-laden evaluations or judgments, nor about distinct actions or thoughts, but about something more akin to the ongoing experiential background against which such action may take place. This brings us very close to much of what Shapiro so brilliantly describes in his writing on the cognitive/affective modes, forms, or structures of what he has called "neurotic styles." What, we may ask, is the typical cognitive/affective style or perceived world of persons in the schizophrenia spectrum, and what does this suggest about their capacity or propensity for autonomy?

Here, as so often in treating the themes of both schizophrenia and autonomy, we encounter a somewhat paradoxical situation. Whereas the person with schizophrenia may be, in some sense, *doomed* to the eccentric nature of his own cognitive processing or lived perceptual world, these eccentricities bear a complex relationship to the issues of both consciousness and volition: For one thing, these eccentricities may themselves involve a disturbance of automatic and an associated heightening of more volitional and conscious forms of mental processing. For another, they are not completely outside the patient's willful or conscious control. A third and final point is that, even if the person with schizophrenia is, in some ultimate sense, temperamentally doomed to a style or stance of eccentricity – perhaps because of innate neurophysiological factors – this does not prevent her from taking this stance up actively and, in some sense, making it her own, thereby animating the style with a certain intentionality (Sass 1992, p. 74).

Perhaps the best way to grasp the first point is to consider the phenomenological psychiatrist Wolfgang Blankenburg's (1971, 2001) description of the loss of "common sense" or "natural self-evidence" in schizophrenia (Stanghellini 2004; Sass 2001). As Blankenburg points out, persons with schizophrenia frequently (perhaps always) lose the ability simply to take-for-granted the practical routines and social conventions that guide so much of normal human conduct, which they seem rather to look on at from outside. "I am like an emperor in a pyramid," said one patient. "I am not involved in the world, merely observing it from outside to understand its secret ways." "I am a detached onlooker," said another (Stanghellini and Ballerini 2007 p. 136).

The patient's sense of being outside conventional ways of acting and perceiving may be, to a large extent, an affliction, a kind of incapacity that is related to certain neuro-cognitive or neuro-affective abnormalities (disorders of the hippocampus-based "comparator" system is one very plausible candidate[22]; diminished *Lebensdrang* is

---

[22] One of most plausible neuro-cognitive approaches to schizophrenia hypothesizes a disturbance of the hippocampus-based "comparator" system – the system that normally enables the cognitive-perceptual system to take familiar information for granted, i.e., to experience it in an implicit manner while directing focal attention toward that which is novel and unexpected (Hemsley 2005). One consequence of disturbance to this system would be disruption of the explicit-focus/implicit-background relationship that is essential to Blankenburg's "natural self-evidence." Stimuli that would normally fade into the background of awareness because of their sheer familiarity, would tend instead to become objects of focal awareness.

another – see below). It is noteworthy, however, that one of the consequences of this incapacity or loss is that the individual often becomes explicitly aware of practical and social conventions that would not normally come to be objects of focal attention. The combination of perplexity and rejection of common sense is suggested in the following statement by a patient: "I admitted the physiological abjuration of common sense, in the moment in which I could admit the desperate effort to understand the tacit codex that is implicit in human actions" (Stanghellini and Ballerini 2007 p. 138). Such things as the arbitrary nature of our ritual of shaking hands, the performative conventions whereby we express the masculinity or femininity of our gender roles, or our use of words, may be consciously perceived and, as such, can come to seem both arbitrary and absurd. Another patient said, "I don't understand why this has to be called a table, and if the sun's out we have to say it's a nice day" (p. 136).

The schizophrenic loss of natural self-evidence certainly makes it difficult for such individuals to engage in *normal* or conventional forms of autonomous action; this should not, however, blind us to the fact that it can also open up the possibility of more radical, albeit "dysfunctional" (if judged from a conventional standpoint) modes of being. Shapiro argues that neurosis and, by implication, all forms of psychopathology[23] tend to "restrict subjective experience" (AR pp. 23–24). True enough, in some respects. Here, however, we see some ways in which schizophrenia-spectrum conditions can also *expand* awareness of features of life that are normally relied upon in an implicit and non-focal fashion – thereby rendering these features more subject to forms of volitional judgment or control. The forms of autonomy this awareness tends to facilitate are not, of course, those that many normal people would choose (this is part of what we mean by calling them "dysfunctional"). Some persons with schizophrenia (or schizoid personality) may, however, have a sense of superiority over what they may perceive to be the bovine or mechanical condition of normal individuals, who seem so completely unaware of and subservient to the rituals and routines they are actually following (see Laing 1965, pp. 49, 102). One patient, for instance, claimed that the vast majority of human beings were not truly living minds but only "organic machines" or "mental vegetables" who lacked a real soul. What appeared to be thinking on their part was, he claimed, really no more than the mechanical retrieval and processing of facts and memories from a memory bank (Sass 1992, p. 334). Quotations from schizophrenic or schizotypal patients in Stanghellini and Ballerini's (2007) study illustrate this same attitude: "Man is merely a heap of memories in a standard hardware." "The brain is a believalogical imbecile" (pp. 138).

Such forms of awareness are not merely passively registered. Indeed, they often give rise to a mode of life in which the person actively attempts to stay independent of grounding conventions, or perhaps to invent new conventions of an idiosyncratic kind ("idiosyncratic convention" is, of course, something of an oxymoron). In this sense the person not only assents but commits himself to a mode of life to which he may, in some sense, also be doomed. Here the views of Binswanger and Blankenburg are relevant.

---

[23] In *Dynamics of Character* Shapiro makes it very clear that he wishes to extend the neurosis model to account for aspects of psychosis.

Binswanger (1956) disagreed with Berze and Gruhle's notion that schizophrenic eccentricity was based on a choice of an antagonistic lifestyle. He argued, rather, that such persons strive to be faithful to their own intrinsic eccentricity (in Stanghellini and Ballerini 2007). In his opinion the characteristic eccentricity results from both an innate peculiarity *and* a deliberate fidelity to this way of being. Blankenburg (1971) had a similar view. He describes a "pseudo-voluntary choice" of alienation, noting that persons with schizophrenia often "flirt" with their psychosis and that their preference for eccentricity contributes in turn to their alienation (pp. 192, 195). Blankenburg's use of the prefix "pseudo" seems overly strong, however; for as both Binswanger and Blankenburg acknowledge, there is a sense in which the patient has a *preference for* and *commits* himself to the particular way of being that happens to be available to him. It is perhaps more accurate to speak, instead, of a "quasi-choice of an entire existential stance." One might ask, in fact, how different this situation is from that of the normal individual: Does he, too, not acquiesce to a mode of functioning (in this case, practical, conventional, imbued with common sense) that he does not so much choose as inherit?

The schizophrenic's basic disconnection from common-sense reality might itself be explained in various ways. I already mentioned the possible role of disturbance of the hippocampus-based "comparator system."[24] Another possibility would be to associate this disconnection with decline in emotional or drive-related factors, as is implied by Eugene Minkowski's (1927) notion of "loss of vital contact" in schizophrenia or, perhaps even more clearly, in Max Scheler's notion of a weakened *Lebensdrang* or life-drive (Cutting 2009; Stanghellini 2010). Both notions have affinities with the concept of "diminished self-affection" (Sass 2001; Sass and Parnas 2003). Diminished *Lebensdrang* would have the effect of unraveling the usual fabric of meaning, since this fabric depends on there being some sense in which things "matter" or have a place in relationship to the ongoing projects and prevailing "appetites" of the subject in question.

The concept of *Lebensdrang*, together with the closely related notion of the passions, nicely illustrates the complementarity of active/autonomous with passive/heteronomous factors. Our passions and vital appetites (expressions of *Lebensdrang*) are, after all, what provide the rationale, meaning, and vital energy for our most intense activity, yet they themselves are, in another sense, passively endured. The very term "passion," with its implication of both passivity and intense directedness, captures both sides of this coin. If schizophrenia *did* involve a basic diminishment of *Lebensdrang,* this could obviously help to account for the seemingly motivation-less passivity characteristic of negative-symptom patients. It might also help us to understand the peculiar quality of some of the strange, motiveless actions that such individuals may carry out – actions that, unlike classic forms of "acting out," can seem to be products of a pure (and often, curiously bewildered)

---

[24] See earlier note re hippocampus-based "comparator" function.

willfulness that lacks much grounding in underlying emotion or desire.[25] "Philip," the young man with schizophrenia mentioned earlier, for example, had once cata-pulted a piece of fried fish high into the air and across the dining room of his school, in what seemed a sort of pure absurdist gesture. Such actions are both more *and* less autonomous, depending on how one understands the implications of a divorce from passionate engagement.[26]

Shapiro is himself very sensitive to the profound interdependence of cognition and affect, which he describes as being "together, aspects of the individual's rela-tionship with the external world" (DC p. 143). He is well aware that, as he puts it, "cognition cannot be separated from cognitive attitude, and [that] cognitive attitude, in turn, cannot be separated from the dynamics of the personality as a whole" (DC p. 115). Thus he speaks of "the organizing effects of purpose." It is slightly unex-pected, then, that Shapiro should assimilate what he calls the schizophrenic patient's lack of "goal-presentation" or "interest" (which, as he notes, is a source of cognitive disruption) to the individual's surrendering of a self-directed attitude or agentic role, rather than acknowledging that this lack of interest might be more straightforwardly rooted in a fundamental diminishment or other alteration of affect or drive (DC pp. 138–140).[27]

Another relevant fact is that, although the experiential orientation in question is, in an important sense, a fact of life with which such persons must contend, it is not *entirely* outside the sphere of their control. Patients report, for example, that they can sometimes diminish or even temporarily eliminate the strangeness of their per-ceptual world or bodily experience in various ways, for example, by engaging in

---

[25]For rich analysis of one such individual, a patient who cut his grandmother's throat despite seem-ing to have no history or current feelings of hostility toward her, see Castel (2009).

[26]See Jouan (2009) for interesting arguments regarding the (paradoxical) need for autonomous actions to be rooted in a kind of passivity, that of a passion or basic commitment that is itself not freely chosen.

[27]An interesting formulation of the latter possibility can be found in *Dementia Praecox or the Group of Schizophrenias*, where Eugen Bleuler (1950) speculates not only that affective decline may be more fundamental than the thinking disturbance in schizophrenia, but that this decline may largely involve defensive shutting-down as protection against disorganizing affect (pp. 41–51, 65–68, 364–369). Shapiro presents evidence that seems very supportive of the fundamental, orga-nizing role of affect- or drive-related factors. He cites Thomas Freeman's observation re catatonic schizophrenia patients that "coherent, fluent, and logical speech appeared when they were angry or under the pressure of a need [such as hunger]." Here, as Shapiro acknowledges, the "momentary emergence of spontaneous purpose, possible under these conditions without self-consciousness, organizes thought and speech" (DC, p. 140).Shapiro also acknowledges that, in schizophrenia, we must consider "an effect in the opposite direction": not "the weakening of the experience of exter-nal reality that follows from the restriction or loss of volition" but rather, "the effect on volitional direction of a loss of clear external objectives" (DC, pp. 144–145). Fair enough. But Shapiro goes on to insist that the "loss of a clear and stable sense of external reality [must itself be] a by-product of the defensive retreat from volitional experience" – a by-product that "may in turn assume pro-portions that deprive the individual of the external objects that volitional direction requires." I hear the ring of special pleading here.

action. The patient Renee, for instance, would throw herself into familiar activity in order to dissipate the surreal "Land of Unreality" that emerged at the height of her psychosis (Sass 1992, p. 73). They may also, at times, *heighten* the sense of worldly strangeness by adopting a stance of contemplative detachment, or may exacerbate a sense of emotional flattening or bodily fragmentation by focusing objectifying attention on kinesthetic or proprioceptive sensations that would normally be lived or inhabited in a more immediate or implicit fashion. The "schizophrenic hyperawareness of body sensations" and bodily alienation need not, therefore, be understood only as a possible *consequence* of the absence of more normal forms of "purposeful movement and purposeful attention," as Shapiro suggests (DC p. 139). It may also involve active, self-directed forms of attention (Sass 1992, Chapter 7; Sass and Parnas 2007).

Shapiro's own hypothesis about the defensive sources of the schizophrenic's denial of autonomy suggest a similar mechanism – a goal-directed albeit not fully conscious "project" whereby the patient brings about a global experiential change. Shapiro's hypothesis invokes a perfectly plausible process that is nevertheless somewhat paradoxical: a teleological, in some sense *active* process (he speaks of symptoms that are "products of a radical surrender of volitional direction of thought that is defensive in origin"; DC p. 135) whereby the person in question attempts to diminish and to deny his own capacity for action. Indeed, it may even be that this extreme (and purposeful) *denial* of volition suggests a particularly acute, underlying awareness of the *fact* of volition. This point is already made by Shapiro himself in his discussion of catatonic schizophrenia – where rigidly scrupulous "self-consciousness and inhibition [appears to extend] to all action" (DC 151). Such individuals, it seems, shudder and freeze before an experience of the absoluteness of freedom that recalls the Kantian notion of the sublime – where the infinitude of personal freedom is felt to rival the infinitude of the universe itself. Shapiro quotes Arieti's description of a catatonic patient for whom, in the period prior to the actual catatonic state, "Every action … became loaded with a sense of responsibility. Every willed movement came to be seen … as a moral issue" (Arieti 1974, p. 161; DC p. 152)."

Conclusion: Alternative Views

We see, then, that it is potentially misleading to characterize schizophrenia simply as a condition of diminished autonomy. Along with prominent symptoms that reveal such a tendency, there are others that suggest exaggeration both of the *sense* of autonomy and of *actual* autonomy – at least if we accept many standard understandings of what "autonomy" might mean. Persons with schizophrenia will not infrequently espouse an ethic of radical independence. Their actions and thoughts will often reveal of kind of exaggerated willfulness and idiosyncrasy. Although the infra-structural level is the most difficult to characterize, here too we find a mode or style of consciousness that can be both conducive to and responsive to forms of radical independence and unconventionality.

Given the presence of what seem to be antithetical tendencies – toward both diminishment *and* hypertrophy of "autonomy" – one may well wonder whether anything more general can be said about autonomy in schizophrenia. As already mentioned, one can certainly say that *normal* autonomy tends to be diminished in schizophrenia. This, however, seems a rather empty statement – neither very dis-criminating (surely many other disorders also involve diminished normal autonomy) nor very precise (it does not specify just *how* or *why* normal autonomy is attenuated).

A somewhat more nuanced way of describing the diverse abnormalities in ques-tion might be to say that they all involve diminishment of the normal *equilibrium between* autonomy and heteronomy or *between* independence and dependence on that which lies beyond the self. The grounding of autonomy (of normal autonomy) within a more fundamental heteronomy has been described by many authors and in various ways, yet is readily forgotten or ignored. Both G. H. Mead and Lev Vygotsky conceive the development of a sense of self as requiring an internaliza-tion of the experience of others. Winnicott's (1958) famous article, "The Capacity to be Alone," argues that the capacities for solitude or independence (at least in their *normal* form) require that one be able to sense the reassuring presence of internalized, nurturing others. The paradoxical tendency – seemingly inherent or inbuilt – to forget the founding dependency is captured by Lionel Trilling's descrip-tion of the grounding of the highly autonomous modern self in the culture that forms it: "This intense conviction of the existence of the self apart from culture is, as culture well knows, its noblest and most generous achievement" (in Menand 2008). It is Kant (1965, orig: 1787), however, in his famous image of a bird's flight, who most succinctly captures the thoroughly non-sensical nature of any claim to absolute autonomy: "The light dove cleaving the air in her free flight, and feeling its resistance, might imagine that its flight would be still easier in empty space" (A5 B8-9).[28] Also relevant is the passage from Merleau-Ponty that appears at the top of this article. In recent years, various philosophers have spoken of "decen-tered" or "relational autonomy" (Jouan and Laugier 2009).

Many of the forms of exaggerated autonomy found in schizophrenia seem to involve a denial of this founding complementarity of autonomy and heteronomy – as if the patient believed, against all reason and experience, that *he* at least might be able to transcend all dependence on other human beings or on surrounding tradi-tions, cultural forms, or even material realities. The solipsism of a patient like Adolf Wölfli (the *art brut* artist mentioned above) – self-enclosed within his virtual uni-verse – is perhaps the most extreme expression of this defiant ambition. It is as if what Wölfli relishes above all else, in his imaginary flights, is the sense of moving through space without the slightest resistance, conjuring worlds at will.

In *Dynamics of Character*, Shapiro (2000) interprets persons with schizophrenia as seeking to bring about an extreme, "anxiety-forestalling surrender of volition and

---

[28] See also Taylor's criticism of the notion of "radical choice" (Taylor 1976).

agency" (p. 133); he contrasts this with the more traditional notion of "a defensively motivated turning-away from reality or the external world" (p. 142). An alternative view might emphasize the desire to deny, not agency *or* the world, but that inextricable mix of freedom and constraint, agency and obstacle, activity and passivity that defines the fabric of a normal *relationship* to social and objective reality. And this, in turn, might imply a somewhat different therapeutic goal and ideal, one in which the virtues of dependency and acceptance, and of the passions, might hold a place equal to those of independence or free-agency.

It is noteworthy in this context that autonomy has emerged as the dominant value in modern and postmodern societies, which are highly individualistic and interiorizing (Gauchet 2003; Taylor 1985). This may be especially true of the USA. Perhaps we are in danger of overemphasizing autonomy's advantages; perhaps also of imposing it too readily as a therapeutic goal and yardstick (often using the rhetoric of "empowerment") to the exclusion of some opposing but ultimately complementary ideals.[29] Overemphasis on the autonomy ideal may, incidentally, be due to institutional changes as well as cultural factors – namely, the near-elimination of the "total institution" for the treatment of chronic mental illness in favor of supposedly more community-based, independent forms of living. It is interesting, in this light, to recall the findings of the World Health Organization cross-cultural studies that found somewhat better life outcomes among patients in underdeveloped countries, perhaps because these cultures and societal settings place less emphasis on the necessity of independence and productive autonomy (Lin and Kleinman 1988). This might suggest that fostering *interdependence* is a more appropriate goal around which to organize treatment. The issue is complex; however, one must also bear in mind findings that suggest that persons with schizophrenia may do better (as indexed by rates of re-hospitalization) when they are *not* required to engage in too much social interaction, but are allowed instead to find their own comfort zone, which typically involves an idiosyncratic lifestyle and rather minimal levels of social interaction (see the ethnographic studies done in Montreal: Corin 1990). Current notions of "recovery" in the treatment of schizophrenia should take care not to overemphasize the ideals of normal role functioning and a conventional sense of identity.

I conclude by mentioning one last defense of the diminished-autonomy hypothesis. If careful analysis of "autonomy" shows that it *presupposes* heteronomy (as just suggested), one might argue that a denial of heteronomy amounts also to a denial of autonomy. *True* autonomy, one might say, just *is* normal autonomy, with its moderate degree of free-agency and its appropriate grounding in custom, interdependence, and the social order. Such a view recalls the "substantialist" and "strong externalist" viewpoint of philosophers who explicitly identify certain objective conditions – such as sanity or mental health – as necessary conditions for autonomy. In an important article, for example, Susan Wolf (1987) argues that the ability to distinguish good

---

[29] For an excellent study of the autonomy ideal and its possible association with psychopathology and conceptions thereof, see Ehrenberg (1998).

from bad and to allow one's perceptions and reactions to be guided by external reality[30] (conditions of mental health that are not necessarily identifiable by the subject himself, or under his control) are among the *essential* criteria for having liberty or free will.[31] Wolf also argues that sanity requires the capacity, not for self-*creation* – which is an impossibility – but for self-*correction* in accord with one's sensitivity to reality and moral demands. Such an approach might well be congenial to David Shapiro; it might in fact already be implicit in his reference to true autonomy as implying "flexibility" (AR p. 74).

Wolf's position (like Shapiro's) is subtly argued and has a strong intuitive appeal. It can be criticized, however, on various grounds. For one thing, it seems to lead to a conflation of descriptive with normative issues, thereby obscuring any possible distinction between personal "autonomy" and such other virtues as engagement, loyalty, good judgment, or other notions of the valued or the good (Jouan 2008, p. 20). From a psychopathological standpoint, her position rather begs the question by simply *defining* autonomy and insanity as mutually exclusive.[32] It may seem at first that the "capacity for self-correction" does provide a clear distinguishing criterion – given that the schizophrenic individual's extreme eccentricity and insistence on absolute independence may be *itself* quite beyond the individual's capacity for self-modification. On reflection, however, the adequacy of this latter criterion seems questionable. After all, one must admit that the practical and conventional orientation of the *normal* individual is not *itself* within such an individual's awareness or under his control; and also that this normal orientation did not come about as the product of any volitional choice. On reflection, in fact, it is hard to deny that there is at least some validity in the view that persons with schizophrenia occasionally adopt toward normal individuals: namely that, in our unthinking acceptance of custom and convention, we do indeed behave a bit like "believaological imbeciles."

The substantialist approach – equating *true* autonomy with *normal* or *sane* autonomy – cannot be refuted by any decisive argument. It should not be allowed, however, to obscure the diversity of meanings that the term "autonomy" can have. Personally, I am dubious about the prospects of discovering *any* fully adequate way of analyzing the nature of "autonomy" – whether for normal individuals or across the spectrum of psychopathology. What is most needed in this domain, it seems to me, is not the analytic approach (of, say, a Donald Davidson or Harry Frankfurt) but the more skeptical or deconstructive spirit of Ludwig Wittgenstein – who would surely view "autonomy" as an irredeemably ambiguous, family-resemblance concept. Such an approach is, in my opinion, fundamentally consistent with the essential spirit and thrust of Shapiro's own perspective, with its distinctive appreciation for

---

[30] In a later work, Susan Wolf describes this as the ability to act in conformity with and on the basis of the True and the Good (Wolf 2005, p. 71).

[31] For a similar approach, see Honneth (1993).

[32] At the end of her article, Wolf (1987) explicitly acknowledges the normative nature of her concept of mental health, and hence of her notion of autonomy.

complexity and nuance. From a psychopathologist's standpoint, the most important thing is, after all, to "save the phenomena," i.e., to avoid any theoretical perspective that might blind us to the complexity and diversity of the actual phenomena at issue. And to describe all forms of schizophrenia (or of psychopathology in general) as manifestations of pseudo- or diminished autonomy – meaning diminished *normal* autonomy – risks effacing the forms of *exaggerated* autonomy that are also common both in schizophrenia and some other conditions. Such a move is too likely to make us neglect symptoms that are neither "passive-reactive" nor "rigid" in the sense of a blind following of rules. These would include experiences (however deluded) of omnipotence, as well as hyperawareness of volitional choice, ways of defying convention, acts of exaggerated volition, and certain expressions of radical independence.

Acknowledgement For helpful comments on drafts of this article, I am grateful to Steven Silverstein, James Walkup, Barnaby Nelson, Shira Nayman, Pierre-Henri Castel, Alain Ehrenberg, Saneke de Haan, and Craig Piers.

References

Arpaly, N. (2004). Which autonomy? In J. K. Campbell, M. O'Rourke, & D. Shier (Eds.), *Freedom and determinism* (pp. 173–188). Cambridge: MIT Press.

Barham, P. (1984). *Schizophrenia and human value*. Oxford: Blackwell.

Berrios, G. E. (1991). Delusions as "wrong beliefs": A conceptual history. *British Journal of Psychiatry 159* (Suppl. 14), 6–13.

Berze, J., & Gruhle, H. W. (1929). *Psychologie der schizophrenie*. Berlin: Springer.

Binswanger, L. (1956). *Drei Formen missglückten Daseins*. Tubingen: Max Niemeyer (quoted in Stanghellini & Ballerini 2007).

Binswanger, L. (1987). Extravagance, perverseness, manneristic behavior and schizophrenia. In J. Cutting & M. Shepherd (Eds.), *The clinical roots of the schizophrenia concept* (pp. 83–88). Cambridge: Cambridge University Press.

Blankenburg, W. (1971). *Der Verlust der natürlichen Selbstverständniskeit*. Stuttgart: Ferdinand Enke.

Blankenburg, W. (2001). First steps toward a psychopathology of 'common sense'. *Philosophy, Psychiatry & Psychology, 8*, 303–315.

Bleuler, E. (1950). *Dementia praecox or the group of schizophrenias* (J. Zinkin, Transl.). New York: International Universities Press.

Bleuler, M. (1978). The schizophrenic disorders. New Haven/London: Yale University Press.

Castel, P.-H. (2009). Folie et responsabilité (Contrepoint philosophique à "Moi, Pierre Rivière..."). In M. Jouan & S. Laugier (Eds.), *Comment penser l'autonomie ? Entre compétences et dépendances*. Paris : PUF.

Christman, J. (1991). Autonomy and personal history. *Canadian Journal of Philosophy, 21*, 1–24.

Corin, E. (1990). Facts and meaning in psychiatry: An anthropological approach to the lifeworld of schizophrenics. *Culture, Medicine, and Psychiatry, 14*, 153–188..

Cutting, J. (2009). Scheler, phenomenology, and psychopathology. *Philosophy, Psychiatry, Psychology, 16*, 143–159.

Ehrenberg, A. (1998). *La fatigue d'être soi: Dépression et societé*. Paris: Odile Jacob.

Frankfurt, H. (1971). Freedom of the will and the concept of a person. *Journal of Philosophy, 68*, 5–21.

Gauchet, M. (2003). *La condition historique*. Paris: Gallimard.

Hackett, P. (1952). *The cardboard giants*. New York: G. P. Putnam's Sons.

Hemsley, D.R. (2005). The development of a cognitive model of schizophrenia: Placing it in context. *Neuroscience and Biobehavioral Reviews, 29*, 977–988.

Heveroch, Dr. (1913). Über die Störungen des Ichtums. Zeitschrift für die gesamte Neurologie and Psychiatrie, 19: 422–496 (cited in Landis, 1964, p. 347).

Honneth, A. (2008). *L'autonomie décentrée : Les conséquences de la critique moderne du sujet pour la philosophie morale*. In M. Jouan (Ed.), *Psychologie morale : Autonomie, responsabilité, et rationalité pratique* (pp. 347–363). Paris: Vrin (original in German, 1993).

Jouan, M. (2008). *Introduction générale*. In M. Jouan (Ed.), *Psychologie morale: Autonomie, responsabilité, et rationalité pratique* (pp. 7–37). Paris : Vrin.

Jouan, M. (2009). *Les limites de l'expression de soi chez Harry Frankfurt : Une lecture de* La Vie des Autres. In M. Jouan and S. Laugier (Eds.), *Comment penser l'autonomie ?*(pp. 319–342). Paris: Presses Universitaires de France.

Jouan, M., & Laugier, S. (2009). *Présentation*. In M. Jouan & S. Laugier (Eds.), *Comment penser l'autonomie?* (pp. 1–16). Paris: Presses Universitaires de France.

Kant, I. (1965). *The critique of pure reason*, Unabridged Edition, translated by N. K. Smith. New York: St Martin's (from 2nd ed., 1787).

Laing, R. D. (1965). *The divided self*. Harmondsworth: Penguin.

Landis, C. (1964). *Varieties of psycho-pathological experience*. New York: Holt, Rinehart & Winston.

Lecours, A. R., & M. Vanier-Clement,M. (1976). Schizophasia and jargonaphasia, *Brain and Language, 3*, 1976.

Lin, K.-M., & Kleinman, A. (1988). Psychopathology and clinical course of schizophrenia: A cross-cultural perspective. *Schizophrenia Bulletin, 14*, 555–567..

Menand, L. Regrets only: Lionel Trilling and his discontents, *New Yorker*, Dec 27 2008.

Merleau-Ponty, M. (1962). *Phenomenology of perception* (Transl. C. Smith). London: Routledge & Kegan Paul.

Minkowski, E. (1927). *La Schizophrénie*. Paris: Payot.

Møller, P., & Husby, R. (2000). The initial prodrome in schizophrenia: Searching for naturalistic core dimensions of experience and behavior. *Schizophrenia Bulletin, 26*, 217–232.

Pfander, A. (1911). Motive and motivation. In A. Pfander (Ed.), *Münchner philophische abhandlungen (Festschrift für Theodor Lipps)* (pp. 163–195). Leipzig: Barth.

Ricoeur, P. (1966). *Freedom and nature: The voluntary and the involuntary* (Transl. F. V. Kovak). Chicago: Northwestern University Press.

Ryan, R. M., Kuhl, J., & Deci, E. L. (1997). Nature and autonomy: An organizational view of social and neurobiological aspects of self-regulation in behavior and development. *Development and Psychopathology, 9*, 701–728.

Sass, L. (1992). *Madness and modernism: Insanity in the light of modern art, literature, and thought*. New York: Basic Books (Harvard paperback 1994).

Sass, L. (1994). *The paradoxes of delusion: Wittgenstein, Schreber, and the schizophrenic mind*. Ithaca/London: Cornell University Press.

Sass, L. (1997). Adolf Wölfli, spatiality, and the sublime. In E. Spoerri (Ed.), *Adolf Wölfli: Draftsman, poet, composer* (pp. 136–145). Ithaca/London: Cornell University Press.

Sass, L. (2001). Self and world in schizophrenia: Three classic approaches. *Philosophy, Psychiatry, Psychology, 8*, 251–270.

Sass, L. (2004). Affectivity in schizophrenia: A phenomenological perspective. *Journal of Consciousness Studies, 11*, 127–147.

Sass, L. (2007). "Person with schizophrenia" or "schizophrenic person": Reflections on illness and the self. *Theory and Psychology, 17*, 395–420..

Sass, L., & Parnas, J. (2007). Explaining schizophrenia: The relevance of phenomenology. In M.C. Chung, K.W.M. Fulford, & G. Graham (Eds.), *Reconceiving schizophrenia* (pp. 63–95). Oxford: Oxford University Press..

Shapiro, D. (1965). *Neurotic styles*. New York: Basic Books.

Shapiro, D. (1981). *Autonomy and rigid character*. New York: Basic Books.

Shapiro, D. (2000). *Dynamics of character*. New York: Basic Books.

Stanghellini, G. (2004). *Disembodied spirits and deanimated bodies: The psychopathology of common sense*. Oxford: Oxford University Press.

Stanghellini, G. (2010). Commonsense, disembodiment, and delusions in schizophrenia. In G. Dimaggio, & P. H. Lysaker (Eds.), *Metacognition and severe adult mental disorders: Crossing from basic research to treatment*, 134–149.

Stanghellini, G., & Ballerini, M. (2007). Values in persons with schizophrenia. *Schizophrenia Bulletin, 33*, 131–141.

Stanghellini, G., & Monti, M. R. (1993). Influencing and being influenced: The other side of 'bizarre delusions'. *Psychopathology, 26*, 165–169.

Strauss, J. (1989). Subjective experiences of schizophrenia. *Schizophrenia Bulletin, 15*, 179–187.

Taylor, C. (1976). Responsibility for self. In A. Rorty (Ed.), *The identities of persons* (pp. 281–299). Berkeley: University of California Press.

Taylor, C. (1985). The person. In M. Carrithers, S. Collins, & S. Lukes (Eds.), *The category of the person: Anthropology, philosophy, history* (pp. 257–281). Cambridge: Cambridge University Press.

Thalberg, I. (1978). Hierarchical analysis of unfree action. *Canadian Journal of Philosophy, 8*, 211–225.

Watson, G. (1975). Free agency. *Journal of Philosophy, 72*, 205–220.

Winnicott, D. W. (1958). The capacity to be alone. *International Journal of Psychoanalysis, 39*, 416–420.

Wolf, S. (1987). Sanity and the metaphysics of responsibility. In F. Shoeman (Ed.), *Responsibility, character, and the emotions: New essays in moral philosophy* (pp. 46–62). Cambridge: Cambridge University Press..

Wolf, S. (1993). The real self view. In J. Fischer & M. Ravizza (Eds.), *Perspectives on moral responsibility* (pp. 151–170). Ithaca: Cornell University Press..

Wolf, S. (2005). Freedom within reason. In J. S. Taylor (Ed.), *Personal autonomy: New essays on personal autonomy and its role in contemporary moral philosophy* (pp. 258–274). Cambridge: Cambridge University Press.

Woods, W. (1938). Language study in schizophrenia, Journal of Nervous and Mental Disease, 87, 290–316.

Reply to Louis Sass

David Shapiro

The main concern of Dr. Sass' thoughtful essay is my contention that schizophrenic symptoms reflect and can be explained as a radical failure of autonomous self-direction and capacity for volitional direction of thought. I characterize the form of this loss of autonomy as an extreme kind of helpless passivity of self-direction. In Sass' view, my characterization of schizophrenia in this way is a simplification of the facts; in particular, he points to a fairly common schizophrenic symptom that is, or seems to be, directly contradictory to what I propose, namely a "heightened" or "exaggerated" experience of autonomy, as in a conviction of great mastery or knowingness. This question involves further, important questions, about the meaning of autonomy and, also, about the relation of this kind of passivity of self-direction to rigidity.

Sass concurs that an impairment of autonomous self-direction, or, as it has been called, willless-ness, is a central schizophrenic symptom. He maintains, however, that this is not the whole story. That any theoretical statement on schizophrenia is not the whole story is hard to refute, but I do not think that the kind of phenomena Sass offers actually substantiates his view. He argues that some schizophrenic individuals instead of the surrender of autonomy to passive helplessness that I describe, show its opposite, a "heightened" or "exaggerated" autonomy. Examples of such heightened autonomy are ideas or feelings of great mastery or control, or special knowingness. Sass suggests the term "alternative autonomy" for this phenomenon as opposed to the "normal autonomy." He anticipates that these exaggerated forms of autonomy might be dismissed as merely defensive, in a compensatory way, but rejects that argument, to my mind correctly, as insufficient. Deluded ideas of mastery or omniscience might well be defensively motivated in an individual whose volitional self-direction is actually impaired, but motivation alone is not enough to explain a defensive process. Any defensive process must also be shown to be a plausible product of more general attitudes or ways of thinking.

It is a fact that exaggerated ideas of the sort Sass calls examples of an alternative type of autonomy, are commonly found in rigid characters, both obsessive compulsive and paranoid. But these ideas turn out not to represent an alternative kind of autonomy so much as being a product of the impaired autonomy characteristic of rigid character. We see, for instance, the seemingly confident dogmatism and stubbornness of some compulsive individuals. The dogmatic person sticks to an opinion, the "right" or, as he sees it, authoritative opinion without regard for common sense, reasonable proportions or particular circumstances. The very purposefulness of their outlook allows a narrowly selective observation and the easy establishment of firm conviction. But this seemingly confident person is thrown into anxiety when he cannot avoid making a personal choice. His leaning on authoritative opinion and narrowly selective confirmation of it constitute at the same time the limitation of his autonomy and the appearance, even the experience, of a heightened or exaggerated knowingness.

In paranoid individuals, a still more rigid cognitive style typically has the result of still greater exaggeration of knowingness and mastery, especially in the form of their knowing suspiciousness and often evident also in a defensive arrogance. But, again, the rigid prejudice that grasps immediately confirming evidence of what is expected, or defensively required, represents an autonomy or volitional direction of attention whose appearance of heightened mastery is in fact a direct symptom of a diminished mastery. Furthermore, the immediacy with which the expected evidence is identified, the clue, increases in direct relation to the rigidity of the expectation. It is not too much to say that increasingly the expected and confirming evidence, more and more purposefully and narrowly selected from its context and therefore less and less constrained by realistic proportions, compels the paranoid individual's attention. At the point of psychosis a word on the radio becomes enough to reveal the message. In other words, the greater the approach to prescience, the greater the actual diminishment of volitional direction of attention, or autonomy. In the extreme case, the immediacy of recognition of an inevitably confirming element reaches the point of a total failure of active, critical judgment and, as one patient said, the threatening message "jumped out" at her from a passing billboard. In short, seemingly active knowingness reveals itself as helpless revelation.

Still, Sass has a point. It is true that a phenomenological difference should not be dismissed and, at least until it reaches extremes in schizophrenia, even the illusion of actively directed thought and action is different from a more frank surrender of autonomy. But I think that difference is very much smaller than Sass believes it to be.

Sass also questions whether my contention of a failure of autonomy in the form of a loss of volitional focus on the object of interest is the correct explanation for the schizophrenic's awareness of what is normally peripheral and unnoticed, such as the sound of word syllables or the brightness of colors. He suggests that this weakness of "goal presentation" or clear focus may just as likely be a result of a general weakness of affective interest. But this phenomenon seems to be observed in acute schizophrenic states in which there is no indication of a general weakness of affective interest. On the contrary, Interest does not seem to be absent, only help-lessly distracted and held. Even the patient Sass quotes, Renee, is "riveted" and frightened by strange perceptions. Similarly in the case of the acutely psychotic patient I mentioned above who reported that a fearful message "jumped out at her" from an advertising billboard.

I am not inclined to say, as Sass assumes I might, that the "yardstick" of mental health is the capacity for autonomy or self-directed action and that degrees of psychopathology correlate with a person's distance from this "ideal." That is because I do not believe that kinds of psychopathology or for that matter various kinds of diminished autonomy can easily be measured on a linear scale. The loss of autonomy in psychopathology is in my view a general result of the individual's estrangement from his subjective life, and that estrangement takes many forms. Thus, the authority of routines and internal rules in the compulsive person obstructs consciousness of spontaneous wishes and feelings, and he tells us that he lives like a train running on a fixed track; in the hysterical character serious, deliberate reflection is inhibited; she is easily suggestible and acts, she says, only according to her emotional reactions. In other words, the general result of these restrictive styles is the individual's loss of full consciousness of his or her own motivational experience; hence, in one way or another, the loss of agency or autonomous self-direction.

The process of defense is not consciously purposeful, although it usually does involve some conscious participation. One cannot say that "the patient brings (it) about." A self-protective reaction does not require knowledge of purpose. The individual personality includes a regulatory system according to which anxiety or stress prompts or triggers some anxiety or discomfort dispelling reaction. It is in line with this general principle that I have proposed that schizophrenia does not involve a breakdown of an existing defense system, as has been thought, but a radical exaggeration of it. (I take it for granted that genetic factors play a part in the liability to such a process.)

The formal separation of neurotic conditions and schizophrenia is not as great as might be thought. The characterological nature of neurotic conditions makes it clear that neurotic defense processes do not involve only the individual's internal relations with himself, but also his cognition and his relationship with the external world in general. The fundamental formal dimensions of the schizophrenic's impaired relationship with the external world – loss of reality, degradation of affective response, weakening of the distinctness of the self (or "ego boundaries"), and limitation of autonomous (or fully volitional) direction of thought and action – are all to be found in the defensive styles of nonpsychotic conditions as well, in much more moderate forms, of course, and often given different names or simply unrecognized. In other words, the rigid and passively reactive neurotic styles in which the experience of personal agency and agency itself are diminished and anxiety thereby forestalled find a correspondence in schizophrenia. This does not mean that schizophrenic and nonpsychotic conditions are different only in degree; it speaks only of a correspondence of essential features. It is this correspondence that lends credence to the hypothesis that the symptoms of schizophrenia, in particular the radical loss of autonomy, constitute a defensive system.

The defensive nature of the schizophrenic loss of autonomy does not, any more than in the dynamics of neurotic conditions, seem inconsistent with symptomatic fluctuations in different circumstances, nor with the possibility of artistic creativeness in connection with such fluctuations, nor with the coexistence of an unacknowledged realistic self-awareness – what Sass describes well as "double bookkeeping." Nor, as far as I can see, is it inconsistent with the inference that these modes of diminished agency originated in early childhood, are retained in normal adult life in spontaneity or unreflective routine, and are also available for defensive aims.

I have used several terms as essentially synonymous with "autonomy," usually in order to convey its particular subjective quality in a given context. As to its further definition, let me add another to the locutions Sass lists. He mentions early in his essay that the purpose of psychotherapy (from the point of view I advocate) must be to increase self awareness and agency. I can hardly imagine that a therapist could describe its purpose in that lofty way and still expect the patient to return. But in the case that patients ask I do sometimes say something like that. I say that the aim of therapy is to help people know clearly what they want and want to do. Perhaps that is the best definition of personal autonomy of all. Judging from what Sass writes, the philosopher Harry Frankfurt might agree.

Rejoinder to David Shapiro

Louis A. Sass

I am grateful for David Shapiro's response to my paper, and have only a few clarifying comments to make in reply.

My first comment concerns the general contention, in my paper, that Shapiro relies very heavily on the notion of "autonomy" to conceptualize both mental health and mental disturbance. I see now, on reflection, that it was perhaps unfortunate to describe Shapiro as treating autonomy as what I called a "yardstick" for mental health. As I discuss in detail in the early part of my article, Shapiro is nothing if not subtle and qualitative in his conception of the mind and human experience; he is clearly not a theorist given to thinking in terms of uni-dimensional or merely quantitative measures. He is not a linear thinker, but one who recognizes that small increments in degree can lead to overall reorganizations of character – as in the transition from obsessive-compulsive to paranoid or from neurotic to psychotic forms of organization.[33] "Yardstick" is thus a rather un-Shapiro-esque and inapt metaphor. But as a point of clarification, I would note (and expect that Shapiro would agree) that my key point about the centrality of "autonomy" in his overall conceptualization, is not at issue. Indeed, in the course of his reply, Shapiro himself suggests that, "in one way or another, the loss of agency or autonomous self-direction" does seem to be a virtually universal characteristic of psychopathology; and slightly later he states that, for him, the point of therapy is clearly to increase both self-awareness and agency, thus implying that agency is *the*, or at least *a*, key criterion of mental health.

A second comment concerns Shapiro's response to my argument for the possible autonomy, even heightened autonomy, to be found at least *some* of the time and in *some* cases of schizophrenia. In characterizing my argument, Shapiro only mentions my assertion that such individuals may often have the *experience* or the *idea* of their own power or capacity for control. I do indeed point this out. But a crucial part of my argument is that such individuals will also (at least at times) engage in *actions* that are consistent with their wishes and claims of autonomy; for as I point out, only then would one be able to argue that such persons have heightened autonomy according to the rather specific philosophical criteria (from Harry Frankfurt and Charles Taylor) discussed in my paper.

As a third comment, I would note that, in his reply, Shapiro focuses on obsessive-compulsive and paranoid phenomena in particular. Paranoia is obviously an important symptom or aspect of many cases of schizophrenia; it is not,

---

[33]Re this point, see Chapter 10.

however, universal or constant in the illness. An important feature of schizophrenia that can be antithetical to the kinds of rigidity on which Shapiro focuses in his reply is the "loss of natural self-evidence" classically described by the German phenomenological psychiatrist Wolfgang Blankenburg. Patients who lose this sense of natural self-evidence may, in a certain sense, have a cognitive style that is *too* free or *too* free-floating, in that they may see more possibilities for interpreting stimulus situations than are compatible with effective action in conventional circumstances; this can be described as a lack of "perspectival abridgment" of consciousness (Sass 1992, p. 144). This is, at the least, a condition radically different from paranoid rigidity – even though, in some cases, it may ultimately give rise to such rigidity, perhaps as a kind of escape or defense.

My fourth comment concerns the issue of loss of goal-presentation, affect, and diminished autonomy. One point made in my chapter was that schizophrenia patients may well represent, in some instances, a diminishment of what Max Scheler termed *Lebensdrang*, the latter referring to a kind of life-drive or impulse that motivates one to seek certain desired objects in the world and to see the world in light of that pattern of desires and drives. It seems to me that it is perfectly possible for a person to experience a diminishment of such *Lebensdrang* while simultaneously experiencing certain kinds of intense affect, such as anxiety or even types of fear. Indeed it is possible that diminished *Lebensdrang* may actually *give rise* to cognitive confusion. This is because the lack of any motivational orientation, of any sense of things *mattering*, will deprive the cognitive/perceptual world of one crucial form of organization; the sense of confusion that results may lead, in turn, to forms of anxiety or a kind of generalized fear. In my view, to understand the realm of affect in schizophrenia, it is necessary to make a distinction between what might be called "emotion" in a relatively narrow sense, and other forms of affect that may be less associated with desire and less directed toward particular targets in the world. Elsewhere I have argued that some of the confusing, even paradoxical-seeming features of schizophrenia can only be understood if one grasps the possibility that such patients may experience, at the same moment, *both* a diminishment of *some* kinds of affect (namely, the truly "emotional" sort) *and* an intensification of affect of other kinds (namely, less targeted, mood-like affects such as ontological insecurity, awe, or a sense of cosmic omnipotence; Sass 2004, 2007).

A fifth and final comment is simply to note that there are a number of points in David Shapiro's response with which I fully agree: namely, regarding the existence of significant affinities between aspects of schizophrenia and of non-schizophrenic or neurotic conditions, and also the important role that defensive processes may play in schizophrenia. Nothing in my own paper is meant to dispute either of these two points; indeed, at the beginning of my paper I say much in appreciation of Shapiro's illuminating discussions of these sorts of issues.

Let me close by saying what a great honor it has been for me to respond to David Shapiro—an author who in my view, has written some of the richest and most clinically relevant works on psychopathology to be produced in the past or current century.

References

Sass, L. (2004) Affectivity in schizophrenia: A phenomenological perspective. *Journal of Consciousness Studies, 11*, 127–147. Also appeared in D. Zahavi (Ed.) (2004). *Hidden resources: Classical perspectives on subjectivity* (pp. 127–147). Exeter: Imprint Academic.

Sass, L. (2007). Contradictions of emotion in schizophrenia. *Cognition and Emotion, 21*, 351–390.

Part III
The Psychology of Defense

Chapter 6
Reconceptualizing Defense, Unconscious Processes, and Self-Knowledge: David Shapiro's Contribution

Morris N. Eagle

Introduction

David Shapiro is an original, lucid, and independent thinker. Although obviously strongly influenced by psychoanalytic theory and practice, Shapiro does not easily fit into this or that psychoanalytic "school." If one had to place him somewhere in the world of psychoanalytic theory, one would locate him in the broad category of ego psychology, a placement partly dictated by the obvious influence on his work of Reich's character analysis and the writings and thoughts of his teacher, Helmuth Kaiser. However, as we will see, Shapiro's thinking defies any straightforward assignment to a particular "school."

I will address the following issues that play a prominent role in Shapiro's work and that also speak to my interests:

1. A reconceptualization of repression from mechanism to character style.
2. From the unconscious to gradations of consciousness: the role of attention and articulation.
3. Third-person versus first-person self-knowledge: from estrangement to personal avowal.
4. The adaptive and maladaptive consequences of defense: the role of context and situation.
5. Defensive style in relation to external trauma compared to inner conflict.

Although the last two issues are not prominently or explicitly present, I believe they are implicit in Shapiro's writings.

M.N. Eagle (✉)
Professor Emeritus, Derner Institute of Advanced Psychological Studies,
Adelphi University, Garden City, NY 11530
and
Distinguished Educator-in-Residence, California Lutheran University,
Thousand Oaks, CA 91362
e-mail: meagle100@aol.com

C. Piers (ed.), *Personality and Psychopathology: Critical Dialogues with David Shapiro*,   135
DOI 10.1007/978-1-4419-6214-0_6, © Springer Science+Business Media, LLC 2011

A Reconceptualization of Repression: From Mechanism to Character Style

As Shapiro (1965) brilliantly elucidated in his classic, *Neurotic Styles*, the individual's "choice of neurosis," including his or her "choice" of defenses and symptoms, is inextricably linked to, indeed, is one expression of, that individual's character style, that is, his or her ways of thinking, experiencing, and behaving. From this perspective, the defense employed by an individual is not a mechanism, but a characteristic way of functioning. For example, given the hysterical character's global and impressionistic style of functioning, one would expect that repression would be his or her characteristic way of dealing with actual and potential unpleasant and distressing experiences. Thus, on this view, repressive defenses are not simply "mechanisms" that an individual employs, but rather constitute expressions of his or her character style.

The heuristic value of viewing repression as a *personality style* rather than a "mechanism" is well illustrated by the history of research on repression. For many years, numerous attempts were made to demonstrate the existence of repression in the experimental laboratory. The assumption seemed to be that as a "mechanism," under the proper conditions, one should be able to trigger and observe repression operating in anyone. This approach led to more than 50 years of essentially wasted effort (Holmes 1990). What passed for repression in the experimental laboratory were such phenomena as greater forgetting of nonsense syllables paired with electric shock – a finding that has little or nothing to do with the psychoanalytic concept of repression – or for that matter Freud (1915), with much of anything in the real world.

The heuristic value of the concept of repression became evident once it was defined in a more clinically meaningful and "ecologically valid" way and once the focus of research was directed to *individual differences in repressive style as a personality variable*. Doing so led to fruitful research and the demonstration of significant links between "repressive style" and ecologically meaningful areas of behavior, including physiological arousal, physical symptoms and illness, autobiographical recall, and styles of thought. Although there is no evidence that Shapiro's work directly influenced this productive shift, it is certainly congruent with the basic orientation of the widely read *Neurotic Styles*.

As Davis (1990) has noted, if repression is real but cannot easily be operationalized in the laboratory, one strategic option is to study repression as a personality trait, identify individuals who characteristically adopt a repressive mode of coping, and then attempt "to demonstrate predictable phenomena associated with (the use of) repression" (p. 388). Weinberger (1990) and others operationally defined a repressor as someone who reports low anxiety (e.g., on the Byrne 1961) and also scores high on defensiveness on self-report measures (e.g., the Marlowe–Crowne Scale). In addition, despite the verbal report of low distress, the repressor characteristically shows *greater* autonomic reactivity and other indirect evidence of anxiety, such as greater speech disruption. In other words, there is a disjunction between report of conscious experience and indices of anxiety.

Employing the above relatively simple and straightforward measures, investigators have been able to lawfully and predictably link repressive style to a variety of other significant variables. Let me provide a few examples: using a phrase-association task, Weinberger, Schwartz, and Davidson (1979) found that repressors showed greater verbal avoidance of affective (i.c., sexual and aggressive) material, significantly longer reaction times, and greater increases during the task on a number of physiological measures (e.g., skin's resistance, heart rate, and frontalis electromyographic activity). Compared to a non-defensive low-anxiety group, repressors reported significantly less negative emotion to hypothetical events that would normally evoke such emotions (Weinberger and Schwartz 1982).

Consistent with these results, Weinberger et al. (1979) found that when asked to describe in a few words the most "outstanding or important characteristics" of their personality, repressors "often defined themselves as individuals who do *not* become upset" and who "often explicitly excluded [the experience of negative affect] from what they defined as their central self-concept" (Weinberger, 1990, p. 348).

Employing the Rorschach Index of Repressive Style (Levine and Spivak 1963, 1964), Luborsky et al. (1965) studied the relationship between repressive style and pattern of eye fixations when subjects inspected each of ten pictures for a 10-s period. They found that repressors literally engaged in less looking-about – their fixations were less scattered. This relationship was particularly strong when pictures were of sexual content. Furthermore, repressors recalled less of the picture, particularly of the sexual pictures. These results are entirely compatible with Szalai and Eagle's (1992) finding that subjects who employ repressive-avoidant defenses attended less to the aggressive dimension of stimulus pictures and therefore had greater difficulty forming an aggressive concept.

In one study (Girdjonnson 1981), repressors showed the greatest discrepancy between subjective report of discomfort and physiological responses when answering a series of potentially embarrassing questions, such as "Do you ever steal things?" This finding of discrepancy between self-report and physiological responses (specifically, self-report of low distress or anxiety), and physiological responses indicating high distress or anxiety has "been demonstrated across a variety of tasks and psychophysiological indices" (Weinberger 1990, p. 356). Some findings in this area are quite impressive. For example, King et al. (1986) reported that in a sample of middle-aged sedentary men and women, repressors had significantly higher resting and submaximal systolic blood-pressure levels than control subjects. Further, and also quite impressive, repressors versus nonrepressors accounted for more of the variance in systolic blood-pressure changes during an arithmetic task than assessments of Type A behavior. Also, repressors had significantly higher total and low-density lipoprotein cholesterol levels than the low-anxious group.

Shedler et al. (1993) reported findings similar to those obtained by King et al. (1986). They found that subjects who look healthy on self-report scales but who are evaluated as distressed on the basis of a clinical interview show significantly higher physiological reactivity (heart rate or systolic blood pressure) during stressful laboratory tasks than both subjects who "look" healthy on both self-report measures and clinical interview and subjects who are distressed on both measures. They also score higher on "verbal defensiveness" on a phrase-association task than the other two groups. The authors describe these people who look healthy on self-report measures, but who are evaluated as distressed on clinical interviews and who show heightened physiological reactivity to stress, as manifesting "illusory mental health" rather than genuine mental health. They conclude that for these subjects, self-report mental health scales "were not assessing mental health…, but instead were assessing defensive denial" (p. 1127). It is clear that the "illusory mental health" subjects of this study are similar to the repressors of other studies. In both cases, the subjects' presentation of themselves as not distressed is belied by contradictory evidence of high distress. Furthermore, the defensive denial of distress seems to exact a physiological cost.

Behavioral indices other than psychophysiological ones also suggest that repressors are more distressed despite their self-report of low anxiety. Thus, they showed more verbal interference while carrying out a verbal task (Weinberger et al. 1979); a greater tendency to show facial expressions associated with anxiety (Asendorpf and Scherer 1983); and a greater impairment on cognitive and perceptual-motor tasks (Boor and Schill 1968).

There is a good deal of evidence that while the use of a repressive style may convince repressors that they are experiencing little distress, this self-deceptive strategy takes its toll. There are a number of studies that indicate that repressors are at greater risk for various physical illnesses than either individuals who acknowledge distress or non-defensive individuals with genuinely low distress. The illnesses for which repressors have been found to be at greater risk include hypertension (e.g., Davies 1970; Schwartz 1990) and asthma (e.g., Mathe and Knapp 1971). Weinberger et al. (1987) have reported a relationship between repressive style and proneness to physical illness in sixth graders.

Some investigators have attempted to identify possible mediating mechanisms between repressive style and greater proneness to physical illness. There is some evidence that repressive style may be associated with heightened release of stress-related hormones such as cortisol (e.g., Temnes and Kreyer 1985) and norepinephrine (e.g., Esler et al. 1977) and with suppression of the immune system (Jamner et al. 1988). There is also evidence that repressors tend to delay seeking diagnostic information and medical treatment (e.g., Hill and Gardner 1980; Willett and Heilbrown 1972).

Thus, the correlation between repressive style and heightened autonomic arousal has generally been interpreted as suggesting that the characteristic use of repression is causally responsible for the heightened arousal. The assumption most frequently made is that the operation of repression exacts a variety of costs, including physiological costs. Thus, Shedler et al. (1993) write that "Psychological defense has physiological costs. It is associated with autonomic reactivity and may be a risk factor for medical illness" (p. 1119).

What is not clear is why repression should be associated with heightened autonomic reactivity. Little is known regarding the specific mechanisms linking repression to autonomic reactivity. Although they do not discuss repression specifically, but rather the general behavior of holding back of thoughts and feelings connected with trauma, Pennebaker et al. (1988) suggest that "the inhibition or active holding back of thoughts, emotions, or behaviors is associated with physical work that, over time, can become manifested in disease" (p. 244). In other words, they suggest that avoidance or inhibition of certain thoughts and feelings is a stressor that renders one susceptible to illness. Their notion of the work involved in the inhibition of thoughts and emotions is quite similar to the psychoanalytic concept of the work of repression. In both cases, the assumption is made that the active chronic avoidance or inhibition of thoughts and feelings involves work that exacts a psychological and physiological cost.

One plausible alternative to the hypothesis that repressive style is causally implicated in heightened arousal is that repressors are predisposed to heightened autonomic reactivity and then deal with this tendency through a repressive coping method, in which the conscious experience of physiological arousal is dampened and minimized. This style, insofar as it permits repressors to function without the disruptive effects of chronic conscious experience of anxiety and heightened physiological arousal, would serve adaptive functions. In this alternative view, the correlation between repressive style and susceptibility to physical illness would be artifactual and would be accounted for by the relationship between the predisposition to heightened physiological arousal and the susceptibility to physical illness. The repressive style would constitute primarily a way of dealing with this general predisposition to heightened autonomic reactivity.

According to this alternative view, the maladaptive aspect of repression would lie, not in the direct physiological cost it supposedly involves, but largely in the fact that it prevents the individual from confronting and dealing with his or her difficulties and with the sources or precipitants of anxiety and autonomic arousal. Pennebaker and Beall (1986) and Pennebaker et al. (1988) present impressive evidence that confronting a trauma (by writing about it) that one has avoided thinking about results in a variety of beneficial effects upon follow-up, including a heightened immune reaction, fewer health center visits, a decline in systolic blood pressure, and a happier subjective state. These follow-up effects occurred despite the fact that immediately after writing about their traumas, these subjects reported higher levels of physical symptoms and negative moods than control subjects.

Pennebaker et al. (1988) hypothesize that by confronting one's thoughts and feelings connected to the trauma, rather than inhibiting or avoiding them, one can better understand and assimilate the trauma. They provide examples of several subjects who, in the course of writing about the same traumas day after day, gradually changed their perspectives and, so to speak, put the trauma to rest. They suggest, seemingly paradoxically, that the active inhibition and avoidance of thoughts and feelings about the trauma is conducive to a continuing obsession with it, while confronting it is more likely to lead to its resolution. This reminds one of Schlesinger's (1970) observation that the best way of preserving a mental content and keeping it active is by repressing it and conversely, the best way of truly forgetting it and putting it to rest is by lifting repression, confronting, and resolving it.

Pennebaker and his colleagues confine their research to the inhibition versus confrontation of thoughts and feelings about trauma. However, their findings and conclusions may also apply generally to thoughts and feelings that are associated with conflict, anxiety, guilt, shame, and other dysphoric affects. Indeed, this is a basic assumption made in psychoanalytic theory – namely, that the confrontation with and assimilation of these thoughts, in contrast to their avoidance and repression, is likely to be therapeutic (although one must qualify this assumption by noting that poorly timed, unmodulated, and hostile confrontations can be destructive rather than therapeutic). The basic goal of psychodynamic psychotherapy is to help people confront thoughts and feelings linked to trauma, conflict, anxiety, guilt, and shame in a setting that will permit them to assimilate and resolve these thoughts and feelings rather than be overwhelmed by them. Pennebaker et al.'s (1988) findings provide support for the legitimacy of this goal.

One can speculate, then, as an alternative to the currently accepted view, that it is not repression and avoidance that directly exact a physiological cost, but rather unresolved conflicts, underlying, even if denied, feelings of anxiety, guilt, and shame, and underlying preoccupations with unresolved traumas. The adaptive function of repression and avoidance would lie primarily in their ability to facilitate functioning without the continued overt intrusion of troubling thoughts and feelings into conscious experience. And the maladaptive consequence of repression and avoidance would lie, not in the direct physiological costs they supposedly entail, but in the chronic and continuing physiological and psychological costs exacted by unresolved conflicts, traumas, and the continued negative emotions and thoughts associated with these conflicts and traumas.

It is interesting to note the connection between this contemporary idea regarding the pathogenic potential of unresolved and unassimilated thoughts and feelings and both the similar pre-psychoanalytic idea regarding the pathogenic significance of mental contents isolated from the center of the personality (Janet 1889, cited in Ellenberger 1970, p.149) and the central psychoanalytic idea of attributing pathogenic potential to the repression of mental contents. These basic ideas have persisted for a very long time and one can understand much current research on repressive style as an attempt to understand why the repression, avoidance, and failure to assimilate certain thoughts and feelings should be associated with various forms of pathology.

From "The Unconscious" to Gradations of Consciousness: The Role of Attention and Articulation

Without explicitly stating that this is what he intends to do, Shapiro formulates a conception of defenses and of unconscious processes that, in important respects, is radically different from a classical psychoanalytic perspective. In part, this difference flows from Shapiro's view of defenses as something people do rather than as subpersonal mechanisms. Let me elucidate Shapiro's formulations and then link these formulations to similar related efforts to reconceptualize defenses and unconscious processes.

First, it seems clear that Shapiro has little truck with the notion of repressed feelings, thoughts, wishes, intentions, and so on being unconscious in the sense of being completely and utterly inaccessible to consciousness. Rather, he describes repression as the "failure to bring…thought content [i.e., an unpleasant fact or possibility], which is, as it were, on the *periphery of attention* (my italics) into sharp focus of attention…" (Shapiro 1965, p. 117). In other words, a repressed thought content is not deeply buried somewhere in "the unconscious," but rather is *not articulated*, not brought "into sharp focus of attention." In viewing conscious awareness versus unawareness in terms of deployment of attention, to a certain extent, Shapiro's thinking converges toward Rapaport's (1954) and Freud's (1950 [1895]) emphasis on the role of attention in rendering a mental content conscious. However, where Rapaport refers to impersonal mechanisms of deployment of "attention cathexis," Shapiro describes habitual ways of people dealing with unpleasant material, the ways they normally do things.

According to the classical view, particularly in the context of drive theory, a repressed mental content (e.g., a desire or wish) continues to strive for expression in consciousness and to gain access to motility and action. This is so because, on the classical view, given our psychobiological nature (i.e., given the nature of drives), simply because a wish is repressed does not mean that it will simply cease to push for expression and gratification. This tension between the opposing forces of the wish striving for expression and the ego forces of defense, disguise, delay, and control is, of course, what makes "the unconscious" a "dynamic unconscious" and what renders the classic conception of an id-ego model.

As far as I can tell, this is not the model adopted by Shapiro. Rather than viewing conflict as one between wish energized by a "blind" id pushing for discharge and ego defenses and structures, on Shapiro's view, certain themes and contents will be expressed only in a fleeting way, because the individual harbors thoughts, feelings, wishes, and so on that he or she will not fully articulate or "spell out."

This view of repressed thought contents as fleetingly conscious and relegated to the periphery of consciousness and of repression as equivalent to not articulating and not being brought "into sharp focus of attention" is quite similar to other formulations, including Fingarette's (1969) reconceptualization of repression as not "spelling out," and in some respects, Stern's (2003) emphasis on not formulating unformulated experiences. Along with Fingarette (1963) and Stern (as well as others), Shapiro essentially replaces the classical psychoanalytic conception of "the unconscious" with such notions as gradations of consciousness, periphery of consciousness, fleeting awareness, and unarticulated and unattended thoughts and feelings. In effect, Shapiro and others with a similar point of view, have returned to James' (1890) critique of unconscious processes and have adopted his replacement of "the unconscious" with the idea of fleeting and momentary states of consciousness. They also come much closer to Sartre's (1956) understanding of defense in terms of "bad faith" – a purposeful form of self-deception. It is also interesting to observe that the view of defense in terms of fleeting awareness and failure to articulate or "spell out" is quite congruent with Freud's early conception of repression (see Erdelyi 1993).

Consider, for example, Breuer and Freud's (1893–1895) account of the Lucy R case: Without going into the details of the case, Freud links Lucy R's conversion symptoms (the smell of burnt pudding and a smell of cigar smoke) to her repressed love for her employer and wishful fantasies that he returned her love. At one point, Freud says to Lucy R: "I believe that really you are in love with your employer, the Director, though perhaps without being aware of it yourself...." (p.117). Lucy R's response is: "Yes, I think that's true" (p.117). Freud queries further: "But if you knew you loved your employer why didn't you tell me?" (p.117). Lucy R responds: "I didn't know or rather I didn't want to know – I wanted to drive it out of my head and not think of it again; and I believe latterly that I have succeeded" (p.117). However, although "she even allowed herself to dwell on the gratifying hopes," once she realized the futility of her hopes, Lucy R "decided to banish the whole business from her mind" (Breuer and Freud 1893–1895, p.118). The point to be noted here is that although Freud refers to Lucy R's *repression*, she is certainly not totally unaware of her feelings of love for her employer and her fantasy that he will ask her to marry him. Rather, she wants to "drive it out of her head," that is, she tries not to attend to these thoughts and fantasies.

The conception of defense in terms of not attending and not articulating or "spelling out" has important clinical implications. Before elucidating these implications, I want to note something about Shapiro's style. His formulations, rather than being based on "top-down" theory, always seem to be derived from his astute clinical observations. These formulations then turn out to have important "bottom-up" theoretical implications.

Let me turn to the clinical implications of Shapiro's conception of defense. If conflictual and anxiety-laden thoughts and feelings are fleetingly experienced and left unarticulated rather than "deeply" unconscious, it would follow that interpretations are best directed, not at the "deep" unconscious, but at the surface, at material that is "almost fully conscious," that the patient, in some sense, knew all along. (See Wachtel 2003, for an insightful discussion of depth versus surface.) Of course, this is precisely the position taken by Gray (1994) and others whose focus is on "close process" defense analysis and who emphasize the importance of interpreting "at the surface." Quite congruent with Shapiro's focus on characterological style, Gray and others with a similar point of view tend not to think of the function of interpretation as uncovering repressed contents, but rather as revealing the patient's style, that is, how he or she deals with conflictual and anxiety-laden feelings and thoughts. As an expression of this point of view, Busch (2001) contrasts the uncovering of repressed contents with helping the patient understand how his or her mind works – in Shapiro's term, his or her ways of thinking, feeling, and behaving.

Third-person Versus First-person Self-knowledge: From Estrangement to Personal Avowal

From Shapiro's perspective, the neurotic individual has feelings, thoughts, aims, intentions, and so on, that are not adequately represented in his or her articulated consciousness. They are unrecognized and unarticulated. As Shapiro (1981) puts it,

"The neurotic process has created an articulation of consciousness that does not represent but in fact distorts actual feelings, wishes, interests, intentions, the actual state of subjective experience" (p. 26). One can say that the individual is *estranged* from aspects of what he or she actually feels, thinks, intends, and so on. Another way to put it is that the individual harbors thoughts and feelings that he or she does not know about, where "know" refers to recognizing and articulating.

I want to expand on this issue of forms of knowing by discussing the distinction between third-person and first-person self-knowledge and its relevance to therapeutic change. As Moran (2001) observes, first-person self-knowledge is characterized by immediacy and the fact that it does not require observational evidence and inference. Although it may occur, normally, one does not observe one's behavior and then infer one's desires, intentions, and wants. For example, I do not normally observe my behavior and then infer that I am thirsty. I just *feel* thirsty. And knowing that I want or intend, say, to go to the library to obtain a particular book does not normally rest on my observation of some aspect of myself. I just know that I want to go to the library. In contrast to first-person self-knowledge, third-person self-knowledge is based on observation and inference and, as such, is not essentially different from the way one acquires knowledge about a third person.

In some respects, the distinction between intellectual and emotional insight parallels the distinction between third-person and first-person self-knowledge. Although intellectual insight as well as third-person self-knowledge may be useful – for example, in bringing some order and meaning to what is experienced as chaotic and meaningless – generally, it does not bring about significant change.

Although he does not employ these terms, Shapiro provides some quintessential instances of people trying to understand their feelings, thoughts, and behavior through third-person self-knowledge, that is, the kinds of observational and inferential processes that are applicable to another person. In the first example, Shapiro (1981, p. 50) cites an obsessive patient who states, "I must be in love with her. She has all the qualities I want in a wife." This is a wonderful example of a kind of self-estrangement characterized by trying to "know" one's feelings on the basis of inference from observational evidence – all the qualities the woman has. It is also an excellent example of someone trying to argue himself into a feeling that he does not fully feel but believes he should feel (Piers, personal communication).

As a second example, Shapiro (1981, p. 21) cites a newspaper report of a successful business executive who has learned from his psychotherapy that his forging of checks was due to "forces of work within me that I was not consciously aware of" and that his professional success "required me to start punishing myself." This sort of knowing is a good example of what Moran refers to as third-person self-knowledge insofar as it is based on an inferential process that could just as easily be applied to a third person. It is also, of course, as third-person self-knowledge often is, a good example of merely intellectual understanding. As Shapiro (1989, pp. 117–118) observes, "mere information or facts, it seems, can produce only that kind of understanding that is called, although quite vaguely, 'intellectual' understanding, and results, at worst, in some superficial change of *behavior*, whereas the sort of change we call therapeutic is supposed to involve changes of feelings and attitude."

What is missing from the third-person self-knowledge described in the above examples that is present in first-person self-knowledge? Again, without using the terms third-person and first-person self-knowledge, Shapiro provides some important insights in addressing this question. He cites Kaiser's observation "that the neurotic person is not completely 'behind' what he says or does" (Shapiro 1981, p. 27). At another point, in describing a rigid dutiful attitude, Shapiro (1981, p. 87) makes a distinction between *carrying out* decisions and *making* decisions. The former can come about simply through following a routine; the latter requires *making a choice*, that is, standing behind one's aim or intention.

There are various ways of not standing behind one's feelings, intentions, etc. One way, illustrated by the above example and characteristic of the rigidly dutiful individual, is by transforming all possible *wants* into *shoulds*. This enables one to escape dealing with what one wants and the anxiety that accompanies the expression of one's wants. Another way, perhaps more typical of the hysterical character, is to fail to articulate or "spell out" one's desires, intentions, etc. Still another way, illustrated by the check-forging business executive, is to intellectualize about unconscious forces that are far removed from one's first-person experiences. All these ways of dealing with conflictual and anxiety-laden feelings and thoughts involve some form of self-estrangement. As Shapiro (1989, p. 3) puts it, "...a reaction by the personality against itself leaves the person who experiences it estranged, cut off, from himself in certain ways."

Let me pursue further this issue of self-estrangement and its relationship to third-person versus first-person self-knowledge. A fundamental assumption that Shapiro makes is that one can distinguish between what a person actually feels, thinks, desires, intends, and so on and what he or she identifies and recognizes as his or her feelings, thoughts, desires, intentions, and so on.

Under ideal conditions, one's actual and identified thoughts and feelings entirely converge. In neurotic conflict, there is a gap between the two. In traditional psychoanalytic theory, this gap between the former is assigned to the unconscious. Accordingly, the goal of psychoanalytic treatment was to remove or narrow the gap between the two through broadening the recognized and identified to include the individual's actual but unrecognized and unidentified feelings and thoughts that had been relegated to "the unconscious." On this view, once "the unconscious" is interpreted and defenses are analyzed and lifted, the individual's hitherto unrecognized and unidentified feelings and thoughts are recognized and identified, that is, are fully and directly experienced in consciousness in a first-person way. But, as we know, this is not quite the way things always work out. As we saw in Shapiro's example of the check-forging business executive, his self-knowledge of his purported self-punishment motives is an inferred one that could just as easily apply to a third-person. There is no evidence that the business executive has any first-person experience of a desire to punish himself. The desire is an inferred one. That the knowledge of his desire was inferred and "handed" to the business executive by his therapist does not really matter. For even if the business executive inferred the desire himself, it would still constitute third-person knowledge.

From Shapiro's perspective, the gap between the actual and recognized is not one between the actual but deeply buried unconscious and the recognized conscious, but rather one between the actual but relatively unattended and fleetingly experienced conscious and the identified and articulated conscious. Hence, on this view, the gap between the two is narrowed not by interpreting the deeply buried – this approach, as we have seen, too frequently leads to intellectualized third-person self-knowledge – but by attending to and articulating or, in Fingarette's (1969) words, "spelling out," the unattended and unarticulated. Hence, in an important sense, in articulating the unarticulated or in formulating the unformulated (Stern 2003), one is primarily identifying and spelling out what the patient, at some level, already knows rather than providing entirely new knowledge. It is not the newness of the knowledge that is critical, but the transformation of the fleeting and unattended into the articulated conscious, with the result that consciousness and personal agency are expanded so that they more adequately represent the full range of one's thoughts, feelings, and desires. Articulated consciousness is now a better representative of who one is and what one thinks, feels, desires, and intends. This is not to say that every aspect of one's feelings and thoughts is, at any given time, represented in articulated consciousness. Rather, a wider range of feelings and thoughts is, when needed, *accessible* to articulated consciousness.

Up to this point, I have referred to the epistemological terms "knowing" and "knowledge." The emphasis has been on different ways of knowing oneself and various implications of these different ways of knowing. However, as Moran (2001) has elaborated, first-person self-knowledge is not simply an epistemological issue, that is, a matter of knowing, but also a matter of *avowing* and endorsing one's feelings, thoughts, intentions, and beliefs. Thus, as Moran (2001) points out, it is not only the non-inferential status and immediacy of first-person self-knowledge that gives it special authority, but also one's *avowal* of what one thinks, feels, believes, and so on. In the language of Kaiser, as cited by Shapiro, the individual "stands behind" his thoughts, feelings, beliefs, and behaviors. This is not the case for the neurotically conflicted individual who cannot "stand behind" much of his or her behavior because much of what he or she thinks or feels is disavowed. To the extent that that is the case, there are severe limits to the authority one's behavior as well as one's statements about one's behavior can have.

Consider an example provided by Sartre (1956) of a married woman who, seemingly unaware, permits her hand to remain in the hands of a man who is trying to seduce her. When his intention is made more explicit (in part, because he is encouraged by her seemingly acquiescent behavior), she reacts with surprise and outrage. Sartre describes the combination of allowing her hand to remain in the man's hand and reacting with surprise and outrage as being in "bad faith" (mauvaise foi). According to Fingarette (1969), the woman has failed to "spell out" both her partial acquiescence to the seduction and her policy to not spell out her acquiescence. In the present context, the point to make is that although the woman is engaged in a seduction, she does not stand behind it, that is, does not avow it. Further, by not avowing, she can, at the same time, both acquiesce in the seduction and be surprised and outraged when it is made explicit.

From Sartre's, Fingarette's, and Shapiro's perspective, in the above example, the issue is not one of making the (repressed) unconscious conscious, but rather of articulating what has been allowed to remain unarticulated, of avowing what was disavowed. This perspective, I believe, is congruent with a particular interpretation of Freud's (1923) replacement or at least supplementation of making the unconscious with "where id was, there shall ego be" as a primary goal of psychoanalytic treatment. When id and ego are divorced from drive theory and translated, in accord with their original German terms "Das Es" and "Das Ich," as, respectively, the "it" and the "I," it becomes clear that id refers to aspects of oneself that have been disavowed and given an impersonal "it" status and ego refers to aspects of oneself that are avowed and experienced as one's own, as "I." From this perspective, one can understand the behavior of Sartre's woman, particularly her outrage, as the product of not only failing to articulate her interest and acquiescence in the seduction, but also of defensively giving her interest and acquiescence an "it" status, in Sullivan's terms, a "not me" status. Further, the therapeutic task, in this case, at least the immediate one, would not be of uncovering deeply buried repressed wishes, but of articulating and avowing her interest and acquiescence in the seduction.

This is not to say that repressed infantile wishes may not, indeed, be involved in the conflictual behavior of Sartre's woman. Let us say that oedipal wishes have been triggered by the man's attempt at seduction. However, the, so to speak, route to identifying these oedipal wishes would still first require an articulation and avowal of her interest and acquiescence in the seduction. One should also note here, parenthetically, the question of the nature of the woman's knowledge of her oedipal wishes. Does such knowledge constitute third-person inferential knowledge? If so, issues of avowal and "standing behind" do not really seem to apply – at least not in the same way that the woman can avow and stand behind her interest and acquiescence in the seduction. Only after she avows her interest and acquiescence, can Sartre's woman meaningfully explore other complex issues such as her motives for her interest and acquiescence, her conflicts and anxiety surrounding her interest, her failure to articulate her interest, and so on.

The Adaptive and Maladaptive Consequences of Defense: The Role of Context and Situation

In this section, I want to take up an issue that, as noted earlier, is not explicitly discussed by Shapiro – at least not in a prominent way – but is implicit in his writings. The issue is the adaptive as well as maladaptive consequences of defense and the role of context and situation in determining these consequences.

Although early on, Freud (1894) viewed repression as pathogenic and compared repressed mental contents to a "parasite," later in his writings, he noted the adaptive as well as maladaptive nature of defense. Thus, although on his view, defense plays a part in neurosis, intact defenses keep anxiety from being consciously experienced. Indeed, according to the Freudian theory of neurosis, it is the *failure* of defense and the "return of the repressed" that leads to the outbreak of anxiety and neurotic symptoms. However, despite the logic of Freud's theory of defense, there is a widespread tendency in the psychoanalytic literature to view defenses as simply pathogenic and to equate health with an absence of defense. From that perspective, analytic work consists largely in analysis of defense (Gray 1994).

This tendency to equate defense with pathology is evident in the assumptions (1) that dealing with various forms of trauma through denial and avoidant defenses is inherently pathological; and (2) that accordingly, the appropriate therapeutic approach to trauma is to help the patient overcome denial and other defenses. This latter assumption is evident, for example, in the emphasis on the necessity of doing the work of grief and mourning following loss and on the importance of recovering and working through memories and experiences of trauma.

There are a number of problems with these assumptions. One major problem is that they are not supported, in any simple way, by empirical evidence. The empirical evidence suggests (1) that repressive defenses or "styles" bestow certain benefits and exact certain costs – in other words, they have both adaptive and maladaptive consequences; and (2) that these adaptive and maladaptive consequences are partly a function of context and situation.

Let me cite some illustrative evidence for each of the above propositions:

1. There is evidence that individuals with a "repressive style" show, on the one hand, greater autonomic arousal and a greater susceptibility to a range of physical illnesses and, on the other hand, a lower likelihood of being diagnosed with anxiety and depression disorders (Lane et al. 1990).[1]
2. During the acute period following a heart attack, patients who show higher denial have better survival records than patients who do not employ denial (Hackett et al. 1968). However, the continued use of denial beyond the acute period is associated with poorer outcome (Levine et al. 1987). In other words, whether denial is adaptive or maladaptive is a function of context.

A striking example of the vital importance of context in determining whether denial is adaptive or maladaptive is provided by Eitinger (1983) who observes that unless one massively denied the utter hopelessness of one's situation, the concentration camp inmate stood little chance of even short term survival. Full awareness of the reality confronted in the concentration camp, Eitinger notes, would interfere with survival. In quite a different context, Taylor and her

---

[1]Although a large number of studies have reported a relationship between a "repressive style" and physical symptoms, Bonanno et al. (1995) and Coifman et al. (2007) reported opposite findings. However, whereas Coifman et al. assessed health status by employing a self-report health inventory – which itself can be biased by repressors' tendency to avoid negative affects and memory of negative events – other studies supporting the relationship between "repressive style" and physical symptoms have relied on more objective measures, for example, number of health center visits and verified illness as judged by the attending nurse (Cousineau and Shedler 2006).

colleagues (e.g., Taylor and Brown 1994) have shown that some "optimal" degree of self-deception in regard to oneself serves as a protection against depression and conversely, that the relative absence of self-deception is associated with a greater susceptibility to depression. The idea that a certain degree of self-deception regarding oneself is necessary to ward off depression and despair is, of course, the central theme of O'Neill's *The Iceman Cometh*. It is only their self-deceptions – "their pipedreams" – that enable the characters in the play to go on living. When their pipedreams, their illusions, are shattered by the truths brought to them by Hickey, the Iceman, they are all overcome with despair.

And, of course, Freud himself seems to suggest that a certain degree of self-deceptive denial in regard to oneself is adaptive and that its absence may be associated with depression. Thus, he writes in regard to the melancholic individual, "He also seems to us justified in certain other self-accusations; it is merely that he has a keener eye for the truth than other people who are not melancholic. When in his heightened self-criticism he describes himself as petty, egoistic, lacking in independence, one whose sole aim has been to hide the weakness of his own nature, it may be, as far as we know, that he has become pretty near to understanding himself; we only wonder why a man has to be ill before he can be accessible to a truth of this kind. For there can be no doubt that if anyone holds and expresses to others an opinion of himself such as this (an opinion that Hamlet held of himself and of everyone else), he is ill whether he is speaking the truth or whether he is being more or less unfair to himself" (Freud 1917 [1915], pp. 246–247).

Although it is clear that avoidance and denial can be adaptive in certain contexts, the evidence indicates that they need to be highly selective and "fine-tuned" in order to serve adaptive functions (Eagle 2000). Thus, the patient who adaptively denies the seriousness and life-threatening nature of his heart attack nevertheless continues to stay in bed, takes his or her medication, and does not decide to jog up and down the hospital corridor. Were denial so extreme and massive that it led to refusal to remain in bed, refusal to take medication, and insistence upon a vigorous jog in the corridor, it would obviously become highly maladaptive and life-threatening. And, in fact, as noted above, deniers do worse on follow-up after leaving the hospital. In the concentration camp situation, too, denial needed to be selective if it was to enhance survival. As Eitinger (1983) notes, "Denying death could be life-saving under certain circumstances, while denying the small seemingly unimportant factors of daily life and struggle would result in certain and premature death" (p. 211).

One can say that the judicious, selective, and fine-tuned use of denial suggests a goodly degree of ego strength, while the massive and undifferentiated use of denial suggests ego weakness. This is similar to the use of any other defense, including repression. That is, the flexible and selective employment of defenses for adaptive purposes, such as the avoidance of massive anxiety, the avoidance of despair and the maintenance of hope (see Breznitz 1983), indicates ego strength rather than pathology. And, contrastingly, the massive and non-selective use of defense is suggestive of ego weakness and pathology.

Defensive Style and External Trauma Versus Inner Conflict

Many of the studies discussed above have largely to do with methods of coping with *external trauma* (although this is not the case in regard to "repressive style," which has mainly to do with denial of anxiety and "unacceptable" thoughts). However, following Freud's relinquishment of his seduction theory, traditional psychoanalytic theory has focused mainly on wishes, desires, and fantasies that are enmeshed in *inner conflict*. Furthermore, a basic assumption of Freudian theory is that because these wishes and desires are often linked to our psychobiological nature, they do not simply disappear when they are defended against. Rather, they remain active and continue to influence our feelings, thoughts, and behavior in some form. Hence, repressive defenses against conflictual inner wishes and desires may have different consequences on behavior than defenses against external events such as loss, trauma, and chronic illness.

The differences between external trauma and conflictual desires may have important implications for how one understands defenses as well as for the nature of effective and appropriate interventions in these two areas. An external trauma, if it is severe, is *inherently* threatening and traumatic. Thinking about it or examining it does not alter that fundamental fact. Contrastingly, a conflictual wish or desire is accompanied by anxiety not necessarily because it is inherently "bad" or threatening, but because its association with the early "danger situations" of parental punishment and disapproval has become internalized (Freud 1926). Hence, it would appear to make more sense to employ interventions designed to help the patient become aware of his/her internalization of parental prohibitions and to bring about the emotional conviction that, as an adult, anxiety and defenses against his/her impulses and desires are no longer necessary. As Friedman (1991) puts it, the analyst brings the good news that the "danger situations" are no longer dangerous.

It is interesting to note that in his treatment of hysteria, presumably brought on by external trauma, one of Janet's (1907) interventions was to replace, through hypnotic suggestion, the traumatic event with a benevolent event. One can see this as an early instance of therapeutic encouragement of presumably adaptive avoidance and denial in regard to external trauma. It would be difficult to envisage a similar intervention in regard to conflictual wishes and desires. In short, it is possible, perhaps likely, that adaptive ways of coping as well as therapeutic interventions may be different for dealing with external traumatic events and conflictual wishes and desires. Not thinking about an external event such as loss or other trauma may be an effective way of avoiding the conscious experience of negative affect. In the case of conflictual desires, however, not consciously experiencing or not thinking about them is likely to have different consequences insofar as at some level, one continues to have these desires. Repressive-avoidant defenses in relation to external events and conflictual desires may share in common the adaptive function of avoiding the conscious experience of anxiety and negative affect. However, they may differ with regard to other more maladaptive consequences. Of course, this hypothesis needs to be investigated empirically.

It seems to me that, although often misdirected, in certain respects, recent findings on repressive-avoidant defenses and "positive illusions" do present challenges to particular interpretations of psychoanalytic theory, and it is these challenges to which I now turn. I recall that almost immediately following 9/11, a veritable army of well-intentioned mental health professionals descended on Ground Zero to offer their services to the victims of the trauma. These professionals, including those who were psychodynamically oriented, assumed that some form of psychological debriefing or working through would be helpful. However, there is little evidence that this approach to trauma is uniformly helpful and indeed, there is evidence that it can be harmful (e.g., Wortman and Silver 1989; Rose et al. 1999).

The evidence that psychological debriefing of trauma can be harmful appears to be contrary to the earlier noted findings of Pennebaker and his colleagues that writing about trauma can be helpful. However, the contradiction is only an apparent one for a number of reasons. For one thing, in the Pennebaker work because the participants were asked to write about traumas from the past, it is likely that the events and experiences they chose to write about were still experienced as unresolved. That is, for some subjects, not thinking about the traumatic event did not appear to succeed in eliminating its lingering impact.

One must also keep in mind that not all participants benefited from writing about their traumatic experience. It may be the case that mainly the participants who benefited were those whose repressive-avoidant defenses did not succeed in adequately dealing with the trauma. The participants who did not benefit from writing about their trauma may have already dealt adequately with it by not thinking about it. In other words, there are individual differences in coping and defensive styles.

It is these individual differences that are overlooked in the assumption that encouraging individuals to confront and "work through" trauma and discouraging their not thinking about it will be uniformly helpful – as if one size fits all. As Bonnano and his colleagues have shown, for some people the use of repressive-avoidant coping and defenses in relation to external trauma such as loss works quite well for them (Bonanno 2005; Bonanno et al. 1995,2002,2005).

Finally, it needs to be noted that unlike the context of the Pennebaker studies, which targeted traumatic events in the individual's past, the debriefing approaches are employed immediately after the traumatic event. Consequently, the individual whose habitual coping and defensive style may be to not think about the event is confronted with and is subject to an approach that is contrary to his or her "natural" coping style and that does not work for him or her.

Quite apart from its impact, the question I want to raise in the present context, however, is whether a psychological debriefing approach can really be legitimately derived from psychoanalytic theory. I think that the psychodynamically flavored rationale for debriefing, stated in a telescoped way goes something like this: Repression, avoidance, and denial are maladaptive because they keep people from facing, expressing, and working through their thoughts and feelings. The implicit assumption here is that allowing thoughts and feelings, particularly negative ones, to remain unconfronted and unexpressed has pathogenic effects on personal functioning. A common "mental health" assumption is that intense thoughts and feelings necessarily evoked by traumatic events must be confronted and worked through by the individual if he or she is to cope effectively with the trauma and move on with his or her life. It is assumed that if such confrontation and working through does not occur, the thoughts and feelings generated by the trauma will continue to operate, unintegrated into the personality, and will exert pathogenic influences.

Although in his early writings Freud (Breuer and Freud 1893–1895) stressed the pathogenic consequences of not confronting and expressing feelings (which he described as "strangulated affect" [p. 255] triggered by external trauma, his main emphasis, particularly in his later writings, was on *inner conflict* between wishes and desires and defenses against consciously experiencing and gratifying them. The clinical rationale for the importance of the psychoanalytic goals of becoming consciously aware of repressed wishes – making the unconscious conscious – and of the defenses against them – defense analysis –; and of integrating them into the personality – where id was, there shall ego be – the rationale for all these goals pertains mainly to thoughts and feelings related to inner conflicts about our wishes and desires rather than to external trauma.

What I am suggesting is that the rush to debriefing interventions in regard to external trauma cannot really be justified by a psychoanalytic rationale. An explicit or implicit attempt to do so rests, I believe, on a misunderstanding – certainly, an oversimplification – of psychoanalytic theory. In particular, it rests on a failure to distinguish between ways of coping with inner conflict regarding one's wishes and desires and reactions to external trauma and on the assumption that the rationale for interventions regarding inner conflict is applicable to interventions dealing with external trauma.

As Shapiro (1989) makes clear, "the neurotic personality or character…is one that reacts against itself; it reacts reflexively, against certain of its own tendencies. It is a personality in conflict" (p. x). One can add that the neurotic suffers from estrangement from various aspects of himself or herself. The self-estrangement is such that it brings about "an articulation of consciousness that does not represent but in fact distorts actual feelings, wishes, interests, intentions, the actual state of subjective experience" (Shapiro 1981, p. 26). Hence, the task of psychoanalysis or psychodynamic psychotherapy is to ameliorate self-estrangement by expanding consciousness so that it better represents the full range of one's feelings, desires, intentions, and so on. The extension of this perspective to areas beyond the domain of inner conflicts and ways of coping with them is, I believe, highly questionable.

In coming to the end of this chapter, I want to return to my introductory comment about Shapiro's work and style. Although influenced by others, Shapiro has gone his own independent way and has produced a body of work that possesses a remarkable coherence and inner unity and integrity. Although Shapiro has not attempted to establish a "school" – that, I am sure, would be anathema to him – his writings are relevant to any "school" that places a premium on lucidity and clinical relevance of thinking.

References

Asendorpf, J., & Scherer, K. (1983). The discrepant repressor: Differentiation between low anxiety, high anxiety, and repression of anxiety by autonomic-facial-verbal patterns of behavior. *Journal of Personality and Social Psychology, 45*(6), 1334–1346.

Bonanno, G. (2005). Resilience in the face of potential trauma. *Current Directions in Psychological Science, 14*(3), 135.

Bonanno, G., Field, N., Kovacevic, A., & Kaltman, S. (2002). Self-enhancement as a buffer against extreme adversity: Civil war in Bosnia and traumatic loss in the United States. *Personality and Social Psychology Bulletin, 28*(2), 184.

Bonanno, G., Keltner, D., Holen, A., & Horowitz, M. (1995). When avoiding unpleasant emotions might not be such a bad thing: Verbal-autonomic response dissociation and midlife conjugal bereavement. *Journal of Personality and Social Psychology, 69*(5), 975–989.

Bonanno, G., Rennicke, C., & Dekel, S. (2005). Self-enhancement among high-exposure survivors of the September 11th terrorist attack: Resilience or social maladjustment? *Journal of Personality and Social Psychology, 88*(6), 984.

Boor, M., & Schill, T. (1968). Subtest performance on the Wechsler Adult Intelligence Scale as a function of anxiety and defensiveness. *Perceptual and Motor Skills, 27*(1), 33–34.

Breuer, J., & Freud, S. (1893–1895). *Studies on hysteria* (Vol. 2). London: Hogarth.

Breznitz, S. (1983). Denial versus hope: Concluding remarks. In S. Breznitz (Ed.), *The denial of stress* (pp. 297–302). New York: International Universities Press.

Busch, F. (2001). Are we losing our mind? *Journal of the American Psycho-Analytic Association, 49*, 739–757.

Byrne, D. (1961). The repression-sensitization scale: Rationale, reliability, and validity. *Journal of Personality, 29*(3), 334–349.

Coifman, K., Bonanno, G., Ray, R., & Gross, J. (2007). Does repressive coping promote resilience? Affective-autonomic response discrepancy during bereavement. *Journal of Personality and Social Psychology, 92*(4), 745.

Cousineau, T., & Shedler, J. (2006). Predicting physical health: Implicit mental health measures versus self-report scales. *Journal of Nervous and Mental Dis*ease, *194*(6), 427–432.

Davies, M. (1970). Blood pressure and personality. *Journal of Psychosomatic Research, 14*(1), 89–104.

Davis, P. J. (1990). Repression and in the inaccessibility of emotional memories. In J. L. Singer (Ed.). *Repression and dissociation*. Chicago: University of Chicago Press, pp. 387–403.

Eagle, M. N. (2000). Repression: Part II. *The Psycho-Analytic Review, 87*(2), 161–189.

Eitinger, L. (1983). Denial in concentration camps: Some personal observations on the positive and negative functions of denial in extreme life situations. In S. Breznitz (Ed.), *The denial of stress* (pp. 199–212). New York: International Universities Press.

Ellenberger, H. F. (1970). *The discovery of the unconscious*. New York: Basic Books.

Erdelyi, M. H. (1993). Repression: The mechanism and the defense. In D. M. Wegner & J. W. Pennebaker (Eds.), *Handbook of mental control* (pp. 126–148). Englewood Cliffs: Prentice-Hall.

Esler, M., Julius, S., Zweifler, A., Randall, O., Harburg, E., Gardiner, H., et al. (1977). Mild high-renin essential hypertension. Neurogenic human hypertension? *New England Journal of Medicine296*(8), 405–411.

Fingarette, H. (1963). *The self in transformation: Psychoanalysis, philosophy and the life of the spirit*. New Yok: Basic Books.

Fingarette, H. (1969). *Self-deception*. New York: Humanities.

Freud, S. (1894). The neuro-psychoses of defense. *Standard Edition, Vol. 3*. London: Hogarth, pp. 41-68.

Freud, S. (1915). *Repression. Standard edition*, (Vol. 14). London: Hogarth.

Freud, S. (1917 [1915]). *Mourning and melancholia*. London: Hogarth.

Freud, S. (1923). *The ego and the id. Standard Edition* (Vol. 19, pp. 12–66). London: Hogarth.

Freud, S. (1926). *Inhibitions, symptoms and anxiety* (Vol. 20). London: Hogarth.

Freud, S. (1950 [1895]). *Project for a scientific psychology* (Vol. 1). London: Hogarth.

Friedman, L. (1991). A reading of Freud's papers on technique. *Psychoanalytic Quarterly, 60*, 564–595.

Girdjonnson, G. H. (1981). Self-reported emotional disturbance and its relation to electrodermal reactivity, defensiveness, and trait anxiety. *Personality and Individual Differences, 2*, 47–52. In P. J. Davis & G. E. Schwartz (Eds.) *Journal of Personality and Social Psychology*, 1987.

Gray, P. (1994). *The ego and analysis of defense.* Nothvale, N.J. Jason Aronson.

Hackett, T. P., Cassen, N.H., & Wishnie, H. A. (1968). The coronary care unit: An appraisal of its psychological hazards. *New England Journal of Medicine, 279*, 1365–1370.

Hill, D. & Gardner, G. (1980). Repression – Sensitization and yielding to threatening health communications. *Australian Journal of Psychology, 32*, 183–193.

Holmes, D. S. (1990). The evidence for repression: An examination of sixty years of research. In J. L. Singer (Ed.). *Repression and dissociation.* Chicago: University of Chicago Press, pp. 85–102.

James, W. (1890). *The principles of psychology* (Vols. 1 & 2). New York: Holt.

Jamner, L., Schwartz, G., & Leigh, H. (1988). The relationship between repressive and defensive coping styles and monocyte, eosinophile, and serum glucose levels: Support for the opioid peptide hypothesis of repression. *Psychosomatic Medicine, 50*(6), 567–575.

Janet, P. (1889). *L'automatisme psychologique.* Paris: Alcan.

Janet, P. (1907). *The major symptoms of hysteria.* New York: Macmillan.

King, A. C., Albright, C. L., Taylor, C. B., Haskell, W. L., & DeBusk, R. F. (1986, October). *The repressive coping style: A predictor of cardiovascular reactivity and risk.* Paper presented at the annual meeting of the Society of Behavioral Medicine, San Francisco.

Lane, R., Merikangas, K., Schwartz, G., Huang, S., & Prusoff, B. (1990). Inverse relationship between defensiveness and lifetime prevalence of psychiatric disorder. *American Journal of Psychiatry, 147*(5), 573–578.

Levine, M. & Spivak, G. (1963). The Rorschach index of ideational repression: Application to quantitative sequence analysis. *Journal of Projective Techniques, 27*, 73–78.

Levine, J., Warrenberg, S., Kerns, R., Schwartz, G. E., Delaney, R., Sontana, A., Gradman, A., Smith, S., Allen, S., & Cascione, R. (1987). The role of denial in recovery from coronary heart disease. *Psychosomatic Medicine, 49*(2), 109–117.

Levine, M., & Spivak, G. (1964). Rorschach index of ideational repression: Application to quantitative sequence analysis. *Journal of Projective Techniques, 27*, 73–78.

Luborsky, L., Blinder, B., & Schimek, J. (1965). Looking, recalling, and GSR as a function of defense. *Journal of Abnormal Psychology 70*, 270–280.

Mathe, A. A., & Knapp, P. H. (1971). Emotional and adrenal reactions to stress in bronchial asthma. *Psychosomatic Medicine33*(4), 323–340.

Moran, R. (2001). *Authority and estrangement: An essay on self-knowledge.* Princeton: Princeton University Press.

Pennebaker, J., & Beall, S. (1986). Confronting a traumatic event: Toward an understanding of inhibition and disease. *Journal of Abnormal Psychology, 95*(3), 274–281.

Pennebaker, J., Kiecolt-Glaser, J., & Glaser, R. (1988). Disclosure of traumas and immune function: Health implications for psychotherapy. *Journal of Consulting and Clinical Psychology, 56*(2), 239–245.

Piers, C. (November 2009). [Personal Communication].

Rapaport, D. (Ed.). (1954). *On the psychoanalytic theory of thinking* (Austen Riggs Center, 11). New York: International University Press.

Rose, S., Brewin, C. R., Andrews, B., & Kirk, M. (1999). A randomized controlled trial of individual psychological debriefing for victims of violent crime. *Psychological Medicine, 29*, 793–799.

Sartre, J. (1956). *Being and nothingness* (H. Barnes, Trans.). New York: Philosophical Library.

Schlesinger, H. (1970). The place of forgetting in memory functioning. *Journal of the American Psychoanalytic Association, 18*(2), 358–371.

Schwartz, G. E. (1990). Psychobiology of repression and health: A systems approach. In J. L. Singer (Ed.). *Repression and dissociation*. Chicago: University of Chicago Press, pp. 405–434.

Shapiro, D. (1965). *Neurotic styles* (Vol. 5). New York: Basic Books.

Shapiro, D. (1981). *Autonomy and rigid character*. New York: Basic Books.

Shapiro, D. (1989). *Psychotherapy of neurotic character*. New York: Basic Books.

Shedler, J., Mayman, M., & Manis, M. (1993). The illusion of mental health. *American Psychologist, 48*(1), 1117–1131.

Stern, D. (2003). *Unformulated experience: From dissociation to imagination in psychoanalysis*. Hillsdale: The Analytic Press.

Szalai, J. & Eagle, M. N. (1992). The relationship between individual differences in defensive style and concept formation. *British journal of Medical Psychology, 65*, 47–57.

Taylor, S., & Brown, J. (1994). Positive illusions and well-being revisited: Separating fact from fiction. *Psychological Bulletin, 116*, 21–27.

Temnes, K., & Kreyer, M. (1985). Children's adrenocortical responses to classroom activities and tests in elementary school. *Psychosomatic Medicine, 47*, 451–460.

Wachtel, P. (2003). The surface and the depths: The metaphor of depth in psychoanalysis and the ways in which it can mislead. *Contemporary Psychoanalysis, 39*(1), 5–26.

Weinberger, D., Schwartz, G.E., & Davidson, R. (1979). Low-anxious, high-anxious, and repressive coping styles: Psychometric patterns and behavioral and physiological responses to stress. *Journal of Abnormal Psychology, 88*(4), 369–380.

Weinberger, D. (1990). *The construct validity of the repressive coping style*. Chicago: University of Chicago Press.

Weinberger, D., Gordon, D., Feldman, S., & Ford, M. (1987, August). *The relationship between family patterns and restraint in preadolescent boys*. Paper presented at the annual meeting of the American Psychological Association, New York.

Willett, E.A., & Heilbrown, M. (1972). Repression-sensitization and discrepancy between self-report and official report of illness. *Journal of Psychology, 81*, 161–166.

Wortman, C. B., & Silver, R. C. (1989). The myth of coping with loss. *Journal of Consulting and Clinical Psychology, 57*, 349–357.

Reply to Morris Eagle

David Shapiro

Dr. Eagle raises five interesting, diverse subjects, both theoretical and practical. I will respond to them in the order he presents them.

Dr. Eagle makes the point, in regard to the concept of repression, that experimental efforts to locate a simple mechanism of forgetting have failed. In contrast, the study of a repressive-avoidant-denying character style has been shown to be associated with a variety of related psychological, behavioral, and physiological effects. I would like to pursue that point further.

Granting that the earlier experimental studies of forgetting were misguided, psychoanalysis itself cannot be completely exculpated from their error. From the beginning in psychoanalysis the concept of repression, and for that matter the conception of defense in general, has implied a restraining action of some sort, a specific counterforce. More generally, the related idea of a capability for delay of tension discharge has deep roots in analytic theory. Yet nowhere is it made clear what such a counterforce or capability for delay consists of. In *Neurotic Styles*, I proposed an alternative understanding of defense in which the idea of a specific defense counterforce is superfluous. Any character style is restrictive; any organizing mode or form of thinking or affect, however adaptive it may be, indeed any adaptive regulatory system, contains a vector of control or restraint. The adaptive capability of concentration or deliberate focus of attention, for example, may be said to constitute in itself a restraint of more passively distractable interest. This is restraint without a restraining force or mechanism. Let us suppose that a child, whose character style, or characteristic attitudes, are developing, encounters continuing anxious circumstances. The further development of this child's ways and attitudes, then, will be in a direction that mitigates that anxiety. One child will become more cautious, another more ingratiating, each, so to speak, relying increasingly on whatever tendencies already exist. In this way, a style will develop that is hypertrophied in a particular direction, often adaptively so, but at the same time restrictive. This is in fact what we see in adult neurotic character.

If not a specific unconscious restraining mechanism or counterforce, what does repression consist of? As Eagle indicates, a style of vague, impressionistic, and highly subjective thinking ("ruled by my emotions") makes the elimination of or inattention to disturbing ideas as easy to accomplish as the romantic exaggeration of attractive ones. This is not so much a matter of specific focused avoidances as of the creation of a generally less sharp and objective and more personally satisfying world. I am not sure that this picture meets the specifications of the traditional concept of repression. But I am confident that it actually exists.

Whether Eagle is right when he says that I have no truck with the unconscious depends on exactly how that term is used. He certainly is right when he speaks of my emphasis on different levels of consciousness, in particular a level of unarticulated and therefore incompletely conscious subjective experience that is distinct from a level of consciously articulated ideas. These are the levels of consciousness that are familiar to me, the levels that determine action and that are, in my opinion, the territory of internal conflict that effective psychotherapy must deal with.

I take for granted that the content and organization of these levels of consciousness at any time does not constitute the entirety of the mind. The content of any particular internal conflict contains and is organized by attitudes, which have deep roots, certainly, in early personal history. More than memory, those attitudes, not themselves necessarily conscious, but shaping consciousness, embody that history. But those attitudes and the particular internal conflicts of the neurotic adult in which those attitudes may be represented are not likely merely to be new editions of the particular conflicts in which they may have historically originated. In the figure of speech I have borrowed from Philip Rieff, oak trees are not acornish. Defensive attitudes, originally self-protective, become restrictive and generate new anxieties and conflicts of a much broader kind than their particular origins. As to the idea of unconsciously preserved early conflicts that now serve as planful and manipulative agents of symptomatic action, I am therefore more than dubious.

The level of unarticulated subjective experience that I speak of is not necessarily freely available to attention and in fact may resist conscious articulation. In that respect it is not equivalent to the usual psychoanalytic understanding of preconscious. However, psychoanalysis also recognizes a "second censorship," between consciousness and preconsciousness, and that kind of spontaneously inaccessible preconscious is comparable to the level of subjective life I have in mind. This level of unarticulated subjective experience is probably equivalent as well to what the psychoanalyst Joseph Sandler has called the "present unconscious," which he distinguishes from an historical unconscious. If I am not mistaken, Sandler, also, regards the "present unconscious" as the main area of therapeutic attention. This level of consciousness, or unconsciousness, is also recognized by Fenichel as the proper initial therapeutic focus. Fenichel, of course, considers it necessary to continue – in my opinion, to burden – the therapeutic work with a further inferential, if not theoretically inspired, construction of a historical narrative. At any rate, I have no particular objection if this level of unarticulated, incompletely conscious, experience is simply described as unconscious. It is sometimes convenient to do so and I occasionally do it myself.

I would like to make a few further comments here about the dynamics of neurotic character. Imagine the sort of person I spoke of above, characterized generally by vague, naive ideas, perhaps expressed in childlike locutions ("grumpy," "discombobulated"), someone I might describe as a hysterical character and whom Eagle might consider a repressor. If one talks with such a person over a period of time, one will gradually become aware that the childlike manner and the naïveté are exaggerated, do not seem completely genuine. As Hellmuth Kaiser put it, the patient does not "talk straight." In other words, the defensive character style is also a persona, not consciously adopted, but reflexive, necessary, in some way self-protective. One realizes that there is more to this apparently childlike person than was first apparent. And, in fact, at unexpected moments she asserts an unusual judgment in a firmer voice ("I'm not the problem! He's the problem!"). But when she does so and, so to speak, discovers herself, she recoils anxiously ("That sounds brazen, doesn't it?"). The sensation of personal authority does not feel safe. I am presenting a picture of psychological dynamics, but it is not a dynamics of particular unconscious wish and defense mechanism; it is a dynamics of unrecognized attitudes. These attitudes are not merely "the surface" of the personality, though they shape the surface of the personality. They are deep structural features of the personality.

Eagle's discussion of the different forms of self-knowledge is very useful. The comparison he makes between first-person and third-person self-knowledge, on the one hand, and so-called emotional and intellectual therapeutic insight, on the other, seems to me exact. The former description could well replace the latter, which is certainly less clear. Even so, first-person self-knowledge/emotional insight remains less than completely sharp, as is evident from the several different ways in which it is described. I shall propose a further clarification in a moment.

The therapeutic ineffectiveness of third-person self-knowledge or intellectual insight has, of course, been a problem for psychoanalytic therapy from the beginning. It was the problem that Wilhelm Reich attacked in his *Character Analysis* ("...the patient may develop a good intellectual understanding and perhaps a theoretical conviction of the correctness of the analytic work...but there is very little change in structure") and was undoubtedly the main stimulus for that work. I would disagree with Eagle when he says that this kind of self-knowledge, if not living up to its original promise, may still be (therapeutically) useful. I think, on the contrary, that it only adds, particularly for obsessional patients (which is to say most office patients), another self-conscious program, that of "being oneself," and more stilted self-direction. What I take to be Eagle's own suggestion that intellectual self-knowledge can be considered a kind of self-estrangement seems consistent with that view.

The aim of therapy is not to instruct but to liberate, not in any grand romantic way, but simply to help people discover what they want to do and feel comfortable doing it. As Eagle says, paraphrasing me, neurotic people are estranged, cut off from their own feelings, even from their own convictions by internal conflict. This is not a matter of the repression of particular wishes or fantasies, but of estrangement, on account of a restrictive style, from whole classes of subjective experience. Thus, we say that rigid people lack spontaneity. But this self-estrangement, as I indicated above, is not subjectively complete. Neurotic patients tell us, sincerely, perhaps too emphatically, that they want to do something – say, quit a job – but with a look of doubt in their eyes. They say that they are sure that things will turn out alright, but search our eyes for reassurance. The man who says that he feels terrible about what happened at the party last night, tries to stifle a flickering smile. When one calls attention to his effort, he indignantly and sincerely denies it ("It's not funny!"). What he thinks he feels is what he "should" feel, but it is not what he actually feels. In short, we see unmistakable evidence of subjective experience or sensation that cannot quite be called unconscious, yet is not consciously recognized or articulated and whose articulation is in fact not necessarily welcome. It is the articulation of such experience that is, in contrast to third-person insight, recognizable to its subject and liberating. It has much the same result, though more deeply felt, as an ordinary spontaneous articulation, a "saying out loud," of what had been only a vague, nascent, perhaps unwelcome thought. This rise in conscious clarity is accompanied by a sense of purposefulness, intention, or agency, an experience of knowing now what one means. It is, in other words, an enlargement of the experience of the self, a full first-person self-awareness.

In this connection, Eagle's suggestion that my view of therapeutic change brings to mind Freud's later statement of psychoanalytic therapy's goal as "where id was, there shall ego be" seems apt. I do think that what I have presented is consistent with the aims of psychoanalysis, if not its contemporary practice.

Eagle raises the question of whether defense or self-deception is necessarily an indicator of pathology or can even be adaptive. He concludes on two grounds that it can be adaptive, or at least not necessarily pathological. The first ground is Freud's theory of neurotic conflict, the second has to do specifically with trauma.

From the standpoint of psychoanalytic theory, Eagle's case that defense is not necessarily pathological is clear. In this theoretical picture, if defense is successful in excluding threatening wishes or fantasies from consciousness, there is no reason to expect the presence of anxiety or clinical symptoms. But this picture of a completely successful exclusion of threat is tenable only if one imagines neurotic conflict to consist of a particular unconscious wish opposed by a particular defense mechanism. It is an unrealistic conception of neurotic conflict and an unrealistic picture of a completely successful defense.

A characterological – I would say also a phenomenological – picture of dynamics, while not necessarily contradicting Eagle's conclusion, is more complicated. The defensive process, consisting of the working of a general restrictive style, is never wholly successful in forestalling anxiety. Nor is that process, as psychoanalytic tradition holds, wholly unconscious, or almost so. Conscious action and attitudes of consciousness are, though without self-awareness, centrally involved in this process. Some degree of conscious, if unwitting, effort is invariably involved in defensive self-deception. The compulsive person, anxious when faced with a personal decision, searches for rules to tell him what he wants to do; the defensively passive and naive person actively avoids opinions, makes a point of letting one know she has none. These self-deceptive efforts will show themselves in some degree of artificiality or stiltedness of behavior. Such signs of defense processes may be subtle and sporadic or conspicuous and more or less continuous. At least up to a certain point of severity, whether one calls them signs of pathology is a matter of definition, and perhaps common sense.

At the same time, from a characterological standpoint, the adaptive value of defensive style, emerging as a special tendency from general ways of being, is not only possible; it is highly likely. Thus, the productiveness of the compulsive, the spontaneity and charm of the hysterical character, even the decisiveness of the psychopathic man of action.

I share Eagle's skepticism regarding the therapeutic value or necessity of debriefing after traumatic experience. Defense or self-deception, however one understands it, is a self-protective reaction, although it is true that it offers self-protection at a cost. Its benefits and cost must be weighed against each other. Whether that cost – in the form, say, of interference with genuine intimacy in important personal relationships – is too great or defense is so fragile and so restrictive to be sustained comfortably are, again, matters of judgment. And, accordingly, so is whether a condition can reasonably be called pathological.

I do not think, though, that an overzealous aim to rout all comforting illusion should be associated, as Eagle does, with a general therapeutic emphasis on the analysis of defense or self-deception. The gradual articulation and relaxation of restrictive attitudes of self-deception is central to effective psychodynamic therapy. No doubt such work can be militant (as it was in the work of Wilhelm Reich) and in that way even abusive, but in principle, the gradual articulation of self-deception, allowing the patient to discover himself, actually stands in opposition to avid efforts to bypass self-protective measures and expose what is hidden, or inferred to be hidden, by them.

As I said above, I share Eagle's doubt of the benefit of "debriefing" victims of trauma. And I generally agree with his view of its apparent theoretical basis as misguided. The case is not open or shut, however. Many, perhaps most, people immediately after or during a shocking event want, even urgently, to talk about it, especially to others who have shared their experience. Whether the comfort that interaction provides is mainly a result of the articulation of the experience in sharing it with others or, as I would guess, the sense of solidarity that is achieved is a question. In any case, such sharing of experience is not at all the same as a professional debriefing by a stranger with his own program. I think, as Eagle does, that pressing people to "talk it out" is at least as likely to interfere, though probably only temporarily, with spontaneous recovery from traumatic experience as to encourage it. But what exactly does spontaneous recovery from trauma consist of? Are not its constituents, such as communicative interaction with others, self-protective or, in this case, self-reparative reactions? Are they not, then, broadly speaking, defense reactions similar to or even identical with the defense reactions involved in neurotic internal conflict?

There is a tendency in our field to consider the experience and treatment of trauma apart from the individuals who are experiencing it. But we do not treat trauma; we treat individuals who have experienced trauma and have assimilated or endured it each in his own way according to his makeup. The experience of trauma is bound to be engaged, virtually from the start, by the dynamics of the personality, which is to say that it will elicit a self-protective or reparative reaction of some sort. That reaction may or may not be successful in dispelling distress. In some individuals it may dispel the immediate distress, but substitute another kind. Thus, some individuals become obsessed with the trauma. They continue to rework it and revive it, cannot allow it to fade, and are preoccupied with it many years afterward. Many victims of certain sorts of trauma (rape victims, holocaust survivors) feel humiliated by the experience and, ashamed, hide it and try to avoid recollection. Some political victims of torture, seem, with some success, to overcome its humiliation and helplessness by cultivating the image of themselves as having survived all that the enemy can inflict; they insist that they be called survivors of torture, never victims. Some holocaust victims and survivors attempt a kind of redress; thus, the desperate need to leave a record as a witness that will speak of their experience and its cruelty and injustice.

These reactions are self-protective, or self-reparative efforts, conscious of their own aims in varying degrees, some successful in dispelling distress and adaptive in that sense, some as I said replacing one kind of distress with another, in some way lesser, kind. Some involve self-deception, some may not. Among the former, one might sometimes speak of a situation-dependent psychopathology that fades along with relief from the traumatic situation. False confessions or political thought reform in the face of coercion are of that sort. They reflect a passive surrender of autonomous judgment that resembles, in exaggeration, neurotic conditions. All of these reactions, inasmuch as they are self-reparative, are reactions to internal conditions, not directly to the external events that evoke those conditions. I do not see any fundamental distinction between them and the defensive reactions of internal conflict.

Reply to David Shapiro

Morris N. Eagle

I appreciate Dr. Shapiro's reply to my chapter and, for the most part, agree with his comments. However, I want to clarify a few matters and respond to several issues that Dr. Shapiro raises in his reply:

1. The early experimental work on repression I refer to in my chapter was not intended "to locate a simple mechanism of [ordinary] forgetting," but rather motivated forgetting, which presumably captures the essence of repression.
2. With regard to the concept of repression as well as of defense, Dr. Shapiro criticizes the notion that they involve "a restraining action of some sort, a specific counterforce" and proposes instead that defense be understood characterologically, or entailing "restraint without a restraining force or mechanism." Although I agree with him that defenses are best understood characterologically, one still wants to know about the processes or mechanism through which defenses are implemented. For example, in a study referred to in my chapter, Luborsky et al. (1965) found that repressors tend to avoid visually fixating on the sexual contents of a presented stimulus. Thus, although the avoidant repressive tendency or "style" is likely a characterological one, it is implemented through the process of "not looking at" rather than some other means. Similarly for the Szalai and Eagle (1992) study cited in my chapter. In addition to learning that people who characteristically and habitually employ repressive-avoidant defenses have greater difficulty forming an aggressive concept, one learns that the greater difficulty is attributable to attending less to the aggressive dimension of stimulus pictures than to some other process.
3. If, as Dr. Shapiro maintains, some kind of "restraining mechanism or counterforce" is not an essential aspect of repression, that is, in Freud's (1915) words, does not require a "constant expenditure of effort" (p. 151), how does one account for the evidence that "repressive style" seems to be associated with physiological costs such as compromised immune response and greater susceptibility to certain physical illnesses – both of which support an active effort that exacts a cost? It may be that a readiness to employ a "restraining mechanism of counterforce" is itself a characterological tendency.
4. I agree with Dr. Shapiro that the concept of "infantile neurosis" notwithstanding, the conflicts of the neurotic adult "are not likely merely to be new editions of the particular conflicts in which they may have historically originated." However, there is likely to be some lawful relationship between the early conflicts of childhood and the conflicts of the neurotic adult, which can be elucidated by longitudinal studies. Indeed, Dr. Shapiro's emphasis on character suggests such a lawful relationship. Also, I believe that there is likely to be greater continuity

between *early and later patterns of coping* with conflict – which Dr. Shapiro refers to as "attitudes" – than the content of conflicts. The findings on the relative stability of attachment patterns supports the idea of continuity of coping patterns.

5. Dr. Shapiro disagrees with my suggestion that, although not therapeutically ideal, third-person self-knowledge may be useful. He is correct that I also state that excessive reliance on third-person self-knowledge can be considered a form of self-estrangement. However, I do believe that, under certain circumstances, third-person self-knowledge can be useful. For example, it can be useful to become aware, through a kind of third-person self-observation, of certain destructive patterns in one's life as a first step in trying to understand and change them. Let me provide a concrete example: A patient with whom I worked came to see that she was always attracted to the wrong man, that is, in her words, to the "party animal" who would inevitably bring her grief. Although the nature of her spontaneous attraction did not change for a long time, her awareness of her pattern with men was an important first step and also played a useful role in avoiding repetitive disappointment and distress.

I do not want to make too much of this point. For, on the whole, Dr. Shapiro and I agree that it is first-person self-knowledge rather than third-person self-knowledge that is liberating and necessary for deeply meaningful change.

6. I agree with Dr. Shapiro that it is more accurate and useful to view defenses and dynamics characterologically rather than in terms "of a particular unconscious wish opposed by a particular defense mechanism." However, there is the possibility – and this is an empirical question – that conflicts in certain content areas (e.g., sex, aggression, assertiveness) especially trigger characterological defenses. In other words, there may be an interaction between content area and defense.

7. I must not have been clear in my chapter. I definitely do not equate "a general therapeutic emphasis on the analysis of defense or self-deception" with "an overzealous aim to route all comforting illusion." I do not believe, however, that one size fits all. I do agree with Dr. Shapiro that "many … people immediately after or during a shocking event want, even urgently, to talk about it, especially to others who have shared their experience." However, one, not everyone copes with trauma that way. And two, as Dr. Shapiro notes, "such sharing of experience is not at all the same as a professional debriefing a stranger …."

The point I was making in my chapter is that the overzealous aim to debrief or to indiscriminately provide "mental health services" to "victims" of trauma that focus on such processes as uncovering, reliving, and doing grief work are based on theoretical notions that do not take adequate account of individual differences in coping with trauma. As the work of Bonnano (e.g., 1995) and Taylor and her colleagues (e.g., Taylor and Brown 1994) shows, some people cope well with loss and other trauma through avoidant means and sometimes through moderately illusory (not entirely realistic) means. There is little reason to denigrate or tamper with these coping methods based on some general view, or perhaps one should say, some Weltanschauung that insists that only a particular coping style is adaptive. In effect,

I am strongly endorsing Dr. Shapiro's statement that "we do not treat traumas; we treat individuals." I would simply add that there are times when one does not need to treat either the trauma or the individual.

8. In my final comment, I want to reiterate my general agreement with what I take to be Dr. Shapiro's central emphasis on what I would refer to as authenticity, as being of one piece. At its most general, but also most profound, psychoanalysis deals, not with this or that particular wish or this or that particular defense, but with self-estrangement. And psychoanalytic therapy, at its most general and also its most profound, deals with the amelioration of self-estrangement. Thus, although it sounds quite mundane, it is, indeed, profound to recognize, as Dr. Shapiro does, that "the aim of therapy … [is] simply to help people discover what they want to do [and I would add, feel] and feel comfortable doing it."

References

Bonanno, G., Keltner, D., Holen, A., & Horowitz, M. (1995). When avoiding unpleasant emotions might not be such a bad thing: Verbal-autonomic response dissociation and midlife conjugal bereavement. *Journal of Personality and Social Psychology, 69*(5), 975–989.

Freud, S. (1915). Repression. *Standard edition* (Vol. 14). London: Hogarth Press.

Luborsky, L., Blinder, B., & Schimek, J. (1965). Looking, recalling, and GSR as a function of defense. *Journal of Abnormal Psychology, 70*, 270–280.

Szalai, J., & Eagle, M. (1992). The relationship between individual differences in defensive style and concept formation. *The British Journal of Medical Psychology, 65*, 47–61.

Taylor, S., & Brown, J. (1994). Positive illusions and well-being revisited: Separating fact from fiction. *Psychological Bulletin, 116*, 21–27.

Chapter 7
Defensive Styles of Thinking to Prevent Dreaded States of Mind

Mardi J. Horowitz

Introduction

Among the most overwhelming or unpleasant human experiences are undermodulated states: mortal terror, darkest despair, towering hostility, and searing shame and guilt. A shift into states that avoid such experiences is accomplished by defensive control processes. The most common of these are inhibition of potential ideas, blunting of representations of emotionality, and distortions of meanings. These defensive maneuvers can be observed in short, medium, and long orders of attunement to the mind of another. This chapter focuses on short order observations, as witnessed in communications with another and as modeled intrapsychically by empathy for the mind of another. By understanding what is happening, here and now in a therapy hour, a clinician may realize how to act to reduce not only short order control processes that are maladaptive, but by so doing gradually modify longer order patterns of characterologically-based defensiveness.

The Context of Theory

Traditional psychoanalytic ideas on defense mechanisms began with the theory of repression of overwhelmingly affective memories such as those of traumatic seductions in childhood. Subsequent revisions added a variety of mechanisms such as projection, identification, role reversal, conversion of passive to active, isolation of affect, and many others. Recognizing defensive stifling of ideas and feelings that might otherwise be expressed became an important aspect of how to

M.J. Horowitz (✉)
Distinguished Professor of Psychiatry, University of California-San Francisco,
San Francisco, CA 94143
e-mail: mardih@lppi.ucsf.edu

C. Piers (ed.), *Personality and Psychopathology: Critical Dialogues with David Shapiro*,
DOI 10.1007/978-1-4419-6214-0_7, © Springer Science+Business Media, LLC 2011

listen to our patients. This close listening led to more refinements as to how a defensive posture was accomplished by mental processes such as momentary inhibitions and facilitations of particular topics.

At the same time that close listening to small order moments of defensiveness clarified cognitive processes, growing recognitions of how to formulate the defensive layers or structures of character were occurring. Over decades, David Shapiro made major contributions to this area as well as the area of short order observations of how a patient communicates. The characterological stances that developed and habituated were ways of self-regulating the self, and these ways might be usefully unpacked during the longer time of a character changing therapeutic process. He saw the short order defenses, such as inhibiting a conflictual topic, as specific instances revealing some of the intricate workings of character based self-regulatory processes (Shapiro 1965, 1981, 2000).

Defensive control process can help a person shift away from dreaded, intense emotions that might otherwise occur. If we think in terms of short, medium, and long term spans of observation in the context of the close-in understanding of minds as occurs in psychotherapy, we may observe a conspicuous shift in state from well modulated expressions to overmodulated reactions in a few seconds. That would be what I mean by short order framing of how defensive control processes work. In terms of medium order framing, we can hear reports about experiences over days, weeks, and months. In these materials, we may observe phasic shifts in the use of defensive avoidances, as in onset and offset of phases of denial, and numbing after the patient experiences a recent traumatic event. Often, the style of defense is both situational and characterological: Habitual avoidances increase in times of crises, but long order observations such as those of Shapiro show how avoidance of strong feelings may be a habitual aspect of characterological compromise formations.

Patients sometimes purchase states of apparent emotional equilibrium at the price of reducing their chances to learn from new experiences. For example, prolonged denial of the implications of bad news may remove fright but it may operate so that it functions as if preventing optimum decisions for how to deal with the crisis. Prolonged avoidance of sexual arousal after having experienced sexual abuse does not lead to chances of learning how to engage in love-making in a safe, healthy, and satisfying way. A period of numbing may be useful to recover equilibrium after being fired; however, prolonged numbing becomes a pathological symptom if it leads to failures to act to regain another job or change one's career. For these reasons, we seek to understand, perhaps counteract, and possibly help the patient to modify defensive operations in the context of treatment.

We may need to differentiate current, stress-induced regressions from habitual defensive styles. That kind of differentiation – of medium and long order defensive stances – may take time. We clinicians may make such inferences through close observation of signs of defensiveness. That, and a wish to understand "how it works," motivates a focus in this chapter on short order observations and how they might be categorized.

Short Order Observations

Inhibiting or distorting expression of an important, unclearly resolved topic before an apt point of closure is one of our best signs of defensive control processes. This was David Shapiro's starting point in his pioneering 1965 work on how to observe neurotic styles, as in the cloudy impressionstic and short-circuiting thinking of a person with a histrionic style. Even a person with such a histrionic style may have working states in which emotions are clearly labeled in words, and shift to states in which a topic is stressful and so the emotions are not labeled in verbal communications. Any such shifts of communication may catch our attention and indicate to us the presence of an active, here and now, episode of conflictual thought and communication.

An increase in ideas that are jumbled, started and stopped, or excessively general rather than self-focused may indicate defensiveness. Discords and contradictions between and within verbal and nonverbal communication of emotion are also important. A person may talk clearly and harmoniously about many topics, but shift into frequent silences, retractions, obscurity, and disjointed ideas when a specific topic is broached. In this way, we gradually observe how signs of defensive control processes link to core themes, ones that are important but unresolved, ones that may re-enact outmoded but nonetheless repeated modes of transaction with others, preventing opportunities for more self integration and intimacy.

Important themes and defensive control processes can also be inferred from stories told about what happens outside the clinical session. A patient who initially came because she abused her child may describe a work failure and then report that when she returned home she had angrily disparaged her child as stupid and inept for breaking a dish. She had placed blame and disgust away from herself. Using role-reversal as a defense might be in the short order moment of therapy be described as shifting within the memory being now reported from a view of the self as inept to viewing the child as inept. Fault is attributed to the child – the child is to blame and not the self – and hostility is placed on the other. In the short order, the role reversal can be reappraised, re-interpreted, and for the moment "revised" in the direction of more realistic and accepting appraisals.

Categories Enable Close Observation of Defensive Control Processes

Clinicians seeing the same videotape of a session with a patient may agree on the manifestations of specific defense mechanisms (Vaillant 1994). In cognitive-behavioral schools of practice, the theoretical construct of defense is seldom specified, although some do regard defenses as important (Young 1994) and obstacles to therapy are considered in such formulations (Persons 1992, 1989). In order to integrate dynamic and cognitive-behavioral concepts, my colleagues and I have aimed at a direct observational approach (Horowitz 1986; Horowitz et al. 1992, 1996; Horowitz and Stinson 1995). This approach represented a convergence of psychodynamic theory with modern cognitive science (Horowitz 1988a, b; Horowitz et al. 1990). The results are categories for observing signs of defensive control processes, a listing of categories of mental activities that can alter emotion.

In general, the defensive control processes that involve *content* (inhibiting attention to topics, concepts, and meanings) form the phenomena of repression, suppression, disavowal, denial, and rationalization. The control processes that involve *form* (mode, time, linkage, and, arousal) lead to phenomena such as regression, autistic fantasy, generalization, isolation, and withdrawal. The control processes that *shift* self and other views can form defenses called projection, projective identification, splitting, dissociation, reaction formation, role reversal, and undoing. (For a fuller discussion of defense mechanisms, see Vaillant (1994); Perry et al. (1989); Singer (1990); Conte and Plutchik (1995); Horowitz et al. (1996); Saklofske and Zeidner (1995); and Horowitz (1988a).

Observing Self Report of Intrapsychic Events and Interpersonal Communicational Style

Tables 7.1 and 7.2 give an example of signs of defensive change in *topics and themes*.

Table 7.1 focuses on what can be subjectively found on conscious reflection and communicated by self-reports of inner experiences. The same issues of control of topics as directly observable in communications are compared in Table 7.2. To repeat, I am presenting the same inferred processes as they might be described from intrapsychic vantage points (Table 7.1) and interpersonal vantage points (Table 7.2). Of course, the interpersonal communications are what both parties in a therapy dyad might observe, although in fact they do interpret what is happening between them somewhat differently. The intrapsychic is

Table 7.1 Contents of conscious experience: Outcomes of control processes

Defensive outcomes			
Control processes	Adaptive	Maladaptive	Failure of regulation
Altering topics	Useful periods of contemplating and not contemplating a stressful topic (dosing); rational balances between internal and external sources of information.	Topics of importance are not insightfully examined; needed decisions are not made; forgetting, disavowal, or denial of a stressful topic that requires resolution.	Intrusion of an emotionally overwhelming topic.

(continued)

Table 7.1 (continued)

Control processes	Defensive outcomes		
	Adaptive	Maladaptive	Failure of regulation
Altering concepts	Useful contemplation of implications and possible solutions to problems; selective inattention to vexing or distressing concepts in order to gain restoration from distressing levels of emotion or loss of morale when problems seen insoluble; useful balancing of emotion by switching between concepts; establishment of a rational order of concepts.	Avoids key concepts; irrelevant details are amplified; moves from the emotional heart of a topic to its periphery in a way that leaves cause and effect sequences distorted or obscured.	Disjointed or confused thought.
Altering the importance to self in a chain of concepts	Weighs alternatives and accepts the best solution to a problem amongst alternatives; accepts realistic estimates; appropriate humor.	Irrational exaggeration or minimization; excessive "sweet lemons" or "sour grapes" attitudes; rationalizes alternative solutions that are less rational than other solutions; inappropriate humor.	Sense of being dazed and experiencing emptiness or chaotic shifts in attitudes.
Altering threshold for disengagement	Takes action when a good solution has been reached; accepts a new reality; makes efforts to practice new ways of thinking and acting, overrides outmoded unconscious ways of thinking and acting; tolerates high levels of negative emotion without derailing a topic, when processing that topic is beneficial.	Terminates contemplation of a topic prematurely; blocks reviews of memories or anticipation of threatening events; selects the emotionally easy but unrealistic choice; makes no choices on how to integrate contradictions.	Uncontrolled impulsive conclusions.

Table 7.2 Contents of interpersonal communications: Outcomes of control processes

| | Defensive outcomes | | |
Control processes	Adaptive	Maladaptive	Failure of regulation
Altering topics	Expresses a potentially stressful topic to another person, to a degree that both can tolerate the emotion or conflict evoked with a balanced focus on self and other.	Unbalanced focus causing disruptive attention to self, or too attuned to other to be sufficiently attentive to topics of importance to self; does not present stressful topic(s); selects obscuring or misleading alternative topic(s).	Sudden plunges into and out of expressing emotionally overwhelming topics.
Altering concepts	Communicates key facts and emotions; contemplates implications and possible solutions to problems; alert to cues of others.	Conceptual reluctance; misleads others who are potentially helpful; gives misinformation; generalized when specifics are indicated; avoids expressing a concept that might prove useful in solving problems; switches facts back and forth; interrupts or overrides other to prevent clarification or useful give and take; refuses to follow useful cues or leads provided by others.	Fragmented and finds it hard to follow conversation.
Altering the importance of self in a chain of concepts	Careful appraisal of alternatives; maintenance of clear changes in values, commitments, and shared meanings.	Vacillates when taking a stance is essential; facile face-saving at the expense of reasonable shared estimates of the truth; rationalizes the irrational.	Disruptive or chaotic shifts in attitudes.
Altering threshold for disengagement	Shares the decision-making process; makes decisions when in the best position to do so; selects the best topics and shows links between topics; accepts lead from others where that is best.	Avoids undesirable actions to prevent inner tensions; acts in an impairing manner to terminate a tense situation prematurely.	Uncontrolled impulsive talk or actions.

"private," but it is our specialized skills as psychotherapists that allow us to examine two or more versions of intrapsychic representations: our own (which topics do we inhibit as we self-reflect) and our empathy based internal modeling of what we think the patient is thinking (which topics do we paraphrase on their behalf as we recognize what they might NOT be saying but might be dimly or intuitively thinking).

Tables 7.3 and 7.4 use alteration of forms of expression to illustrate intrapsychic and interpersonal observation of defensive control processes. Table 7.3 focuses attention on what can be known consciously by our self reflections, by our empathic internal model of what the patient might be intrapsychically experiencing, and what the patient might self-reflect upon his or her own intrapsychic experiencing. While Table 7.3 is perhaps closer to how it might work in mental processes, we are more reliable in categorizing what is communicated, and that is what is used for the processes shown in Table 7.4 which, as I said, focuses on communication signs.

In addition to the form and content of thinking, defensive control processes can change the organization of a state of mind by activating different unconscious person schemas, perhaps as role relationship models of self in transaction with others (Horowitz 1991). This changes the relative activity of role models and transaction for self and others and so the organizers of a given state of mind. These are effective but sometimes irrational ways of warding off entry into a dreaded state of mind by evocation of the organizational principles for a preferable one.

The most common short order defensive control processes at this level of person schematic organization of information involve role reversal as in taking a strong active role rather than a weak passive one. For example, the role of perpetrator, to the subject, may be preferred to the role of being a victim, if these seem to be the only available unconscious choices, or if there are unconscious motives to get some kind of revenge for having felt like a victim (see Tables 7.5 and 7.6).

Counteracting Common Defensive Styles

I followed David Shapiro in noting defensive styles in different prototypical personality disorders in my books *Personality Styles and Brief Therapy*, *Stress Response Syndromes*, and *Treatment of stress Response Syndromes*. While a personality disorder typology helps general formulation, psychotherapists can be helped by observing the general play of inhibitions and distortions, and counteracting the medley of defensive control processes in active usage. The clinician simultaneously contains the patient's negative affect within the safety of an established therapeutic alliance. In turn, the alliance is constantly strengthened by making the clarification of difficult topics, with negative emotions, tolerable in working states of mind rather than dreaded, out-of-control states.

Table 7.3 Form of conscious experience: Outcomes of control processes

Defensive outcomes

Control processes	Adaptive	Maladaptive	Failure of regulation
Altering mode of representation	Selective representation in all modes; lexical explanations; restorative imagery; somatic preparation.	Omission of useful modes; excessive numbing by avoiding images; avoids understanding images in words; prolonged escapist use of imagery or bodily enactions.	Intrusive and excessively vivid images (flashbacks), pseudo-hallucinations, hallucinations; enactive expression of raw emotions.
Altering time span	Looks at plans one step at a time to avoid being emotionally overwhelmed by long-term implications; relates an event to an entire life span to avoid being overwhelmed by long-term implications.	Denies urgency of a threat; disavows long-range implications to self; focuses on past or future to avoid need to make present decisions and take necessary actions.	Chaotic sense of time.
Altering logic level	Balance between rational planning and restorative or creative fantasy.	Excessive preoccupation with small logical steps and details or with fantasy.	Confusion.
Altering level of action planning	Restorative changes between activity and thought; prompt action at appropriate signs of opportunity; useful restraint.	Preoccupation with thinking to avoid important perceptions; preoccupation with perception to avoid necessary thinking; excessive action to avoid thought; excessive thought to avoid action; paralysis of action in favor of endless rumination.	Impulsive action and/or thought; no action.
Altering arousal level	Balance between arousal and rest cycles.	Excessive hypervigilance and compulsive worry or avoidant sleeping, reverie and lethargy.	Frenzied or exhausted states of mind.

Table 7.4 Form of interpersonal communications: Outcomes of control processes

Defensive outcomes			
Control processes	Adaptive	Maladaptive	Failure of regulation
Altering mode of representation	Coherent mix of verbalization, facial signals, imagery metaphors, and bodily gestural movements.	Disruptive image metaphors; flat verbiage; discordant prosodic across words, voice, face, and body, leading to distortion, confusion, or a sense that something is warded off or being concealed.	Jumbles different expressive media; impulsive inaction of emotional signals.
Altering time span	Discusses coherent framing of time as to past, present, future, or imaginary perspectives.	Disruptive or confusing shifts in temporal perspective.	Chaotic timing of actions.
Altering logic level	Balance between rational planning (reflexive analyses) and restorative or creative fantasy (brainstorming); restorative humor or banter.	Disruptive or confusing shifts between analytic reasoning and fantasy; avoidant humor, joking, or banter.	Inability to follow a thread of meaning.
Altering level of action planning	Appropriate and shared choices of when to talk and when to act; taking turns in a dialogue.	Avoidant disruption of turn-taking in a dialogue; acting out without recognition or sharing intentions in a dialogue; avoidant dialogue when acting is indicated; restless jittering to avoid thinking and feeling.	Impulsively excessive actions.
Altering arousal level	Appropriate lulls, silences, excitements, and turn-takings; useful cycles of activity and inactivity in complementary actions.	Excessive speed or slowing of actions to avoid useful confrontations.	Unavailable to shared communication because of excessive excitement or blunting.

Table 7.5 Schemas that organize conscious experience: Outcomes of control processes

Defensive outcomes			
Control processes	Adaptive	Maladaptive	Failure of regulation
(a) Altering self schemas	Improved understanding of situation; enriched sense of identity.	Excessively grand or inferior beliefs about self; takes on a negative self schema to avoid identity diffusion; "subpersonalities."	Identity diffusion, states of depersonalization.
(b) Altering schema of other person	Enriched understanding of the intentions, motives, and predictable patterns of other.	Disregard of nature of other to preserve fantasy or personal stereotypes; changes the object of a feeling, wish, or source of threat from a more pertinent to a less pertinent one (displacement).	Impoverished understanding of other as a center of feelings and initiative.
(c) Altering role relationship models	Resilient change in internal working model of a current situation; useful learning through identification, mourning, resolving transferences.	Reverses roles inappropriate to the situation; switches working models into all-good or all-bad views of the relationship; changes the agent or source of an activity, wish, or feeling from self to other or other to self (role-reversal, projection).	Annihilation anxiety or panic on separations, states of derealization.
(d) Altering value schemas (critic role)	Sagacious monitoring and judging of self and others, and of future critique of present choices; maintains useful vows and commitments; emancipatory self-reflections.	Unrealistic devaluation or idealization of self and/or other; switches values so rapidly that doubt paralyzes action.	Inability to evaluate moral consequences.
(e) Altering executive-agency schema	Restorative sense of being a part of something beyond self; intergenerational sense of responsibility for others.	Excessive surrender of best interests of self; excessive self-centeredness.	States of alienation.

Table 7.6 Schemas that organize interpersonal communications: Outcomes of control processes

Defensive outcomes

Control processes	Adaptive	Maladaptive	Failure of regulation
(a) Altering self schemas	Increase in competence and resilience within a situation; improved fit of behavior to the situation.	Jarring shift in "personality"; acting in a too-superior or too-inferior way; uses others as if they were part of, or extension of the self.	Intentional signals are confusing.
(b) Altering schema of other person	Increase in understanding of the intentions, motives, and predictable patterns of other (empathy); ability to "read" another during an interaction.	Reacts to an internal misperception of the other; provokes the other to conform to an internal misperception (projective identification); short circuits to an inappropriate all-good or all-bad view of other; changes the object of a feeling, wish, or source of threat from the most pertinent one to a less pertinent one (displacement).	Chaotic views about what to expect from another in a situation.
(c) Altering role relationship models	Useful trials of a new pattern for a situation.	Disguises or undoes an intended script sequence by running an alternative, compromise, or opposite one (undoing, passive aggression); shimmering alternations of contradictory patters; pretense of roles that are not felt authentically; preservation of an inappropriate script rather than acting flexibly as the situation unfolds; switches working models into all-good or all all-bad views of the relationship; changes the agent or source of an activity, wish, or feeling from self to other, or other to self.	Inability to use relationships with others to stabilize a sense of identity.
(d) Altering value schemas (critic role)	Points out the following of, or deflection from, values, rules, and commitments by self and others, in order to improve future situation.	Irrational assumptions of other's values to avoid social tension; inhibition of spontaneity by excessive monitoring; attributes blame irrationally outward to protect self-esteem.	Impulsive, punitive, revenge behaviors (on self or others).
(e) Altering executive-agency schema	Acts responsibly to care for others and to care for self as situations demand.	Unrealistic abnegation of self; suddenly selfish or altruistic acts that disrupt relationships.	Inability to responsibly care for others.

Some generalizations from such work on personality typologies can help clinicians when they are helping a person work through a life crisis or traumatic experience rather than aiming at a slower, longer treatment to modify character structure. Such generalizations are summarized for three common typologies in Tables 7.7, 7.8, and 7.9.

Table 7.7 Obstacles to therapy with people who habitually inhibit ideas

Defensive style	Therapeutic counter
Global or selective inattention with impressionistic rather than accurate discourse about the events.	Encourage talk and provide verbal labels. Ask for details, then construct cause-and-effect sequences.
Limited disclosure due to inhibitions of ideas.	Encourage verbal production through clarifications.
Short circuit to erroneous conclusions.	Keep the topic open and emphasize step-by-step decision-making.
Misinterpretations based on past stereotypes of self and others.	Interpret what is realistically likely, and differentiate that from what is most dreaded, and what is ideally desired. Differentiate reality from fantasy; clarify time frames, distinguishing past from possible futures.

Table 7.8 Obstacles to therapy with people who habitually avoid emotion

Defensive style	Therapeutic style
Excessively detailed but peripheral approach to talking about emotional stressors.	Ask for personal impressions and meanings.
Avoids disclosure of emotion.	Interpret linkage of emotional meanings to ideational meanings. Focus attention on mental images, emotions, and felt reactions.
Juggles opposing sets of meanings back and forth.	Hold discussions on one valence of a topic. Interpret defensive shifting and the meanings it conceals.
Endless rumination without reaching decisions about how to act.	Interpret reasons for warding-off reaching decisions, and for impulsive actions rather than carefully chosen ones. Encourage action planning in relation to imagined outcomes.

Table 7.9 Obstacles to therapy with people who distort reality for self-enhancement

Defensive style	Therapeutic counter
Focuses on praise and blame and is deceitful.	Avoid being provoked into either praising or blaming, and do not accuse of lying.
Avoidance or disavowed information that deflates self-concepts.	Use tactful timing and wording to counteract denials and deceits.
Slides meanings about who did what to whom, that is, the importance of what the other person did may be exaggerated to blame them for what the self-minimized to reduce self-criticism.	Consistently redefine meanings and encourage realistic appraisals while bolstering against shame.

(continued)

Table 7.9 (continued)

Defensive style	Therapeutic counter
Excessive attention to finding routes to self-enhancement.	Cautiously deflate grandiose meanings while emphasizing realistic skills and capacities.
Dislocates bad attributes of self to another.	Clarify who is who in terms of acts, intentions, and expectations.
Forgives self too easily when some remorse is realistically justified. Denies any culpability in causing or reacting to stressors.	Support self-esteem with a genuine interest in the patient while working toward an appropriate sense of responsibility. Help patient plan for realistic acts of remorse without excessive shame in instances of realistic "guilt."

Conclusion

David Shapiro's approach was inspirational in focusing the author's attention on defensive control processes. This chapter has focused on short order observations. The goal has been to understand what is going on, how it works, in terms of intrapsychic models and interpersonal models of the same mental processes. These mental processes were categorized as those effecting the contents of what was thought or enacted, the form of thought or sequential communication, and the person schematic organizers of intrapsychic representations and interpersonal transactions.

References

Conte, H. R., & Plutchik, R. (1995). *Ego defenses: Theory and measurement*. New York: Wiley.

Horowitz, M. J. Levels of interpretation in dynamic psychotherapy. *Psychoanalytic Psychology, 3*, 39–45, 1986.

Horowitz, M. J. (Ed.) (1988a). *Psychodynamics and cognition*. Chicago: University of Chicago Press.

Horowitz, M. J. *Introduction to psychodynamics: A new synthesis* (1988b). New York: Basic Books.

Horowitz, M. J. (1991). *Person schemas and maladaptive interpersonal patterns*. Chicago: University of Chicago Press.

Horowitz, M. J., Markman, H. C., Stinson, C. H., Ghannam, J. H., & Fridhandler, B. A. (1990). Classification theory of defense. In J. Singer (Ed.), *Repression and dissociation: implications for personality theory, psychopathology and health*. Chicago: University of Chicago Press.

Horowitz, M. J., Cooper, S., Fridhandler, B., Perry, J. C., Bond, M., & Vaillant, G. (1992). Control processes and defense mechanisms. *Journal of Psychotherapy Practice and Research, 1*(4), 324–336.

Horowitz, M. J., & Stinson, C. H. (1995). Defenses as aspects of person schemas and control processes. In H. Conte & R. Plutchik (Eds.), *Ego defenses: Theory and measurement* (pp. 79–97). New York: Wiley.

Horowitz, M.J., Znoj, H., & Stinson, C. (1996). Defensive control processes: Use of theory in research, formulation, and therapy of stress response syndromes. In M. Zeidner & N. Endler (Eds.), *Handbook of coping* (pp. 532–553). New York: Wiley.

Perry, J. C., Augusto, F. & Cooper, S. H. (1989). Assessing psychodynamic conflicts: I. Reliability of the ideographic conflict formulation method. *Psychiatry*, *52*, 289–301.

Persons, J. B. (1989). *Cognitive therapy in practice: A case formulation approach*. New York/London: W.W. Norton.

Persons, J. B. (1992, September). A case formulation approach to cognitive-behavior therapy: Application to panic disorder. *Psychiatric Annals*, *22* (9), 470–473.

Saklofske, D. H., & Zeidner, M. (1995). *Personality and intelligence*. New York: Springer.

Shapiro, D. (1965). *Neurotic styles*. New York: Basic Books.

Shapiro, D. (1981). *Autonomy and rigid character*. New York: Basic Books.

Shapiro, D. (2000). *Dynamics of character*. New York: Basic Books.

Singer, J. L. (Ed.). (1990) *Repression and dissociation: Implications for personality theory, psychopathology, and health*. Chicago: University of Chicago Press.

Vaillant, G. E. (1994). Ego mechanisms of defense and personality psychopathology. *Journal of Abnormal Psychology*, *102*(1), 44–50.

Young, J. E. (1994). *Cognitive therapy for personality disorders: A schema-focused approach* (3rd ed.). Sarasota: Professional Resource Exchange, Incorporated.

Reply to Mardi Horowitz

David Shapiro

Dr. Horowitz's paper has two closely related aims; both are related to psychotherapy, but I would like to consider them separately. The first, which occupies most of the paper, is to describe particulars of various defense processes as they may appear in, or be suggested by, the immediate behavior of the patient. He makes the important point that these processes, often regarded as entirely internal, manifest themselves interpersonally as well. In all of this, he aims to help the therapist recognize the dynamics of the patient as it shows itself in the "here and now." It is an approach to understanding patients and to doing psychotherapy that is of course very congenial to me. I think this kind of understanding is experienced by the patient with a reactive immediacy, quite different from intellectual insight, that itself constitutes change. Thus, the therapist says, "You seem to be struggling not to cry;" instantly the tears flow freely, the posture relaxes, the voice changes. Even though such change may be only momentary, it is an increment of more general, lasting change.

But I think something is missing in Horowitz's observations, as they are presented in his tables, that will seriously affect their usefulness to therapists. His observations are too objective, too abstract. Even the direct observations of defensive speech or behavior contain virtually no mention of the way something is said or done. He speaks of empathic inferences from behavior of the quality of conscious experience, but his descriptions of behavior are not themselves empathic. There is "flat verbiage" or "avoidant humor." But is the verbiage flat in the way of a dutiful report or is it in the manner of a resigned spirit? Or is it, again something quite different, perhaps confidently businesslike? Is the avoidant humor forced? Does the patient glance at the therapist to see whether his performance is successful? Is it driven? Is it spoken fast, exuberantly, in a loud voice? This is the kind of listening and noticing that is required of a therapist. For that matter, it is the kind of listening that occurs in normal everyday life, although usually without much notice. Empathy begins not in conscious inference from behavior; but in the perception of behavior itself.

The second point has to do with the method of treatment. Horowitz, in this paper, emphasizes that he is speaking of the treatment of "stress induced" reactions, reactions to a life crisis, perhaps to trauma. Apart from his specific therapeutic recommendations for such treatment, this emphasis raises the important question of the difference, if there is or should be any, between such therapy and therapy whose aims are more far reaching. My own view is that there are no essential differences between these if one is dealing consistently with the "here and now." The nature of what is "here and now" will naturally be different – I should say unique – in every case, but the method is the same. Horowitz, I think, does not share that view.

Horowitz's aim in "stress induced" cases of this kind is clearly to reach the underlying and, as he puts it, unmodulated emotional reaction to the crisis or trauma, with the hope of modifying those emotions in the therapeutic situation. I take it that it is in this specific context that he makes recommendations for "counteracting" defense styles, which he regards as "obstacles" to therapy. It seems to me that this point of view in regard to defense is inconsistent with his own understanding, as well as my own. Horowitz clearly believes that defensive processes or styles are aspects of the general working of the personality; in fact, that these styles have adaptive possibilities as well as defensive ones. That these aspects of the personality serve defensive ends can mean that they restrict expression of the emotional reaction to crisis or trauma, but it cannot mean that they are obstacles to therapy. We are, after all, not treating crisis or trauma, but people. These are people who have experienced crisis or trauma according to their own ways, ways that have not been equal to modulating or dispelling the immediate distress of that experience. We are interested in having an effect on those ways, perhaps only a small effect if time is limited, but sufficient to dispel that distress. Those ways of defense, or attitudes, are, in other words, the object of therapeutic work, not an obstacle to it. In this matter, I believe that Dr. Horowitz aims at the wrong target.

Part IV
Self-Deception

Chapter 8
Self-Deceptive Speech: A Psycholinguistic View

Michael F. Schober and Peter J. Glick

In "On the psychology of self-deception," David Shapiro (1996) considers a man talking about a difficult decision he has made. The man says: "I *know* I did the right thing!" with exaggerated emphasis on "know," and he says it more loudly than he would in ordinary conversation. Shapiro characterizes this as the man's attempt to dispel his own doubts, as much to convince himself of the content of what he is saying as to convince his listener; it is thus an attempt at self-deception. In this case, it is an unsuccessful attempt, as evidenced by the man's following up, after a pause, with "I think."

Shapiro sees this as one example of self-deceptive speech, a kind of speech that has several qualities that distinguish it from speech with typical communicative aims. Self-deceptive speech of this sort can be characterized by repetition ("I *know* I did the right thing! I *know* I did!") and by surprising affective disconnects: either notably less affect in the saying than the content would typically warrant (e.g., speaking of being furious without any concomitant sign of anger), or alternatively what Shapiro describes as a melodramatic and artificial feel to the descriptions and gestures. As Shapiro (1996) recounts from prior clinical observation, e.g., from Hellmuth Kaiser in the 1950s, self-deceptive speakers do not "seem to express what they actually thought or felt. The tears sometimes seemed forced or worked up; the story of childhood sounded rehearsed; the angry account of yesterday's event, as one listened to it, had the quality of a public oration" (p. 788).

Another quality of this kind of speech, Shapiro (1996) proposes, is that it comes off as self-directed rather than listener-directed: the speaker is "addressing himself through the listener" (p. 790). Shapiro describes two manifestations of the inwardness of self-deceptive speech. In one version, the speaker does not seem to be attending to the listener at all. His speech has unusual prosodic characteristics that do not take the listener into account (as when our example speaker speaks unusually loudly), and he does not look at the listener in the ordinary way that speakers do. The listener can feel as if he or she is irrelevant to the speaker for the moment, and

M.F. Schober (✉)
Dean and Professor of Psychology, New School for Social Research, Department of Psychology, Office of the Dean, 6 E. 16th St., 10th floor, New York, NY 10003
e-mail: schober@newschool.edu

C. Piers (ed.), *Personality and Psychopathology: Critical Dialogues with David Shapiro*, DOI 10.1007/978-1-4419-6214-0_8, © Springer Science+Business Media, LLC 2011

that the speaker would not notice any reaction the listener might have. In the second version, the speaker gazes intently at the listener as if hoping for confirmation and support for what he is trying to convince himself of; if that confirmation is not perceived as sufficiently forthcoming, through even slight hesitation by the listener, the speaker may work even harder at the self-convincing. Shapiro argues that despite the fact that in this second version the speaker is attending closely to the micro-reactions of the listener, the speech act is still self-directed rather than listener-directed, in that the listener is only being treated as a mirror for self-diagnosis rather than as a real interlocutor.

In Shapiro's view, self-deceptive speech is effortful, even if it is not consciously and deliberately planned, and it necessitates conscious activity because it involves speech and interaction. But speakers are not aware, or fully aware, of their self-deceptive activity; self-deceptive speech lies in a murky borderland between what is conscious and non-conscious, and what is effortful and automatic.

Shapiro's notion of self-deceptive speech does not find a straightforward counterpart in the mainstream of psycholinguistic views on the nature of speech planning and intention, nor in standard pragmatic models of communication. It is, by nature, a notion at the boundaries of ordinary language use. Even if the empirical basis of the phenomenon is not as firmly established as would be needed to convince corpus-based or experimental researchers of its generality, the issues it raises resonate in important ways with psycholinguistic questions and findings about the nature of and limits of language use. In this chapter, we explore these resonances, as well as describe our own empirical corpus-based explorations of self-deceptive language (or should it be called defensive language?), which demonstrate that it seems to have distinctive lexical characteristics (Glick and Schober 2007).

Finally, we will argue that under some circumstances the boundaries between self-deception, other-deception, motivated self-presentation that does not reach the level of deception, and simply choosing among legitimate alternate conceptualizations are quite unclear. Understanding when and how these differ will require greater clarity about the range and kinds of communicative situations in which speakers find themselves, as well as about how interlocutors contribute to speakers' self-deceptive utterances.

Self as Audience

Shapiro's notion of self-deceptive speech requires a speech system in which a speaker in the presence of an addressee can have herself as her primary audience, at least at the moment of the self-deception. This contrasts, presumably, with the ordinary communicative case where the speaker treats her addressee as a full interlocutor. At first blush this seems paradoxical: How can a speaker produce an utterance with the intention of conveying information to herself? Is it possible for a speaker to simultaneously know and not know what she intends? And is it possible *not* to consider one's partner in an interactive situation? Much current thinking about the nature of speech planning and production, and of interactive language use, does not address these questions directly, but some proposals suggest what mechanisms or structures might allow such a bifurcation.

One issue at stake is the notion of a *communicative intention*. The standard approach (see Levelt 1989, for an excellent overview) is that speakers communicate intentions through speech, but not all intentions are communicated (as Levelt says, thank heaven! p. 59) and there are other ways of communicating intentions besides through speech. Communicative intentions, following Grice's approach, are special, in that they always involve an extra purpose of *intention recognition*. That is, for an intention to be communicative the speaker must also intend that the addressee understands what the speaker is saying *because of* the utterance – not because the addressee could otherwise infer the speaker's intention from other actions or behaviors or displays.

The intentions implicated in an utterance can be complex and multilayered. Beyond the main intentions in an utterance there can also be "side intentions" that are backgrounded as associations and embellishments (see Levelt 1989, p. 137). Communicative side intentions can include reasons for a speaker's actions, plans or decisions, and are often encoded in additional grammatical structures beyond the main ones (different clauses, different temporal frames). Non-communicative side intentions often involve the impression the speaker wishes to make on her interlocutor, most often positive social goals like being seen as knowledgeable, pleasant, powerful, humble, or competent. These kinds of self-presentational intentions are usually not encoded in the surface structure of a speech act; making them explicit and grammatical would undermine them. For example, a speaker desiring to be seen as pleasant would be unwise to make the direct claim of pleasantness.

What would this analysis make of the "I *know* I did the right thing!" example? On the surface, the speaker is making an assertion for the interlocutor with the communicative intention of asserting that he knows he did the right thing. If the speaker "really" believes this, then it is a straightforward communicative intention. If the speaker really does not believe this, then he is lying and this is a case of other-deception. He may also have side intentions for his interlocutor of appearing decisive and correct. The fact that Shapiro (and possibly the addressee present at the moment of the speaker's utterance) interprets the utterance as a failure shows that the side intention has gone awry; the inappropriateness of the paralinguistic form of the utterance (too loud) further helps undermine any such side intention. One could also propose that the very syntactic form of the utterance presupposes that there had been a prior accusation or question about the legitimacy of the speaker's judgment; for this (presumably invented) example we don't have a full record of prior discourse, but presumably this utterance would feel far less self-deceptive if it were a response to a direct question: "Do you know that you did the right thing?" Perhaps one part of what makes the utterance seem self-deceptive is that it is answering a question that hadn't been asked.

In any case, to consider this a case of self-deception, where the speaker is trying to convince himself of what he is saying, we must consider the speaker himself to be another addressee in the interaction, and to have a dual role of speaking and listening at the same time. Is there evidence for such a split?

Mainstream psycholinguistic theorizing actually *does* have a role for an internal addressee: what has been called the Monitor or Editor (see Levelt 1989, among many others). The idea is that in speech planning and execution there are monitoring processes that keep track of the extent to which what one is articulating matches what one intends, at all levels of planning and execution (Levelt 1989): Does the ordering of what one is saying fit the larger communicative aims? Does the syntactic structure of one's message cohere? Does one's lexical selection fit what one is intending to say? Is one making any speech errors in grammar, word choice, or pronunciation? The evidence suggests that there are both internal self-monitoring processes that prevent certain kinds of errors from being produced overtly and external self-monitoring processes that catch errors after they have been uttered (and which then allow going back and correcting oneself).

Both internal and external self-monitoring processes require a kind of mental bifurcation, in that the monitoring allows a view of what is about to be or has been produced that is separate from the processes that produced it. In the case of external self-monitoring, the processes involved are most likely the same processes involved in comprehending speech uttered by another; that is, the speaker hears what she herself has said and can judge the extent to which what she is saying does or does not fit her intentions. (Evidence shows that the effectiveness of this kind of monitoring is reduced when the speaker's hearing is interfered with, see Lackner and Tuller 1979.) In the case of internal self-monitoring, the debates are trickier; some argue that a special set of monitoring processes need to be separate from other production and comprehension processes, while others would argue that not only does it make sense that the production system should use the same processes as the comprehension system, but that proposing separate systems leads to the kinds of logical homunculus problems that make dualistic theories of mind untenable (see Levelt 1989, for review). More recently, Pickering and Garrod (2004) have proposed that one of the main features of the mental processes of language users in dialogue is that speakers' production systems and listeners' comprehension systems are tightly interlinked, and that part of the interlinking lies in speakers' being able to attend to their own utterances in the same way that listeners do.

But for psycholinguists the role of the monitor is *not* typically assumed to act at the level Shapiro is talking about, where high-level intentions could be unknown to the speaker. Researchers in language production (see, e.g., Nozari and Dell 2009; Oppenheim and Dell 2008, among many others) have most often focused on "lower" levels of production–comprehension interaction as evidenced in phonological, lexical and syntactic errors and repairs. (It makes sense that this is where the research would have focused, as these kinds of issues are more tractable in empirical lab research and in analyses of large-scale corpora of speech errors.) The evidence from these kinds of studies is that the speech monitoring system is quite sensitive to the lexical character-istics of what is being said; speakers are more likely to produce speech errors that are words within the language rather than non-words, and more likely to produce errors that are semantically related to prior discourse and to the contextual situation (e.g., Baars et al. 1975; Motley 1980; Motley et al. 1981). Speakers seem not only to moni-tor for relatively "dry" aspects of the correctness of their speech output, but also for its social appropriateness. They are less likely to produce taboo words as speech errors than non-taboo words (Motley et al. 1982); the evidence suggests that the taboo word is actually created prior to articulation and the taboo word is then "retracted" before articulation in ways that produce particular speech errors.

In general, it looks as if there can indeed be relatively independent processes that produce an utterance and that then monitor or edit what is produced, either prior to articulation or afterward. (This point is not without controversy; monitoring functions could also be modeled as more central in the production process.) It also seems that the monitor can check for aspects of what has been produced that do not seem to be available to the initial processes that produced it; this suggests that there can be a split between what the producer "knows," at least temporarily, and what the monitor observes. But in all these cases the monitor is the wiser process, the one that comes along and cleans up the mess created by the less careful (or more time-pressured) production mechanism. It is not that the production mechanism is trying to convince the monitor of something that the monitor has yet to be convinced about.

So it seems that the internal audience for Shapiro's self-deceptive utterance is not the same sort of monitor that psycholinguists propose. In Shapiro's example, one could argue that the addition of "I think" is an after-the-fact effort reflecting the monitor's wisdom in recognizing how the initial utterance sounded, and so the monitor and the internal audience are the same thing. (And, simultaneously, the monitor is protecting the initial production mechanism from looking inappropriate or foolish to an external audience.) On the other hand, one could argue that, particularly in cases with no amendment like "I think," the Shapiro notion of self-deceptive speech is describing a failed monitor that does not recognize the discrepancy between what is intended and what is known, and does not see the utterance from any sort of external perspective. In any case, to our knowledge, there is no laboratory or corpus-based psycholinguistic evidence that demonstrates the kind of bifurcation in high-level intention production and comprehension that Shapiro proposes.

What the psycholinguistic literature *does* discuss are the kinds of failures to take one's audience into account that Shapiro argues go along with self-deception: speaking at inappropriate volume, saying more or less than the listener needs, failing to attend to one's partner. A sizable empirical literature has been investigating the extent to which and ways in which speakers succeed and fail at partner-directed language use (for reviews see Brennan and Hanna 2009; Brennan et al. 2010; Keysar et al. 1998; Krauss and Fussell 1996; Pickering and Garrod 2004; Schober 2006; Schober and Brennan 2003) in initial and subsequent moments of processing. The debates are far from resolved, but a notable proposal is that communicative language always starts out planned egocentrically and that speakers adapt to their partner's informational needs only at a later stage of the processing. (The debates are about when and whether this is so; mounting evidence suggests that when relevant information is available, speakers cognitively adapt to their partners from the very first moments of processing.) Following this line, one could characterize what is going on in the Shapiro examples as the speaker's failing to take the addressee's communicative needs and the social situation into account. That is, the addressee who feels that the speaker is not attending to them is picking up on a set of phenomena that do happen often enough in ordinary conversations. Under this interpretation the question would be how one should interpret the speaker's failure to adjust – is it characterological? Is it momentary? Or is it the norm, and only when all the circumstances are right do speakers fully adjust to their partners?

At a quite different level of analysis, one could conceive of the "I *know* I did the right thing" moment as a display that invites the interlocutor's support or confirmation, along the lines of the "ostensible" speech acts (see Isaacs and Clark 1990) that interactional psycholinguists consider. On this view, some speech acts, like many an invitation to "do lunch some time," involve a complicated multilayered social game, in which players who understand the game well know that what the speaker intends is not really what is on record (an invitation to lunch) but a kind gesture that ought to be turned down. Of course, the invitation is public and "on record" and so can't be withdrawn, which is why the game requires both parties to participate in the pretense if the game is to be played well, or else unintended results (lunch plans) or undesired offense (feeling rejected) can occur. On this sort of analysis, one could argue that the self-deceptive statement "I *know* I did the right thing," on record, is a statement of the speaker's belief; off record, it is a request for validation and affirmation that the speaker hopes the addressee will support. The "I think," as the kind of hedge that speakers can use to request input from their interlocutors (see Brennan and Ohaeri 1999), provides further evidence of the off record validation request. A willing partner in the ostensible act would collude by providing validation ("Of course you did the right thing!"). An unwilling or doubtful partner will not comply, and the speaker is stuck; he cannot, in any way that is socially acceptable, make explicit or insist upon the indirect validation request (just as the ostensible lunch-inviter cannot respond "Oh, I didn't really want to have lunch with you").

Obviously, we do not yet have a full picture of which psycholinguistic processes would be involved in self-deception as Shapiro describes it, either at the levels of internal and external self-monitoring or at the levels of partner adaptation or indirect speech acts. Although psycholinguists would describe interactive behaviors like inappropriate volume and failure to monitor the addressee's facial feedback as particular kinds of error in self-monitoring, there are not good accounts of *when* people succeed and fail at self-monitoring. There is good evidence that what speakers monitor varies during the course of an utterance, because it is not possible to monitor for everything all the time; there are cognitive limitations (see Levelt, chapter 12). And as a general principle when people are under greater cognitive load, or have greater working memory limitations, their processing becomes less efficient and accurate. So a reasonable proposal is that under notable cognitive load a speaker may fail to monitor. For Shapiro, the argument could be that trying to convince oneself of something that deep down you do not really believe leads to a particularly high cognitive load.

Lexical Features of Defensive Speech

Even without a full account of the psycholinguistic processes or structures that would be involved in truly self-deceptive speech, we can come closer to an account of what the qualities of that speech would be. As Shapiro has described the nature of self-deceptive speech, there are certain behavioral and paralinguistic features that go along with it, and there may also be structural features, like repetition. To what extent have these clinical observations been validated using methods that psycholinguists would find definitive?

Although there is not much work of a psycholinguistic flavor (see Nelson and Horowitz 2001, for a rare example), there is clinical research on understanding the nature of defensive speech, which is a closely related (if not identical) notion (for discussion of whether all defensiveness is self-deceptive, and all self-deception defensive, see Barrett et al. 2002; Paulhus 1988; Sackeim 1988; Sackeim and Gur 1978; Shapiro 1989, among others). (We acknowledge that "defensive speech" has a more other-oriented flavor than "self-deceptive speech," and does not highlight the possible links between self-deception and other-deception that are worth exploring.) Building on this research, we (Glick and Schober 2007, 2011) have carried out analyses of the lexical characteristics of speech coded as defensive by clinicians, and we have found that it does seem to have some distinctive qualities compared to speech judged to be non-defensive.

In our study, we examined an audio corpus of 63 interviews of undergraduates that had been reliably coded for defensive behavior (Christensen 2003). In each interview, participants had been asked a series of 23 questions about potentially threatening experienced events, like "Describe a time when you've broken your own moral code." Later, researchers coded participants' audiotaped responses to these questions using a four-point scale that was designed to reveal defensive processes (Barrett et al. 2002), by focusing on the content, quality, and coherence of the verbal reports. Thus, we had a corpus of over 1,400 responses coded for how defensive they were.

We carried out lexical analyses on transcripts of the five questions in the interviews that elicited the most defensive answers using Pennebaker, Francis, and Booth's (2001) Linguistic Inquiry and Word Count (LIWC) tool, which is a dictionary-based word counting program. LIWC's dictionary, which was empirically developed and which has now been used in hundreds of studies, includes 74 different categories both of grammatical classifications (e.g., first person pronouns, past tense verbs) and content categories (e.g., family words, positive emotion words). We compared different responses to the same questions by people classified as more and less defensive, as well as different responses characterized as more and less defensive by the same participants; our analyses thus focused on 299 lengthy responses from the corpus.

The results indicated that participants classified as defensive used words differently than their counterparts classified as non-defensive. Across questions and participants, there was consistent and robust evidence that defensive speech had more words that LIWC classifies as cognitive mechanism words (such as *cause, know, ought*) and more exclusive words (such as *but, except, without*) than non-defensive speech. There was also some less conclusive evidence to suggest that defensive language was wordier, used more negation words (*no, never, not*), and repeated the same words more often.

Closer examination of what LIWC is picking up provides hints of what might be going on here. First, defensive speakers' greater use of cognitive mechanism words is consistent with the proposal that they may be attempting to protect their self-concept by offering reasons, justifications, and mitigations for their answers. For example, a participant who had been asked about a time when she broke the rules offered the following explanation as part of her answer (cognitive mechanism words in italics):

> And so I *think* what they did was really unfair to me *because* usually what they do to students who who cheat is they they have them take the test all over again and in this case it was one little part on one little question and it was an equation. I *admit* it was wrong *but* the action they took was far too severe and so ever *since* then I've viewed the school as extremely hypocritical.

Here, the defensive participant refused to take full responsibility for her actions and instead externalized blame and culpability to an outside source. Such a justification seems to be indicative of defensive speech.

Second, in a similar fashion, the increased presence of exclusive words also may be attributed to defensive people's need to distance themselves from potentially incriminating or harmful information. In another example, a participant offered this as part of his response to describe a time when he broke his own moral code (exclusive words in italics):

> I don't like liars at all and it's not so much *that* I've lied recently *but* I've kind of hid things from my girlfriend now. It I mean it was for her own good I mean and she'll know today so *but* I've been like keeping it from her…

Here, the participant seems to defend himself against perceived criticism for lying to a significant other. To minimize the impact he reinterprets the events offering instead a modified view of his behavior. There is a partial admission of guilt but not without attempts at mitigating the severity of his actions.

Third, secondary findings from our study suggested that defensive speech may include other lexical markers. There was some evidence to suggest that defensive speakers were wordier and used more negation words, and that their utterances exhibited greater textual cohesion. Defensive justification may require more words to explain the reasons behind an action: a lengthy rationale to argue that the speaker's thoughts, feelings, or behaviors are not as detrimental or guilt-inducing as they sound. Negation words (*no, never, not*), like exclusive words, can be seen as evidence of a person's attempt to linguistically distance him/herself from an unwanted thought, feeling or behavior, and as such may aid in controlling the idea or perception of a disturbing external event (Vaillant 1992).

Of course, this is an analysis of defensive speech in a very particular setting – a research clinical interview – and so more will need to be done to find out whether these characteristics are similar to those found in other settings. And, of course, these analyses focus on the lexical characteristics of that speech, and not the paralinguistic or other aspects that Shapiro argues are important features of self-defensive speech. Nonetheless, they provide initial support for the idea that there are stable characteristics of a mode of discourse that is usually characterized more through case study analysis, and that with the right sampling methods we can start to understand those characteristics more systematically.

What is notable is that the lexical profile we see for defensive/self-deceptive language is different from that identified for other-deception (lying) (Berry et al. 1997; Burgoon et al. 2003; Hancock et al. 2008). When people lie, the evidence is that they say less, use fewer first-person pronouns, more negative emotion words and fewer exclusive words (DePaulo et al. 2003; Newman et al. 2003). Unlike other-deceivers, our defensive speakers say more, use *more* exclusive words rather than less, and they do not differ in their use of first-person pronouns or negative emotion words from nondefensive speakers or when they are not speaking defensively. To the extent that our findings reflect a generalized profile of how defensive people talk, we can speculate that the processes involved in other-deception (which lead to the lexical form of what is said) are different from those involved in self-deception. That is, even though liars also seem to distance themselves from what they are saying, for example by referring to themselves less often, the kind of distancing they are doing may be different. This make sense; liars do not want the addressee to recognize that anything unusual is going on, whereas defensive speakers do, and they want the addressee's understanding or exoneration.

The research on other-deceptive language use has another intriguing finding that may be relevant to self-deception: the linguistic profile of the person being lied to looks different from the profile of a person who is being told the truth (Hancock et al. 2008). That is, there seems to be detectable evidence of the lie in what the interlocutor says, even when the interlocutor has no awareness that the speaker is lying. More specifically, the target of a lie tends to match their linguistic style to the liar more closely than when being told the truth. Some dimensions of this style matching include reducing their use of first person pronouns, causal terms and sentence complexity, while increasing their use of negations, just like the liar. The person being lied to also asks questions more when being lied to than when being told the truth, although this does not seem to help their ability to detect lies (Hancock et al. 2008).

The possibility that the recipient of self-deceptive or defensive language may actually show evidence of the self-deception in their own speech, whether or not they are aware that something unusual is going on, suggests that the interlocutor's role in defensive and self-deceptive language is worth considering more directly. We propose that a full account of self-deceptive speech should include its discourse context, and how the interlocutor's prior utterances, ongoing behavior, and reactions might be affecting the self-deceptive utterance.

What Kind of Communicative Moment?

The kind of speech that Shapiro examines falls into under-explored territory that is not discussed by the mainstream of theories of language use. We are curious about the range of situations in which this kind of speech happens, the kinds of interpersonal moments; surely there are moments in which it is less likely to occur. We assume, for example, that a speaker is less likely to say "I *know* I did the right thing" to a child at a birthday party or in a casual transaction at the supermarket with a clerk than in a confessional moment with a friend or spouse, an ethnographic interview, or a psychotherapy session. That is, even if the speaker is treating their addressee operationally as a sounding board rather than a real interlocutor, we assume that there are nonetheless particular partners with whom the kinds of topics of discussion that could merit self-deception are still less likely to occur.

What our theories of language use lack is a taxonomy of situations that classify different kinds of interpersonal moments with different affordances, and thus which circumstances lend themselves to the expression of self-deception. To our thinking, it will be useful to understand more about those kinds of moments and their communicative dynamics, as it is not only the speaker's utterance but the addressee's being treated without regard in particular ways that characterize self-deceptive speech. Understanding when these moments shade into other-deception or are characterizable simply as "spin" or positive self-presentation will help flesh out a theory of self-deception.

Consider, for example, the moment during a clinical interview or survey interview when a patient or respondent is asked to report about a potentially sensitive or embarrassing behavior, as happens regularly when respondents are asked questions like: "How many sex partners have you had in the last 12 months?" The evidence is that different interviewing circumstances lead to different levels of reporting in large-scale surveys (and thus different national or regional estimates of sexual activity in the population): the average reported number of sex partners is notably different when people answer the question on a computer in a self-administered survey than when they answer to a human interviewer face to face or on the telephone; women report more sexual partners and men fewer (e.g., Tourangeau and Smith 1996; see Tourangeau and Yan 2007, for a review). Of course, we can't know which number is more likely to be the true answer, but the common interpretation is that most American women are embarrassed to report having had many sex partners and men are embarrassed to report fewer; somehow the self-administered computer interview frees respondents to reporting more accurately, perhaps because it is perceived as unable to judge or condemn. This sort of finding extends to various other kinds of sensitive questions and to questions about psychological distress, with respondents in some circumstances reporting more depressive and anxious symptoms to computers than to humans (see e.g., Epstein et al. 2001; Moum 1998; Rosen et al. 2009); and of course it raises questions about the usual wisdom that face to face interviews are the gold standard for creating rapport and eliciting honest responding.

Imagine that a respondent reports a particular number of sex partners to a human interviewer, and that she might have reported a higher number to a computer. What exactly might be going on here? There is a range of interpretations. One interpretation is that the respondent reporting the lower number is presenting a version of herself that is consistent with her desired self rather than her actual self, that is, that she is simply lying to look better. Another interpretation is that the respondent, faced with an intolerably embarrassing moment, is self-deceiving or lying to herself: telling herself what she wishes were true, even though a part of her knows that the truth is different than what she is presenting.

One could also account for this as neither deception nor self-deception, but rather as a legitimate (and truthful) self-presentation based on the respondent's leeway in deciding which behaviors to count as sexual acts. That is, while some physical encounters unambiguously count as having a sex partner by any sensible definition, others are murkier and could be counted differently depending on one's personal or community definitions. Notoriously, there seems to be a generational difference on whether oral sex counts as sex, but various kinds of what was once called "petting" might be counted if one is particularly stringent or wants to report a high number of partners, but could be discounted if one wants to report a lower number. In this case, either a higher or lower number could be justifiable to report; either number could be consistent with providing an answer that is faithful to what the respondent believes the question author intended to be asking. Even if each answer represents a particular perspective or "spin" on the matter that presents the respondent in a different light, that is quite a different matter than other-deception or self-deception.

This kind of communicative issue arises more frequently than one might think, given the definitional variability across people and situations. For example, we have found (Suessbrick et al. 2005) that people's interpretations of what counts as smoking a cigarette are astonishingly variable when they are asked whether they have smoked 100 cigarettes in their entire lives; some count only tobacco cigarettes and others include clove cigarettes, cigars, and marijuana; some include any cigarettes they finished and others count cigarettes from which they took just one puff; some include only cigarettes they bought and others include cigarettes they "borrowed." The interpretation differences are enough to affect answers to the question; 10% of our respondents changed their answer from yes to no or no to yes when asked to count only tobacco cigarettes and count any from which they had taken even a single puff. In this case, we would be hard pressed to consider these alternate reports as deceptive or self-deceptive, or even unsavory "spin"; they seem to reflect different boundaries for what counts in a category and what does not, and perhaps different levels of flexibility in how solid those boundaries are in different communicative situations.

In contrast, a different moment in our tobacco interviews seems, on the surface, far more connected with a sense of self-deception. Current smokers in the survey were all asked whether they intended to quit smoking within the next 12 months. All of them answered that yes, they did. Next they were asked whether they intended to quit smoking within the next 6 months. A large majority reported that they did not, although often after a pause, and quite often with a rueful laugh, as if they had been caught at having been insincere a moment earlier when reporting their intention to quit in 12 months. That moment of saying "yes" to intending to quit in 12 months seems a legitimate candidate as a moment of self-deception given the immediately subsequent answer and the affect that went with it. But one could also ask whether it should better be considered other-deception, or politeness (wanting to be agreeable to the hint that the question assumes) or motivated self-presentation: wanting to present oneself in the best light to a human interlocutor, or wanting to be the person one wishes to be. Or, more complicatedly, whether in the murky moment of answering "yes" several of these might be at play.

In any case, we propose that considering a range of examples of polite responses, clear lies, self-presentations with "spin," and cases of speech characterizable as defensive or self-deceptive will help us to lay out this particular interpersonal terrain, and clarify which moments are unambiguous and which fall into the communicative borderland. Shapiro's characterization of self-deceptive speech presents a challenge to the mainstream of psycholinguistic accounts that is worth taking up. We propose that understanding more about the audience for these acts, what the speaker believes about the audience, and how the audience's ongoing behavior affects the speaker are likely to be an important part of the puzzle.

Acknowledgments We thank the New School for Social Research for helping to support the writing of this chapter, and Susan Brennan, Fred Conrad, Jeff Hancock, Craig Piers, and Rebecca Rosen for helpful comments on an earlier version.

References

Baars, B. J., Motley, M. T., & McKay, D. (1975). Output editing for lexical status from artificially elicited slips of the tongue. *Journal of Verbal Learning and Verbal Behavior, 14*, 382–391.

Barrett, L. F., Williams, N. L., & Fong, G. T. (2002). Defensive verbal behavior assessment. *Personality and Social Psychology Bulletin, 28*, 776–788.

Berry, D. S., Pennebaker, J. W., Mueller, J. S., & Hiller, W. S. (1997). Linguistic bases of social perception. *Personality and Social Psychology Bulletin, 23*, 526–537.

Brennan, S.E., Galati, A., & Kuhlen, A. (2010). Two minds, one dialog: Coordinating speaking and understanding. In B. H. Ross (Ed.), *The Psychology of Learning and Motivation, Vol. 53* (pp. 301–344). Burlington: Academic Press.

Brennan, S. E., & Hanna, J. E. (2009). Partner-specific adaptation in dialog. *Topics in Cognitive Science, 1*(2), 274–291.

Brennan, S. E., & Ohaeri, J. O. (1999). Why do electronic conversations seem less polite? The costs and benefits of hedging. *Proceedings of the International Joint Conference on Work Activities, Coordination, and Collaboration (WACC '99)* (pp. 227–235). San Francisco: ACM.

Burgoon, J. K., Blair, J. P., Qin, T., & Nunamaker, J. F. (2003). Detecting deception through linguistic analysis. *Intelligence and Security Informatics, 2665*, 91–101.

Christensen, T. C. (2003). *Experiencing sampling procedures: Are they probes to autonetic awareness?* Unpublished doctoral dissertation, Boston College, Boston.

DePaulo, B. M., Lindsay, J. J., Malone, B. E., Muhlenbruck, L., Charlton, K., & Cooper, H. (2003). Cues to deception. *Psychological Bulletin, 129*, 74–118.

Epstein, J. F., Barker, P. R., & Kroutil, L. A. (2001). Mode effects in self-reported mental health data. *Public Opinion Quarterly, 65*, 529–549.

Glick, P. J., & Schober, M. F. (2007). *Lexical content of defensive speech.* Paper presented at the 17th annual meeting of the Society for Text and Discourse, Glasgow.

Glick, P. J., & Schober, M. F. (2011). *Lexical characteristics of defensive speech.* Manuscript in preparation.

Hancock, J. T., Curry, L., Goorha, S., & Woodworth, M. T. (2008). On lying and being lied to: A linguistic analysis of deception. *Discourse Processes, 45*, 1–23.

Isaacs, E. A., & Clark, H. H. (1990). Ostensible invitations. *Language in Society, 19*, 493–509.

Keysar, B., Barr, D. J., & Horton, W. S. (1998). The egocentric basis of language use: Insights from a processing approach. *Current Directions in Psychological Science, 7*, 46–50.

Krauss, R. M., & Fussell, S. R. (1996). Social psychological models of interpersonal communication. In E. T. Higgins & A. Kruglanski (Eds.), *Social psychology: Handbook of basic principles* (pp. 655–701). New York: Guilford.

Lackner, J. R., & Tuller, B. H. (1979). Role of efference monitoring in the detection of self-produced speech errors. In W. E. Cooper & E. C. T. Walker (Eds.), *Sentence processing: Psycholinguistic studies presented to Merrill Garrett.* Hillsdale: Lawrence Erlbaum.

Levelt, W. J. M. (1989). *Speaking: From intention to articulation*. Cambridge: MIT Press.

Motley, M. T. (1980). Verification of "Freudian slips" and semantic prearticulatory editing via laboratory-induced spoonerisms. In V. A. Fromkin (Ed.), *Errors in linguistic performance: Slips of the tongue, ear, pen, and hand*. New York: Academic.

Motley, M. T., Baars, B. J., & Camden, C. T. (1981). Syntactic criteria in prearticulatory editing: Evidence from laboratory-induced slips of the tongue. *Journal of Psycholinguistic Research, 10*, 503–522.

Motley, M. T., Camden, C. T., & Baars, B. J. (1982). Covert formulation and editing of anomalies in speech production: Evidence from experimentally elicited slips of the tongue. *Journal of Verbal Learning and Verbal Behavior, 21*, 578–594.

Moum, T. (1998). Mode of administration and interviewer effects in self-reported symptoms of anxiety and depression. *Social Indicators Research, 45*, 279–318.

Nelson, K. L., & Horowitz, L. M. (2001). Narrative structure in recounted sad memories. *Discourse Processes, 31*, 307–324.

Newman, M. L., Pennebaker, J. W., Berry, D. S., & Richards, J. M. (2003). Lying words: Predicting deception from linguistic style. *Personality and Social Psychology Bulletin, 29*, 665–675.

Nozari, N., & Dell, G. S. (2009). More on lexical bias: How efficient can a "lexical editor" be? *Journal of Memory and Language, 60*, 291–307.

Oppenheim, G. M., & Dell, G. S. (2008). Inner speech slips exhibit lexical bias, but not the phonemic similarity effect. *Cognition, 106*, 528–537.

Paulhus, D. L. (1988). Self-deception: Where do we stand? In J. S. Lockard & D. L. Paulhus (Eds.), *Self-deception: An adaptive mechanism?* (pp. 251–257). Englewood Cliffs: Prentice Hall.

Pennebaker, J. W., Francis, M. E., & Booth, R. J. (2001). *Linguistic Inquiry and Word Count (LIWC): LIWC2001*. Mahwah: Erlbaum.

Pickering, M. J., & Garrod, S. (2004). Toward a mechanistic psychology of dialogue. *Behavioral and Brain Sciences, 27*, 169–190.

Rosen, R. L., Schober, M. F., & Conrad, F. G. (2009). *Mode effects in questions about stigmatized behaviors and personal distress*. Paper presented at the 64th annual conference of the American Association for Public Opinion Research, Hollywood.

Sackeim, H. A. (1988). Self-deception: A synthesis. In J. S. Lockard & D. L. Paulhus (Eds.), *Self-deception: An adaptive mechanism?* (pp. 146–165). New York: Prentice-Hall.

Sackeim, H. A., & Gur, R. C. (1978). Self-deception, self-confrontation, and consciousness. In G. E. Schwartz & D. Shapiro (Eds.), *Consciousness and self-regulation: Advances in research* (Vol. 2, pp. 139–197). New York: Plenum.

Schober, M. F. (2006). Dialogue and interaction. In K. Brown (Ed.), *The encyclopedia of language and linguistics* (2nd ed., pp. 564–571). Oxford: Elsevier.

Schober, M. F., & Brennan, S. E. (2003). Processes of interactive spoken discourse: The role of the partner. In A. C. Graesser, M. A. Gernsbacher, & S. R. Goldman (Eds.), *Handbook of discourse processes* (pp. 123–164). Mahwah: Lawrence Erlbaum.

Shapiro, D. (1989). *Psychotherapy of neurotic character*. New York: Basic Books.

Shapiro, D. (1996). On the psychology of self-deception. *Social Research, 63*, 785–800.

Shapiro, D. (1996). On the psychology of self-deception. *Social Research, 63*(3), 785–800.

Suessbrick, A., Schober, M. F., & Conrad, F. G. (2005). When do respondent misconceptions lead to survey response error? In *Proceedings of the American Statistical Association, Section on Survey Research Methods*. Alexandria: American Statistical Association.

Tourangeau, R., & Smith, T. W. (1996). Asking sensitive questions: The impact of data collection mode, question format and question context. *Public Opinion Quarterly, 60*, 274–304.

Tourangeau, R., & Yan, T. (2007). Sensitive questions in surveys. *Psychological Bulletin, 133*, 859–883.

Vaillant, G. E. (1992). *Ego mechanisms of defense*. Washington, DC: American Psychiatric Press.

Reply to Michael Schober and Peter Glick

David Shapiro

There can hardly be a subject matter more important to effective clinical work than self-deceptive speech. The reason is simple, though it involves a major change in the conception of the dynamics of psychopathology. We are able to see now that those dynamics are not constituted of particular unconscious conflicts within the person, separated from that person's attitudes and purposeful behavior. To the contrary, the individual's purposeful action is involved in a central, self-protective way in the pathological dynamics. It is often rationalized and in any case is aimed unwittingly at dispelling anxiety whose nature is unknown to its subject. This self-protective action is represented in the therapy hour itself and consists largely of self-deceptive speech. In that speech the patient reassures himself, without realizing that he is doing so; defends himself against charges, not knowing that they are of his making; persuades himself that he really wants what he thinks he should want. Well trained therapists are able recognize these dynamics, at least some of the time. But, how? We do not know all that makes self-deceptive speech recognizable or what, if anything, makes it distinguishable from conscious deception. This is the area that Schober and Glick look into and in which they offer an experimental study. It is clearly an area where dynamic psychology and psycholinguistics meet.

As Schober and Glick point out early in their essay, the psychology of self-deception requires some conception of self-monitoring of speech and thought, and therefore, as they put it, some kind of "mental bifurcation" is implied. The complicated question arises of whether the internal monitor is to be imagined as a separate institution. Schober and Glick, if I understand them correctly, lean carefully toward the assumption of independent processes for the production of speech and monitoring it, although they are obviously conscious of the logical risks of a dualistic conception. Clinicians, however, have a special reason for rejecting the idea of a separate self-monitoring institution. Homunculus-like conceptions of internal forces or agencies to which responsibility for action is assigned have played a problematic role in dynamic psychology. I am referring in particular to the conception, especially present in early psychoanalysis, of unconscious forces or agencies pursuing *their* aims in symptomatic behavior. It is a conception that works directly against the therapeutic goal of reviving the patient's experience of *his* reasons, not those of an unconscious force within him, for doing what he does.

The concept of a separate self-monitoring agency for self-deception, an agency that knows what not to know, is not only logically dubious, but also unnecessary. As I said in my paper *On the Psychology of Self Dece*ption (1996), "Regulatory monitoring and even regulatory action do not necessarily require understanding, and intention does not have to be knowledgeable. We jerk our hand from the hot plate not because we are afraid of damage to the skin, but because it hurts" (p. 786).

In other words, an internal monitoring effect requires only a signaling system, not a knowledgeable one. Specifically, it requires only an organization of attitudes which will respond with discomfort to the incipient articulation of ideas inimical to it. The individual's character or personality constitutes such a monitor. Inasmuch as such a discomfort or anxiety will then trigger, according to the personality, a corrective reaction, such as self-deceptive speech ("I *know* I did the right thing"), capable in principle of forestalling that conscious articulation, the monitoring and corrective actions are one. (Schober and Glick, incidentally, presume this example of mine to have been invented. It was not. The speaker was a free lance professional who frequently faced difficult job choices. In this instance, he had rejected the bird-in-the-hand at least partly because he considered that choice to be "weak.")

Schober and Glick consider the monitoring function in self-deception to be of a different sort from the kind familiar in psycholinguistics for the avoidance of speech errors. Their reason for that view is not clear to me. I should think that a signaling conception of monitoring comparable to the process I proposed for self-deception would be applicable as well for the correction of language errors. That would require, presumably, an existing structure of lexical, and perhaps social, standards sensitive to errors or transgressions. While the subjects and the effects of monitoring are certainly quite different in the two cases, their formal relationship may not be so distant. I say that admittedly prompted by a general supposition that the processes involved in self-deceptive speech must be ordinary psycholinguistic processes put to special use.

It is a curious thing about the experimental study Schober and Glick report that from the standpoint of a clinician it was more successful than might have been expected. To a clinical observer, after all, the most obvious distinction between self-deceptive speech and ordinary communicative speech (and lying) is not in the difference of the words used, but the different ways the same words are used. For that reason, I would think that formal or structural features of speech are more likely to show distinctions between self-deceptive and communicative speech than the use of particular words. Schober and Glick mention that possibility also and demonstrate it with findings such as greater wordiness and repetition in self-deceptive speech. Perhaps the use of many qualifying clauses would be another such feature. Of course, the separation between particular word content and structural features is not absolute; certain words like "but," "really" or "never," possibly the unusual use of adverbs and adjectives in general, suggest unnecessary emphasis or wordy complication. At any rate, though they may have fished in unpromising waters, Schober and Glick have made a catch. They have produced evidence of lexical distinctions and in that way have confirmed, as they say, the distinctness of a self-deceptive style of speech.

Schober and Glick raise additional interesting questions concerning the effects of the particular audience on self-deceptive speech and vice versa. Altogether, the relationships of the self-deceiving speaker to himself and to his listener are of great interest. In this connection, I found especially interesting their anecdote telling of the smoker's rueful laugh during the survey when he recognized, and abandoned, his self-deception. I have seen a good natured and rueful laugh of exactly that kind many times as a psychotherapist at the moment a patient becomes conscious of his own self-deception. It is the patient's laugh at himself as he abandons an effort that he had not noticed himself making and now, seeing it, regards as pointless. That laugh in psychotherapy – and I have no doubt also in the survey interview – expresses a significant alteration not only in the individual's emotional state of mind but, also, in his cognitive state. His voice sounds more relaxed and conversational. He no longer looks away as he speaks or looks only for signs of confirmation; he looks with recognition at the listener and the listener in turn has the distinct impression of now being seen. This cognitive change occurring as it does at the moment the self-deception is abandoned brings into relief the speaker's peculiar cognitive state before its abandonment.

Reply to David Shapiro

Michael F. Schober and Peter J. Glick

We appreciate David Shapiro's thoughtful reply to our chapter, and we agree with him that any processes involved in self-deception should indeed be extensions of basic cognitive and psycholinguistic processes. Like him (and various psycholinguists), we are also uncomfortable with an overly dualistic notion of the monitor. Nonetheless, we believe that it will be a challenge for a theory of self-deception to detail how a monitor for high-level intentions really can be construed in a non-dualistic way. Even though it would be parsimonious if all monitoring processes, from lowest to highest levels, were continuous in terms of mental representation and processes, there is as yet no evidence that demonstrates such continuity. How one conceives of the "self" in self-deception that is deceivable is thus a complicated affair. We believe that Shapiro's alternative "reflex" notion (of a non-knowledge-able signaling system) is attractive, but many more details are left to be worked out before such a model fully connects with what is known about language planning and processing.

As for what Shapiro calls our fishing expedition, we are less surprised than he that we find in our data lexical evidence for a defensive style of speech, as lexical markers are concomitants of syntactic and discourse-level phenomena. Nothing in our findings requires that this style of speech be lexically driven rather than being a "linguistic fingerprint" or trace of the cognitive phenomena involved. On the other hand, language production involves many intertwined layers or cascades of macro- and micro-planning, with discourse-level intentions and syntactic choices not only driving but being driven by lexical choices. So we would not rule out that these effects could be lexical or at least have lexical components; we would expect to see evidence for a discourse style at multiple levels.

We are glad to know that the example "I *know* I did the right thing!" wasn't invented. From our perspective, it would be fascinating to see a full transcript not only of the patient's but also of Shapiro's verbal and paralinguistic behaviors throughout the interaction; it would also be useful to understand more of what happened before. We assume that there could be much to learn from a close look at what the therapist contributes to such a moment – both in the patient's beliefs about how the therapist is likely to respond (which could be based as much on carry-over from other conversational partners as from the therapist) and in how the therapist's behavior at the moment could make a difference. Presumably the effects of the therapist's overtly challenging the self-deceptive speech and colluding in it would be evident; presumably if the therapist merely listened with no visible change in expression this could also be interpreted as a signal by the patient. Even the physical setting – chair or couch – could presumably make a difference not only in what the patient thinks is going on, but in how responsive the therapist is and how the patient interprets a therapist's silence (DiNardo et al. 2005). As we see it, the very particular conversational goals that the interlocutors bring to this conversation – which may not match (Russell and Schober 1999) – surely are at play in making sense of the peculiar kind of moment into which Shapiro so intriguingly delves.

References

DiNardo, A. C., Schober, M. F., & Stuart, J. (2005). Chair and couch discourse: A study of visual copresence in psychoanalysis. *Discourse Processes, 40*, 209–238.

Russell, A. W., & Schober, M. F. (1999). How beliefs about a partner's goals affect referring in goal-discrepant conversations. *Discourse Processes, 27*(1), 1–33.

Chapter 9
Neurotic Self-Deception as a Reproductive Strategy

Lawrence Josephs

> If deceit is fundamental in animal communication, then there must be strong selection to spot deception and this ought, in turn, to select for a degree of self-deception, rendering some facts and motives unconscious so as not to betray – by the subtle signs of self-knowledge – the deception being practiced
>
> Trivers (1976, p. xx)

Freud originally tried to ground psychoanalysis in the principles of evolutionary biology as Freud was quite familiar with Darwin's work (Makari 2008, p. 111). Unfortunately, some of those principles proved erroneous such as Lamarck's belief in the inheritance of acquired characteristics, Haeckel's idea that ontogeny must recapitulate phylogeny, and the assumption that natural selection selects groups rather than individuals (Nesse and Lloyd 1992). In addition, Freudian thought has frequently been charged with excessive biological reductionism and determinism that tends to minimize the ways in which human personality functioning is socially constructed (Cushman 1996). Freud's attempts at reconstructing the prehistorical evolution of the human mind, as in *Totem and Taboo* (Freud 1912–1913), have been characterized as "phylogenetic fantasies" (Freud 1915/1987). As a consequence, evolutionary thinking in psychoanalysis has gone out of fashion with some notable exceptions (Slavin and Kriegman 1992). Nevertheless, concepts such as psychological adaptation and psychological homeostasis that utilize ideas originally derived from biology are routinely employed in the psychoanalytic literature without much reflection on the status of those ideas in contemporary evolutionary thinking.

> Contrary to what many people have been taught, evolution has nothing to do with the survival of the fittest. It is not a question of whether you live or die. The key to evolution is reproduction. Whereas all organisms eventually die, not all organisms reproduce. ... Organisms do not compete among themselves for scarce resources or survival. Rather, they compete for genetic representation in subsequent generations. ... As a consequence, what is or is not adaptive has to be measured in terms of its impact on reproduction. An adaptive trait is one that confers a reproductive advantage
>
> Ash and Gallup (2008)

L. Josephs (✉)
Professor, Derner Institute of Advanced Psychological Studies
of Adelphi University Garden City, Long Island, NY 11530
e-mail: josephs@adelphi.edu

C. Piers (ed.), *Personality and Psychopathology: Critical Dialogues with David Shapiro*,
DOI 10.1007/978-1-4419-6214-0_9, © Springer Science+Business Media, LLC 2011

Hartmann (1939) introduced the adaptive viewpoint in his classic, *The Ego and the Problem of Adaptation*, in order to extend the link between psychoanalysis and biology. Hartmann suggested that "We call a man well-adapted if his productivity, his ability to enjoy life, and his mental equilibrium are undisturbed" (p. 23). Evolutionary psychologists have critiqued this view of adaptation because it assumes that "psychological mechanisms would evolve merely to achieve mental relief, regardless of the utility of the actions they motivated," (Daley and Wilson 1987, p. 135) that is the trait's contribution to insuring genetic representation in subsequent generations. For example, emotion researchers have discovered that our negative evaluations appear to be more potent than our positive evaluations (Baumeister et al. 2001). "It would make evolutionary sense for the individual to be more responsive to pain than to pleasure, to danger rather than safety. Without such a bias, the chances of survival would seem to be diminished" (Oatley et al. 2006, p. 172).

Psychoanalysts have defined adaptation as "the capacity to cope appropriately and advantageously with the environment" (Moore and Fine 1990, p. 5). Of course, one cannot evaluate the advantageousness of an adaptation unless one asks the question of advantageous to what ends. Psychoanalytic views of adaptation implicitly tend to be either intrapsychically restorative (i.e., what is advantageous to restoring mental equilibrium/ homeostasis by reducing conflict and disturbing affect), socially conformist (i.e., what is advantageous for socially appropriate interpersonal coping/ social adjustment), and/ or survivalist (i.e., what is advantageous for individual survival). Psychoanalysts rarely pose the question of what is advantageous for achieving genetic representation in subsequent generations.

As we shall see, psychoanalysts beginning with Freud and continuing through the work of Shapiro, have tended to view the primary adaptive function of self-deception, as of any other defensive process, as a means of emotional self-regulation that functions to maintain psychological homeostasis. In contrast, evolutionary psychologists assume that the primary adaptive function of self-deception is interpersonal as an adaptive aid to more successfully deceiving others. Self-deception is adaptive because it enhances reproductive success to the extent that having a capacity to deceive others enhances reproductive success. Concealment as a strategy of tactical deception appears to have evolved as a fundamental feature of human reproductive physiology. For instance, human females are unique among primates in that ovulation is concealed rather than clearly advertised in large, colorful, and highly visible genital swellings during ovulation, as in chimpanzees our closest primate relative. In hominid evolution, sexual selection favored progressively less visible genital swellings during ovulation that made it progressively more difficult for male sexual behavior to be differentially responsive to reliable clues of ovulation.

A reproductive strategy is what humans must successfully implement to win a desirable mate, retain a desirable mate, and raise children to maturity that will successfully reproduce (Buss 1994; Hrdy 1999). As a species, humans are "cooperative breeders" (Hrdy 1999) who tend to go for a quality over quantity reproductive strategy; usually giving birth to only one slowly maturing offspring at a time in whom there tends to be high investment from both parents, grandparents, other kin, as well as close allies. Given the socially cooperative nature of human reproductive strategies there would need to be strategic concealment of whatever is self-interested, opportunistic, and/or exploitative in one's own reproductive strategies. Unwitting exposure of one's strategies of tactical deception would be a major strategic blunder among cooperative breeders who are likely to harshly punish covertly uncooperative individuals whose deception has been exposed. It will be proposed that individual character styles may have evolved in part as competing adaptations for reproductive success that rely in part upon strategies of tactical deception, buttressed by self-deception, so as not to betray the deception being practiced by the subtle signs of self-knowledge that psychoanalysts have become so adept at discerning.

Strangers to Ourselves

We now know that the manifest content is a deception, a façade

Freud (1925, p. 130)

In *The Interpretation of Dreams*, Freud (1900) proposed a model of the mind in which neurotic self-deception was central to psychological functioning. The manifest content of the dream, the conscious and verbally formulated memory of the dream, was thought to reflect a disguised manifestation of the gratification of forbidden wishes. Freud applied this topographic model of the mind to the understanding of symptoms, character traits, parapraxes, jokes, and psychoses. Thus many aspects of consciousness serve as a façade, a self-deception that maintains a socially acceptable but essentially illusory view of who we are that repudiates our truer, less reputable motives. Self-deception serves a defensive function by alleviating the intense anxiety that would result from conscious awareness of our true intentions. Self-deception maintains psychological homeostasis by preventing the eruption of traumatically overwhelming levels of anxiety that might flood the ego. In this sense self-deception can be adaptive as a means of emotion regulation though self-deception would seem maladaptive to the extent that it entails at least a partial failure of reality testing and diminishes the sense of personal agency (Shapiro 2000).

Freud grounded his theory of human nature in evolutionary biology. Freud's (1915) first dual instinct theory pitted the reproductive instinct versus the ego instincts, roughly paralleling Darwin's (1871) suggestion that two processes guide evolution, natural selection (i.e., adaptations for survival) and sexual selection (i.e., adaptations for reproduction). Our sexual and aggressive fantasies may reflect our own narcissistic self-interest (Freud 1914), what we ideally wish we could do to successfully reproduce and survive in a socially competitive world if we were unimpeded by social, moral, or realistic constraints. Thus, our sexual and aggressive wishes conflict with and are constrained by the concessions we feel compelled to make to get along with other people, which is also a basic survival need (see Freud 1930, *Civilization and Its Discontents*).

Self-deception serves to maintain an illusory view of our own social acceptability when open expression of our sexual and aggressive desires would likely make us targets of the moral aggression of others. Self-deception serves to defend against our fear of the abandonment, rejection, physical abuse, shame, and guilt that morally offended and punitive individuals, originally the disciplinary parents, would inflict upon us for openly expressing and attempting to actualize our forbidden sexual and aggressive fantasies. The superego (Freud 1923) reflects the internalization of punitive parental authority so that we threaten ourselves with various frightfully disturbing punishments to the extent we are inclined to openly express our forbidden desires. Self-deception quells our fear of the many dreaded "situations of danger" (Freud 1926) that our perfervid imaginations conjure up to dissuade us from further open expression of our forbidden tendencies.

The Anxiety Forestalling Function of Self-Deceptive Speech Acts

It becomes apparent that the neurotic personality reacts against itself, with the consequence that the neurotic person does not know himself. It is not a case, as it once seemed, of a rational adult being affected by an estranged voice of his childhood. It is a case of an adult who does not recognize his own adult voice

Shapiro (1989, p. 172)

David Shapiro (1965) in his landmark publication, *Neurotic Styles*, picked up where Wilhelm Reich (1933) left off, focusing on character style as a holistic mode of defensive functioning. Reich suggested that neurotic symptoms are expressions of an underlying neurotic character so that one had to understand the dynamics of "character as a total formation" in order to understand a patient's symptoms. That total formation served a defensive function that Reich referred to as "character armor." Shapiro defined a neurotic style as "a form or mode of functioning" reflecting "ways of thinking and perceiving, ways of experiencing emotion, modes of subjective experience in general" (p. 1). Shapiro suggested that these "modes of functioning are detached from the content of the infantile conflict, which is their presumed origin, and achieve, in this respect at least, an autonomy or independence from that original conflict" (p. 7).

Character style, whatever its presumed origins, becomes a self-generating, self-reinforcing, and self-sustaining self-regulatory strategy to the extent that it successfully forestalls the development of anxiety, at least in the short-term. Yet in the long term, defensive rigidities of character (i.e., obsessional/paranoid styles) or defensive passive reactiveness (i.e., hysteric/impulsive styles) might lead to even greater vulnerability to anxiety. The more one relies on a defensive constriction of conscious experience to forestall the experience of anxiety, the less anxiety tolerance one possesses, and the less anxiety tolerance one possesses, the more one is inclined to further rely on defensive strategies of anxiety management thereby creating a vicious cycle. Shapiro (1981, 1989, 2000) has been making this original argument with ever greater clarity, eloquence, and force in his subsequent publications.

Shapiro's understanding of character results in a characterological understanding of the operations of self-deception. The defensive constriction of consciousness to forestall the experience of anxiety leads to self-estrangement and therefore self-deception in regards to one's true thoughts, feelings, and motives. It is not so much the buried infantile fantasies, conflicts, and traumatic memories from which the defensively constricted person is alienated but "unarticulated adult attitudes, subjective experience, and subjective dynamics" (Shapiro 1989, p. 172). For the character analyst "actions speak louder than words." The person's real thoughts, feelings, and motives are reflected in her actions not necessarily in what she says about her actions. The story that patients tell about their actions may reflect "self-deceptive speech acts."

> The speech act may be, in other words, not so much an expression of the individual's relationship with another person as an expression of his momentary relationship with himself. It may be, in fact, less an expression of his thoughts or feelings than an unrecognized reaction against them, an effort to dispel or revise them. Speech then becomes a continuation of the dynamics of self-deception

> (Shapiro 1989, p. 63)

Shapiro (2000) suggests that all self-deception may be constructed in speech, either to oneself or to a listener. Shapiro observed that the person engaged in self-deceptive speech acts is highly attuned to the reactions of the listener, feeling relieved when obtaining a confirming response and discomforted when obtaining even the slightest hesitation. "He is addressing himself through the listener" (p. 37). Thus self-deceptive speech acts place considerable interpersonal pressure on the listener to buttress the speaker's self-deception to the extent the speaker becomes upset, anxious, defensive, or indignant when confirmation is not forthcoming. Self-deceptive speech invites collusion with the self-deception so the listener can avoid the interpersonal discomfort of feeling held responsible for undermining the operation of the speaker's anxiety forestalling constrictions of self-awareness, a discomfort that may threaten to undermine the listener's own anxiety forestalling operations.

Shapiro has implicitly developed an interpersonal theory of the mutual regulation of self-deception, though he hasn't formulated his contribution in those terms. He does not view the self-deceptive speaker as implicitly trying to make the listener feel any particular way as in Kleinian/ Bionian theories of unconscious communication through projective identification. Shapiro implies that the self-deceptive speaker is oblivious to the listener's feelings as long as the listener supports the speaker's defensive organization, which we often do unreflectively as a matter of social *politesse*. Failure to support the self-deception could lead the speaker to anxiously worry about what the listener is really thinking and feeling but not saying, generating interpersonal tension.

Self-Deceptive Speech as an Adaptive Form of Social Manipulation

> When an individual plays a part he implicitly requests his observers to take seriously the impression that is fostered before them. ... One finds that the performer can be fully taken in by his own act; he can be sincerely convinced that the impression of reality which he stages is the real reality

> Goffman (1959, p. 17)

Shapiro focusing mostly on the adaptive homeostatic/anxiety forestalling function of self-deceptive speech does not develop the possibility that there may also be an adaptive interpersonal function of self-deceptive speech acts. Sociologists like Goffman (1959) suggest that the main function of interpersonal communication is "impression management." The function of interpersonal communication is to successfully convince others that our public persona is our true self so that others will treat us as we wish to be treated. Similarly, evolutionary psychologists believe that the adaptive function of animal communication is effective social manipulation. Social communication is not simply the transmission of factual information without any personal agenda. It is always transmission of information to others in the hope of advancing one's own self-interests. Thus deceptive communication successfully passing as honest communication may be an effective way of advancing one's own self-interests.

> If you lived in a group, as humans have always done, persuading others of your own needs and interests would be fundamental to your well-being. Sometimes you had to use cunning. Clearly, you would be at your most convincing if you persuaded yourself first and did not even have to pretend to believe what you were saying. The kind of self-deluding individuals who tended to do this flourished, as did their genes

McEwan (1997, p. 112)

Nesse and Lloyd (1992) note that if self-deception "gives an advantage by increasing the ability to deceive others and if being deceived by others is sometimes disadvantageous, then natural selection should increase the ability to detect deception. This will, in turn, shape ever more subtle abilities to deceive, which will shape still more sophisticated abilities to detect deception. Such evolutionary 'arms races' between the ability to deceive and the ability to detect deception are well known in other species" (p. 606). Shapiro's contribution surely contributes to this evolutionary "arms race" by providing excellent advice about how to detect the subtle nonverbal signs of self-deceptive speech acts, whereby the speaker is dissimulating her true thoughts, feelings, and intentions. This arms race occurs in the consulting room. Psychoanalytic listening, in general, may constitute a sophisticated refinement of the highly developed deception detectors that all humans possess. Yet we try to thwart the successful operation of others' deception detectors by implicitly pressuring others to confirm our self-deceptive speech acts by making them feel socially awkward and anxious if they don't. We unconsciously try to induce others to selectively ignore all the ways in which we say one thing but do another. Character analysts try to overcome this subversion by training themselves to selectively ignore the content while selectively attending to the process. Focusing on style instead of content results in more accurate discernment of concealed intent. In contrast, trying to decode symbolic verbal communication that is open to multiple and contradictory interpretations tends to lead to uncertainty as to the "true" underlying meaning of the patient's verbal discourse.

Is Self-Deception Content Neutral?

> Human reasoning is well designed for detecting violations of conditional rules when these
> can be interpreted as cheating on a social contract
>
> Cosmides and Tooby (1992, p. 205)

Shapiro makes clear that self-estrangement silences the "adult voice" though one does not get a clear sense from reading Shapiro of exactly what that adult voice would be saying once it is freed to speak its mind freely. Shapiro rightly critiques the common psychoanalytic view that the inner voice from which the adult is alienated is the voice of an "inner baby" frozen in time who must be unearthed. Character analysis is not archaeological reconstruction of a buried past through historical understanding but understanding the dynamics of one's own neurotic character in the here-and-now, how one is defensively estranged from one's true thoughts and feelings in the moment. Shapiro provides us a compelling formulation of the process of self-deception but is largely silent on the topic of the content of self-deception, what adults really want, really think, and really feel when they are not estranged from their true selves.

Evolutionary psychologists posit that humans "want" (i.e., at some ultimate metapsychological level) what all living organisms want, which is to maximize their inclusive fitness (Hamilton 1964). Human motivations have been shaped by evolution to be gratified by pursuing the things that will maximize replicating our genes in the environment of evolutionary adaptedness, either by reproducing ourselves or by facilitating the reproduction of close kin with whom we share many genes in common. "Kin altruism" arises because it can be within one's own inclusive self-interest to make personal sacrifices to advance the reproductive interests of one's close kin (Hamilton 1964). Cooperative social relationships with individuals with whom one doesn't share any genes in common could evolve through the process of "reciprocal altruism" (Trivers 1971). The idea is that if I make sacrifices for you in the moment, you will return the favor by making sacrifices for me in the future. The problem with reciprocal altruism is that individuals could successfully exploit the system by only pretending to be a reciprocal altruist, by taking favors which are never returned. Cheating creates selection pressure for individuals to develop "cheater detection mechanisms" to differentiate the truly cooperative from the pseudo-cooperative. Recent research has been successful in discovering just such cheater detection mechanisms in humans (Cosmides and Tooby 1992).

Self-deception might therefore evolve in the service of successfully simulating a genuine reciprocal altruist when unconsciously one is hoping to get away with undetected cheating. Thus self-deception would most likely be activated whenever it would seem to be in one's inclusive self-interest to cheat people who are treating one cooperatively rather than be genuinely cooperative oneself. There would seem to be no need for self-deception whenever it is in one's inclusive self-interest to act in genuinely cooperative and/ or altruistic ways. Darwin (1871) noted that sexual selection is essentially a competitive enterprise; one may be competing for both quality and quantity of both mates and offspring so that someone else's reproductive success may mean one's own reproductive failure. In contrast, social cooperation based on reciprocal altruism as well as kin altruism is a "win-win" strategy in which we advance our own interests by advancing the interests of others, even if it involves some self-sacrifice. So there may be some inherent tension between advancing our own interests by helping others and advancing our own interests by defeating or exploiting others. Self-deception is likely to be activated whenever it seems more profitable to advance our interests by defeating or exploiting others than by helping them. Self-deception in the service of deceiving others facilitates evasion of the sophisticated "cheater detection mechanisms" through which others consciously and unconsciously scan our communicative behavior for the most subtle clues of dissimulation.

Deception as a Reproductive Strategy

All is fair in love and war

Certain aspects of romantic courtship may reflect an exercise in what primatologists and social psychologists call "Machiavellian intelligence" (Wilson et al. 1996). Romantic courtship may be seen as a strategic predatory activity that involves acts of tactical deception as we aim to seduce the targets of our romantic desires. We try to win our romantic partners by putting forward our ideal selves as best we can and seducing our partners into believing that our ideal selves are in fact our real selves. We hide what is less than optimal and play to our strengths by exaggerating them if our actual romantic desirability is not quite as optimal as we had hoped. We unconsciously put out "dishonest" or false signals of physical and psychological desirability that we try to pass for the real thing intuitively appreciating that potential romantic partners are searching for "honest" indicators of romantic desirability that we may not possess ourselves. We achieve mating success if somebody buys into our false self as though it were real. Once a romantic attachment is formed, romantic disillusionment does not necessarily lead to relational dissolution because as Fairbairn (1952) suggested it may be better to have a bad object than no object at all, especially once offspring have arrived.

Freud sometimes likened romantic love to a psychotic delusion. Fisher (2004) has suggested that the purpose of romantic love, the honeymoon period of a relationship, is to keep a couple together long enough for a strong attachment to form. By the time the honeymoon is over and the couple is seeing each other more realistically, it is difficult to break up without experiencing considerable separation anxiety. Thus the self and other deception, the unrealistic idealization entailing impaired reality-testing and impaired judgment as well as the diminished sense of volitional agency in letting one be unreflectively swept away by romantic passion may serve an adaptive function in the establishment of long-term monogamous bonds.

Courtship seems to involve some gender specific forms of self and other deception. Males may pretend that they are more interested in a long-term relationship than they really are because they believe women will be more inclined to sexually gratify them the more committed they appear to be. Women may pretend that they are less interested in commitment than they really are because they believe men might be scared off by too much pressure to make a commitment (Buss 1994).

Reproductive success is not just about winning a desirable mate but also requires an ability to prevent mate defection through infidelity or divorce by exercising effective mate retention tactics. Mate retention may be facilitated by pretending to be more in love than one really is to allow one's partner to live with a false sense of security. Pretending that one is less in love than one really is may succeed in making a dependent partner even more insecure and clingy. Feigning romantic interest in others may provoke jealousy in the hopes of inspiring frantic efforts to win back a potentially straying partner. Pretending to be less angry than one really is may be a way of avoiding conflicts that might eventuate in relational dissolution. A betrayed spouse may deceive himself or herself in regard to sneaking suspicions of a partner's infidelity if a "don't ask don't tell" policy might save the marriage. Thus couples often act as though honesty is not necessarily the best policy for keeping a long-term relationship going. Self-deception about this state of affairs may allow a couple to bask in the comforting illusion that they possess a reasonably open and honest relationship based on high levels of reciprocal altruism. They collude in denying the implicitly adversarial aspect of the marital relationship in which each partner engages in manipulative forms of marital communication in order obtain a tactical advantage over the other partner.

Reproductive success is not only about successfully winning, retaining, and maintaining a tactical advantage over a desirable mate. It also means successfully raising children to maturity that will be reproductively successful themselves. Trivers (1973, 1974) suggested that parents will demonstrate discriminative solicitude towards those offspring whom they judge as possessing the greatest reproductive potential, which in some cultures may be the first born child or sons as opposed to daughters. Thus parents inevitably play favorites with their children. It may be in the parents' self-interest to deceive themselves and their children as to the true state of affairs, to create an illusion that all children are loved equally, in order to maintain family harmony despite surreptitiously playing favorites. Thus self-deception in the service of deceiving the one's we love appears to be a ubiquitous reproductive strategy, be it with short-term sexual partners, long-term partners, or even one's own children.

Character Style as a Reproductive Strategy

Evolutionary psychologists would not be the first to look at character style as an interpersonal adaptation. The early interpersonalists, Sullivan, Horney, and Fromm, developed a way of looking at characterological functioning as an interpersonal strategy of adapting to one's family and one's culture by identifying with certain social role assignments. These analysts rejected the biological determinism of Freudian theory. They believed that humans evolved to become highly social and cultural animals because establishing complex social organizations through culturally acquired learning generated maximum flexibility for adapting to variable and unpredictable environments. Interpersonalists believed that humans acquired greater behavioral plasticity than other animals by becoming less instinctually driven. In contrast, William James suggested that to behave flexibly humans must have more rather than less instincts than other animals (Tooby and Cosmides 1992, p. 93). For the interpersonal school as well as the contemporary relational school, Darwinian processes of sexual selection take a back seat to the quest for secure and positive relationships with others that insure individual survival as in Bowlby's (1988) attachment theory.

Shapiro developed his characterological viewpoint as an extension of the ego psychology of Anna Freud, Fenichel, Hartmann, Rapaport, George Klein, etc., a viewpoint that tends to de-emphasize Freud's Darwinian Id as well as the interpersonal viewpoint of the so-called cultural school. Contemporary evolutionary psychology has generated what one might call a Darwinian social psychology (Barkow et al. 1992). For evolutionary psychologists, both personality and social psychology are the study of adaptations for reproductive success as well as for survival. From this perspective, character styles may be seen as having evolved at least in part as competing strategies of relating to others in the implicit service of one's own reproductive self-interests. Adaptive reproductive strategies may be discerned in emotions like sexual jealousy that motivate mate guarding behavior or interpersonal behaviors such as flirting in order to seduce a desirable romantic partner. Character styles may reflect stable individual differences in the behavioral strategies that may facilitate successful reproduction under certain ecological conditions.

We can look at the various character styles as particular reproductive strategies, each of which possesses its own unique forms of self-deception in the service of deceiving others. Each character style reflects a particular way of appearing to seem like a genuine reciprocal and/or kin altruist while surreptitiously trying to advance its' own self-interested reproductive agenda at the expense of others. For example, obsessives try to present themselves to others as persons who would religiously and conscientiously play by the rules so are therefore eminently trustworthy. The obsessive might seem like a good candidate for a long-term romantic relationship who would never "cheat" and would dutifully fulfill marital and parental responsibilities. Their compulsive conscientiousness might inspire confidence that they couldn't break the rules even if they consciously wanted to. Yet in long-term relationships obsessives tend to be experienced as overly controlling, fault-finding, and emotionally withholding and may act in passive-aggressive ways through which resentment of the "rules" of the relationship is implicitly expressed. Thus obsessives may implicitly exploit the trust which others naively place in their exaggerated conscientiousness in order to try to covertly dominate others who have become reliant on them while evading playing by the rules in passive-aggressive ways which they rationalize. Here we see a strategy of attracting mates as well as of covertly controlling long-term partners and children in the service of one's repudiated interest in domineering others while covertly extricating oneself from certain inconvenient obligations.

Hysterics present themselves to others as essentially innocent, wholesome, friendly, and nonthreatening individuals, the kind of person you could absolutely trust to be especially agreeable and accommodating in a long-term relationship. The fact that their natural disposition seems so completely superficial, naïve, and unreflective might lead one to assume that they were entirely lacking in the capacity to take advantage of someone in coldly calculating or Machiavellian ways. In fact their suggestibility and gullibility may make it seem as though they could be easily manipulated and exploited to one's own advantage. Yet in long-term relationships it may emerge that hysterics are not so agreeable and accommodating. They may be experienced as rather dependent and angrily entitled when their dependency needs are not met. It may also seem in retrospect that they seemed to have promised more than they could realistically deliver so there is some sense of false advertising, of promises made and promises broken. To confront these issues openly is only to be met with shock and indignation, as though one is unfairly impugning the good character of an essentially innocent individual. The hysteric strategy has been long known to work well in seducing potential mates and may potentially succeed in advancing their self-interests with long-term partners and children by feigning shattered innocence anytime they are held accountable for benefits accrued on the basis of promises made but never kept.

As Shapiro has often noted, paranoid styles reflect intensifications of obsessional rigidities while impulsive styles reflect intensifications of the hysteric's passive reactiveness. Paranoids imply that if others don't try to take advantage of them behind their backs that they can be trusted to respond in kind, providing a seeming basis for a relationship of reciprocal altruism. It would seem that forming a cooperative alliance with a paranoid individual would be establishing a wise coalition with a formidable adversary in any aggressive encounter who you would always want on your side of a conflict. For paranoid individuals one is either friend or foe, generating a sense of relief and safety as long as one remains on the paranoid individual's good side. Yet in long-term relationships paranoid strategists might be prone to striking out preemptively, rationalizing that it is better to seduce and betray others before others seduce and betray them (Josephs 2006). Freud (1922) linked paranoia to projection of the impulse to infidelity suggesting that paranoid sexual jealousy constituted a disguised reflection of the paranoid individual's own cheating tendencies. Thus paranoid individuals may seduce potential mates with the idea that they would never abuse the other's trust as long as the other remains trustworthy. Yet in long-term relationships they may falsely accuse partners and children of having abused their trust in order to rationalize their own abusive treatment of long-term partners and children. Rationalized abuse serves to sadistically control the behavior of individuals upon whom paranoids feel dependent for their own reproductive success but whom they don't feel entirely safe trusting to their own devices in dread of being cheated themselves.

The impulsive individual seduces others into colluding with their "get rich quick schemes," how to enjoy all the pleasures of life in the moment without having to worry about the long-term consequences. Impulsive individuals are quick to provide false reassurance that thinking about long-term consequences is only a form of neurotic worry that should be selectively disregarded in order to enjoy a carefree life to its fullest. Of course, in long-term relationships with impulsive individuals it soon becomes apparent that one has been "conned" into living in a "fool's paradise" that one ultimately regrets. The impulsive strategy may be effective in sweeping up others into grand romantic passions, often buttressed by alcohol and drugs that cloud one's better judgment. In long-term relationships, partners (i.e., like the co-dependent enabling spouse of an alcoholic) as well as children (i.e., like the parentified child of an alcoholic) often find themselves feeling responsible to clean up the mess generated by the impulsive person's poor judgment. Thus impulsive persons may succeed in being able to intensively focus on pursuing and gratifying their own short-term self-interests while having found a way to make the people who have become dependent upon their long-term success responsible for looking out for and taking care of the impulsive person's own long-term self-interests, an implicitly parasitic form of adaptation.

None of these underlying reproductive strategies are socially acceptable for they all involve surreptitious violations of the social norms of reciprocal as well as kin altruism upon which social cooperation is based. Certainly we feel cheaters should be punished for being immoral or at least shamed for being immature. If there is indeed a just world, these self-serving strategies should eventuate in tragic defeat (i.e., should prove ultimately maladaptive). Yet the Bible long ago raised the troubling question of why the wicked should prosper while the righteous suffer. The Darwinian answer to that question is that although genuine social cooperation may lead to reproductive success in most circumstances; surreptitiously cheating the one's we love has led to sufficient reproductive success over the course of human evolution that it remains in human nature as an "evolutionary stable strategy" (Dawkins 1976, p. 69) that remains available for automatic unconscious deployment under certain ecological conditions.

From the perspective of ego psychology, the main benefit of a defensive style is the reduction of anxiety. The disguised gratifications afforded by a defensive style have been referred to as "secondary gain" (Freud 1901). From the evolutionary perspective, the potential reproductive benefits of a defensive style are "primary gains," advances in one's own self-interests that may come at the expense of the self-interests of others. For example, deceptive reproductive strategies as effective means of social manipulation may enable one to successfully obtain a mate that seems "out of one's league," prevent a mate from defecting on the basis of false pretenses, and exploit one's children to advance one's own self-interests such as by choosing marital partners for one's adult children that may be more in the parents' than the child's best interests. Signal anxiety (Freud 1926) would then reflect an intuitive assessment of the likelihood of getting caught violating legitimate expectations of reciprocal altruism and/ or of kin altruism and therefore being exposed to the punitive moral aggression of others who realize to their great chagrin that they have been successfully duped, betrayed, and cheated by someone whom they foolishly trusted. Incipient conscious awareness of one's own forbidden cheating tendencies could portend increasing likelihood of public exposure through the nonverbal leakage of the subtle signs of self-knowledge.

Implications for Character Analysis

Patients are likely to seek psychotherapy when their reproductive strategies seem to be failing and they are suffering from feelings of anxiety, depression, and frustration as a consequence of that perceived failure. Horney (1950) was one of the first character analysts to note that patients come to treatment unconsciously trying to obtain the analyst's support in maintaining and actualizing the patient's "neurotic solution." In trying to make their current reproductive strategy work, patients may unconsciously resist insight into the self-defeating nature of their reproductive strategy, resist attempting to switch to what might be a more successful reproductive strategy, and/ or resist coming to terms with their feelings of reproductive failure if implementing a more successful strategy is ultimately beyond their capacity. Helping patients in this way is challenging as there is considerable self-deception as to the true nature of the patient's unconscious reproductive strategy and the patient places considerable interpersonal pressure on the would-be character analyst to support the patient's self-deception.

As Shapiro rightly notes, character analysis does not necessarily require historical reconstruction of childhood influences that may have shaped one's character in one way or another. It is not the childhood experiences but rather the current adult attitudes (i.e. the adult attitudes that justify the currently activated but repudiated reproductive strategy) that maintain a characteristic way of functioning in the present. In fact, there are many significant variables having little to do with childhood experience that successfully predict adult romantic prospects such as physical attractiveness, health, social status, and age (Buss 1994). In general, young, healthy, beautiful, affluent, intelligent, and creative individuals have better romantic prospects than old, unhealthy, ugly, poor, stupid, and unimaginative individuals. One's mate value in a sexually competitive marketplace is an exquisitely shame sensitive issue around which there may be considerable self-deception, be it defensively overvaluing or undervaluing one's mate value. Improving one's personality through psychotherapy may significantly enhance one's mate value to people who appreciate character traits in a romantic partner like self-reflection, warmth, willingness to share resources, commitment, empathy, humor, emotional stability, reliability, moral integrity, honesty, self-acceptance, self-assertiveness, and adaptive flexibility. Yet displaying a personality that epitomizes mental health is unlikely to entirely compensate for deficiencies in other areas for which there may be few realistic remedies other than plastic surgery, winning the lottery, or discovering the fountain of youth.

In conclusion, Shapiro must be applauded for his incisive analysis of how character style serves to forestall anxiety through a defensive constriction of consciousness that results in self-estrangement and self-deception. Those intrapsychic processes manifest themselves interpersonally in self-deceptive speech acts. Evolutionary considerations enable us to place those seminal insights in a broader adaptive/interpersonal context by viewing neurotic self-deception as an adaptation that aides in deceiving others by decreasing the probability of inadvertent betrayal of the deception being practiced by minimizing the leakage of the subtle nonverbal signs of self-knowledge. In simpler words, to be a good liar you have to be good at lying to yourself. Neurotic character can be viewed as an adaptation for reproductive advantage when that advantage can only be gained by violating the social requirements of reciprocal and/or kin altruism, a violation that arouses an intense dread of becoming a target of the moral aggression of the naively trusting people whom one hopes to successfully deceive and cheat.

References

Ash, J., & Gallup, G. (2008). Brain size, intelligence, and Paleolithic variation. In G. Geher & G. Miller (Eds.), *Mating intelligence: Sex, relationships, and the mind's reproductive system* (pp. 313–336). New York: Erlbaum.

Barkow, J., Cosmides, L., & Tooby, J. (1992). *The adapted mind: Evolutionary psychology and the generation of culture.* New York: Oxford University Press.

Baumeister, R., Bratslavsky, E., Finkenauer, C., & Vohs, K. (2001). Bad is stronger than good. *Review of General Psychology, 5*, 323–370.

Bowlby, J. (1988). *A secure base: Clinical applications of attachment theory.* London: Routledge.

Buss, D. (1994). *The evolution of desire: Strategies of human mating.* New York: Basic Books.

Cosmides, L., & Tooby, J. (1992). Cognitive adaptations for social exchange. In J. Barkow, L. Cosmides, & J. Tooby (Eds.), >The adapted mind: Evolutionary psychology and the generation of culture (pp. 163–228). New York: Oxford University Press.

Cushman, P. (1996). *Constructing the self, constructing America: A cultural history of psychotherapy.* New York: Addison Wesley.

Daley, M., & Wilson, M. (1987). The Darwinian psychology of discriminative parental solicitude. *Nebraska Symposium on Motivation, 35*, 91–144.

Darwin, C. (1871). *The descent of man and selection in relation to sex.* London: Murray.

Dawkins, R. (1976). *The selfish gene.* New York: Oxford University Press.

Fairbairn, R. (1952). *Psychoanalytic studies of the personality.* London: Routledge.

Fisher, H. (2004). *Why we love? The nature and chemistry of romantic love.* New York: Owl Books.

Freud, S. (1900). *The interpretation of dreams* (Standard Edition, pp. 4–5). London: Hogarth Press.

Freud, S. (1901). *The psychopathology of everyday life* (Standard Edition, Vol. 6, pp. vii–276). New York: W. W. Norton.

Freud, S. (1912–1913). *Totem and Taboo* (Standard Edition, Vol. 13, pp. 1–161). New York: W. W. Norton.

Freud, S. (1914). *On narcissism: An introduction* (Standard Edition, Vol. 14, pp. 73–102). London: Hogarth.

Freud, S. (1915). *Instincts and their vicissitudes* (Standard Edition, Vol. 14, pp. 111–140). London: Hogarth.

Freud, S. (1915/1987). *A phylogenetic fantasy: Overview of the transference neurosis* (I. Gruberish-Simitis, Trans. and Ed.). Cambridge: Belnap.

Freud, S. (1922). *Some neurotic mechanisms in jealousy, paranoia, and homosexuality.* (Standard Edition, Vol. 18, pp. 221–232). London: Hogarth.

Freud, S. (1923). *The Ego and the Id* (Standard Edition, Vol. 19, pp. 1–66). New York: W. W. Norton.

Freud, S. (1925). *Some additional notes on dream interpretation as a whole* (Standard Edition, Vol. 14, pp. 123–138). London: Hogarth.

Freud, S. (1926). *Inhibitions, symptoms, and anxiety* (Standard Edition, Vol. 20, pp. 75–175). New York: W. W. Norton.

Freud, S. (1930). *Civilization and Its Discontents* (Standard Edition, Vol. 21, pp. 59–145). New York: W. W. Norton.

Goffman, I. (1959). *The presentation of self in everyday life.* New York: Anchor.

Hamilton, W. (1964). The genetical evolution of social behavior. *Journal of Theoretical Biology, 7,* 1–52.

Hartmann, H. (1939). *Ego psychology and the problem of adaptation.* New York: International Universities Press, 1958.

Horney, K. (1950). *Neurosis and human growth.* New York: Norton.

Hrdy, S. B. (1999). *Mother nature: Maternal instincts and how they shape the human species.* New York: Ballantine Books.

Josephs, L. (2006). The impulse to infidelity and oedipal splitting. *International Journal of Psychoanalysis, 87,* 423–437.

Makari, G. (2008). *Revolution in mind: The creation of psychoanalysis.* New York: Harper.

McEwan, I. (1997). *Enduring love.* New York: Nan Talese.

Moore, B., & Fine, B. (1990). *Psychoanalytic terms and concepts.* New Haven, CT: Yale.

Nesse, R. & Lloyd, A. (1992). The evolution of psychodynamic mechanisms. In J. Barkow, L. Cosmides, & J. Tooby (Eds.), *The adapted mind: Evolutionary psychology and the generation of culture* (pp. 601–626). New York: Oxford University Press.

Oatley, K., Keltner, D., & Jenkins, J. (2006). *Understanding Emotions.* Malden: Blackwell.

Reich, W. (1933). *Character analysis.* New York: Orgone. 1949.

Shapiro, D. (1965). *Neurotic styles.* New York: Basic Books.

Shapiro, D. (1981). *Autonomy and rigid character.* New York: Basic Books.

Shapiro, D. (1989). *Psychotherapy of neurotic character.* New York: Basic Books.

Shapiro, D. (2000). *Dynamics of character: Self-regulation in psychopathology.* New York: Basic Behavioral Science.

Slavin, M., & Kriegman, D. (1992). The adaptive design of the human psyche: Psychoanalysis, evolutionary biology, and the therapeutic process. New York: Guilford.

Trivers, R. (1971). Reciprocal altruism. In *Natural selection and social theory* (pp. 3–55).

Trivers, R. (1973). The Trivers-Willard effect. In *Natural selection and social theory* (pp. 111–122).

Trivers, R. (1974). Parent-offspring conflict. In *Natural selection and social theory* (pp. 123–153).

Trivers, R. (1976). Foreword. In Dawkins, R. (Eds.), *The selfish gene.* New York: Oxford University Press.

Wilson, D., Near, D., & Miller, R. (1996). Machiavellianism: A synthesis of the evolutionary and psychological literatures. *Psychological Bulletin, 119,* 285–299.

Reply to Lawrence Josephs

David Shapiro

I have been skeptical of much that I have read and heard of evolutionary psychology and Dr. Josephs' article has not persuaded me that my doubts are unfounded. He makes assumptions and develops inferences that are conceivable, but not necessarily convincing. Plausibility is not enough. The most fundamental of these assumptions, which seems to be a regular feature of evolutionary psychology, is that any adaptive capability must have evolved on account of its adaptive, or reproductive, success. The assumption seems to go further, that any capability must be adaptive since it is an evolutionary product. Neither of these assumptions is justified. Structural evolutionary developments have side effects which may have acquired adaptive value or may not be adaptive at all. I believe such side effects, at least those that have acquired some adaptive value, are given the name "spandrels" by Stephen J. Gould and Richard Lewontin, after the architectural term denoting certain incidental effects that result from essential structural features.

Self-deception and deception as well seem to me to fall well within that category. At least no structural basis, no basis other than their existence, is offered to support the assumption that they have evolved on account of their adaptive or reproductive value. They both seem likely to be side effects of the development of human self-awareness. In fact, despite its value in certain circumstances—some psychologists have argued the value of self-deception for a positive outlook—it is on the whole probably not adaptive at all. One usually thinks of the human ability to make realistic judgments unclouded by self-deception as critical to survival. As against Josephs' specific argument that self-deception has evolved to make the adaptive capacity for deception easier and more effective, one thinks of the psychopathic confidence man for whom conscious deception, quite unsupported by self-deception, is most fluent of all.

Josephs raises the interesting and important matter of the social, that is, interpersonal, advantages of defensive styles. Certainly these do exist; I have pointed out some of them; for example, the industry of compulsive characters, or the decisiveness of psychopaths which makes them effective "men of action." Josephs indicates others that may have specific value in attracting mates. I do not doubt that there are some general, probably evolutionary, characterological tendencies favored more in one sex than the other—although now that I think of it the only one that comes to mind is a greater aggressiveness in men, though even that difference is obviously very rough and, equally obvious, subject to cultural conditions. And, probably, any such gender difference will also be expressed in some general differences in defensive style. But, again, the proposition that any such differences in defensive style are themselves evolutionary products on account of their presumed desirability to the other sex, as opposed to side effects, is not convincing. The mate-desirability of the defensive exaggerations of maleness and femaleness that Josephs cites is clearly culturally affected—the flighty, superficial female is certainly less representative of the gender now than it once was and it was never equally evident in all classes, races, or social settings. Actually, the assumption that the defensive styles of an exaggerated kind of maleness or femaleness have evolved on account of being desirable to the other sex suffers from another problem. These defensive exaggerations are largely inseparable from other features of the defensive style that would seem to be far from desirable or adaptive in that way. The rigid man is likely to be indecisive in some circumstances and sexually mechanical; the passive woman may often be a less than good enough mother.

There is one matter of fact in Dr. Joseph's article that I would like to correct. The method of psychotherapy that I originally learned from Hellmuth Kaiser and advocate does not involve selectively ignoring the content of the patient's speech and attending only to the style. The point is, rather, that one can only understand the significance of what the patient says, its point, by attending also to how it is said.

Spandrel or Adaptive Design?

Lawrence Josephs

Personality variation is relevant to reproductive life-history strategy. ...The adaptationist framework predicts stable personality traits – that traits are classifiable by the adaptive problems they were designed to solve and that traits evolve as a function of the adaptive problems faced by the organism over evolutionary time.

Figueredo et al. (2005, pp. 870–871)

David Shapiro's skepticism is warranted in that the onus is on evolutionary psychology to prove that its speculative theories are not "just so stories" without empirical justification. Shapiro is correct to point out that evolutionary psychologists distinguish between adaptations and spandrels. The criteria for establishing the adaptive value of a trait is "evidence of special design" (Williams 1966), that is the possession of some special species specific problem-solving machinery that solves an evolutionary long-standing problem. The question is then one of whether there is accumulating empirical support for the idea that a particular personality style as a reproductive strategy possesses special design features. Most research on psychopathological traits is biased towards elucidating how those traits are costly rather than adaptive, though evolutionary psychology assumes cost-benefit trade-offs in the evolution of all traits.

Evolutionary psychology employs converging lines of evidence to support its hypotheses. For a personality style to be viewed as an adaptation for reproductive advantage it would need to be demonstrated that: (1) The personality style possesses a significant heritable component. (2) The personality style reliably emerges cross-culturally, perhaps linked to universal sex differences in prevalence rates. (3) The personality style has identifiable, partially heritable, neurophysiological correlates. (4) It possesses a reliable life history/developmental trajectory demonstrating adaptive benefits at the predicted points in the life cycle. (5) It is context sensitive in that it is reliably activated in predisposed individuals in environmental contexts in which its activation would maximize reproductive advantage. (6) There is supporting paleontological, archaeological, or anthropological evidence of its phylogenetic history from examination of the fossil record or observations of current hunter-gatherer societies. (7) There are analogs in our closest primate ancestors, like chimps or bonobos, so that the adaptive value of the personality trait is observable in other species.

As illustration of this approach to evolutionary theory testing, we can briefly and partially review some of the converging lines of evidence for impulsive character style as a sexually selected adaptation for reproductive advantage. The evolutionary hypothesis would be that an impulsive character style that facilitates implementation of an opportunistic mating strategy is adaptive in environmental contexts in which a quantity over quality reproductive strategy with low parental investment is on average more likely to lead to a greater number of descendants than a quality over quantity strategy with high parental investment. Males as the parent with less obligatory parental investment would have more to gain from such an opportunistic mating strategy than would females [see Triver's (1972) parental investment theory].

Psychopathic related personality dispositions have shown moderate to high heritability (Blonigen et al. 2003). Antisocial/ impulsive styles appear cross culturally with men showing these traits much more so than women in all cultures (Campbell 1999). Basal testosterone levels in men and women predict relative strength of sex drive as well as dominance, and twin studies suggest that basal testosterone levels have a significant heritable component in both men and women (Mehta et al. 2008). Dabbs and Morris (1990) found significant correlations between testosterone levels and antisocial behavior in lower class men. Antisocial/ impulsive styles begin in childhood with conduct disordered behavior, intensifies during adolescence and young adulthood, and incrementally subsides with age (Shavit and Rattner 1988). It is associated with early puberty, early onset of sexual intercourse with multiple casual partners, early parenthood with multiple partners, and relatively low parental investment (Rowe 2001). It is more likely to manifest itself in predisposed individuals in resource poor, father absent homes with child abuse or neglect than in environmental contexts that facilitate successful implementation of monogamous strategies (Walsh 2006). Forensic fossil evidence for murder goes as far back as 50,000 years (Trinkaus and Zimmerman 1982). Male chimps form gangs to murder males from other troops, engage in infanticide which induces ovulation in females from competing troops who are then impregnated. Subordinates engage in tactical deception demonstrating Machiavellian intelligence when it comes to sex and food to evade the retaliation of the dominants (De Waal 2007).

The scientific question is then if sufficient evidence of "special design" has been accumulated to suggest that impulsive character style is an adaptation rather than a spandrel. Given that impulsive individuals are high risk takers with less longevity than those high in conscientiousness (Larsen and Buss 2008, p. 163), such a style would not seem to have evolved as an adaptation for longevity but more likely for its early age reproductive benefits, despite the all too obvious costs. Non-evolutionary theories have difficulty accounting for why men everywhere tend to be more antisocial risk takers than women, the universal age curve in antisocial tendencies, and the promiscuous, partially testosterone-driven, mating strategy resulting in early parenthood with multiple partners with low parental investment.

In addition, it is not obvious that con artists lie without self-deception. Such individuals tend to be grandiose gamblers who rationalize their exploitation of the gullible thus deluding themselves about the likelihood of getting caught as well as their own moral culpability. The testable empirical question is whether con artists who believe their own lies demonstrate less nonverbal leakage of the contrary emotion, like dread of being caught and punished, than con artists who don't believe their own lies (see Ekman 2001 on the detection of lies through facial expressions).

Emotions that cannot be regulated cannot be concealed from others. Blind and sighted children as young as 4 years of age have learned to conceal their feelings if the context dictates (Cole 1986). If self-deception facilitates emotion regulation as Freud first suggested and if emotion regulation facilitates context sensitive emotional concealment beginning in early childhood as the developmental literature suggests, then self-deception facilitates emotional concealment as Trivers (1976) first hypothesized. Such an important insight into human nature should be assimilated by psychodynamic theory as interpretative work becomes biased when analysts are more attuned to the obvious costs than the implicit adaptive functions of a defense mechanism like self-deception.

References

Blonigen, D. M., Carlson, S. R., Krueger, R. F., & Patrick, C. J. (2003). A twin study of self-reported psychopathic personality traits. *Personality and Individual Differences, 35*, 179–197.

Campbell, A. (1999). Staying alive: Evolution, culture, and women's intrasexual aggression. *Behavioral and Brain Sciences, 22*, 203–214.

Cole, P. M. (1986). Children's spontaneous control of facial expression. *Child Development, 57*, 309–1321.

Dabbs, J. M., & Morris, R. (1990). Testosterone, social class, and antisocial behavior. *Psychological Science, 1*, 209–211.

De Waal, F. (2007). *Chimpanzee politics: Power and sex among the apes*. Baltimore: Johns Hopkins.

Ekman, P. (2001). *Telling lies: Clues to deceit in the marketplace, marriage, and politics*. New York: Norton.

Figueredo, A., Sefcek, J., Vasquez, G., Brumbach, B., King, J., & Jacobs, W. (2005). Evolutionary personality psychology. In D. M. Buss (Ed.), *The handbook of evolutionary psychology* (pp. 851–877). Hoboken: Wiley.

Larsen, R. J., & Buss, D. M. (2008). *Personality psychology: Domains of knowledge about human nature*. New York: McGraw Hill.

Mehta, P., Jones, A., & Josephs, R. (2008). The social endocrinology of dominance: Basal testosterone predicts cortisol changes and behavior following victory and defeat. *Journal Personality and Social Psychology, 94*, 1078–1093.

Rowe, D. C. (2001). *Biology and crime*. New York: Roxbury.

Schavit, Y., & Rattner, A. (1988). Age, crime, and early lifecourse. *American Journal of Sociology, 93*, 1457–1470.

Trinkaus, E., & Zimmerman, M. R. (1982). Trauma among the Shanidar Neanderthals. *American Journal of Physical Antropology, 57*, 61–76.

Trivers, R. (1972). Parental investment and sexual selection. In B. Campbell (Ed.), *Sexual selection and the descent of man: 1871–1971* (pp. 136–179). Chicago: Aldine.

Trivers, R. (1976). Foreword. In Dawkins, R. (Ed.), *The selfish gene*. New York: Oxford University Press.

Walsh, A. (2006). Evolutionary psychology and criminal behavior. *Missing the revolution: Darwinism for social scientists*. New York: Oxford University Press.

Williams, G.C. (1966). *Adaptation and natural selection: A critique of some current evolutionary thought*. Princeton: Princeton University Press.

Part V
Extensions and Empirical Applications

Chapter 10
David Shapiro's Characterology and Complex Systems Theory

Craig Piers

David Shapiro's work, most notably *Neurotic Styles* (1965), has influenced generations of psychologists, psychiatrists, and other students of the mind from diverse theoretical orientations. His broad appeal is typically thought to rest in his rich phenomenological description of various character styles. While true, careful reading of *Neurotic Styles* and Shapiro's (1981, 1989, 2000) subsequent body of work reveals a holistic, systemic theory of character that has theoretical and clinical importance. Shapiro describes neurotic character as a self-regulating dynamic system that diminishes the individual's conscious experience of autonomy (sense of separateness from the external world) and self-direction (sense of acting in accord with conscious aims or intentions). From within this framework, Shapiro then sees symptoms as consequences, and defenses as conspicuous expressions, of these same restrictive, self-regulating dynamics.

Independently, complex systems theory (CST), through its rigorous study of biological, social, and inanimate systems, has identified several system dynamics and properties that are quite compatible with Shapiro's systemic theory of character. CST demonstrates that a system's *character*, defined as its relatively stable, system-wide organization and structure, emerges from the spontaneous coordination of the system's constitutive subsystems. Furthermore, CST shows that the emergence of systemic organization brings with it system-wide differentiation and the elements necessary for intra-systemic (internal) conflict. Finally, CST demonstrates that nonlinear reciprocal relationships between critical variables drive qualitative, discontinuous, and non-proportional change in a system's overall organization.

This chapter reviews each of these ideas and then explores their relationship to Shapiro's work. I propose that CST not only offers an independent formalization of many of Shapiro's central ideas, but I also point to instances where CST provides a more detailed account of the processes underlying Shapiro's theory and clinical observations.

C. Piers (✉)
Senior Supervising Psychologist, Thompson Health Center, Williams College,
105 Knoll Road, Williamstown, MA 01267
e-mail: craig.piers@williams.edu

C. Piers (ed.), *Personality and Psychopathology: Critical Dialogues with David Shapiro*,
DOI 10.1007/978-1-4419-6214-0_10, © Springer Science+Business Media, LLC 2011

While beyond the scope of this chapter, it is interesting to note that recent neuroscientific research has suggested that the brain's dense network of neurons exhibits many of the same dynamics and properties that are reviewed in this chapter (Edelman 1992, 2004; Freeman 1995, 2007; Kelso 1999; Lachaux et al. 1999; Bressler and Kelso 2001; Kozma et al. 2005; Kelso and Engstrom 2006; Grigsby and Osuch 2007). This suggests that CST could provide a bridging language or a unifying set of dynamic concepts that allows us to link a systemic theory of the mind to current neurobiological accounts of the brain. This, in turn, suggests an even more intriguing possibility: if we succeed in faithfully translating psychodynamics and neuro-dynamics into the language of CST, we may then bring this understanding to the larger, ongoing, and multidisciplinary effort to identify a small set of universal, system-invariant and scale-invariant processes and properties that account for complex, adaptive systems of all kinds.

A Way of Thinking

With the use of computer models and simulations, CST attempts to elucidate the fundamental features and dynamics of systems. This has included an effort to identify the necessary ingredients for the development of system-wide organization, coherence, and stability, as well as the change processes that result in qualitative, irreducible, and virtually unpredictable transitions in the overall organization of a system. In so doing, CST emphasizes an adaptive system's spare and elegant design. As computer models and simulations have demonstrated, with very little built into their basic design, systems – particularly self-organizing ones – can produce remarkably complex behavior. This way of thinking has tremendous intuitive appeal when we consider biological, adaptive systems.

What am I getting at? When designing and building a model to simulate the behavior of a complex, adaptive system, it is tempting to try to load in – at the front end or design phase – a response to every conceivable circumstance. This works fine when we can identify precisely the exact nature of all the components comprising the system. But when we want to study systems that include an unpredictable element – that is, make the model a closer approximation of adaptive systems in the real world – the model very soon breaks down or freezes up because it encounters circumstances that were not anticipated in the design phase. Of course, we could just keep adding new modules to address specific circumstances. But when it comes to unpredictable environments, our work would be unending and soon our models would collapse under the weight of their sheer size.

This simple observation indicates that this cannot be the design of biological systems honed by evolution. Rather the fundamental design of adaptive, biological systems must be more elegantly and sparely designed and in such a way that they are able to generate novel responses to unanticipated circumstances. When it comes to modeling, this means that building in less of the right stuff, produces more robust and adaptive responses. So when we model a system, the key is to start simple, and then, only slowly, add little details to the model's design, one at a time. What we find is that at some critical point – often suddenly and far earlier than we anticipated – the model's behavior crosses a threshold of complexity and produces adaptive responses. The simple message from CST is: with less in, you can get more out.

Applying this insight to the mind has led me to conclude that we need not front-load – that is, load into our theories of mind – features and processes that account for every conceivable expression. Rather, an understanding of self-organizing systems encourages us to identify a small set of elementary subsystems that combine and recombine in radically different ways in response to changing internal and external conditions, ultimately arriving at a novel, adaptive, and relatively stable organization of states, all in the absence of prefigured instructions, commands, or blueprints.

Review of Complex Systems Theory

My interest in dynamic systems, most certainly set in motion by Shapiro's systemic understanding of character, has brought me to the literature on cellular automata (CA). CA are spare, bare-boned, and rigorously-defined computer models comprised of interconnected cells or elementary subsystems (Ilachinski 2001; Wolfram 2002; see Piers 2007, for an application to the mind). My interest in CA is based on the fact that *despite* their simplicity, they are capable of rather complex behavior, and *because* of their simplicity, they may provide insight into the fundamental nature and dynamics of systems more generally.

To provide just a bit more detail about their design, a CA's elementary subsystems can be defined in their entirety by three simple parameters: a *state parameter*, which sets the number of microstates available to each subsystem[1]; an *interaction parameter*, which sets the extent of interconnection and communication between subsystems; and *transition rules*, which spell out the conditions that must be met for the subsystem to transition from one microstate to the next. Just three parameters. What is fascinating is that with this simple, three-parameter system, we are able to simulate, in clear terms, many of the dynamic properties of far more complex systems. To offer just a few examples, models such as this have been used to simulate the apparent "collective intelligence" in hiving bees and in colonies of ants and termites (Goodwin 1994; Resnick 1994), the emergence of synchronized flashing in Malaysian fireflies and the coordinated patterns of birds in flight (Strogatz 2003), the skewed distribution of wealth and the spread of disease in social systems (Epstein and Axtell 1996), and the organized and meaningful patterns that emerge in the firing of the brain's interconnected network of neurons (Freeman 1995, 2007; Bressler and Kelso 2001; Kozma et al. 2005).

Essentially, these three parameters define and set a system's primitives. The first two parameters set limits or constraints on the elementary subsystems' range of

---

[1] I call these "microstates" to distinguish them from the "macrostate" the system organizes itself into at any one moment in time.

expression and scope of influence, respectively. The third parameter, transition rules, builds into the subsystems simple biases or preferences in the form of conditions that the subsystem requires to transition between its available microstates. Of course, while these are built in at the level of the elementary subsystem, these constraints and biases determine what the larger system becomes capable of, though not in any straightforward, linear way, as we will see.

At this point, it is reasonable to wonder what relationship the parameters of these highly idealized models have with other complex systems, such as social groups, the economy, or, of special interest to us, character. Well, with some translation, if we understand a CA's "state" and "interaction" parameters as setting functional limitations or constraints on the subsystem, we can see them as approximating the constraints of real-world, biological systems.[2] As Demos (2007) reminds us, the human eye responds only to a narrow band of wavelengths in the electromagnetic spectrum, the human ear can detect sound only through a certain frequency range, and human short-term memory can hold on an average seven pieces of information. In other words, these represent constraints on the perceptual, auditory, and cognitive subsystems, respectively. Of course, there are human skeletal and muscular features that also set functional constraints: take, for example, the joints in our arms and legs. Constraints provide the outer limits or boundaries of a system, a critical element for the development of internal organization. Importantly, constraints also guarantee that certain gross formal similarities will arise between systems of the same class.

Finally, in biological systems, the "transition rules" approximate elementary tendencies, preferences, or biases – what Gerald Edelman (1992) calls "values." An example in the human infant is the perceptual preference for dark-light contours and contrasts. Oliver Sacks writes that elementary values or biases serve to "differentially weight experience," making the infant prefer some aspects of experience and withdraw from others (cited from Ghent 2002). A subsystem's values are selected through evolution because of the fitness they offer their possessors in terms of survival, adaptation, and reproduction.

Having described the basic design of CA and their possible relevance to our study of the mind, what do these simple, elegant models demonstrate? Most importantly, they appear to provide clues about the sources and nature of system-wide organization and structure. From a wide range of parameter setups, CA have demonstrated that system-wide organization and structure arise spontaneously from the nondirected coordination of a system's interacting and mutually influencing subsystems. Put differently, the spontaneous coordination of a system's disparate, yet interacting, subsystems (with their built-in constraints and values) give rise to system-wide organization, coherence, and structure, in the form of a macrostate. As we move forward and begin to apply CST to the mind, a single macrostate should be thought of as a coordinated state of mind. Sometimes states of mind are fleeting, sometimes enduring. It is when macrostates, or coordinated states of mind, are

---

[2] Although Thelen and Smith (1994) and Demos (2007) do not write about CA, their developmental accounts of constraints and biases have assisted me greatly in my translation of CA into biological systems.

observed and mapped over time that they reveal the mind's relatively stable, overall organization – its character.

There are different ways of measuring or characterizing subsystem coordination. For instance, with subsystems that cycle through different phases or microstates, the degree of coordination between subsystems can be measured based on each subsystem's cycling speed (for example, cycles per second or hertz). In this case, subsystems are coordinated when they spontaneously come to share the same cycling speed, despite having a range of possible cycling speeds available in their repertoire. Another common measure of coordination is "relative phase" or the calculated difference in phase between two subsystems (Kelso 1999). With relative phase, subsystems are coordinated when the difference in phase between two subsystems remains fixed or unchanging over time. Likewise, if the relative phase between two subsystems varies widely either spatially or temporally, we conclude that they are not coordinated.

But how might we characterize subsystem coordination when considering the mind? The mind's subsystems include the perceptual, cognitive, affective, and motor subsystems. Each subsystem has a full range of expression, both in their formal qualities (for example, a way of thinking or feeling) and in their content (for example, a particular thought or feeling). Therefore, coordination between the mind's subsystems would be evident in a relatively fixed range of expression across the subsystems. Returning to the measurement of "relative phase," but modifying to measure "relative range," two of the mind's subsystems would be coordinated when the difference in their respective range of expression remains relatively fixed or unchanging over time.

Macrostates (momentary system-wide organization) have several important features. One, a macrostate is *self-organized*; it arises spontaneously without prefigured instructions or blueprints. In other words, there are no instructions embedded within the system telling it to organize itself into a particular macrostate. With regard to CA, the built-in constraints and simple values do not instruct the system to arrive at a particular macrostate. Rather, at a single moment in time, the entire system becomes organized through the coordination of interacting subsystems. Self-organization is an example of a selectional process, as opposed to an instructional process (Edelman 2004). That is, the stable, coordinated macrostate, representing a temporary systemic solution, was selected out of a massive number of possible macrostates, given current conditions and the subsystems' intrinsic and varied constraints and values.

Two, a self-organized macrostate is *emergent*; it is qualitatively different and irreducible to the subsystems that gave rise to it (Goldstein 2007). This means that with the emergence of a macrostate, the system as a whole develops features and capabilities unavailable to any one subsystem in isolation. An oft-cited example of emergence is human consciousness, widely considered an emergent property of the brain's dense network of neurons. That is to say, individual neurons do not contain little bits of consciousness, that when added up across the billions of neurons that comprise the brain, produce consciousness. Rather, consciousness is an emergent property, and as such, qualitatively different and irreducible to the network of neurons that gives rise to it.

Three, a self-organized, emergent macrostate is *differentiated* into second-order subsystems. Macrostates, in other words, rarely evince uniform and unvarying coordination across the entire system, with all aspects of the system moving in lockstep.

Rather, more often than not, we see emergent islands of coordinated activity separated by oceans of different, but nonetheless, coordinated activity. What separates or distinguishes one area (islands) from the other (oceans) is the nature of their respective coordination. In short, embedded within the macrostate's overall coordination, we see the emergence of second-order subsystems, each with its own degree of coordination. Differentiated, second-order subsystems are emergent because they represent, on a scale smaller than the macrostate, the coordination of activity across elementary subsystems, and in that way, bring with them properties and dynamics unavailable to any of the elementary subsystems. Thus, with differentiation comes the development and enhancement of difference and specialization at the level of the macrostate. When thinking about differentiation, it is tempting to emphasize the separation, isolation, or independence of one second-order subsystem from another. Yet because the entire system is involved in arriving at the differentiated macrostate, the second-order subsystems are utterly interdependent, or dependent on their uncoordinated (with them) neighbors for their continuation. Change in coordination of any of the parts leads to change rippling across the entire system and potentially altering the coalitions that have developed between aspects of the system.

A self-organized, emergent, differentiated macrostate is a snapshot of the system's overall coordination at a moment in time. To determine whether there is stability or continuity in the system's coordination, we observe and map the macrostate's overall degree of coordination of over time. Importantly, when the overall degree of coordination of successive macrostates is mapped, the system's discernible, identifiable, and *dynamically stable* organization – the system's character – is revealed. "Dynamically stable" may seem like a rather odd phrase. After all, "dynamic" means changing and "stable" means unchanging. The dynamic or changing aspect of the system's organization, on the one hand, is evident in the fluctuating degree of coordination in the macrostates across time. That is, the degree of coordination of evolving macrostates rarely repeats exactly over time. The stable or unchanging aspect of the system's organization, on the other hand, is evident in the way the fluctuating macrostates become organized around a central value. Put differently, while the degree of coordination fluctuates, the fluctuations remain within certain limits, seemingly attracted or tethered to a centralized macrostate or set of macrostates. It is the bounded, constrained nature of these fluctuating macrostates that reveals the system's organization over time. I refer to the system's dynamically stable organization as its character, because the word character appropriately describes the system's relatively stable and discernible, overall organization.

An important implication of a system's emergent, dynamically stable character is that, while strictly determined by the elementary subsystems, it comes to constrain the expression of the subsystems in a top-down fashion. That is, the system's organization constrains the range of expression of the subsystems due to the latter's "enslavement" or "entrainment" to the system's overall organization (Kelso 1999). Thus, we see circular causality, wherein the whole, while completely dependent on the parts, comes to constrain the expression of the parts. A system's capacity to restrain fluctuations is related to its differentiated organization into second-order subsystems, because breaking into areas with varying degrees of coordination allows the system to restrain a wider range of fluctuations. Later when discussing the mind, I propose that in addition to constraining the subsystems' range of expression, the emergence of a dynamically stable organization of the mind is accompanied by the individual's newfound capability to increase or decrease the degree to which the elementary subsystems' range of expression is restrained. This is because autonomous self-direction emerges as a feature of the mind's organization, and as such, the individual is able to exert, within certain limits, top-down influence.

CST refers to a system's overarching dynamically stable character as an *attractor*. An attractor is a geometric representation of the organized, constrained pattern of fluctuating macrostates that the system settles into over time (see Piers 2000, 2005, for extended discussion). For example, the simplest attractors include the "point attractor," where, from any set of initial conditions, the system winds down to a single, repeating macrostate over time, and a "limit cycle attractor," where the system ends up cycling through a repeating sequence of macrostates. "Strange attractors" are the most complex of the attractors, so named because the evolving macrostates' degree of coordination never repeats, but they still all remain constrained or bounded by an overall organization. That is, mapping the macrostates' non-repeating degree of coordination over time reveals that the system still has a dynamically stable organization, but one that is complex. The strange attractor's complexity is related to its fractionated (fractal) dimensionality – a set of dimensions that cannot be captured by a whole number (Mandelbrot 1982; see Piers 2000, for a more extended discussion). The important point to take away is: systems whose behavior conforms to a strange attractor have *both* an unlimited number of macrostates in their repertoire and a discernable, albeit complex, dynamically stable character. Elsewhere, I have suggested that strange attractors aptly describe the way individuals are recognizable as the persons they are across time and context (evident in the continuity in their "way of being" or character), even in the midst of their vast multiplicity (Piers 2005).

The stability of an attractor is related to its tolerance for, or capacity to restrain, internally generated discordant fluctuations – macrostates with a degree of coordination that are atypical or uncharacteristic of the system. An attractor's stability can be ascertained by asking two questions: (1) how quickly does the system return to its more characteristic pattern of fluctuating coordination following the occurrence of a discordant fluctuation and (2) how discordant can a fluctuation in coordination be without changing the system's overall organization? This analysis is used to determine the attractor's "basin of attraction." Very stable attractors, for example, have wide, steep, and deep basins of attraction that are able to capture and restrain even widely discordant fluctuations.[3] As such, attractors are ways of describing and

---

[3] Imagine a ball rolling along the inside of a bowl. If we place the ball anywhere along the side of the bowl, over time the ball will settle at the bowl's bottom. The questions then become: (1) if go in and bump the ball on its way toward settling at the bottom, how long would it take the ball to resume its previous trajectory?; and (2) how much force is required to push the ball over the side and out of the bowl? These questions are asking about the width, steepness and depth of the attractor's basin of attraction, and by extension, the stability of the system's overall organization.

studying the conservative quality of systems – those aspects that resist change and restrain fluctuations. Furthermore, the presence of attractors, with their basins of attraction, signals the presence of self-regulatory processes that work to maintain a system's current organization going forward. Importantly, from this discussion we can see that self-regulation is an emergent property of the system's character, meaning that it is not present in any one of the subsystems.[4]

While attractors provide a way of characterizing a system's continuity over time, to understand how systems change, we need to return again to the subject of intrinsic fluctuations: the continuous (albeit restrained) presence of internally generated variability in coordination. Fluctuations in coordination exist in all "coupled" systems and are related to the range of ways elementary subsystems can become coordinated given their constraints and biases – a range in coordination that is constrained by the system's overall organization, but never fully stamped out. Discordant fluctuations – ones that fall outside the system's attractor but within its basin of attraction – create a dynamic tension within the system because they probe and test the stability of the system's current organization. Importantly, the organization of adaptive systems differs from maladaptive systems in terms of the degree of fluctuation that can be tolerated. Restated in the language of attractors, the system's tolerance for discordant fluctuations is determined by its basin of attraction. Some tolerance for discordant fluctuations is a sign of the system's adaptiveness because fluctuations represent adaptations or adjustments that the system as a whole is making in response to ever-present variations in internal or external conditions. A system that suppresses all fluctuation, as well as a system that is tolerant to only a limited degree of fluctuation, are both maladaptive, because they suggest insensitivity to small changes in conditions that are presumed to be going on all the time.

Returning to the subject of system-wide differentiation for a moment, it is important to appreciate that a system's tolerance for discordant fluctuations corresponds directly to the nature of the system's differentiated second-order subsystems, because both arrive simultaneously with the emergence of the system's organization. An adaptive system's organization stabilizes somewhere between two *maladaptive* poles of coordination. At one end of the spectrum, overall, single uniformity in coordination prevails, which entails the absence of both fluctuation and differentiation. At the other end, only small pockets of coordinated activity prevail, entailing low tolerance for discordant fluctuations and a highly fragmented or splintered overall differentiation into numerous, small second-order subsystems. Adaptive systems, by contrast, settle into a pattern of fluctuating coordination, characterized by an optimal tolerance for fluctuation and optimally sized second-order subsystems. They do so not because of a prefigured plan or instruction, but *precisely* because this organization is able to restrain a wide range of fluctuations, and as such, is dynamically stable, resilient, and responsive.

Internally generated, discordant fluctuations have different meanings depending on your point of view. Seen one way, discordant fluctuations represent the possibility

---

[4]This last statement is perhaps somewhat misleading because it deemphasizes the scale-invariant nature of generic system properties like self-regulation.

for qualitative transformation and change in a system's organization – a sign of the system's momentarily restrained potential. Seen another way, discordant fluctuations represent a potential threat to the system's organization. Whether seen as suppressed potential or as organizational threats, the presence of discordant fluctuations means that built directly into the system's organization are the seeds for its own dissolution. Furthermore, it is the system's current organization that delineates the very form the fluctuations will take – fluctuations are unique to, and defined by, a system's current organization.

Discordant fluctuations perturb the dynamic stability of a system's organization when they approach the outer limits of the system's tolerance for fluctuation. In response to some of these disturbances, I suggest that some systems – such as human character – respond by either contracting or expanding their tolerance for fluctuations, that is, their basin of attraction. A system's capacity to modify its basin of attraction is related to the emergent nature of its organization. As is the case with emergent phenomena, with the emergence of system-wide organization, a system gains new capabilities – in this case, a capability to change, within certain limits, its basin of attraction in a top-down fashion.[5]

When a system contracts or expands its tolerance for discordant fluctuations, it may work temporarily to quiet those fluctuations, even give the system time to relax back to its former organization. But contracting or expanding its tolerance can also set in motion a destabilizing cycle, because the net effect of contracting or expanding its basin of attraction is an increased potential for discordant fluctuations. After all, a system's overall organization has no effect on the subsystems' constraints and biases, or the range of ways elementary subsystems can spontaneously coordinate their functioning in response to changing internal and external conditions. It *constrains* that range, but does not determine it. When the system contracts or expands its basin, it destabilizes its formerly dynamically stable organization, and as such, diminishes its capacity to restrain fluctuations. A diminished capacity to restrain discordant fluctuations can lead to their proliferation. Thus, the destabilizing cycle takes the following form: the presence of even more fluctuation following the contraction (or expansion) of the basin leads the system to contract (or expand) even further, which, in turn, leads to an increased potential for even more discordant fluctuations. In other words, contracting (or expanding) the basin of attraction sets off a positive feedback cycle, leading to an acceleration of contraction (or expansion) and ever-increasing destabilization of the system's overall organization.

The relationship between the degree of contraction (or expansion) and the destabilization of the system's organization is a *nonlinear* one. That is, an incremental change in contraction (or expansion) does not correspond to a proportional, incremental destabilization of the system, in any one-to-one way. Rather, once the degree of contraction (or expansion) exceeds a certain threshold, the system's overall

---

[5]This may become clearer when we describe human character as a dynamically stable organization, because, as I have indicated, with the emergence of overall organization, the individual acquires the capability for conscious self-direction – the capability to regulate, within certain limits, aspects of character.

organization is lost. What one notices is the presence of a critical threshold or tipping point beyond which even a small change in the degree of contraction (or expansion) leads to the destabilization of the entire system.

Systemic, qualitative, and discontinuous change occurs when discordant fluctuations overwhelm the strength or "stickiness" of the system's organization. In fact, a sign of impending system-wide change is escalating and widening fluctuation or variability in coordination (Thelen and Smith 1994; Kelso 1999). Once the current organization is destabilized, coordination varies widely until such time that the system as a whole discovers a new, emergent, dynamically stable organization – one that keeps fluctuating macrostates to tolerable levels, a tolerable level that is newly defined by the system. With the emergence of a new dynamically stable organization, not only has the system's tolerance for discordant fluctuations become redefined, but the degree of relatively stable, system-wide differentiation also changes. In fact, the change in the system's overall differentiation is what allows the system to again restrain and stabilize fluctuations.

It is important to note, however, that while discordant fluctuations may push the system to change, they do not completely determine the ultimate shape of the system's new organization. Rather, discordant fluctuations destabilize the system's current organization forcing it to find a new dynamically stable organization. The system's new organization is also determined, in part, by whether it is discovered while changing in a contracting or expanding direction. In the contracting case, the new organization will be more restrictive, less tolerant to discordant fluctuations, and splintered into small, second-order subsystems of coordination. In the expanding case, the new organization is more adaptive, more tolerant to fluctuations, and differentiated into larger, second-order subsystems. Larger second-order subsystems, it should be understood, indicate greater and more optimal coordination of the elementary subsystems.

We have now covered, to my mind, the most relevant aspects of CST. It is important to appreciate that research in CST has simulated most of these system features and properties with simple, rigorously defined models of interacting subsystems with intrinsic values and constraints.

Shapiro's Character Theory and CST

Much like CST, Shapiro depicts character as a complex adaptive system. Implicit in Shapiro's conceptualization are the concepts of self-organization, emergence, attractors, and intrinsic, system-delineated, and discordant fluctuations. Implicit in Shapiro's view, as well, is an appreciation of the nonlinear, reciprocal relationships between critical variables. For instance, this is present in his discussion of the transition from obsessive to paranoid character, and in his conjecture about the onset of schizophrenia.

Shapiro's systemic view could be further refined by the inclusion of the central role of coordination because, in CST, spontaneous coordination is the source of the system's emergent and dynamically stable organization and, importantly, its associated differentiation and internally generated fluctuations. This is important because differentiation, or in Shapiro's language, "objectification of the external world," is central to the development of autonomous self-direction. Similarly, the defensive curtailment of agency in neurosis is associated with decreased differentiation, resulting in what Shapiro refers to variously as the "loss of self-object polarity" or a loss of an objective attitude toward the external world.

Character as a Self-Organized, Emergent Attractor

The concepts of self-organization, emergence, and attractors fit comfortably within Shapiro's conceptualization of neurotic character. Let us take them in turn.

Self-organization is not only the nondirected and unscripted emergence of a macrostate, but also the nondirected emergence of an organized set of fluctuating but constrained macrostates over time, evident in the system's dynamically stable character. The system's character, in other words, is not directed into being from above. Rather the system's organization represents a system-wide solution (revealed in an attractor and its basin of attraction) based on the coordination of elementary subsystems with their various and sometimes competing constraints and biases. In the same way, neurotic character is an unintended, nondirected, relatively stable organization of attitudes (a dynamically stable, relatively enduring systemic solution) that emerges from the coordination in functioning of perceptual, sensory, cognitive, affective, and motor subsystems with their own constraints and biases. Consistent with the idea of self-organization, character is embodied, rather than intended, selected, or coordinated by the individual. While individuals do not choose the nature of their neurotic character, they do become unwittingly complicit in perpetuating, and sometimes intensifying, its restrictive dynamics.

Shapiro's view of character includes emergence in at least three respects. One, his view of neurotic character is non-reductive. Character is seen as different in kind and more encompassing than any early, however traumatic, set of experiences that may have had a hand in shaping it. Character also has its own internal, self-regulating dynamics, which means that it is not sustained by an ongoing link to its original, earlier sources. In addition to being irreducible to particular early experiences, character is also irreducible to developmentally earlier organizations of the mind. While it is true that Shapiro sees particular character styles (obsessive, hysterical, paranoid, etc.) similar in some respects to two fundamental and developmentally earlier prevolitional modes – the passive-reactive and rule-based modes – character styles are conceived of as defensively modified variants of these modes ("hypertrophied," in Shapiro's language) and in that way, different in kind and irreducible to them. Character styles are similar to prevolitional modes inasmuch as both share as a central feature the diminished experience of autonomous self-direction. Yet, the former emerge for defensive reasons, while the latter emerge for developmental reasons.

Two, the development of character, conceived of as dynamically stable organization of attitudes, brings with it properties previously unavailable to the mind, an idea that is consistent with emergence. For instance, the experience of autonomous self-direction, for Shapiro, emerges simultaneously with increasing objectification of the external world. Autonomous self-direction is emergent because it is a property of system-wide organization and differentiation, and in that way, not present in any of the elementary subsystems that gave rise to it.

Three, Shapiro touches on the circular causality discussed in relation to emergence when he describes the way character constrains the range of expression (through entrainment) of perceptual, sensory, cognitive, affective, and motor subsystems – those subsystems whose coordinated functioning resulted in the emergent organization of character. That is, character styles are accompanied by particular ways of perceiving, thinking, feeling, and acting, all of which has an internal coherence. For instance, in obsessive individuals, sharply focused attention accompanies precise, analytical thinking, constrained emotional expression, and sometimes, rigid, robotic movement. In these ways, the emergent character style constrains or narrows the range of expression of each of the subsystems.

Finally, CST's discussion of attractors with their basins of attraction provides a clinically useful way of illustrating and conceptualizing Shapiro's discussion of neurotic character's conservative, self-regulating elasticity. Recall that sampling and mapping the system's fluctuating but constrained macrostates over time reveals attractors and their basins, or the system's character. The width, steepness, and depth of an attractor's basin of attraction provide a way of describing the dynamic stability of character and its vulnerability to perturbation. Clinically, character's self-regulating elasticity is observed when patients work to dilute their awareness of discordant and conflictual aspects of subjectivity, often through self-deceptive speech acts, and the way they often return to characteristic ways of organizing experience, even following moments of insight.

Development of Autonomy

Autonomous self-direction is central to Shapiro's (1981, 2000) theory of character and he has written extensively on both its development and defensive curtailment in all forms of psychopathology. Shapiro's developmental account of autonomous self-direction is related to its reciprocal relationship with the objectification of the external world, or what I have described as the differentiation of the system into second-order subsystems. For Shapiro, the experience of the externality of objects allows for the possibility of interest in objects, and thus, opportunities for self-directed (volitional) action. Acting on the world of external objects based on intention, in turn, leads to still further differentiation of self from the external world, as well as greater discrimination between external objects. Through this reciprocal relationship, ever-increasing differentiation and autonomous self-direction emerge.

Of note, Shapiro (1981) writes of the emergence of volitional self-direction as gradual and incremental: "The emergence of intentionality...is too gradual to be marked with any precision" (p. 41). This seems unlikely, and inconsistent with Shapiro's own description of the way neurotic character can undergo qualitative and discontinuous transitions in its overall organization driven by nonlinear, reciprocal relationships between critical parameters (discussed below). It is difficult to precisely mark the advent of intentionality, but it would be more internally consistent to link this difficulty to its nonlinear emergence.

Shapiro's developmental account of the dynamics underlying the objectification of the world would be enhanced by incorporating an understanding of self-organized coordination, which leads to the individual's dynamically stable character and associated differentiation. I suggest that autonomous self-direction and differentiation are both properties that accompany the emergence of system-wide organization, and that system-wide organization emerges in the child from the repeated coordination of the perceptual, sensory (including proprioceptive), cognitive, affective, and motor information uniquely associated with the child's activity. It is the coordination of this information, in contrast to the coordination of information associated with the experience of external objects, which leads to the nonlinear (non-gradual) emergence of differentiation and autonomous self-direction – properties of the child's developing character.

With this said, I would like to sketch a simple model for the development of autonomous self-direction. The infant is equipped at birth with elementary perceptual, sensory, cognitive, affective, and motor subsystems, all of which have built-in constraints and biases approximating CA models.[6] With regard to the primitive "values" or biases, the infant is intrinsically interested in *differences*. This is a systemic bias that includes an interest in contrasts, contours, change, novelty, and violation of expectations and contingencies (Demos 2007). I see all these specific expressions as aspects of an intrinsic interest in differences because, at a fundamental level, each expression requires that the infant appreciates, and is interested in, differences in and between events, states, or experiences.

And lastly, I want to build one more element into our model of the developing infant. Let us assume that pleasure is associated with any experience or activity that accentuates differences in its various forms. This reinforcing component would lead the infant to attempt to repeat any activity that accentuated differences. It is easy to see how this would guarantee that the coordination of the subsystems involved in early self-initiated actions would be especially pleasing, because, as a participant, there would be a heightened accentuation of difference in the form of self-object contrast or polarity. By building in this reinforcing process, we end up

---

[6] I recognize, of course, that each of these elementary subsystems also mature and become more refined over the course of development, which brings to the entire system new constraints and capacities. In fact, I would suggest that intra-subsystem development unfolds in much the same way as I am describing the overall system, and is even further augmented by a subsystem's coordination with other elementary subsystems. It is my view that the fundamental dynamics of development and change are the same at every level of scale.

with an infant who *appears* to prefer being an active agent. In other words, my model does not build into the infant an intrinsic interest in being an active agent. Rather, he or she *becomes* an active agent. By repeatedly acting on the world (driven by pleasure), self and the external world of objects become increasingly articulated and differentiated through the coordination of information associated with each. We have in essence a built-in reinforcing, positive feedback cycle that sets the right conditions for increasing levels of differentiation and the emergence of autonomous self-direction. Finally, it should be noted that the advent of autonomous self-direction changes the experience of the intrinsic interest in differences. That is, the emergent capacity for volitional, self-directed action moderates and comes to shape the experience of this bias. While the bias still informs and influences the individual's action, the individual determines what influence it will have.

Psychodynamics of Character

CST is largely consistent with Shapiro's description of the dynamics of character. A critical aspect of Shapiro's theory of neurosis is the experience of autonomous self-direction, which, along with differentiation, I have suggested are properties of the system's emergent character. In that sense, they all arrive together. Shapiro suggests that associated with these developments is an increased conscious awareness of possibilities, choice, and importantly, personal responsibility. This sets the stage for conflict arising between competing wishes and desires, which can lead, in some people, to pathological levels of anxiety. In the context of pathological levels of anxiety, relatively stable neurotic character emerges as a self-regulating dynamic system which forestalls or dispels anxiety by diminishing conscious awareness of whole classes of subjective experience that are associated with the experience of agency. Restated in the language of CST, neurotic character emerges as a dynamically stable organization of the mind because it successfully binds, restrains, and dilutes the experience of agency – keeps those experiences at tolerable levels. Consistent with CST, Shapiro indicates that these estranged, threatening, and destabilizing aspects of subjectivity are delineated by the system's current organization. Just as in CST, these discordant, conflictual fluctuations do not have a separate source but are internally generated and defined by the system's current, restrictive organization.

As Shapiro (1981, 2000) indicates, the experience of agency is not a stable quality of our organized and changing coordinated states of mind. Rather, the experience of agency fluctuates. The degree to which we experience agency is largely determined by the familiarity of the task or conditions at hand. In unfamiliar, novel, or challenging situations, for instance, agency is felt more keenly. In this way, and in the language of CST, coordinated states of mind in which the experience of agency is heightened are discordant, potentially destabilizing fluctuations. Similar to the way we have defined discordant fluctuations, these states of mind fall outside character's attractor but within its basin of attraction. This is plausible if we assume that (1) an individual's subjective experience of a coordinated state of mind is accompanied by a sense of "doing" the coordinating and (2) that the subjective experience of doing is different depending on whether the coordinated state of mind falls on the attractor or within its basin of attraction. Coordinated states of mind that fall on the attractor are more characteristic or typical states of mind, and in that way, more automatic or habitual. As such, there is a diminished experience of active coordination or agency. Those states of mind that fall off the attractor, but within the basin of attraction, are less typical, and in that way, the subjective experience of coordination or agency is heightened.

The underlying dynamics driving the emergence of neurotic character are very similar to the contracting, destabilizing cycle described earlier. High levels of anxiety related to agency move the individual to embody ways of thinking and modes of behavior ("ways of being") that restrict or diminish the conscious experience of agency. From the perspective of CST, diminishing agency experience is equivalent to the system becoming less tolerant to discordant fluctuations, or contracting the degree of agency experience that is tolerable. The effect of restricting or contracting the experience of agency is not the loss of a specific experience. Rather, whole classes of subjective experience associated with agency become discordant and potentially destabilizing. This can set in motion a destabilizing cycle where ever-growing restrictiveness is matched by ever-growing fluctuations. When the degree of restrictiveness exceeds a critical threshold, the system's former dynamically stable character is destabilized, leading to the emergence of a new, more restrictive character. As we reviewed earlier, it is more restrictive because it was discovered through a contracting cycle.

For the most part, emergent character styles are dynamically stable because they successfully keep discordant and destabilizing fluctuations in the experience of agency to tolerable levels.[7] But neurotic character can also undergo qualitative and discontinuous transitions in its organization. These shifts occur when discordant aspects of subjective experience threaten to exceed tolerable levels – that is, the experience of agency is amplified by especially threatening and character-specific circumstances. Shapiro suggests that at such moments, neurotic character "tightens" or becomes even more restrictive of agency experience. In the ways we have reviewed, this can set off another contracting, destabilizing cycle. In sum, neurotic

---

[7] Paul Wachtel's (2008) "cyclical-contextual model," for which he credits the influence of Horney and Shapiro (Chap. 2), provides a way of understanding the stability of neurotic functioning. Wachtel's explication of dynamically reinforcing cycles is congruent with my discussion of feedback cycles – in fact, more fully rounds out the picture of the psychodynamics. Wachtel highlights the role of "negative feedback cycles," system dynamics that dampen, neutralize, or correct departures (discordant fluctuations) from the system's stable state and result in the reinforcement and stability of the neurotic cycle. In this chapter, my emphasis has been on "positive feedback cycles," system dynamics that amplify departures (discordant fluctuations) from the system's stable state and drive qualitative change. An appreciation of both types of feedback cycles is required for a more complete understanding of the psychodynamics of *stability* and *change*.

character can go through nonlinear, qualitative shifts in its overall organization driven by ever-increasing restrictiveness, or contraction of agency experience. Shapiro describes exactly these types of nonlinear changes in his discussion of the transition from obsessive and paranoid character, and the onset of schizophrenia.

The earlier discussion of the nonlinear, reciprocal relationship between increasing contraction and the destabilization of the system's overall organization, may point to a difference between Shapiro's conceptualization and CST. Based on my reading of his work, Shapiro suggests a direct relationship between differentiation and autonomous self-direction, with one directly affecting the other. From the perspective of CST, however, the relationship is less direct. Autonomous self-direction and differentiation emerge simultaneously as properties of the system's character. When character becomes increasingly restrictive of agency experience, this does indeed effect differentiation, but by destabilizing the system's overall organization and leading to its reorganization into a more restrictive character – a system with less tolerance for fluctuations and whose differentiation is splintered into small second-order subsystems. As we discussed, smaller second-order subsystems entail less than optimal coordination of the elementary subsystems.

A splintered differentiation of the mind into small second-order subsystems aptly describes the relative lack of coordination across attention, perception, thought, affect, and movement, seen in all forms of psychopathology, but most clearly in the case of schizophrenia.[8] The emergence of this splintered differentiation means that information across the elementary subsystems is not optimally coordinated. The relative absence of multimodal coordination is evident in many of the symptoms associated with schizophrenia. These symptoms include distractibility or the inability to direct one's attention; the capture of attention by extraneous cues, including bodily sensations that typically go unnoticed; the peculiarities of schizophrenic speech, including tangential speech, loose associations, and word fragments; and a degraded, flattened emotionality. Each of these symptoms points to a splintered or less than optimal coordination across the elementary subsystems. In Shapiro's (2000) language, schizophrenia is the result of mounting restrictiveness to agency experience, which eventuates in the relative absence of active, purposeful focus and the associated loss of the external objects required for volitional self-direction. In a sense, ever-growing restrictiveness reverses the very process that brought about self-directedness and differentiation. With the relative absence of volitional self-direction, coordination of information across subsystems is lost.

Having reviewed how the overall organization of neurotic character can change through increasing restrictiveness or the contraction of agency experience, it is important to appreciate that qualitative, discontinuous change in the system's overall organization can happen in the opposite direction, as well. In CST, this occurs when discordant fluctuations are amplified through the expansion of the system's basin of attraction.

---

[8]Through research that examined the coordination of neuronal activity, Bressler (2003) speculated that decreased coordination would be associated with schizophrenia as compared to controls. This was later experimentally confirmed by Uhlhaas and colleagues (2006).

I suggest that the amplification of discordant fluctuations in the expanding case – or the amplification of aspects of subjective experience associated with agency – occurs when the individual directs his or her attention to, and becomes increasingly interested in, these fluctuations. The individual's experience of agency is heightened at such moments not only by his or her interest in formerly estranged aspects of experience associated with agency, but also by the very experience of *directing* his or her attention. That is, the individual receives a double dose of agency experience – one that actually builds on itself. When this amplifying cycle crosses a critical threshold, the current restrictive organization becomes unstable and leads to the emergence of a new dynamically stable organization – an organization of mind that has greater tolerance for fluctuations and more optimal differentiation.

It may appear that I have introduced a new parameter, ad hoc, to explain the bidirectional, qualitative, and discontinuous transitions that can occur in character – an individual's capability to contract or expand his or her tolerance for fluctuations in the experience of agency. But by returning to the simple model I outlined earlier for the development of autonomous self-direction, we can see that the model already accounts for it. Driving the development of autonomous self-direction – as an intrinsic bias – was a preference for *differences* in various forms. I suggest that this intrinsic interest in differences becomes an interest, later in life, in discordant, contrasting fluctuations. Of course, as I have indicated, the emergence of autonomous self-direction comes to moderate this bias or preference. That is, the individual becomes able to direct his or her attention to, or away from, discordant fluctuations. With this said, the rest follows naturally. Self-directed interest in fluctuations – interest in experiences associated with agency – leads to their amplification, and in turn, the possibility for a qualitative change in the overall organization of character into a more responsive and adaptive system. By contrast, restricting or contracting fluctuations leads to the emergence of a more restrictive and maladaptive organization.

Moving briefly to the subject of psychotherapy, this previous point suggests what might be therapeutic about psychotherapy. The therapist's interventions may be effective based on the extent to which the therapist draws the patient's attention to, and the patient becomes interested in, the ways he or she is actively engaged in diminishing the experience of agency. By directing the patient's attention in this way, the therapist is in essence amplifying discordant, conflictual fluctuations. The continued escalation of discordant fluctuations driven by the patient's interest in them can, at some critical point, lead to a qualitative shift in the patient's character. With that said, most of the therapist's interventions only bump the system, because given character's self-regulating elasticity – its basin of attraction – it is more likely that the patient's character will capture and restrain the bump, thus leaving its over-all organization intact.[9]

---

[9] Although I do not develop the idea here, the psychotherapy dyad is also a coupled dynamic system – just at a higher level of scale. As such, we can describe and understand the dynamics and features of the psychotherapy dyad with the same model. Robert Galatzer-Levy's (2009) recent conceptualization of the psychotherapy dyad as "coupled oscillators" is a fascinating and excellent example of this way of thinking.

Clinical Nonlinearities

Nonlinearities abound in Shapiro's theory of development and character. Perhaps Shapiro's systemic approach gave him a suitable vantage point to observe nonlinearities that were previously overlooked. Consider his discussion of character styles as defensive, adapted variants of prevolitional modes. Shapiro (2000) has argued that slight variations in the nature and quality of organizing attitudes can lead to qualitatively different organizations of character. For instance, while obsessive, paranoid, and hypomanic character styles are all founded on a set of "rule-based attitudes," qualitative differences between these character styles are driven by the degree of their respective rigidity. Similarly, psychopathic and hysterical character styles emerge from a set of "passive-reactive attitudes," and their qualitative differences are based on differences in the degree of their immediacy of reaction. In each of these instances, Shapiro details the ways in which a difference in degree can become a difference in kind (Piers 2007).

In his intriguing conjecture about the discontinuous and qualitative transition from neurosis to psychosis, Shapiro bases this transition on a nonlinear, reciprocal relationship between autonomous self-direction and self-object polarity. In his view, when character tightens or becomes more restrictive of agency experience, there is a corresponding loss of self-object polarity. Shapiro suggests that once the degree of restrictiveness passes a critical threshold, the external objects required for the experience of self-direction are lost. This leads to acceleration in restrictiveness until the mind arrives at a new dynamically stable, albeit maladaptive, organization of the mind. For Shapiro, psychosis is not the dissolution of mind's defensive organization, but rather its radical reorganization driven by the same underlying restrictive dynamics.

Conclusion

The reader could reasonably ask, "Why go to all the trouble of learning this new, often dense, language? Shapiro's theory was perfectly clear to begin with." My aims have been threefold. One, demonstrate that CST, with its use of a completely different methodology, has independently formalized many aspects of Shapiro's theory of character as a complex dynamic system. Two, point to instances where CST further explicates the dynamics of character. Three, and most ambitious, faithfully translate the psychodynamics of character into the language of CST so that links could be forged between the study of character and CST's multidisciplinary effort to identify a unifying set of concepts that account for complex, adaptive systems of all kinds. Given the reader may well feel that there is no need for an independent formalization of Shapiro's theory, and that CST does not further elucidate (and may obscure) the dynamics of character, perhaps he or she will be intrigued by the larger effort.

I close with a question for Dr. Shapiro, having to do with a subject not directly addressed in this chapter. If we conclude that all forms of psychopathology are driven by the same underlying restrictive dynamics, we are left to wonder why some individuals go through nonlinear, qualitative transitions in the nature of their psychopathology, while others do not. In the more specific case, why do some obsessive patients become paranoid, or even psychotic, while others do not? Is it an innate biological vulnerability? And if so, what is its psychological expression?

Acknowledgments My thanks to Mindy Greenstein and Everett Waters for their very helpful comments on earlier drafts of this chapter.

References

Bressler, S. L. (2003). Cortical coordination dynamics and the disorganization syndrome in schizophrenia. *Neuropsychopharmacology, 28*, S35–S39.

Bressler, S. L., & Kelso, J. A. S. (2001). Cortical coordination dynamics and cognition. *Trends in Cognitive Sciences, 5*, 26–36.

Demos, E. V. (2007). The dynamics of development. In C. Piers, J. P. Muller, & J. Brent (Eds.), *Self-organizing complexity in psychological systems* (pp. 135–164). New York: Jason Aronson.

Edelman, G. (1992). *Bright air, brilliant fire: On the matter of the mind.* New York: Basic Books.

Edelman, G. (2004). *Wider than the sky: The phenomenal gift of consciousness.* New Haven: Yale University Press.

Epstein, J. M., & Axtell, R. L. (1996). *Growing artificial societies: Social sciences from the bottom up.* Washington, DC: Brookings Institution Press.

Freeman, W. J. (1995). *Societies of brains: A study in the neuroscience of love and hate.* Hillsdale: Lawrence Erlbaum.

Freeman, W. J. (2007). A biological theory of brain function and its relevance to psychoanalysis. In C. Piers, J. P. Muller, & J. Brent (Eds.), *Self-organizing complexity in psychological systems* (pp. 15–36). New York: Jason Aronson.

Galatzer-Levy, R. M. (2009). Good vibrations: Analytic process as coupled oscillations. *International Journal of Psychoanalysis, 90*, 983–1007.

Ghent, E. (2002). Wish, need, drive: Motive in light of dynamic systems theory and Edelman's selectionist theory. *Psychoanalytic Dialogues, 12*, 763–808.

Goldstein, J. (2007). Emergence and psychological morphogenesis. In C. Piers, J. P. Muller, & J. Brent (Eds.), *Self-organizing complexity in psychological systems* (pp. 111–134). New York: Jason Aronson.

Goodwin, B. (1994). *How the leopard changed its spots: The evolution of complexity.* New York: Simon & Schuster.

Grigsby, J., & Osuch, E. (2007). Neurodynamics, state, agency and psychological functioning. In C. Piers, J. P. Muller, & J. Brent (Eds.), *Self-organizing complexity in psychological systems* (pp. 37–82). New York: Jason Aronson.

Ilachinski, A. (2001). *Cellular automata: A discrete universe.* River Edge: World Scientific.

Kelso, J. A. S. (1999). *Dynamic patterns: The self-organization of brain and behavior.* Cambridge: MIT Press.

Kelso, J. A. S., & Engstrom, D. A. (2006). *The complementary nature.* Cambridge: MIT Press.

Kozma, R., Puljic, M., Balister, P., Bollobas, B., & Freeman, W. J. (2005). Phase transitions in the neuropercolation model of neural populations with mixed local and non-local interactions. *Biological Cybernetics, 92*(6), 367–379.

Lachaux, J. -P., Rodriguez, E., Martinerie, J., & Varela, F. J. (1999). Measuring phase synchrony in brain signals. *Human Brain Mapping*, *8*, 194–208.

Mandelbrot, B. B. (1982). *The fractal geometry of nature*. San Francisco: W. H. Freeman.

Piers, C. (2000). Character as self-organizing complexity. *Psychoanalysis and Contemporary Thought*, *23*, 3–34.

Piers, C. (2005). The mind's multiplicity and continuity. *Psychoanalytic Dialogues*, *15*, 229–254.

Piers, C. (2007). Emergence: When a difference in degree becomes a difference in kind. In C. Piers, J. P. Muller, & J. Brent (Eds.), *Self-organizing complexity in psychological systems* (pp. 83–110). New York: Jason Aronson.

Resnick, M. (1994). *Turtles, termites and traffic jams: Exploration in massively parallel micro-worlds*. Cambridge: MIT Press.

Shapiro, D. (1965). *Neurotic styles*. New York: Basic Books.

Shapiro, D. (1981). *Autonomy and rigid character*. New York: Basic Books.

Shapiro, D. (1989). *Psychotherapy of neurotic character*. New York: Basic Books.

Shapiro, D. (2000). *Dynamics of character: Self-regulation in psychopathology*. New York: Basic Books.

Strogatz, S. (2003). *Sync: How order emerges from chaos in the universe, nature, and daily life*. New York: Theia.

Thelen, E., & Smith, L. B. (1994). *A dynamic systems approach to the development of cognition and action*. Cambridge: MIT Press.

Uhlhaas, P. J., Linden, D. S. J., Singer, W., Haenschel, C., Lindner, M., Maurer, K., & Rodriguez, E. (2006). Dysfunctional long-range coordination of neural activity during gestalt perception in schizophrenia. *The Journal of Neuroscience*, *26*(31):8168–8175.

Wachtel, P. L. (2008). Relational theory and the practice of psychotherapy. New York: Guilford.

Wolfram, S. (2002). *A new kind of science*. Champaign: Wolfram Media, Inc.

Reply to Craig Piers

David Shapiro

Dr. Piers has undertaken a brave project. I say brave because it is a project that strikes out into new territory and, I suspect – and judging from his concluding remark, he does as well – that it is likely to receive a puzzled, not terribly sympathetic, reception by many of his colleagues. I think otherwise. In my opinion, it is a particularly interesting and unusual piece of work. Prompted by my own studies, Piers constructs a conception of character and psychopathology based on abstract, that is to say, highly general, principles of contemporary complex systems theory. My work on character and psychopathology has focused on formal principles – styles or modes, especially of thinking – that describe the relations among a variety of symptoms and other mental contents. The application of this formal point of view has demonstrated the characterological basis of symptoms and traits and has led to a general conception of character and its dynamics or self-regulation. It is a conception that is different from traditional psychoanalytic dynamics of particular unconscious conflicts of drive and defense. It is a picture of a consciously purposeful individual whose ways of thinking and attitudes, though generally not consciously articulated, are central to his self-regulation. This is the picture of self-regulation that Piers understands in the still more abstract formal terms of complex systems theory.

Piers has in fact demonstrated that many of the features of that view of self-regulation in psychopathology can be deduced from simple parameters according to the propositions of complex systems theory. He has convincingly deduced from systems theory such conceptions as dynamically stable systems; circular causality; purposeful, but unwitting, perpetuation of neurotic conditions; defensively diminished (he speaks of contraction) autonomy; the elasticity of character organization; and the nonlinear emergence, after small formal changes, of qualitatively new psychological organization – all these concepts describing phenomena of psychopathology. Perhaps "deduced" is not the right word; the derivations do not always seem to me inevitable, but they do seem plausible. In other words, Piers' analysis makes a persuasive case that the basic phenomena we recognize as self-regulation in character can be understood as having been generated by the repeated and extended operation of a few principles on a few givens. This holds as well for development, and specifically the development of autonomy. There is no tiny oak tree in the acorn; a few principles at work, repeatedly, are sufficient for its development.

I have some questions for Piers; some are matters of understanding, some are matters of doubt. I do not understand what he means by a "splintered differentiation of the mind." I do not see, either, why the awareness of difference should be considered the primary given in the infant's cognition. Why not awareness of bright color, or movement? Also, Piers asserts that the experience of autonomy is strongest in connection with novelty or challenge. Strong, yes, but strongest? I would say that the experience is strongest in confronting decision or choice, which may or may not be novel or intrinsically challenging. But these are quibbles; there are more important questions.

What are the aims of and prospects for this project? Piers lists three aims of which he considers the third, relating the study of character to other complex systems, to be the most ambitious and, I think he believes, the most important. The idea brings to mind, to my mind at least, and I imagine to Piers', the possibility of linking individual psychological tendencies, particularly early tendencies, to biological variations. We assume that the infant comes into the world with particular biologically provided mental capabilities and tendencies that become manifest in psychological development. It is, in my opinion, a certainty that these constitutional mental capabilities and tendencies can only be defined in formal terms; they cannot consist of specific ideational contents. In other words, the linking of the psychological with the biological must be done through the formal study of psychological characteristics. I have no idea whether Piers' kind of formal analysis or my own has the potential to be of use toward such an end, but I am convinced that a formal analysis of some kind offers its only possibility.

Piers closes his essay with a question to me: why do some obsessive individuals become paranoid, even psychotic, while others do not? I do not have an answer to that question, and many others like it, but it could as well be Piers' question to answer. It is, again, a question that must be answered by the study of formal differences, such as, in this case, presumably subtle differences in the quality of characteristic mode of thought. Piers has so far not applied his formal principles to the analysis of specific clinical conditions, but probably that is the greatest value of abstract formal analysis: to lead us back to a greater understanding of particular phenomena. It may be that the principles and the vocabulary that Dr. Piers enunciates are as yet not up to that daunting task. However that may be, I think he has made his case so far.

Rejoinder to David Shapiro

Craig Piers

I appreciate Dr. Shapiro's reply and will respond to his comments, both small and large.

First to his "quibbles." Dr. Shapiro had difficulty understanding my meaning of a "splintered differentiation of the mind". Let me try to clarify my meaning. CA simulations indicate that differentiation emerges in systems from the spontaneous (self-organized) coordination of information arising from constitutive subsystems. Systemic coordination is rarely uniform across the entire system, however. Rather, system-wide coordination is regularly comprised of different areas of coordination, forming what I referred to as second-order subsystems. That is, embedded within overall, system-wide coordination, which can be rigorously defined, are different degrees of coordination between second-order subsystems, which can also be defined. Second-order subsystems represent the coordination of primitive subsystems at a smaller scale than the system's overall coordination. Thus, we arrive at multiple measures of coordination: one for the entire system, and values corresponding to each of the second-order subsystems. The emergence of second-order systems, via nonuniform, system-wide coordination is the basis for differentiation.

With this understood, it is important to appreciate that *adaptive* systems organize themselves somewhere between two maladaptive poles of differentiation. At one end of the spectrum, the system's organization is characterized by unvarying, uniform coordination across the entire system – thus the absence second-order subsystems or differentiation. At the other end of the spectrum, highly compartmentalized, fragmented, or "splintered" differentiation emerges, characterized by small pockets of coordination. The differentiation of adaptive systems falls between these two poles, representing optimal coordination of primitive subsystems. Thus, when I wrote of a "splintered differentiation of the mind", I was suggesting that the mind becomes organized consistent with the second of the maladaptive poles described above, revealing small, segmented islands of coordination, or put differently, less than optimal coordination of information arising from the mind's primitive subsystems (perceptual, sensory, cognitive, affective, and motor subsystems). This splintered differentiation (or less than optimal coordination), I went on to suggest, may well describe the less than optimal coordination across attention, perception, thought, affect, and movement observed in varying degrees in all forms of psychopathology. In this way, it may also capture Shapiro's discussion of *self-estrangement*, inasmuch as self-estrangement is an individual's defensive alienation from aspects of his or her own subjective experience, or, in the language of complex systems, the defensively motivated lack of optimal second-order coordination.

In his reply, Dr. Shapiro wonders why I proposed a preference or orientation to *differences* as a primary bias or value in the infant. As an alternative, Shapiro wonders why "bright colors" or "movement" would not be appropriate. From my perspective, both bright colors and movement qualify as possible pathways for detecting differences or variance in and between events or internal states. That is, preferences for bright colors or movement serve as potential sources for detecting contrasts, or differences. As I went on to write, it is this preference for differences that provides a basis for differentiation, and in turn, the experience of autonomous self-direction.

Dr. Shapiro writes that, from his perspective, the experience of autonomy is strongest when confronting choice or decision, rather than my more limited case of experiences of novelty or challenge. I accept and agree with Shapiro's comment. Heightened experiences of agency are often associated with experiences that are not altogether unfamiliar. I would add that experiences of heightened agency include any experience that requires more of the individual than falling back on automatic or unreflective routine or habit.

Finally, let me address Dr. Shapiro's question about the larger aims of and prospects for my work. Thus far, my work represents an effort to translate commonly observed clinical phenomena, many of which Shapiro has explicated, into the formal language of complex systems. If the translation is apt, it suggests several possible lines of study. Most importantly, a shared language will facilitate the exchange of ideas and learning across disciplines. Also, if the phenomena are similar, it suggests similar underlying dynamics. Research into complex systems, particularly the findings derived from computer models, indicates that complex phenomena arise from, as Shapiro described succinctly in his reply, "the repeated and extended operation of a few principles on a few givens." To my mind, this formal way of thinking about systems and their dynamics is different, and points the way toward new understanding and methodologies. To build on this way of thinking, the work that lies ahead is in identifying the relevant principles and givens in psychological systems, and linking these findings to other research on the mind.

Chapter 11
I Don't Want to Want to: Intentionality and Craving in Addiction

Mindy Greenstein

What does it mean to crave something? And what is the relationship between desire and choice? These questions lie at the heart of the vast field of addiction research. Clinicians and researchers from many different theoretical schools ask why substance abusers focus on the immediate positive short-term effects of the substance rather than the devastating long-term effects they know will follow. Less attention is paid, however, to the subjective experience of the craving or urge associated with this addictive behavior, or to the context of attitudes and decisions required for it to occur. Perhaps, this is why Marlatt and Witkiewitz (2005) describe *craving* as "possibly the most widely studied and the most poorly understood concept in the study of drug addiction" (p. 18).

The Disease Model, for instance (e.g., Goodwin 1985; Schuckit 1980), which held sway for many years, argues that addicts simply have no choice. They have a genetically and biologically determined disease that results in uncontrolled and uncontrollable consumption. In this view, there is neither desire nor choice, as craving is merely a genetically determined and biologically mediated response triggered by the first drink. This is experienced as an involuntary physical demand for more alcohol in order to forestall withdrawal symptoms (Jellinek 1952).

Marlatt and Rohsenow (1980), however, showed that the relationship between the first drink and the sense of craving is not necessarily physiological at all. They reviewed a series of double balanced placebo studies in which alcoholics who believed they were drinking an alcoholic beverage, whether or not they actually were ingesting alcohol, began to crave it, while alcoholics who drank alcohol but who believed they were drinking nonalcoholic beverages did not experience craving.

Thus, behavioral models focus instead on external cues, treating *craving* as a conditioned response elicited by the environment. Knowledge of a drug's pleasurable or analgesic effects serves as a positive reinforcer for further drug use, particularly when combined with the desire to avoid aversive withdrawal reactions (cf. Ludwig 1985, 1988; Siegel 1983). Mello (1975) goes so far as to describe the

M. Greenstein (✉)
Consulting Psychologist, Department of Psychiatry and Behavioral Science,
Memorial Sloan-Kettering Cancer Center, 1275 York Avenue, New York, NY 10065
e-mail: greenstm@gmail.com

C. Piers (ed.), *Personality and Psychopathology: Critical Dialogues with David Shapiro*,   247
DOI 10.1007/978-1-4419-6214-0_11, © Springer Science+Business Media, LLC 2011

experience of craving as an "explanatory fiction" that is merely an epiphenomenal reaction to conditioned behavior, though other behaviorists regard this dismissal as too extreme (cf. Ludwig 1988; Wilson 1981). In either case, addiction is seen not as an inborn disease, but as an attempt at adaptation to aversive stimuli. Marlatt and colleagues (1983; Marlatt and Gordon 1985; Marlatt and Donovan 2005) take a nuanced approach to the issue of choice, suggesting that while addicts may not be responsible for the addiction itself, they do nevertheless make choices in their response to the cues that elicit their destructive behaviors.

Still, these theories cannot account for individual differences found in the response to those substances. Johanson and Uhlenhuth (1981), for example, found that even people who are enjoying the reinforcing effects of some drugs may still decide not to use them. In their study, subjects who were given amphetamines over a period of time chose to use them less and less over successive administrations even though they continued to report positive mood effects of the drugs. Falk (cited from Peele 1988) suggested that the drug state probably interfered with the pursuit of their other activities. In other words, finding the effects of the drug pleasant did not necessarily lead to taking them more.

Recent psychoanalytic models similarly focus on addiction as an attempt at adaptation, but to internal deficits. According to these models, people abuse drugs in an attempt to self-medicate their failures in self-regulation (Khantzian 1985, 2003, 1999/2007; Wurmser 1974, 1978). Having failed to internalize the soothing or nurturing aspects of their primary caretakers, addicts look instead to the drug to provide that soothing.

Varied as these models are, they fail to explain or describe adequately the mind of the addict or the subjective psychological processes involved in drug addiction. As Shapiro (1992) and Caccioppo and Berntsen (1992) argue, for example, biological models elucidate only a "permissive substrate," ordinarily in the form of an incentive, for the behaviors in question. The behavioral and psychoanalytic models similarly explain not why some people actually *take* drugs, only why they might *want* them. "In adult human beings, even strong impulses account only for strong temptations; they do not in themselves account for actions" (Shapiro 1981, p. 9). A particular incentive alone, in humans, is in itself not enough to account for complicated actions or series of actions with serious consequences. DiClemente (2003/2006) points out:

> There are virtually hundreds of little decisions that are made daily and weekly to ensure access to the behavior. Arranging schedules, making excuses, sneaking off for periods of time, and minimizing consequences are all part of the process of protecting continued engagement in the addiction (p. 52).

Thus, the models discussed cannot fully account for the behavior itself, or the constellation of attitudes and decisions that are required for the behavior. They ignore the person who is acting and the coalition of attitudes, goals, and other individual factors that are likely to be involved in such consequential action. More generally, their formulations ignore the psychology of action, or the path from thought or urge, to behavior.

It is in his elaboration of the subjective qualities and processes of impulsive characters that Shapiro's theory is relevant to this discussion (1965, 1981). There is strong evidence of a relationship between substance abuse and impulsivity (Tarter 2005; deWit 2009; Khantzian 1999/2007; Moehller et al. 2001). Shapiro's description offers a window into the phenomenology of the experience of addiction and the process of choice itself. He suggests that it is both the process and the experience of intentionality that are impaired in the impulsive character. This paper argues that these same processes are involved in the experience of craving in substance abusers as well.

Craving and Intention

There has been relatively little useful consideration of the subjective experience and psychological processes implied by such terms as *craving*, *desire*, or *intention*. Abelson (1988) addresses more directly the philosophical issues related to these concepts. He contrasts the experience of what he refers to as *full-blooded desire* with a *tropism*, or a desire that is physiologically determined. Full-blooded desire, according to Dennett (1978, cited in Abelson), refers to an end-state in which internal processes have mediated between stimulus and overt response. These internal processes involve a system of relative reasoning and self-monitoring, in which possible responses are judged in terms of other desired states and are either reinforced or inhibited. For Abelson, full-blooded desire requires the possibility of having contrary desires, without which, it is a "pale tropistic surrogate" (p. 22).

> Imagine an entity that has no capacity for desire,….it selects means toward achieving end-state G, and it monitors its successes and failures,… for example, a chess-playing computer. But it couldn't care less whether or not it wins. Nevertheless it seems to make every effort to win, and it usually does win. How do we know that it doesn't *want* to win, that it doesn't have a *desire* for victory? I think the answer is that we cannot conceive of any non-physical conditions under which it would *forbear* from trying to win. No one could bribe it or rationally persuade it to make less of an 'effort.'… its apparent efforts… for that reason, are not full-blooded efforts but mere tropisms that are not motivated by desire. *Full-blooded desire is subject to defeat by contrary desires* (pp. 23–24, italics mine).

In other words, Abelson suggests, full-blooded desire requires the *possibility* that the person might act in a different way, that the person has a matrix of desires which might move him or her to inhibit action if incompatible. From this standpoint, the disease theory represents addiction as no more than a "pale tropistic surrogate." As Peele (1988) and Mello et al. (1968) point out, however, addicts have shown that in fact they can and do sometimes control their level of intoxication, suggesting that, at least in some instances, the desire to use is, in fact, subject to defeat by contrary desires. Peele (1985) goes so far as to argue that the addict chooses to act in line with his own value system, thereby fulfilling Abelson's requirements for "full-blooded desire."

Shapiro's (1965, 1981) exploration of the issues of intentionality and impulsive action from a characterological standpoint suggests a different conclusion. He argues (1992) that understanding addictive action requires understanding the characterologically determined subjective context in which the temptation to act is experienced. His theory of impulsive character suggests that while addicts make choices in an objective sense, they sincerely may not *feel as if* they make those choices.

In particular, Shapiro argues that the motivational process and experience of impulsive characters are different from those of the non-impulsive individual. He proposes that there is an actual attenuation of the process of self-direction and that the experience of deliberateness and intentionality is further diminished defensively. In Abelson's terminology, impulsive individuals *experience* their actions as if they were the result of tropisms rather than full-blooded desires, while *in actuality* they fall in between these. While impulsives may actually desire to act, these individuals are constrained by a combination of their point of view and defensive motivation to experience their actions as lacking in deliberateness. Shapiro further suggests that the marionette-like viewpoint of disease theorists and many psychodynamic theorists fails to recognize this style and accepts at face value the feeling of addicts that they cannot help what they do. Thus, he contends that many experienced clinicians, "cannot quite swallow the idea of [the impulsive's] innocence and cannot help noticing that they do not altogether regret what their impulses choose to do with them… *what these people really cannot help is their inclination, under certain circumstances of motivation, to feel, 'I can't help it'"* (pp. 21–2, italics mine).

In a similar vein to Abelson's and Dennet's accounts, Shapiro (1981) maintains that the normal pathway connecting motivation to action begins with a feeling or urge that, in itself, doesn't necessarily trigger behavioral action. Rather, it generates an awareness of the *possibilities* of action, resulting in some form of conscious intention, which then may in turn give rise to action. It is this pathway that is foreshortened in impulsive characters, and that the current reviewer argues is foreshortened in many addicts as well.

The Impulsive Character Style

The impulsive style is characterized by an attenuated sense of the deliberateness of one's actions, sometimes reaching the point of an experience of irresistible impulse (Shapiro 1965). A person with this character style does not experience cravings and irresistible urges as eruptions or intrusions into an otherwise normal set of executive functions, as the biological and behavioral theorists would argue. Instead, they are unrecognized and disclaimed intentions on the part of the impulsive person. Further, these disclaimed intentions are merely one aspect of a general mode of functioning rather than an isolated trait. In other words, according to this model, the addict's experience of impulses is made possible by an *actually* diminished intentionality. Actual intentionality is sufficiently diminished to permit a disclaimer of intentionality altogether.

An "irresistible impulse" or craving, then, is an unrecognized decision to act. Perhaps, the addict's diminished intentionality is not simply defensive, as psychoanalytic theorists have argued. Perhaps, instead, any defensive disclaimer develops out of proclivities of style that already existed. Tarter et al. (2003), for example, found impulsivity in childhood related to later substance abuse. The defensive externalization of responsibility that is frequently noted in addicts (Miller 1989, 1990a, 1990b, 1991; Denzin 1987, etc.) is from this standpoint also made possible by the diminished sense of personal responsibility.

Normally, Shapiro argues, the appearance of an urge or whim signals the beginning of a complex though somewhat automatic process (1965, 1981, 2000). It appears in the context of relatively stable long-term interests and goals. It may accrue interest as it is integrated into this context and may lead to a decision for action or it may be modified or abandoned. It is this reflective and integrative process that transforms a half-formed whim into an active experience of intention, or a trope into a full-blooded desire. This integrative process is impaired in the impulsive character, and, often, in the addict.

Shapiro notes that the impulsive character's interests and goals tend to be limited to the immediate or short range (see also Miller 1989, 1990). Svebak and Kerr (1989) similarly found that impulsive individuals lacked specific goals. A general absence of planning, associated with a diminished sense of deliberateness, has also been found by Barratt (1993) and Miller (1990). This exacerbates transient motivations and discontinuity in actions. The temporal continuum connecting interests and actions of the past, present, and future is corrupted. Thus, Wilson et al. (1989) find addicts to have difficulty in their time perspective, while Barrat (1985) suggests that impulsives tend to underestimate time.

Without an integrated experience of their past, present, and future actions or aims, such individuals experience themselves as passive responders rather than active actors. Their general mode of doing things is to give in and their interests are erratic and abrupt rather than stable and continuous. Thus, a particular impulse is experienced in a very different context than would be the case for someone without this style of functioning. The normal modulating context is not present, the integrative process is short-circuited, and the normal experience of choice or "full-blown desire" is absent or greatly diminished.

The common findings of low frustration tolerance in such individuals can be explained from this standpoint. It is the existence of competing long-term interests that allows one to postpone the satisfaction of whims; without such interests, delay or forbearance becomes much less tolerable. Indeed, without such interests or consideration of long-term consequences, there is little point in forbearance – with no sense of future ahead of them, such people may see no reason to keep from indulging themselves. This is consistent with the finding that substance abusers discount delayed reinforcement in favor of immediate reinforcement, even if the former would normally provide greater incentive (deWit 2009). It also is consistent with Manganiello's (1978) finding of a foreshortened time perspective in opiate addicts.

The findings of Alexander and his colleagues (1978, 1982, 1988) are suggestive in regard to Shapiro's discussion of choice and intention. Rats with an induced morphine addiction stopped preferring the morphine solution when given a choice between it and another similar-tasting solution, as long as they were placed in bigger cages with more activities and social opportunities, i.e., when they had a *choice* of activities in line with other interests. The well-known sociological finding that low socioeconomic inner-city populations confronted by dim prospects are overrepresented in addicted populations is also consistent with this understanding (Robins 1978). Perhaps, people growing up in such an environment may be less likely to develop long-term goals. Without the expectation that gratification might come in the future, they may fail to develop an internal system of long-term interests and goals, rendering them more likely to live impulsively in the present.

This is not to say that substance abuse can't sometimes be found in people with more rigid characters. Such individuals may experience their addictions in the context of a hyper-deliberateness rather than a lack of it, and might not have the same subjective experience of craving as many substance abusers do. It is the latter experience that this theory is meant to address.

Aspects of Impulsive Style

Shapiro suggests that a regular characteristic of impulsive action is speediness, further diminishing the subjective sense of deliberateness and personal responsibility. Molto et al. (1993) found impulsives to be quicker in time taken to answer personality questionnaires while Bachorowski and Newman (1990) found them to be faster on motor tasks. Newman et al. (1987) found that speed was related to impulsives' poor performance on a computerized card game; when forced to take more time after feedback, they showed great improvement.

Similar tendencies toward speed have been found in various addicted populations. Tiebout (1954) has noted that alcoholics tend to "do everything in a hurry" (p. 612), while Peele (1985) also finds that rapid onset of response is a key ingredient for substance abusers as is "fast action" for gamblers. The noted reliance on routine or automatic sets of techniques in addictive behavior also allows greater speed of action without the necessity of prolonged decisions (Peele 1985; Solomon 1977; DiClemente 2003).

Shapiro notes an impairment in impulsive characters of some qualitative aspects of concentration, in that attention is easily captured by those aspects perceived to be relevant to their immediate interests and aims. DeWit (2009) finds substance abusers suffer lapses in attention, while Ludwig (1985) describes the addict's attention as being "dramatically captured" by the drug he uses (p. 54). This is not to suggest, it must be noted, a lack of intelligence per se. However, it does suggest the possibility of an intelligence that might be better suited to the execution of short-term immediate aims as they arise, rather than to long-term goals requiring planfulness or reflection (Miller 1990a, 1990b; Shapiro 1965).

A cognition that is captured by whatever stimuli are immediately striking implies a discontinuity in one's temporal experience; awareness is dominated by the present, with the past and future shrinking in significance. Thus, at the moment of choice or impulse, this type of person is not in a position to learn from the outcome of past behaviors, and is more likely to opt for short-term solutions regardless of long-term consequences. Further, a person is less likely to develop an array of stable interests when current interests are restricted to the immediate and ephemeral. Within such a context, the impulsive or addict cannot help but respond passively to his or her urges since he or she has no intentional perspective from which to view them. This individual's internal life is necessarily labile and his inclination is not to plan but to act.

In viewing substance abuse against the backdrop of a generally impulsive style, one can see the development of addiction from two perspectives. First, people whose sense of personal agency is already compromised are further discomfited by any feelings of deliberateness; being "under the influence" reduces such anxiety since it reduces the sense of personal responsibility for one's actions. At the same time, this style of action also makes it easier to find oneself "giving in" to cravings. Thus, the relationship between addiction and deliberateness is cyclic; the need to diminish intentionality makes it desirable to use drugs while an already impaired sense of intentionality makes it easier to give in to impulses and urges to use drugs. This is consistent with deWit's (2009) and Khantzian's (1999/2007) suggestion that impulsivity is both a determinant and a consequence of drug use.

Testing the Theory

To empirically test aspects of theory, I analyzed the Thematic Apperception Test narratives of substance abusers and matched controls (Cards 1 and 13mf) for evidence of an underlying impulsive style (1994). As Westen (1991) argues, an individual's responses to the TAT reflect his own schemata for the ways in which people interact with the world. Aspects of the impulsive character that were discussed above, such as the experience of passivity, tendencies toward speedy activity, and nondeliberateness of action, were expected to be reflected in both the content and form of their stories, as compared with controls'.[1]

While some of the hypotheses were not supported, the majority were. For instance, speed appeared to be implicated in the addicts' storytelling, although not necessarily in the speed at which they spoke. Instead, they tried to get the task over with in the shortest and simplest way possible. Their stories were significantly shorter and were significantly more likely to omit required story elements, i.e., beginning, middle, end, and thoughts and feelings of characters. Analysis suggested these omissions were not due to distractibility or disruption in memory. This speedy and incomplete storytelling is consistent with a style involving speedy or abrupt actions as well as diminished reflectiveness and deliberateness of actions.

---

[1] For more detailed description of the study design, methods, coding criteria and findings, see Greenstein (1994).

Furthermore, substance abusers were significantly less likely to take responsibility for the content of their stories. This was assessed by comparing their use of *metareference hedges* relative to controls'. *Metareference hedges* are words and phrases that "dilute the force of the speech act itself," so that statements are accompanied by "mitigating effect[s]" through which, "one refuses to confront… one's own opinions" (Lakoff 1977, pp. 228–230). For example, substance abusers were more likely to use words or phrases such as *Maybe he killed* her … *It sort of looks like… the card makes it look like…*" or general references to what the tester might want them to say. Such phrases reflect the speaker's diminished feeling of responsibility for the story he or she is making up.

By the same token, the actions of addicts' protagonists were significantly less likely to be the result of deliberation or intention. These characters were less likely than controls' protagonists to act in an intended and desired way, and they were less likely to know and act on their feelings. For instance, "he killed her without realizing it" as opposed to "he murdered her." Further, the agency of substance abusers' TAT protagonists' actions and feelings also reflected greater ambiguity than controls'. As an example, "He killed his girlfriend… He's flipping out" -- where it isn't clear whether the killing is actually caused by losing oneself or whether it's the direct result of anger and a wish to hurt the victim (whom the protagonist had caught having an affair).

These findings may suggest an interesting empirical window into the dynamics of the diminishing of a feeling of personal agency and deliberateness in action. It is possible that they reflect the process of defensively avoiding the active/agentive role. The reliance on ambiguity might be an attempt to ward off the experience of intentionality in the course of storytelling.

In the example of the ambiguous role noted above, for instance, the subject noted that the protagonist was "flipping out," after the killing has occurred. The subject does not say that flipping out has caused the act, but seems to allow it as a mitigating circumstance, as if to diminish intention after the fact. This ambiguity suggests that their diminished agency is not merely an existing and stable condition – i.e., not simply a static experience of passivity – but, instead, must be maintained, and the experience of intentionality forestalled, by quick action and, perhaps, alcohol or other drugs. This is consistent with Shapiro's (1965) argument that the impulsive person must avoid reflection and deliberateness in order to forestall the experience of agency.

Another aspect of Shapiro's theory is the existence in the impulsive person of an impaired sense of the future. He proposes a paucity of long-term interests in impulsive people, further compromising the processes of planful action. This hypothesis, however, was not supported by the data; while addicts did exhibit less sense of future orientation than controls, these differences were not significant.

Looking at the data more globally further supports a relationship between Shapiro's concept of impulsive character and substance abuse. A discriminant analysis performed on all the variables studied (speed, metareference hedges, personal agency, etc.) revealed that as a whole, the variables reliably differentiated the two groups. Specifically, the variables as a whole correctly predicted 19 out of the 20 subjects.

Conclusion

Subverting the normal process of intentionality and the experience of agency, are a number of elements, including the time one takes to deliberate upon one's possibilities for action as well as the extent to which one has and knows one's own long-term interests and goals. The present study generally supported the hypothesis that such a subversion occurs to some extent in the substance abuser's subjective experience. Addicts were shown in the study to exhibit elements of speed and abruptness both in the content and telling of their TAT stories. Quick or abrupt actions, performed with less deliberation and thus less likely to be experienced as intentional, allow judgment to be compromised before further consideration might inhibit the action.

In addition, the study supported the notion that addicts *feel* less deliberate in their actions, though not absolutely lacking in intentionality. The language they used in storytelling reflected a diluted sense of personal responsibility for making up the story; it suggested that the card or the tester may have been more responsible than they themselves for the story being told. Thus, one can infer that the storytellers are themselves less likely to know and act on their feelings. The evidence suggests that they, like their characters, feel that their actions are not quite directed by their own decision.

While the evidence suggests that addicts do not experience their actions as having been wholly intended by them, it also suggests that they do not necessarily experience themselves as totally passive, but may require a continuing defensive attempt to forestall feelings of intentionality. In the words of Abelson, ambiguous agency may reflect a melding of intention and tropism, or, as Marlatt & Gordon (1985) propose, addicts "set up a game plan of which they are unaware" (p. 188). The intoxicating effects of drugs may figure in this effort or "game plan," as Marlatt implies in his discussion of attribution theory as it relates to addiction.

Viewing addictive behavior through the prism of Shapiro's theory of impulsive character illuminates some of the psychological elements of the addict's adaptation. The present study suggests that addicts may avoid the deliberation which might otherwise be assumed to precede their behavior. For instance, even if a future alcoholic has a biologically predisposing sensitivity to alcohol, he may not weigh the fact of his previous reaction to the substance, and, on that account, limit himself to a safe number of drinks. Instead, this individual may simply respond to a desire to drink by drinking, without reflection about future consequences, and may experience that act as an irresistible impulse or craving. As Marlatt (1985) and Peele (1985) argue, the first drink or drug may in fact facilitate further drug use by virtue of the addict's own sense of not being the agent in control, that is, believing he has no control further allows him to abandon it.

Substance abuse has been notoriously slow to respond to psychological treatments, regardless of the school of thought. Shapiro (1965, 1981) and Greenstein (1994) suggest that the therapeutic process should include attention to the processes of action themselves and perhaps particularly to the diminished experience of agency, both its causes and effects.

In general, there is much use for further experimental testing of addicted people, focusing on the way in which they process and subjectively experience external cues and internal mental states. While self-report questionnaires may represent what addicts think they feel, they do not do full justice to the way in which they actually experience themselves in the world. Understanding better how substance abusers act and what their attitudes are – both conscious and unconscious, articulated and unarticulated – is necessary to the development of a more sophisticated understanding of this often intractable problem.

References

Abelson, R. (1988). *Lawless mind*. Philadelphia: Temple University Press.

Alexander, B. K., Coambs, R. B., & Hadaway, P. F. (1978). The effect of housing and gender on morphine self-administration in rats. *Psychopharmacology, 58*, 175–179.

Alexander, B. K., & Hadaway, P. F. (1982). Opiate addiction: The case for an adaptive orientation. *Psychological Bulletin, 92*, 367–381.

Alexander, B. K. (1988). The disease and adaptive models of addiction: A framework evaluation. In S. Peele (Ed.), *Visions of addiction*. New York: Free Press.

Bachorowski, J. & Newman, J. P. (1990). Impulsive motor behavior: Effects of personality and goal salience. *Journal of Personality and Social Psychology, 58*(3), 512–518.

Barrat, E. S. (1985a). Impulsiveness defined within a systems model of personality. In C. B. Spielberger & J. M. Butcher (Eds.), *Advances in personality assessment* (Vol. 5). Hillsdale: Erlbaum.

Barratt, E. S. (1993). Impulsivity: Integrating cognitive, behavioral, biological and environmental data. In W. McGown, J. L. Johnson, & M. B. Shure (Eds.), *The impulsive client: Theory, research and treatment*. Washington, DC: American Psychological Association.

Caccioppo, J. T., & Berntsen, G. G. (1992). Social psychological contributions to the decade of the brain: The doctrine of multilevel of analysis. *American Psychologist, 47*, 1019–1028.

Denzin, N. K. (1987). *The alcoholic self*. Newbury Park: Sage.

DiClemente, C. C. (2003/2006). *Addiction and change: How addictions develop and addicted people recover*. New York: Guilford.

Goodwin, D. W. (1985). Alcoholism and genetics: The sins of the fathers. *Archives of General Psychiatry, 42*, 171–174.

Greenstein, M. (1994). *Intentionality and irresistible impulse in addiction*. Unpublished doctoral dissertation, New School for Social Research, New York.

Jellinek, E. M. (1952). The phases of alcohol addiction. *Quarterly Journal of Studies on Alcohol, 13*, 673–684.

Johanson, C. E., & Uhlenhuth, E. H. (1981). Drug preference and mood in humans: Repeated assessment of d-amphetamine. *Pharmacology, Biochemistry and Behavior, 14*, 159–163.

Khantzian, E. J. (1985, November). The self-medication hypothesis of addictive disorders: Focus on heroin and cocaine dependence. *American Journal of Psychiatry, 142*(11), 1259–1264.

Khantzian, E. J. (2003). The Self-Medication hypothesis revisited: The dually diagnosed patient. *Primary Psychiatry, 10*(9), 47–54.

Khantzian, E. J. (1999/2007). *Treating addiction as a human process*. Northvale: Jason Aronson.

Lakoff, R. (1977). Women's language. *Language and Style, 19*(4), 222–247.

Ludwig, A. M. (1985). Cognitive processes associated with spontaneous recovery from alcohol. *Journal of Studies on Alcohol, 46*(1), 53–58.

Ludwig, A. M. (1988). *Understanding the alcoholic's mind*. New York: Oxford University Press.

Manganiello, J. A. (1978). Opiate addiction: A study identifying three systematically psychological correlates. *International Journal of the Addictions, 13*(5), 839–847.

Marlatt, G. A. (1983). The controlled drinking controversy: A commentary. *American Psychologist, 38*, 1097–1110.

Marlatt, G. A., & Rohsenow, D. J. (1980). Cognitive processes in alcohol use: Expectancy and the balanced placebo design. In N. K. Mello (Ed.), *Advances in substance abuse* (Vol. 1). Greenwich: JAI.

Marlatt, G. A., & Gordon, J. (Eds.) (1985). *Relapse prevention.* New York: Guilford.

Marlatt, G. A., & Donovan, D. M. (2005). *Relapse prevention: Maintainance strategies in the treatment of addictive behaviors.* New York: Guilford.

Marlatt, G.A. & Witkiewitz, K. (2005). Relapse prevention for alcohol and drug problems. In G.A. Marlatt & D.M. Donovan (Eds.). *Relapse Prevention: Maintenance Stratagies in the Treatment of Addictive Behaviors.* New York. Guildford.

Mello, N. (1975). A semantic aspect of alcoholism. In H. D. Cappell, & A. E. Leblanc (Eds.), *Biological and behavioral approaches to drug addiction.* Toronto: Addiction Research Foundation.

Miller, L. (1989). Neurocognitive aspects of remorse: Impulsivity-compulsivity-reflectivity. In E. M. Stern (Ed.), *Psychotherapy and the remorseful patient* (pp. 63–76). New York: Haworth.

Miller, L. (1990a). Neuropsychodynamics of alcoholism and addiction: Personality, psychopathology and cognitive style. *Journal of Substance Abuse Treatment, 7*, 31–49.

Miller, L. (1990b). *Inner natures: Brain, self and personality.* New York: St. Martin's.

Miller, L. (1991). Predicting relapse and recovery in alcoholism and addiction: neuropsychology, personality, and cognitive style. *Journal of Substance Abuse Treatment, 8*, 277–291.

Moehller, F. G., Dougherty, D. M., Barratt, E. S., Schmitz, J. M., Seann, A. C., & Grabowski, J. (2001). The impact of impulsivity on cocaine use and retention in treatment. *Journal of Substance Abuse Treatment, 21*(4), 193–198.

Marlatt, G.A. & Witkiewitz, K. (2005). Relapse prevention for alcohol and drug problems. In G. A. Marlett & D. M. Donovan (Eds.). Replase prevention: Maintanance Strategies in the Treatement of Addictive Behaviors. New York: Gildford.

Molto, J., Segarra, P., & Avila, C. (1993). Impulsivity and total response speed to a personality questionnaire. *Personality and Individual Differences, 15*(1), 97–98.

Newman, J. P., Patterson, C. M., & Kosson, D. S. (1987). Response perseveration in psychopaths. *Journal of Abnormal Psychology, 96*, 145–148.

Peele, S. (1985). *The meaning of addiction.* Lexington: Lexington Books.

Peele, S. (1988). *Visions of addiction.* New York: Free Press.

Robins, L. N. (1978). The interaction of setting and predisposition in explaining novel behavior: Drug initiations before, in and after Viet Nam. In D. B. Kandel (Ed.), *Longitudinal research on drug use.* Washington, DC: Hemisphere.

Schafer, R. (1967). *Projective testing and psychoanalysis.* New York: International Universities Press.

Schuckit, M. A. (1980). Alcoholism and genetics: Possible biological mediators. *Biological Psychiatry, 15*(3), 437–447.

Shapiro, D. (1965). *Neurotic styles.* New York: Basic Books.

Shapiro, D. (1981). *Autonomy and rigid character.* New York: Basic Books.

Shapiro, D. (1992). Toward a structural theory of psychopathology. *Social Research, 59*(4), 799–812.

Shapiro, D. (2000). *Dynamics of character: Self-regulation in psychopathology.* New York: Basic Books.

Siegel, S. (1983) Classical conditioning, drug tolerance and drug dependence. In Y. Israel, F. B. Glaser, H. Kalant, R. E. Popham, W. Schmidt, & R. G. Smart (Eds.), *Research advances in alcohol and drug problems.* New York: Plenum.

Solomon, R. (1977). The evolution of non-medical opiate use in Canada II: 1930–1970. *Drug Forum, 6*, 1–25.

Svebak, S., & Kerr, J. H. (1989). The role of impulsivity in preference for sports. *Personality and Individual Differences, 10*, 51–58.

Tarter, R., Kirisci, L., Mezzich, A., Cornelius, J., Pajer, K., Vanyukov, M., Gardner, W., & Clark, D. (2003). Neurobehavior disinhibition in childhood predicts early age onset of substance use disorder. *American Journal of Psychiatry, 160*, 1078–1085.

Tarter, R. E. (2005). Psychological evaluation of substance use disorders in adolescents and adults. In R. J. Frances, S. I. Miller, & A. H. Mack (Eds.), *Clinical textbook of addiction disorders*. New York: Guilford.

Tiebout, H. M. (1954). The ego factors in surrender to alcoholism. *Quarterly Journal on Studies on Alcohol, 15*, 610–621.

Westen, D. (1991). Clinical assessment of object relations using the TAT. *Journal of Personality Assessment, 56*(1), 56–74.

Wilson, A., Passik, S., Faude, J., Abrams, J., & Gordon, E. (1989). A hierarchical model of oppiate addiction: Failures of self-regulation as a central aspect of substance abuse. *The Journal of Nervous and Mental Disease, 177*(7), 390–399.

Wilson, G. T. (1981). The effects of alcohol on human sexual behavior. In N. K. Mello (Ed.), *Advances in substance abuse* (Vol. 2). Greenwich: JAI.

deWit, H. (2009). Impulsivity as a determinant and consequence of drug use. *Addiction Biology, 14*(1), 22–31.

Wurmser, L. (1974). Psychoanalytic considerations of the etiology of compulsive drug use. *Jornal of The American Psychoanalytic Association, 22*: 820–843.

Wurmser, L. (1978). *The hidden dimension*. New York: Jason Aronson.

Reply to Mindy Greenstein

David Shapiro

Dr. Greenstein's study has more than one kind of significance. It is, first, of course, a clear presentation of the subjective dynamics of addiction and, as well, a confirmation of those subjective dynamics. What is particularly convincing and unusual is her use not only of ideational content from the TAT, but formal evidence of behavior style. The principles of Greenstein's analysis can also clarify several popular and, also, psychiatric muddles including ideas of willpower or a separate faculty of will and the idea of loss of impulse control in general, implying as it does a defeated wish to control. The experience of violent "loss of control," for instance, is a defensive self-deception made easier for some by the attenuation, or avoidance, of regular processes of deliberate action. I shall return to that subject in a moment.

The additional significance of the theory Greenstein applies to the problem of addiction has to do with defensive dynamics in general. The defensive style she describes, or any defensive style for that matter, can be considered a psychological structure, in the architectural sense: the structure is what holds the building up. And like any structure, it needs maintenance. A defensive style is generally stable, but from time to time internal discomfort or anxiety impels some action which constitutes reinforcement of that stability. That is what I have meant by the self-regulatory nature of restrictive neurotic styles. The rigid character, for instance, reacts to such discomfort or anxiety by becoming more rigid; in the extreme case that can even mean a transition from a severe obsessional condition to a paranoid one. Generally speaking, however, self-regulation of this sort is rather subtle; the conscientious obsessional person, when anxious, worries more intensively or more continuously. The interesting thing about addiction is that defensive reinforcement, aimed at dispelling anxiety, includes an external element, the drug. The use of the drug therefore constitutes an objective measure of this aspect of subjective dynamics or self-regulation.

The defensive process of externalization of responsibility is well known in psychiatry, but the psychological condition that makes it possible or leads to it is not at all well recognized. This condition, as Greenstein points out, is, again, the attenuation and subjective faintness of the experience of personal agency, often accomplished by a quickness of action that obviates the possibility of reflection. One can express this relation in a simple formula: the less full the experience of personal agency, the greater the tendency of externalization. This holds for a variety of conditions, as well as the addicts Greenstein has studied, and the specific quality of the externalization varies accordingly. The case of the psychopath is quite straightforward: the holdup man, oblivious of his own choice, says, "As soon as I get out, somebody shoves a gun in my hand." The flighty, romantic, hysterical character, lacking in a sense of her own personal authority, invests more easily than most the object of her romantic interest with irresistible attractions, or her teacher or therapist with unfailing authority.

There is another condition in which this relation between a diminished personal agency and the externalization of responsibility is strikingly, and in a particularly interesting way, in evidence, the manic or hypomanic. The experience of these individuals is typically of being carried away by a flood of ideas evoked by external circumstances, often seen as opportunities. The condition is one of a driven spontaneity, but the subjective experience is of an immediate, involuntary reactiveness to what is external (a hypomanic man says, "I can look at nothing without receiving some idea from it leading to an impulse to action.").

Altogether, Dr. Greenstein's subject opens a large area of psychiatric and psychological interest. In fact, its implied revision of concepts like self-control opens significant moral and even legal questions as well.

Chapter 12
Activity, Passivity, and the Subjective Experience of Hypomania

Andreas Evdokas and Ali Khadivi

The literature on hypomania and mania, especially in the context of bipolar illness, is quite extensive. However, very little attention has been directed toward the subjective experience of such a state. This state might include feelings of elation, absence of inhibitions, liberation from constraints, freedom from self-criticism, effortless accomplishment, and the like. Traditionally, hypomania is viewed as a milder version of mania, which itself is seen as the counterpart of depression in bipolar illness (Goodwin and Jamison 1997; American Psychiatric Association-DSM IV-TR 2000). As such, it is usually considered biochemical in nature and genetically determined. According to this view, the manic or hypomanic state occurs and is experienced passively, much like a fever. Allowance is made for environmental stressors, but only as precipitants or triggers, especially in early episodes. However, in this chapter we will present empirical evidence that demonstrates that hypomanic experience is in fact not a strictly passive one, and that such a state, or at least some of its subjective qualities, may be actively fostered, actively prolonged, and/or actively intensified (Shapiro 2000). It is not, of course, proposed that individuals deliberately plan to achieve a psychiatric condition, but that they find immediate relief or satisfaction in the subjective state produced by such activity.

The experience of a hypomanic state includes characteristic patterns of feelings, thoughts, actions, language, and perceptions (Goodwin and Jamison 1997; Kraepelin 1921/1976; American Psychiatric Association-DSM IV-TR 2000). It will be argued that for some individuals such a state may be self-induced and sustained by various kinds of activity (Shapiro 2000; Evdokas, 1997). Numerous autobiographical accounts describe the appeal of such states and the subjective reluctance to give them up (Jamison 1995; see Shapiro 2000, for review of several accounts). This is particularly true of the less severe hypomanic states which are marked by feelings of elevated mood, rapid cognition, increased productivity and originality of thinking, increased energy, and heightened sense of sexuality. In one account, Jamison (1995) describes the experience of manic states as follows:

A. Evdokas (✉)
Assistant Professor of Psychiatry, Department of Psychiatry, Bronx-Lebanon Hospital Center/
Albert Einstein College of Medicine, 1650 Grand Concourse, Bronx, NY 10457
e-mail: aevdokas@bronxleb.org

C. Piers (ed.), *Personality and Psychopathology: Critical Dialogues with David Shapiro*, 261
DOI 10.1007/978-1-4419-6214-0_12, © Springer Science+Business Media, LLC 2011

> The intensity, glory and absolute assuredness of my mind's flight made it very difficult for
> me to believe, once I was better, that the illness was one I should willingly give up....It was
> difficult to give up the high flights of mind and mood, even though the depressions that
> inevitably followed nearly cost my life....When I am my present "normal" self, I am far
> removed from when I have been my liveliest, most productive, most intense, most outgoing
> and effervescent. In short, for myself, I am a hard act to follow (p. 91).

The possibility that such a subjective state may be sought and produced does not imply that biological factors do not play a significant role. Nor do we suppose that this state would be attractive to, or achievable by, everyone. We do assume, however, that both individual character and biology are determinants of its possibility. As such, it is profitable to look more closely at the subjective experience and the generation of such states. The phenomenological study of hypomanic conditions can provide additional clues as to possible underlying causality including any biological processes. Examination of the subjective experience of such states may also increase our capacity to understand and more effectively treat such conditions.

In considering the hypothesis of an active effort to produce and sustain hypomanic states, it is useful to look at the analogue that exists in the cognitive view of the mechanism of depression (Beck 1976, 1979, 1987). It has been shown that depressed patients actively engage in self-critical ideation which is not a consequence of, but contributes to, intensified feelings of passivity, helplessness, and poor self-regard. This ideational activity in turn leads to further dysphoric affect. Simply put, the idea behind cognitive intervention for depression is to make the patients aware that they are actively engaging in such negative thinking and to systematically try to change their thinking. This presumably interrupts the intensification or perpetuation of depressive experience. We are suggesting that an active process, comparable to the depressive, may exist in the generation and sustaining of hypomanic states, although not necessarily a strictly cognitive one. Hypomanic and manic conditions are commonly associated with depressive episodes. There is reason to think that for individuals threatened with depression, typically individuals with severely punishing consciences, the possibility of an escape from critical self-reflection would be especially appealing (Shapiro 2000). In this chapter, we will suggest that the suspension of a self-critical attitude can be facilitated by certain kinds of intentional activity.

Two aspects of activity are particularly important in understanding the subjective experience of hypomanic and manic states. First, activity may take the form of consciously and directly aiming to sustain a hypomanic subjective quality. For example, an individual may intentionally drink alcohol, use mood-altering drugs, or generally be noncompliant with treatment. Second, constant and intense activity, regardless of its specific nature, may contribute to hypomania because it may suspend the capacity for critical self-reflection.

Psychoanalysis, Mania, and Activity

Early psychoanalytic thinking provides a model of mania, which is not solely a biological one. According to this view, suspension of the punishing effect of the superego will ultimately induce elation (Freud 1921; Abraham 1924; Fenichel 1945). Freud (1921) writes:

> On the basis of our analysis of the ego it cannot be doubted that in cases of mania the ego and the ego ideal have fused together, so that the person, in a mood of triumph and self-satisfaction, disturbed by no self criticism, can enjoy the abolition of his inhibitions, his feelings of consideration for others, and his self reproaches (p. 820).

According to Freud (1921), this phenomenon can easily be observed in what he refers to as the "herd instinct" and "group mind" (p. 4). Influenced by Le Bon (1895/1920), McDougall (1920), and others, he suggests that participation in tightly knit groups such as a church or an army contributes to the dissolution of an individual's ego ideal. Factors that contribute to this are diffusion of responsibility, emotional contagion, and suggestibility. Under these conditions "the mental superstructure...is removed, and the unconscious foundations, which are similar in everyone, stand exposed to view" (Freud 1921, p. 9). As a result, "the individual is brought under conditions which allow him to throw off the repressions of his unconscious instinctual impulses...in which all that is evil in the human mind is contained as a predisposition" (Freud 1921, p. 9).

This last statement may be more indicative of Freud's own moralistic view of the human mind, and evil is not necessarily a main ingredient of these group-induced hypomanic states. However, his argument is compelling, and unfortunately numerous accounts exist in which group phenomena such as the ones alluded to by Freud do occur. During wartime, newspaper headlines bring our attention to atrocities committed by conquering forces on innocent civilians. For example, eyewitness accounts of atrocities committed during the recent Balkan war (*The New York Times*; Drakulic 1992, December 13, p. D17; *The New York Times*; Kinzer 1995, July 17, p. A1) describe the perpetrators as having committed these crimes while being in an elated or intoxicated mood.

In the psychoanalytic view, the suspension of self-criticism is considered unconscious, and it is ultimately attributed to a certain periodic biological necessity. It is further suggested that this biological necessity may be responsible for the unconscious motivation for culturally sanctioned celebrations, such as carnivals, which are considered to represent unconscious societal attempts to achieve this. However, according to this view, motivated suspension of self-criticism through activity as well as its biological underpinning are unconscious, and are therefore presumed to be experienced passively.

In discussing the activity and subjective experience of a hypomanic state, Shapiro (1960), originally used the analogy of someone riding a wild horse who feels out of control, but deceives himself that he is a great rider. This view is more in keeping with the traditional view of hypomanic experience, despite the emphasis on describing some of its subjective qualities. However, in what appears to be a change of mind, Shapiro (2000) has since revised his view. In describing this revised view, and using Shapiro's (1960) original analogy, we would argue that the rider instead goads the horse to achieve and sustain an exhilarating sensation of buoyancy and unconstrained speed. Building on the work of David Shapiro, we will present empirical evidence of his later theory and describe our attempts to induce such sensation on a diminished scale in a nonpsychiatric population.

Substance Abuse and Mania

The imagery of a depressed or dejected person, tormented by horrible feelings of guilt and severe self-criticism, who turns to alcohol or drugs as a means of escape is a common one. Numerous such depictions exist in both literary and cinematic fiction. This "commonsense" belief has historically held an enduring explanatory power in terms of a generalized understanding of substance abuse as an attempt to escape the subjective experience of depressive feelings. This belief is consistent with the "self-medicating" hypothesis first discussed by Freud (1884/1974), which has persisted in more recent theories of substance abuse and treatment (Khantzian, 1985; Khantzian et al. 1990). According to this idea, patients attempt to self-medicate their symptoms of depression or other painful or unacceptable feelings. There is evidence that some individuals actively consume alcohol or drugs not solely to dispel depression, but with the conscious aim of inducing, perpetuating, or intensifying hypomanic or manic-like states.

In recent years, several studies have emerged that specifically examine this issue. A general finding is that, contrary to common expectations, bipolar patients are more likely to engage in substance abuse behavior when they are manic or hypomanic than depressed (Anthony and Helzer 1991; Winokur et al. 1998; Angst 1998; Estroff et al. 1985). An exhaustive review of this literature is beyond the scope of this chapter. Rather, we will focus on some studies that examine the relationship between substance abuse and mania, and more specifically, illustrate the use of substances to induce, intensify, or perpetuate a manic or hypomanic state and to some extent focus on the subjective experience of the patients.

In Weiss and Mirrin's (1986) study of 30 cocaine abusers, seven patients were diagnosed as having either cyclothymic or bipolar disorder, and five of the seven stated that "they used cocaine more frequently when endogenously 'high' than when depressed or euthymic" (p. 493) and that they "enjoyed the elated mood states associated with hypomania or mania and found that cocaine augmented their euphoria" (p. 493). Weiss and Mirrin (1986) discuss the unique difficulty in treating such patients, who find their hypomanic or manic states pleasurable enough to "warrant augmenting them with cocaine" (p. 496). In a similar study, Gawin and Kleber (1986), using similar assessment instruments and number of subjects (30), found comparable prevalence rates of affective disorder in cocaine users, with manic depressives comprising about 17% of the total sample. Gawin and Kleber's (1986) patients reported histories of "prolonged periods of 'functional hypomania' during which they did well personally and professionally, without full manic symptoms" (p. 110). Cocaine use during these times did not precipitate manic states. However, as dysthymic cycles occurred, cocaine was initially used to reestablish hypomanic functioning. Subsequently, when patients understood the "potentially harmful effects of cocaine" (Gawin and Kleber 1986, p. 111) they were able to abstain from its use when in a dysthymic state, but were likely to continue using it when in a hypomanic state. Based on patient accounts, they argue that poor judgment, while in a hypomanic state, may have contributed to the recurrence of cocaine use. This argument however, is not inconsistent with the observation that cocaine use may serve a mood-regulating function in cyclothymic patients primarily by aiding in reestablishing a hypomanic state at the onset of a dysthymic state or by extending hypomanic states in order to delay or prevent their extinction. A possible limitation of the above studies is that they are based on retrospective accounts, which may be susceptible to inaccuracies. However, they are important in the sense that they focus on the subjective experience of patients.

Rottanburg et al. (1982) compared 20 psychotic patients with high urinary cannabinoid levels upon admission to a psychiatric hospital to 20 matched cannabinoid-free patients of a similar diagnosis. They found that cannabis patients had significantly more hypomanic symptoms and had significantly less schizophrenic-like symptoms such as auditory hallucinations, flattening of affect, and incoherent speech. The cannabis patients showed significant improvement in their mental state as measured again a week later. In discussing their findings, the authors limit themselves to asking whether cannabis caused this psychosis or whether it helped induce it in "predisposed individuals." In any case, it would be reasonable to assume that if cannabis contributes in inducing a hypomanic-like state, it may be willingly consumed by patients motivated to enter such a state, especially if they are "predisposed." Harding and Knight (1973) present case studies of four patients who were hospitalized with acute psychotic symptoms following increased use of cannabis use. Prior to their hospitalization, all patients experienced hypomanic symptoms, which led to increased cannabis use. At the time of admission, psychotic symptoms were prevalent but with an absence of mood elevation. However, within 3–4 days of admission, these symptoms were replaced by hypomanic symptoms. They concluded that increased marijuana consumption may be symptomatic of a manic illness. Using a perspective approach to studying this further, Baethge et al. (2008) examined the sequencing of cannabis use and the onset of mania/hypomania and found that increased cannabis use preceded or coincided with manic/hypomanic states but did not follow them.

In an early study on the relationship between affective disorder and alcoholism, Pitts and Winokur (1966) observe that in mania "periodic excessive Alcoholic ingestion occurs together with other evidences of euphoria, overactivity and poor judgment" (p. 37). However, they do not provide specific information as to what led to their observation, and it is unclear if they are suggesting a cause-and-effect relationship. In a review of the early research, Mayfield and Coleman (1968) report studies with similar observations (Sherfey 1955; Kraines 1957) and conclude that drinking is "positively and consistently related to elation and negatively and inconsistently related to depression" (p. 473). Similar results were found in other studies which were more experimentally rigorous (Hensel et al. 1979; Dunner et al. 1979; Helzer and Pryzbeck 1988). Helzer and Pryzbeck (1988) present data based on the Epidemiologic Catchment Area (ECA) study (Regier et al. 1984) which is based on a sample size of 20,000 individuals. They investigated alcoholism and psychiatric comorbidity and found that there is a strong degree of association between alcoholism and mania but not with depression and dysthymia. Unfortunately, some of the above studies at best provide only speculation as to why increased alcohol consumption is associated with manic or hypomanic-like states or limit themselves to just describing the association. However, in the sequencing study of substance abuse and affective disorder discussed earlier, Baethge et al. (2008) found evidence that, contrary to cannabis use, alcohol use preceded or coincided with depression.

Overall, based on a review of the current literature, it is hard to make any definitive conclusions as to the role of drugs or alcohol in manic or hypomanic conditions. It is reasonable to assume that they may have a disinhibiting effect in individuals who generally experience pleasurable hypomanic states and are consumed in order to induce, enhance, or extend them. On the other hand it may also be the case that individuals who experience irritable or uncomfortable states of mania consume drugs or alcohol for their sedative qualities in order to attenuate the severity of the experience (Jamison 1993, p. 39). In light of this, it would seem profitable to pay more attention to the accounts of patients' subjective experience of these states and do so in a systematic way.

Lithium Carbonate Noncompliance and Activity

There are situations in which activity to sustain a hypomanic state may involve behaviors which initially appear to be passive. Such seems to be the case with lithium treatment noncompliance. In certain situations, the act of noncompliance itself may be understood as an active attempt on the part of an individual to sustain a hypomanic state. Polatin and Fieve (1971) describe three clinical cases of noncompliance. One patient who was particularly creative felt that lithium carbonate was inhibiting him "therefore acting as a 'brake' on his creativity" (Polatin and Fieve 1971, p. 865). Another said that she was "intellectually chained" by it (Polatin and Fieve 1971, p. 865). The authors conclude that the hypomanic phase can be so productive and enjoyable that bipolar patients would prefer to risk the recurrence of depression rather than eliminate the possibility of experiencing a hypomanic state. Jamison (1995) describes her own experience of this:

> Even though I was a clinician and a scientist, and even though I could read the research literature and see the inevitable, bleak consequences of not taking lithium, I for many years after my initial diagnosis was reluctant to take my medications as prescribed....It was difficult to give up the high flights of mind and mood, even though the depressions that inevitably followed nearly cost my life (p. 91).

Schou and Baastrup (1973) argue that some individuals resist lithium treatment because they feel it makes them "bland" or "flat," or that it renders them less sexually responsive. They describe a patient who, concerned about becoming indifferent, complained: "Doctor, I am a communist and I *must* get excited when I discuss" (p. 66).

The above-mentioned studies are primarily based on self-report or conjecture but do convey the subjective experiences of individuals faced with the dilemma of giving up the possibility of experiencing manic or hypomanic sensations by complying with treatment.

An Attempt to Induce a Hypomanic-Like State

We designed a study to induce a hypomanic-like state that did not involve chemical or physiological arousal or other mood induction techniques such as the Velten Mood Induction Procedure (Velten 1968). Participants without any history of hypomania were simply asked to perform a cognitive-perceptual task, in this case the Rorschach test, under conditions which sought to reproduce aspects of the subjective experience of hypomanic states.

It has been argued that the Rorschach test can be more appropriately considered a method for assessing the workings of the mind rather than a test (Weiner 1995). It can reveal an individual's subjective states including perceptual, cognitive, and associational processes, from which inferences can be made regarding underlying characteristics of specific personality types and discrete mental states. It has been shown that individuals in a hypomanic-like state experience exposure to Rorschach cards in unique ways, and give correspondingly unique sets of responses that reveal thought processes and content that is unique to hypomanic experience (Solovay et al. 1987; Shenton et al. 1987; Khadivi et al. 1997). In an autobiographical account of what this experience is like Jamison (1995) writes:

> He held up Rorschach cards before the class and asked us to write down our responses....My mind was flying high that day, courtesy of whatever witches' brew of neurotransmitters God had programmed into my genes, and I filled page after page with...very strange responses...a recital of...odd associations....Some of them were humorous, but a few of them were simply bizarre....He had never encountered such "imaginative" responses....It was my first lesson in appreciating the complicated, permeable, boundaries between bizarre and original thought. (pp. 47–48)

Our expectation was that a variation in the standard administration procedure would induce a hypomanic-like state by simulating some of the qualitative characteristics of such states. More specifically, subjects were asked to give responses to a set of Rorschach cards under two slightly different speed-pressured conditions. They were asked to respond to the cards as quickly as they could, giving as many responses as they could, continuously, under time-pressure conditions. This procedure would presumably minimize or suspend the subject's self-criticism, generally increase activity level, speed-up cognitive processes, and ultimately induce a hypomanic-like state. It was expected that subjects would subjectively experience a hypomanic-like state and that this would also be evident in their Rorschach responses. Some subjects were asked to give as many responses as they could within 60 s of the presentation of each card ("high-pressure" group), others were asked to give as many responses as possible without any time limit ("modified high-pressure" group), while others were given standard instructions (control group). Also, none of three groups received an inquiry. It was hypothesized that this forced, "speeded-up," cognitive-perceptual activity, which minimizes the possibility of self-reflection especially in the group with no time limit, even if not self-motivated, would induce in the subjects a mild hypomanic-like subjective experience. The responses obtained under these conditions could then be compared qualitatively to the kinds of responses that the literature reports as characteristic of manic or hypomanic responses to the Rorschach under ordinary conditions. Additional self-report measures were also taken as to the person's subjective experience before and after the experimental induction phase specifically in terms of how much pleasure and arousal they felt.[1]

It was hypothesized that subjects in the "high-pressure" and "modified high-pressure" conditions would report experiencing greater arousal and pleasant feelings after the experimental manipulation rather than prior, and would do so to a greater extent than subjects in the control group. Contrary to expectations, none of the three groups reported increased arousal. It is possible that subjects may have experienced an increase in arousal during the manipulation which may have dissipated by the time it was assessed.

Subjects in the "modified high-pressure" group did report experiencing more pleasant feelings after performing the experimental task and did so to a greater extent than subjects in the other two groups. However, an increase in the experience of pleasant feelings was only obtained for subjects in the "modified high-pressure" group and not for subjects in the "high-pressure" group. The failure to obtain this for subjects in the latter group can be attributed to the nature of the experimental task itself. Unlike subjects in the "modified high-pressure" group, subjects in the "high-pressure" group were given a time limit of 60 s during which they were instructed to give as many responses as they could to each Rorschach card. In most cases, subjects were finished with their responses before the end of the 60 s period and had to wait for the remaining time to elapse with nothing else to do but stare at the card in silence. It is reasonable to assume that subjects in this condition were more self-critical during this period than subjects in the other group. This may have counteracted the effect of speeded-up activity on their subjective experience of pleasant feelings.

It was hypothesized that, compared to the control group, subjects in the two experimental groups would engage in more Combinatory Thinking; that is, they would more actively combine various aspects of the blot in novel and unique ways, often describing unlikely combinations in a playful or flippant manner. The results supported this hypothesis.

It was further hypothesized that subjects in the experimental groups would produce more Combinatory Thinking than other forms of thought disorder. As predicted, both experimental groups produced significantly more Combinatory Thinking than any other form of thought disorder. Here are some examples of responses given exhibiting Combinatory Thinking:

an angel and a butterfly mixed, hands up towards heaven, sort of connect at an angle, these 2 people are jugglers (Card I)
a big tree monster looking, like standing on a big piece of like a glass floor and underneath it, looking up at it, it's also, oh it has a head on top and a head on the bottom so it's reversible (Card V)

---

[1] For more detailed description of the study design, methods, instruments used, and findings, see Evdokas (1997).

oh dear, oh nice colors, gosh, I see, Russia, that's Siberia, this is Siberia here, Siberia with feet and some kind of creatures over Siberia bridging something, bridging the abyss, the red is um what is the red& well it could be a metaphoric exhibit, this is Siberia standing over Communism with some kind of creatures bridging the abyss ok (laughs) that's it (Card IX)

I don't know they look like some kind of cross between a crab and an insect or something and they have long antennae and they have the a, the a, they're grabbing whatever that is in the middle, and on either side there's a royal blue creature with a, let's see, with many legs and on its back is some sort of warrior and clasped in his hands are some sort of green tool of destruction, in his arms and they're charging forth towards something, I don't know perhaps they have a noble cause that they're fighting for (Card X)

ahh ooh, um what is that it's pretty but not quite, it looks like red peppers, green peppers, and blossoms, and a sea urchin imprint, nature again I suppose, this is Portugal, kind of, or it's the Adriatic Sea, um more creatures on top, I see the imprint of sea urchins with leaves so it's past and future, and red peppers, and blossoms and green peppers, kind of a piquant Portugal with past and the future (Card X)

It is interesting to note that subjects in the "modified high-pressure" group scored significantly higher on Combinatory Thinking than subjects in the "high-pressure" group. This finding can again be attributed to the fact that subjects in the "modified high-pressure" group were less self-critical than subjects in the "high-pressure" group. Finally, again as predicted, the control group did not show any significant difference in their score on the two categories of thought disorder.

Overall, the above findings suggest that, as a result of the experimental manipulation, subjects selectively produced more Combinatory Thinking than any other type of thought disorder. This is consistent with the expectation that the type of thought disorder produced would be characteristic of hypomanic-like states and not other types of thought disorder (Solovay et al. 1987; Shenton et al. 1987; Khadivi et al. 1997).

It was also hypothesized that subjects in the two experimental groups would give Rorschach responses with more affective content than the responses of subjects in the control group. The data supported this hypothesis. Here are some examples of responses given exhibiting affective content:

a giant, on a beanstalk, a giant trying to make me laugh with his position (Card IV)

two men laughing about a joke (Card VI)

two ogres laughing at each other (Card IX)

flames, burning, chemical flames emitting smoke of green and red, the face of a beast bearing down on us exhaling with great with great belligerent energy about to charge, nuclear explosion (Card IX)

It was further hypothesized that the responses of subjects in the experimental groups would have more affective content than non-affective content. However, the data indicated that subjects in all three groups gave responses with significantly greater affective content than non-affective content (however the difference between affective and non-affective content was significantly greater for the two experimental groups than for the control group).

Overall, this finding supports the hypothesis that the thematic content of Rorschach responses produced, as a result of the experimental manipulation, would selectively be characteristic of hypomanic-like responses and not characteristic of other kinds of psychological states (Khadivi et al. 1997).

General Discussion and Clinical Implications

An integration of the individual findings reveals that subjects in the "modified high-pressure" group were unique in reporting greater experience of pleasant feelings after the experimental manipulation, rather than before. This finding is consistent with a pleasurable subjective experience of a hypomanic-like state. However, it is interesting to note that both experimental groups gave Rorschach responses, which are characteristic of hypomanic-like states. Therefore, the two experimental groups differ only to the extent that subjects in the "modified high-pressure" group reported subjectively experiencing this state as pleasurable.

As mentioned earlier, methodologically, the experimental manipulation for the two groups differs only as to the presence or absence of a Rorschach response time limit. It was also suggested that, as a consequence of a time limit, subjects in the "high-pressure" group may have been more self-critical. It is reasonable to speculate that suspension of self-criticism may be a crucial factor in determining whether a subjective state, which in cognitive and physiological terms is consistent with a hypomanic-like state, will be experienced subjectively as pleasurable or not.

This finding may be of particular clinical importance in understanding the discrepancy between some individual subjective accounts of hypomanic- and manic-like states. The degree of suspension of self-criticism may be an important contributing factor as to whether or not a hypomanic or manic-like state is subjectively experienced as pleasurable. Given the clinical importance of this possibility, it would seem profitable to study this further.

The findings generally support the view that a hypomanic-like state may be induced by activity that minimizes the possibility of self-reflection, suspends self-criticism, and speeds up cognitive processes. Even though in the context of this study the activity was not self-motivated, the possibility that a hypomanic-like experience was induced by activity suggests that individuals may actively engage in such activity of their own volition, if they are so motivated. This may be the case especially for those individuals threatened with depression or those with a severely punishing conscience. Clearly, more can be gained in the future by going beyond descriptions of cognitive processes and physiology in understanding the nature of hypomanic-like states, and paying attention to the interplay between subjective experience of mood states and the effect of activity.

References

Abraham, K. (1924). A short study of the development of the libido, viewed in the light of mental disorders. In: *Selected papers of Karl Abraham*. London: Hogarth.

Angst, J. 1998. The emerging epidemiology of hypomania and bipolar II disorder. *Journal of Affective Disorders, 50*, 143–151.

Anthony, H. S., & Helzer, J. E. 1991. Syndromes of drug abuse and dependence. In Robins, L. N. & Regier, D. A. (Eds.), *Psychiatric disorders in America* (pp. 116–154). New York: The Free Press.

American Psychiatric Association. (2000). *Diagnostic and statistical manual of mental disorders* (4th ed., Text Revision). Washington, DC: Author.

Baethge, C., Hennen J., Khalsa, H.-M. K., Salvatore, P., Tohen, M., & Baldessarini, R. J. 2008. Sequencing of substance use and effective morbidity on 166 first-episode bipolar I patients. *Bipolar Disorder, 10*, 738–741.

Beck, A. T. 1976. *Cognitive therapy and the emotional disorders*. New York: International Universities Press.

Beck, A. T. 1979. *Cognitive therapy of depression*. New York: Guilford.

Beck, A. T. 1987. Cognitive models of depression. *Journal of Cognitive Psychotherapy Quarterly, 1*, 5–37.

Drakulic, S. 1992, December 13). Rape after rape after rape. *The New York Times*, p. D17.

Dunner, D. L., Hensel, B. M., & Fieve, R. R. 1979. Bipolar illness: Factors in drinking behavior. *American Journal of Psychiatry, 136*, 583–585.

Estroff, T. W., Dackis, C. A., Gold, M. S., & Pottash, A. L. C. 1985. Drug abuse and bipolar disorders. *International Journal of Psychiatry Medicine, 15*, 37–40.

Evdokas, A. 1997. *An attempt to induce a hypomanic-like state in normal subjects through rapid production*. Ann Arbor: VMI

Fenichel, O. 1945. *The psychoanalytic theory of neurosis*. New York: Norton.

Freud, S. (1884/1974). Uber coca. In R. Byck (Ed.), *Cocaine papers* (pp. 49–73). New York: Stonehill.

Freud, S. 1921. *Group psychology and the analysis of the ego* (The Standard Edition). New York: Norton.

Gawin, F. H., & Kleber, H. S. 1986. Abstinence symptomatology and psychiatric diagnosis in cocaine abusers. *Archives of General Psychiatry, 43*, 107–725.

Goodwin, F. K., & Jamison, K. R. 1997. *Manic depressive illness* (2nd ed.). New York: Oxford University Press.

Harding, T., & Knight, F. 1973. Marijuana modified mania. *Archives of General Psychiatry, 29*, 635–637.

Helzer, J. E., & Pryzbeck, T. R. 1988. The co-occurrence of alcoholism with other psychiatric disorders in the general population and its impact in treatment. *Journal of Studies in Alcohol, 49*, 219–224.

Hensel, B., Dunner, D. L., & Fieve, R. R. 1979. The relationship of family history of alcoholism to primary affective disorder. *Journal of Affective Disorder, 1*, 105–113.

Jamison, K. R. 1993. *Touched with fire: Manic depressive illness and the artistic temperament*. New York: Free Press/Maxwell Macmillan International.

Jamison, K. R. 1995. *An unquiet mind*. New York: Alfred A. Knopf.

Khadivi, A., Wetzler, S., & Wilson, A. 1997. Manic indeces on the Rorschach. *Journal of Personality Assessment, 69*(2), 365–375.

Khantzian, E. J. 1985. The self-medication hypothesis of addictive disorders: Focus on heroin and cocaine dependence. *American Journal of Psychiatry, 142*, 1259–1264.

Khantzian E. J., Halliday, K. S., & McCauliffe, W. E. 1990. *Addiction and the vulnerable self*. New York: Guilford.

Kinzer, S. 1995, July 17). Conflict in the Balkans: The refugees: Bosnian refugee's accounts appear to verify atrocities. *The New York Times*, p. A1.

Kraepelin, E. 1921/1976. *Manic-depressive insanity and paranoia* (R.M. Barkley, Trans.). New York: Arno.

Kraines, S. H. 1957. *Mental depressions and their treatment*. New York: Macmillan.

Le Bon, G. 1895/1920. *The crowd: A study of the popular mind*. New York: Macmillan.

Mayfield, D. G., & Coleman, L. L. 1968. Alcohol use and affective disorder. *Diseases of the Nervous System, 29*, 467–474.

McDougall, W. 1920. *The group mind*. New York: G. P. Putnam.

Pitts, F. N., & Winokur, G. 1966. Affective disorder-VII: Alcoholism and affective disorder. *Journal of Psychiatric Research, 4*, 37–50.

Polatin, P., & Fieve, R. R. 1971. Patient rejection of lithium carbonate prophylaxis. *JAMA, 218,* 864–866.

Regier, D. A., Farmer, M. E., Rae, D. S., Locke, B. Z., Keith, S. J., Judd, L. L., & Goodwin, F. K. 1984. Comorbidity of mental disorders with alcohol and other drug abuse. *JAMA, 264,* 2511–2518.

Rottanburg, D., Robins, A. H., Ben-Arie, O., Teggin, A., & Elk, R. 1982. Cannabis associated with psychosis with hypomanic features. *Lancet, 2,* 1364–1366.

Schou, M., & Baastrup, P. C. 1973. Personal and social implications of lithium maintenance. In T. A. Ban, J. R. Boissier, G. J. Gessa, H. Heiman, L. Hollister, H. E. Lehman, I. Munkrad, H. Steinberg, F. Sulser, A. Sundwall, & O. Vinar (Eds.), *Psychopharmacology, sexual disorders, and drug abuse* (pp. 65–68). Amsterdam: North-Holland.

Shapiro, D. 1960. A perceptual understanding of color response. In M. Rickers-Ovsiankina (Ed.), Rorschach psychology (pp. 154–201). New York: Wiley.

Shapiro, D. 2000. *Dynamics of character.* New York: Basic Books

Shenton, M. E., Solovay, M. R., & Holzman, P. 1987. Comparative studies of thought disorders: II. Schizoaffective disorder. *Archives of General Psychiatry, 44,* 21–30.

Sherfey, M. J. 1955. Psychopathology and character structure in chronic alcoholism. In O. Diethelm (Ed.), *Etiology of chronic alcoholism* (pp. 16–42). Springfield: Charles C. Thomas.

Solovay, M. R., Shenton, M. E., & Holzman, P. 1987. Comparative studies of thought disorders: I. Mania and schizophrenia. *Archives of General Psychiatry, 44,* 13–20.

Velten, E. 1968. A laboratory task for induction of mood states. *Behaviour Research and Therapy, 6,* 473–482.

Weiner, I. B. 1995. Methodological considerations in Rorschach research. *Psychological Assessment, 7,* 330–337.

Weiss, R. D., & Mirrin, S. M. 1986. Subtypes of cocaine users. *Psychiatric Clinics of North America, 9,* 491–501.

Winokur, G., Turvey, C., Akiskal, H., Coryell, W., Solomon, D., Leon, A., Mueller, T., Endicott, J., Maser, J., & Keller, M. 1998. Alcoholism and drug abuse in three groups – bipolar I, unipolars and their acquaintances. *Journal of Affective Disorders, 50,* 81–89.

Reply to Andreas Evdokas and Ali Khadivi

David Shapiro

As Drs. Evdokas and Khadivi note, my understanding of hypomanic conditions has changed in a critical way since my Rorschach paper of 1960. The change partly reflects a change in the nature of my clinical work since then. My earlier view was of hypomania as essentially a passive process, a kind of affective and ideational surge, often rationalized as creativeness. This view, which was not far from the traditional psychiatric view, was influenced especially by my intensive experience, at the time, with psychological tests, particularly the Rorschach test. I was impressed by what seemed an inundation of excited affect and energy in the reported subjective experience of hypomanic subjects and was apparent in the quality of the test production as well. But this is an incomplete picture of hypomanic excitement and elation. Observers of this excitement uniformly agree that it also has a forced, artificial, driven quality. There are, in other words, two outstanding formal aspects of hypomanic excitement. One is, as I first described, simply a subjective experience of elation, an excited, liberated sensation of being, as one patient put it, "flooded" with ideas. But the other aspect is of a hyperactive and deliberately uncritical drivenness of thought, speech, and activity. I have described the condition altogether as one of *driven spontaneity*. This purposeful driven activity ("above all, staying on the move"), clearly aimed at achieving relief from self-critical reflection, points to a reversal of the usual view of hypomanic activity as an effect of elation and places it, rather, as an effective cause of elation and a defensive effort.

The fact that driven and uncritical, but still purposeful reactiveness can be experienced as virtually, even actually, involuntary ("flooded"), and exultantly so, needs explanation. The phenomenon is only a special, extreme instance of the more general relation between volitional action and personal agency. As one sees in impulsive characters, even to some extent in hysterical characters, any attenuation of volitional thought processes results in a diminished experience of personal agency or responsibility. In the quick reactions of psychopathic individuals, for instance, a diminished reflective deliberateness has the result usually described as externalization of responsibility (the holdup man is asked why he beat his victim; the answer: "He resisted"). When activity is speeded up and the actual process of looking things over and deciding becomes radically foreshortened, the normal experience of agency may be replaced by an experience of being flooded or swept away by ideas about whatever the individual sees or encounters. Perhaps, there is an individual threshold for such experience comparable to the one at which still pictures displayed in rapid succession are seen as in motion.

Drs. Evdokas and Khadivi have attempted to produce a reduced version of hypomanic dynamics, as I have described those dynamics, experimentally. They have arranged conditions of externally required hyperactivity in a procedure, the Rorschach test, designed to reveal mood and thought process. Their arrangement requires thinking and reaction under a condition, the requirement of speedy response, that can be expected to limit the possibility of a self-critical attitude. I think their experiment is a qualified, but very interesting and very promising success. Within the imposed limits of such an experiment (its reliance on normal subjects, the permissible limits of experimental discomfort) some striking effects were obtained. These included both expressions of high mood and, at least as important, what is called, technically, combinatory thinking, a kind of arbitrary and unconvincing "creativeness." That combinatory thinking ("oh, dear, oh, nice colors, gosh. I see Russia, that's Siberia, Siberia with feet...") strikes me as exactly the kind of imme- diately reactive, uncritically ambitious Rorschach response I recall from my psycho- logical testing experience.

Evdokas and Khadivi have also investigated important data concerning the use of alcohol and drugs by people diagnosed as bipolar to produce or sustain high mood. As Evdokas and Khadivi point out, their use, presumably consciously aimed simply at feeling good, or better, is consistent with the perhaps less conscious aim of liberation from self-critical thoughts. Indeed, it is consistent with the common social use of alcohol, diminishing self-consciousness with the result of a mild elevation of mood.

The evidence that depressed individuals are less interested in using alcohol or drugs than bipolar people who are already in a hypomanic state, is especially inter- esting, because it is at first surprising. Why not the other way around, those in greater need having the stronger motivation? But Evdokas and Khadivi show that extensive data in the other direction are consistent. I share their doubt that this can be explained as a cognitive effect of diminished judgment in the hypomanic case. It is far more likely that the difference reflects the eagerness and energetic determi- nation of those already in fragile high spirits to sustain them, as Evdokas and Khadivi indicate, as well as the hopelessness and disinclination to action of those severely depressed. This difference, it seems to me, may be important for a special reason. It may tell us something about the differences between the psychological makeup and state of those individuals who are simply severely depressed and those in whom we see, for better or worse, a hypomanic defense.

Appendix A
On Two Fundamental Categories
of Psychopathology

David Shapiro

Sid Blatt (Blatt 1974; Blatt and Shichman 1983; Blatt and Blass 1992) and I (Shaprio 1981, 2000) have by different routes arrived at the same conclusion, that there are two fundamental categories of psychopathology. He calls them fundamental configurations, I call them modes or styles (actually, Blatt uses these terms as well). The psychiatric conditions to which our respective categories refer are, I believe, essentially identical.

It seems to me that there is reason for satisfaction and assurance in this congruence, Blatt's conclusions drawing on his and his colleagues' systematic investigations and the psychoanalytic developmental model, mine essentially a formal model relying on clinical tests and observation. Our theoretical conceptions of the categories are not necessarily incompatible, coming, so to speak, from two different angles. However, on a certain important point concerning both etiology and dynamics they clearly diverge. In what follows I want mainly to discuss that point of divergence. The larger areas, the areas of congruence, will be obvious and will need only brief description.

Blatt's concept of two configurations, which he calls anaclitic and introjective, is based both on symptomatic content – the typical problems and preoccupying issues characteristic of each – and formal features such as the defense mechanisms and cognitive style associated with that content. Blatt posits that the two pathological configurations are defensive exaggerations of two fundamental developmental lines, the need for satisfying relationships with others and the need for adequate and stable self-definition. These developmental lines and the problems associated with them originate in particular developmental stages; hence, the terms anaclitic and introjective. His conception is therefore etiological.

My conception is more conservative, some would say limited. I have less confidence in the psychoanalytic developmental model, especially as it is applied to adult psychopathology, and I have little to say about etiology. My fundamental modes, the rigid mode, and the passively reactive mode describe the two general forms of activity and thought characteristic of adult psychopathology.

D. Shapiro (✉)
Professor Emeritus, New School for Social Research, 80 Fifth Avenue, New York, NY 10003
e-mail: ShapiroD@newschool.edu

C. Piers (ed.), *Personality and Psychopathology: Critical Dialogues with David Shapiro*,   275
DOI 10.1007/978-1-4419-6214-0, © Springer Science+Business Media, LLC 2011

The content of Blatt's two fundamental configurations is well known. In the introjective category the primary issues, as I said, are those of identity, self-control, self-definition, and self-worth (Blatt and Shichman 1983). This configuration characterizes mainly obsessive–compulsive and paranoid conditions. Its dynamics are identified with problems of several developmental levels. A source of the seemingly excessive ideational and motor self-control seen in obsessive–compulsive conditions, for example, is thought to lie in problems of the anal stage of development. Blatt's anaclitic category comprises those conditions in which the primary concerns are with establishing and maintaining interpersonal relationships (Blatt and Shichman 1983). This configuration includes hysterics, whose concerns may originate in problems of the oedipal level, and infantile characters, whose problems are thought to originate earlier, at the oral stage.

Of the two fundamental modes that I describe, the rigid mode includes obsessive-compulsive and paranoid conditions, as well as certain additional varieties or offshoots of these, such as masochistic characters (Shapiro 2000, 1981). The passively reactive mode includes hysterical characters and also various sorts of passive and impulsive individuals, who would probably fit Blatt's description of infantile characters (Shapiro 1965, 2000). The general congruence of my fundamental modes with Blatt's fundamental configurations therefore seems quite clear, although there are some, I think minor, differences in categorization. For example, Blatt places borderline cases in the anaclitic category, whereas I regard the diagnostic term of borderline as too vague symptomatically to permit any clear definition of form. I have therefore omitted it. But I place schizoid conditions in the passive reactive category.

Now I want to consider the divergence between Blatt's conception and mine. It concerns, as I mentioned, the dynamics of psychopathology and perhaps also its etiology. In Blatt's view the general form (cognitive style, etc.) of the configuration as well as the content of the preoccupying issues are expressions of the defensive exaggerations of its developmental line. The motivations represented in these defensive exaggerations originate in the dynamics of early childhood. My view is in the other direction. Thus, Blatt derives the traits of (what I call) the rigid character from the exaggerated need for self-definition whereas I, conversely, think that the exaggerated need for self-definition and the content of the issues associated with that need are more easily and more plausibly derived from the nature of rigid character. The analogous point holds for the anaclitic or passively reactive configuration. Further, although I cannot offer alternative suggestions for the etiology of each of these character forms, I think it doubtful that they are the heirs of childhood dynamics as Blatt proposes.

Consider the rigid mode. Individuals that I characterize in this way are, to one extent or another, rule directed. That is, they live with a continual awareness, or at least a peripherally conscious sensation, of authoritative rules: moral rules, rules of propriety, rules against waste, and general rules of efficiency, even rules of correct thinking and proper feelings. The most common subjective experience of these rules is contained in the thought "I should." This characteristic is often considered to reflect a severe or excessive conscientiousness or superego. But it is more correctly described as a rigid, that is, rule-based, conscientiousness, as opposed to a more autonomous conscientiousness, a conscientiousness of conviction. Other symptomatic traits commonly include a reluctance to depart from routine, dogmatism, special emphasis on self-control and willpower (I shouldn't "give in" to myself), and stubbornness (I shouldn't "give in" to others). When it is not possible to locate authoritative rules that are decisive, that is, when a personal choice and its accompanying experience of personal agency or responsibility is unavoidable, these individuals are characterized by anxiety and indecision.

The rules by which the rigid character lives, or tries to live, are often embodied in authoritative figures whom the rigid person attempts to emulate and identify himself with. He asks himself: What would (the admired person) do? In this way, he tries to determine the "right" thing to do. The effort to live according to these rules and emulate these figures often requires the exercise self-control, "strength of will" or "willpower." The rigid person's image of himself and self-respect are dependent upon his success in this emulation; that is, his success in believing himself to resemble these emulated figures and believing that what he thinks he should do is what he actually wants to do. He is therefore constantly evaluating himself against these standards.

The obsessive–compulsive person's efforts, or struggles, of will, are directed against himself. They are directed against his own "weakness," his inclination to do what he should not do, or his disinclination to do what he thinks he should. In the paranoid case, however, where the rigidity is more extreme and less stable, the struggle of will becomes largely a struggle with external figures. External figures are trying to make him "give in" by force or temptation, to overcome his will or weaken it.

Is this rigid mode actually "introjective"? Yes and no, it seems to me. Certainly the rules that the rigid individual imposes on himself are largely, though not necessarily, as I shall point out in a moment, internalized versions of originally external rules, and the images that he emulates must be constructed around real or imaginatively elaborated figures of the past. But the situation is more complicated than it may seem.

There is, for example, little evidence that a rigid conscientiousness necessarily reflects an internalization of rigid or strict parental control. Sometimes it probably is; the example of the famous paranoid schizophrenic Schreber is a case in point (Shapiro 1981). But often, judging by clinical evidence, it apparently is not. We know, in fact, that the construction of and rigid adherence to rules is a regular stage of cognitive development; things must be done just so. We know further that for children of low intelligence such rules are especially rigid. In fact, Kurt Lewin, in his famous study of retarded children observed that their strict adherence to the rules of play had on this account the "appealing appearance of moral rectilinearity [sic] (1935, pp. 204–205)." To some extent these rules presumably are internalized versions of adult regulations, although concrete and exaggerated versions. But some rules that children live by originate with them simply out of cognitive limitations, and are often puzzling and bothersome to their parents. Those rules often seem to be based on the authority of precedent: it has been this way, therefore this is the only right way.

Of course such rules do not arise out of the same motivation and do not fulfill the same function as those in rigid adult psychopathology. Nevertheless, the fact remains that the internal experience of authoritative figures or rules as they are experienced in rigid character may not be the direct or simple product of introjection. It seems at least as likely that those rules and emulated images are the later constructions of a rigid character, a type of character whose actual sources and development are more complicated. Neurotic character is a complicated, self-regulating, relatively stable organization of attitudes and modes. It seems to me unlikely that such an organization should rest on the relatively slender foundation of developmental dynamics.

Similar questions arise in the case of the anaclitic category. The concerns and problems of those in this category are understood to be largely with interpersonal relationships, in contrast to those in the introjective category whose problems are largely with themselves. But again one has to ask whether the general form of personality, the defense mechanisms, cognitive style, and the rest, associated with those symptoms can be the direct products or expressions of earlier relational problems and particular developmental dynamics. There is, again, an alternative, namely, that the nature of the interpersonal issues and problems of these individuals can be derived from the general character form.

Consider the example of hysterics. These are people characteristically concerned with pleasing (or not displeasing) others; they are much influenced by others' opinions, especially by figures of authority; they are often preoccupied by romantic attachments and problems of intimacy. Those are among the interpersonal symptoms and traits of hysterical character. Now, consider the example of hysterics as a special category of the more general passively reactive mode.

Hysterical style is a style in which a deliberateness of action and deliberateness of thought or reflection are comparatively inhibited. Deliberateness of action and thought are in fact often consciously disdained in favor of a comparatively immediate reactiveness. It is a defensive mode in which the experience of personal agency or personal responsibility, the clear sense of one's intention, is diminished and anxiety is in that way forestalled (Shapiro 2000). These people tell us that they are guided by their emotions and that they think "intuitively" rather than logically. They are indeed characterized by an emotionality commonly described as volatile and by a mild impetuousness. In short, the anxiety forestalling style of these people is of a somewhat childlike, often disarming spontaneity and, in their unreflectiveness, a mild irresponsibility. The image and sensation that they have of themselves is often of an appealing child, lacking personal authority in a world of weightier and more serious grownups.

It is in the nature of this unreflective and emotionally reactive character form to turn away from introspection and toward external figures and events. It is in the nature of this character form to be involved with those figures and events subjectively and personally. It is, further, in the nature of one who feels like a child to turn toward those who seem like grownups, to lean on them or wish to lean on them and therefore to be anxious to avoid displeasing them.

These are among the symptomatic effects that follow from this general style and they are precisely the symptoms that may otherwise – it seems to me unnecessarily – be counted as effects of early relational problems. To see these (and other) symptomatic traits as particular expressions of the general character form still allows us to recognize that early relationships will contribute to, perhaps determine, their specific content. And we presume that personal history and family dynamics will be a determinant of the general mode of reactiveness itself, within the context of biological constitution. But assumption that the general quality of the adult psychopathology is the heir of the child's early problems of relationships circumvents the intervening development of character.

The fact is that adult symptoms, precisely because they are expressions of adult character, differ in fundamental ways from the developmental problems that may have been their source. A restrictive character has developed. Once that character has developed, the dynamics of the pathology have changed. What evokes anxiety now is not limited to revivals or representations of the original sources of the neurotic character. Anxiety is evoked now by whatever threatens the attitudes and stability of that character, a much more extensive category.

It is true that interpersonal issues are typically uppermost in the hysteric's conscious thinking. But the hysterical style and self-image of the flighty, appealing child who is not to be taken too seriously can be threatened by issues that are not essentially interpersonal. The careful observer will find that it is a manner that from time to time requires some effort to maintain. The thoughtless utterance or vague idea will be interrupted by a witty remark or a penetrating, perhaps aggressive, observation, only to be followed by an anxious retreat ("Gee, I hope I'm not becoming a tough New Yorker"). Similarly, when the rigid obsessive–compulsive individual is confronted by a personal choice for which there is no objective guide, as trivial perhaps as which movie to see, he is thrown into anxiety. We have no reason to assume that this is so because that choice represents or revives the memory of, say, some aggressive fantasy. It seems more reasonable, and certainly more economical, to understand such anxiety as the rule-directed person's reaction to a situation that has no "right" solution.

I would like to make one further point about the two fundamental categories of psychopathology with which Sid Blatt would certainly agree. Rigidity and passive reactiveness in adult psychopathology may easily but mistakenly seem to be polar opposites. Actually they are very closely related. They stand together as opposites of full personal autonomy, or full consciousness of autonomous self-direction. Both draw on modes of activity and thought that are characteristic of early childhood and that continue to be available in normal adult life as well. But these modes, in the case of psychopathology, are defensively employed, restrictive, and hypertrophied. Both modes attenuate volitional processes, diminish the experience of personal agency and in that way forestall anxiety. In the one case, self-direction is ceded to the authority of rules and emulated figures. In the other case, self-direction is ceded to the immediate reaction to external circumstance, in effect to external animators. The distinction between the two categories, from this point of view, is not sharp and one should not be surprised to see evidence of both modes or symptoms of both categories in every kind of psychopathology. We are reminded by the attenuation of volitional processes and the diminished experience of personal agency in both modes that all forms of psychopathology have much more in common than their symptomatic diversity would suggest.

References

Blatt, S. J. (1974). Levels of object representation in anaclitic and introjective depression. *The Psychoanalytic Study of the Child, 29*, 107–157. New Haven: Yale University Press.

Blatt, S. J., & Blass, R. B. (1992). Relatedness and self-definition: Two primary dimensions in personality development, psychopathology, and psychotherapy. In J. W. Barron, M. N. Eagle, & D. L. Wolitsky (Eds.), *Interface of psychoanalysis and psychology* (pp. 399–428). Washington, DC: American Psychological Association.

Blatt, S. J., & Shichman, S. (1983). Two primary configurations of psychopathology. *Psychoanalysis and Contemporary Thought, 6*, 187–254.

Lewin, K. (1935). Dynamic Theory of Personality. New York: McGraw Hill.

Shapiro, D. (1981). *Autonomy and rigid character*. New York: Basic Books.

Shapiro, D. (2000). *Dynamics of character: Self-regulation in psychopathology*. New York: Basic Books.

Appendix B

Books

(2005). *Color Response in the Rorschach Test.* Japan: University Education Press (in Japanese).

(2000). *Dynamics of Character: Self-regulation in Psychopathology.* New York: Basic Books. Translated into Russian.

(1989). *Psychotherapy of Neurotic Character.* New York: Basic Books. Reissued with new Introduction (2000); Translated into Italian and Japanese; Two chapters also reprinted in Conoscere Il Carattere (1996); Audio cassette, *Essentials of Behavior*, in production.

(1981). *Autonomy and Rigid Character.* New York: Basic Books/ Harper Torchbooks; Translated into Russian; Audio cassette, *Essentials of Behavior*, in production.

(1965). *Neurotic Styles.* New York: Basic Books/Harper Torchbooks; Reissued with new Introduction (2000); Translated into Italian, Spanish, French, German, Romanian and Castilian; Audio cassette, *Essentials of Behavior* (2003).

Articles

(2006). Self-reproach and personal responsibility. *Psychiatry: Interpersonal and Biological Processes,* 69(1), 21–25.

(2003). The tortured, not the torturers, are ashamed. *Social Research,* 70(4), 1131–1148.

(2002). Theoretical reflections on Wilhelm Reich's "Character Analysis". *American Journal of Psychotherapy,* 56(3), 338–346.

(2001). OCD or obsessive-compulsive character? *Psychoanalytic Inquiry,* 21(2), 242–252.

(1996). On the psychology of self-deception. *Social Research,* 63(3), 785–800.

(1996). The "self-control" muddle. *Psychological Inquiry,* 7(1), 76–79.

(1996). Character and psychotherapy. *American Journal of Psychotherapy,* 50(1), 3–13.

(1994). Paranoia from a characterological standpoint. In *Paranoia: New psychoanalytic perspectives,* J. M. Oldham & S. Bone (Eds.), Madison, CT: International Universities Press, 49–57.

(1992). Toward a structural theory of psychopathology. *Social Research,* 59(4), 799–812.

(1992). Therapeutic "difficulties" from a characterological view. *Contemporary Psychoanalysis,* 28(3), 519–524.

(1985). Psychotherapy and subjective experience. *Psychiatry: Journal for the Study of Interpersonal Processes,* 48(4), 311–317.

(1984). Review of "The Discovery of Being" by Rollo May. *Contemporary Psychology,* 29(11), 917.

(1977). Speech characteristics of rigid characters. *Language and Style,* 10(4), 262–296.

C. Piers (ed.), *Personality and Psychopathology: Critical Dialogues with David Shapiro,*   281
DOI 10.1007/978-1-4419-6214-0, © Springer Science+Business Media, LLC 2011

(1975). Dynamic and holistic ideas of neurosis and psychotherapy. *Psychiatry: Journal for the Study of Interpersonal Processes,* 38(3), 218–226.

(1974). Review of "The Manipulator: A Psychoanalytic View" by Ben Bursten. *Contemporary Psychology,* 19 (6), 479–480.

(1972). On psychological liberation. *Social Policy,* 4(2), 9–15.

(1970). Motivation and action in psychoanalytic psychiatry. *Psychiatry: Journal for the Study of Interpersonal Processes,* 33(3), 329–343.

(1962). Aspects of obsessive-compulsive style. *Psychiatry: Journal for the Study of Interpersonal Processes,* 25(1), 46–59. Reprinted in *Handbook of Character Studies: Psychoanalytic Explorations* (1991), M. Kets de Vries, F. R. Manfred & S. M. Perzow (eds.). Madison, CT: International Universities Press, 261–284.

(1960). A perceptual understanding of color response. In *Rorschach Psychology,* M. Rickers-Ovsiankina (ed.), New York: Wiley, 251–301. Reprinted in revised edition, 1975. Reprinted together with "Color response and perceptual passivity" (see below) and commentary as *Color Response in the Rorschach Test,* (2005). Japan: University Education Press.

(1959). The integration of determinants and content in Rorschach interpretation. *Journal of Projective Techniques,* 23, 365–373.

(1956). Color response and perceptual passivity. *Journal of Projective Techniques,* 20, 52–69.

(1955). A hysterical character disorder in a housewife. In *Clinical Studies of Personality,* R.E. Harris & A. Burton (eds.). New York: Harper, 178–190.

(1954). Special problems of testing borderline psychotics. *Journal of Projective Techniques,* 18, 387–394. Reprinted in *A Rorschach Reader* (1960), M. H. Sherman (ed.), New York: International Universities Press, 101–110.

(1950). A study of the influence of the social field on individual behavior. *Genetic Psychology Monographs,* 42, 161–230.

Index

CPSIA information can be obtained at www.ICGtesting.com
Printed in the USA
LVOW010005010513

331714LV00002B/32/P